£18.99

British Counterinsurgency

British Counterinsurgency
2nd Edition

John Newsinger

palgrave
macmillan

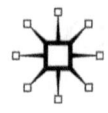

© John Newsinger 2015

All rights reserved. No reproduction, copy or transmission of this publication may be made without written permission.

No portion of this publication may be reproduced, copied or transmitted save with written permission or in accordance with the provisions of the Copyright, Designs and Patents Act 1988, or under the terms of any licence permitting limited copying issued by the Copyright Licensing Agency, Saffron House, 6–10 Kirby Street, London EC1N 8TS.

Any person who does any unauthorized act in relation to this publication may be liable to criminal prosecution and civil claims for damages.

The author has asserted his right to be identified as the author of this work in accordance with the Copyright, Designs and Patents Act 1988.

First published 2015 by
PALGRAVE MACMILLAN

Palgrave Macmillan in the UK is an imprint of Macmillan Publishers Limited, registered in England, company number 785998, of Houndmills, Basingstoke, Hampshire RG21 6XS.

Palgrave Macmillan in the US is a division of St Martin's Press LLC, 175 Fifth Avenue, New York, NY 10010.

Palgrave Macmillan is the global academic imprint of the above companies and has companies and representatives throughout the world.

Palgrave® and Macmillan® are registered trademarks in the United States, the United Kingdom, Europe and other countries.

ISBN: 978–0–230–29823–1 (hardback)
ISBN: 978–0–230–29824–8 (paperback)

This book is printed on paper suitable for recycling and made from fully managed and sustained forest sources. Logging, pulping and manufacturing processes are expected to conform to the environmental regulations of the country of origin.

A catalogue record for this book is available from the British Library.

A catalog record for this book is available from the Library of Congress.

*To Jack Newsinger (1921–82) and
Mary Newsinger (1925–2015)*

Contents

Introduction to the 2nd Edition		1
1	At War with Zion	5
2	The Running Dog War: Malaya	33
3	The Mau Mau Revolt	62
4	Cyprus and EOKA	88
5	The Struggle for South Yemen	112
6	The Unknown Wars: Oman and Dhofar	136
7	The Long War: Northern Ireland	157
8	America's Wars: Afghanistan and Iraq	201
Notes		243
Select Bibiliography		275
Index		277

Introduction to the 2nd Edition

When this book was first published in 2002, the Introduction commented on how the major counterinsurgency campaigns that the British state had waged in Palestine, Malaya, Kenya, Cyprus, South Yemen, Dhofar and Northern Ireland since 1945 had produced a largely celebratory literature. The general argument of this literature was that Britain's campaigns had been conducted with considerable success. This contrasted with the French experience in Indo-China and Algeria, with the Dutch in Indonesia, with the Portuguese in Angola, Mozambique and Guinea-Bissau, with the Americans in Vietnam and with the Russians in Afghanistan. The British, it was argued, knew how to conduct counterinsurgency campaigns and, moreover, conducted them without bringing dishonour on their cause through the use of massacre and torture. This was a distortion of the historical record. First of all, the post-war record included important defeats in Palestine and South Yemen, and included the British failure, despite overwhelming numerical and material superiority, to successfully destroy their opponents in Cyprus and Northern Ireland.

Another important point was that starting with the Labour government of 1945–51, the British took the decision to withdraw rather than confront full-scale rebellion and insurgency in any large, heavily populated Imperial territory. The decision to withdraw from India and Burma, for example, saved the British Empire from its Algeria, from its Vietnam, from its Afghanistan. If the Conservative Party had been returned to power in 1945, there is every likelihood that it would have provoked revolutionary war in India and Burma on a scale that would have completely dwarfed any of the colonial wars that actually did take place post-1945. These wars would certainly have ended in costly defeats. Moreover, the scale of the fighting would have inevitably ensured that they were accompanied by a level of atrocity such as that associated with the French war in Algeria and the American war in Vietnam. The British reputation for comparative restraint would have never taken off. The emphasis here is very much on the word comparative. The claim that the British waged counterinsurgency operations humanely, always practising the minimum use of force and seeking to win hearts and minds, was always a myth. But it was a myth that was given legs by the small scale of the wars that the British chose to fight, the weakness of their opponents and the corresponding low level of British casualties. Nevertheless, where necessary, considerable force was used, sometimes successfully, sometimes not; moreover, the war in Kenya, it is by now generally acknowledged, was conducted with a terrible severity by any standard, certainly comparable with the worst excesses of the French in Algeria or of the Americans in Vietnam. Indeed, a good case can be made that minimum force was generally interpreted by the British as allowing as much force as was considered necessary.

Success, partial success or failure in British counterinsurgency campaigning was not dependent on any supposed military superiority in waging these campaigns, but rather on the ability to establish a large enough political base among sections of the local population so as to enlist their support and assistance in the defeat of the insurgents. Put crudely, but nevertheless accurately, divide and rule remained the key to success in the wars that accompanied the end of the British Empire. The point is also worth making that Britain's post-war counterinsurgency campaigns took place in a context of Imperial retreat, of admittedly often reluctant decolonisation but nevertheless still decolonisation.

It seems fair to say that when *British Counterinsurgency* was first published, the critical stance it took towards the post-1945 campaigns was very much a minority stance. This is no longer the case. Indeed, there is a new consensus today, one that is openly dismissive of the notion that the British were humane counterinsurgents practising minimum force, winning hearts and minds, or particularly successful. Instead, coercion has moved centre stage. As David French put it: 'The cornerstones of most British counter-insurgency campaigns were coercion and counter-terror, not kindness and economic development...waging counter-insurgency operations by employing coercion and intimidation continued to be a mainstay of British practice after 1945'.[1] This new consensus is a product of the work of a number of other scholars as well, including David Anderson, Caroline Elkins, Huw Bennett, Andrew Mumford, Benjamin Grob-Fitzgibbon and others.[2] Certainly it has been a welcome change. This new consensus has been so successful, in fact, that it has recently been argued that there never was a celebratory consensus anyway![3]

What is also important, however, is to acknowledge the context within which this new consensus has emerged, a context that facilitated it and gave it more than academic credibility. Whereas the British counterinsurgency campaigns in Palestine, Malaya, Kenya, Cyprus and South Yemen could all be seen as fighting retreats, Tony Blair's New Labour government took the decision to effectively hand the British Army over to the United States for deployment in the American wars of aggression in Afghanistan and Iraq. These were conflicts that no post-war British government would have participated in of its own volition. However, in order to further the so-called special relationship, the British government committed British troops to fight alongside the Americans in the 'War on Terror', an ideological construct intended to justify military action against governments the US regarded as threatening its interests. The British government and the British military wilfully surrendered their strategic judgement to the most incompetent post-war US administration led by the worst post-war President; indeed, many would say this involved one of the most incompetent US administrations ever and arguably the worst President ever.[4]

In retrospect, the idea of letting George W. Bush decide where British troops should fight seems even more preposterous now than it did at the time. This failure was compounded by a refusal to actually put into the field enough troops and resources for them to have any serious chance of accomplishing the tasks that they had been volunteered for. The result was defeat in both Basra and in Helmand, defeats that paradoxically seriously compromised the very 'special relationship' the original deployments were meant to strengthen and sustain. Indeed, today, because of these defeats, the Americans no longer regard the British as worthwhile military assets. As Andrew Mumford put it, 'Basra pulled the mask away from the hitherto rosy popular trans-Atlantic perception of British competence at counter-insurgency' and pointed 'to an increasingly inescapable conclusion that the British are not as good at counter-insurgency as was previously assumed'.[5] And, of course, far from these initial campaigns in the War on Terror actually defeating the terrorists, they have, as many predicted at the time, led to a dramatic increase in their strength and support. In Aaron Edwards's nice phrase, the invasion of Iraq served as 'a force multiplier for terrorists like Al Qaeda'.[6] While the politicians obviously bear the main responsibility for these bloody fiascos, the generals are also culpable for promising to deliver without ensuring adequate resources. And, of course, throughout the whole dismal affair, every effort was made to mislead, manipulate and manage public opinion. In this respect, an area that urgently needs to be explored is the relationship between the Ministry of Defence and News International. One is inevitably reminded of H. R. McMaster's account of decision-making during the Vietnam War, his appropriately entitled *Dereliction of Duty*.[7] This recent history of defeat and failure provides the context for the new consensus.

What this new edition of *British Counterinsurgency* will attempt is to once again examine the challenges the British faced in Palestine, Malaya, Kenya, Cyprus, South Yemen, Dhofar and Northern Ireland, incorporating as far as possible the latest research. There is also an additional chapter examining the British participation in America's wars in Afghanistan and Iraq.

1
At War with Zion

When the Second World War finally came to an end, the British found themselves confronted by a challenge from the Yishuv, the small Zionist settlement in Palestine. This challenge, tacitly supported by the United States, was to compromise the British Empire's overall position in the Middle East and thereby begin the process of its dissolution in the region. This failure to overcome the Zionist challenge is one of the most humiliating episodes in immediate post-war British history. How was it that the Yishuv was able to inflict such a defeat on a British military establishment fresh from its victories over Germany and Japan?

Exercising the Mandate

At the time the challenge was mounted, the British considered Palestine to be a territory of vital strategic importance, providing a military base from which to dominate the rest of the Middle East. In this way oil supplies and oil profits could be secured and any threat from the Soviet Union could be countered. Such was the region's importance that in the event of war with the Russians the British planned a hurried withdrawal from continental Europe but intended to defend the Middle East at all costs, according the area a priority second only to the defence of the British Isles themselves.[1] The incoming Labour government hoped to be able to control the region informally, by means of a series of unequal relationships with a network of Arab client states, but a large military presence was still regarded as essential. Only British troops could, in the last resort, it was thought, ensure that friendly governments remained in power and defend against external attack in the event of another world war. The Mandate over Palestine was seen as providing the British with a degree of freedom of action which they were in the process of losing in Egypt and would not possess anywhere else in the region. There was certainly no expectation that the British position was soon to crumble.[2]

British policy was fatally compromised by the Zionist settlement in Palestine, a settlement that had initially been sponsored as a counterweight to Arab nationalism. The Balfour Declaration of 1917 committed Britain to supporting the establishment of a European Jewish colony in a land overwhelmingly inhabited by Arabs. While the settlement initially stagnated, the numbers seeking entry rose dramatically with the rise of Nazism in Germany. Whereas in 1931 there were only 4075 Jewish immigrants, by 1935 the number had risen to 66 472. Denied entry to other European countries or to the United States, German and Central European Jews increasingly came to look to Palestine as a safe haven.[3]

Arab opposition to this colonisation of their homeland culminated in the great revolt of 1936–39, the first Intifada, which led to what was, in effect, the reconquest of the Mandate by British troops. The insurgency was only suppressed with great difficulty and considerable brutality, costing over 3000 lives. The British turned to the Zionist settlers for assistance in the campaign, recruiting some 19 000 Jewish police and encouraging the activities of the Special Night Squads, Jewish murder gangs, trained by a British officer with strong Zionist sympathies, Orde Wingate. The Arab revolt was defeated and the Palestinians left disarmed, disorganised and leaderless to confront a Yishuv that was to increase dramatically in strength and determination during the Second World War.[4]

At the time, however, while the Palestinian Arabs might well have been defeated militarily, the scale of their revolt, together with the hostility of the Arab states to the Zionist colony, won a significant political victory in the shape of the 1939 White Paper. With war imminent in Europe, the British felt the need to conciliate Arab opinion. The White Paper limited Jewish immigration, restricted Jewish settlement and promised independence to an Arab Palestine within ten years.[5] This commitment was condemned at the time by British Zionist sympathisers, among them Winston Churchill, as a betrayal of the Balfour Declaration and was, of course, bitterly opposed by all elements of the Yishuv.

The Zionist movement was divided in its response to the White Paper, with the Jewish Agency and the rival Revisionist movement taking very different stands. The Jewish Agency functioned as the effective settler government in Palestine, had the allegiance of the overwhelming majority of the Jewish population and was determined to overturn the White Paper by diplomatic methods. The Agency was sympathetic to the British Empire, which was still regarded as a friend and protector, and rallied to the British war effort against Nazi Germany, the enemy of all Jews. Settlers were encouraged to enlist in the British armed forces and an attempt was made to persuade the British to establish a distinct Zionist army brigade. Altogether some 32 000 settlers served in the British armed forces, fighting in Greece, North Africa and Italy. Within the Jewish Agency, this stance was strongly associated with Chaim Weizmann. It was to be challenged as the war progressed by more militant elements, led by David Ben Gurion, who looked increasingly to the United States for help in pressurising a recalcitrant Britain. While the war continued, however, the Jewish Agency remained committed to the British Empire on whose victory its very survival depended.[6]

Having made use of the settlers to help in the defeat of the Arab revolt, once war broke out, and in line with the White Paper policy, the British withdrew their encouragement of Zionist paramilitary forces. There was a crackdown that drove the Jewish Agency's militia, the Haganah, underground, imprisoning a number of its cadres and seizing whatever arms could be found. Defeat in Europe and the German threat to the Middle East led to yet another change in British policy. The Haganah was once again recognised and an elite formation, the Palmach, was formed from its ranks and trained in partisan warfare by officers from the Special Operations Executive (SOE). This force was to organise resistance if the German Afrika Korps should overrun Palestine. A number of volunteers also played a part in Britain's undercover war against the Axis. As far as the Jewish Agency was concerned, however, the most important development was the eventual establishment of a Zionist brigade within the British Army in 1944 which went into combat in Italy the following year. This was regarded as a diplomatic triumph presaging the abandonment of the White Paper policy and there was considerable confidence that, once the war was over, Britain would return to its Zionist commitment. After all, Churchill was known to be sympathetic, and the Labour Party, his coalition partner and the only alternative government, was committed by its 1944 conference to a Zionist policy more extreme than that advocated by the World Zionist Organisation itself.[7]

On the right of the Zionist spectrum was the minority Revisionist movement established by Vladimir Jabotinsky, an admirer of Benito Mussolini and Italian Fascism. The Revisionists had their own paramilitary forces, the Irgun Zvei Leumi (IZL), which had carried out indiscriminate bombings and shootings against the Arab population during the Arab revolt and who were prepared to fight the British in 1939 in order to overturn the White Paper policy. With the outbreak of war, however, the main body of the Revisionist movement rallied to the British Empire and suspended hostilities. Indeed, the IZL commander, David Raziel, was killed on a SOE operation in Iraq in May 1941.[8]

LEHI and IZL

The exception was a small breakaway terrorist group, the Lohamei Herut Israel (LEHI), usually known after its founder, Abraham Stern, as the Stern Group or by the British as the 'Stern Gang'. This tiny organisation identified the British Empire as Zionism's main enemy and throughout the war continued a terrorist campaign of assassinations and bombings against the Palestine police and the administration. The LEHI went so far as to offer its services to Nazi Germany, proposing to act as a fifth column in the German conquest of Palestine in return for an agreement to resettle Europe's Jews there. Its politics, a peculiar amalgam of anti-imperialism and fascism, were informed by a mystical belief that the Jewish people would have to be redeemed by sacrificial violence. They were actually proud to call themselves 'Terrorists'.[9]

On its own the LEHI never constituted a serious threat to British control over Palestine. The organisation never numbered more than a few hundred members during the war, and it was extremely unpopular with the rest of the Yishuv both because of its continuing terrorist activities and because of its fundraising through armed robbery and extortion. This hostility ensured that the police received the necessary intelligence effectively to cripple the organisation. It became involved in a bloody vendetta with the Criminal Investigation Department (CID), a vendetta in which Stern himself was a casualty, shot dead while in custody in January 1942.[10] By the middle of that year further arrests and shootings appeared to have eliminated the organisation.

The situation began to change in 1944. By this time it was clear that the Allies were winning the war and that the Yishuv was no longer under direct threat from the Nazis. The impact of the Holocaust was also changing attitudes, with a growing number of people convinced that British refusal to allow Jewish refugees into Palestine had sentenced them to death. Britain was from this point of view an accessory to the Holocaust. Together these factors contributed to the revival of the Revisionist paramilitary formations.

The LEHI regrouped under the leadership of a three-man executive consisting of Yitzhak Shamir, Nathan Yellin-Mor and Israel Scheib. The organisation quickly returned to its vendetta with the Palestine police. More important, however, was the reorganisation of the IZL, a much more substantial force that had almost disintegrated in the early years of the war with so many of its leading cadres following Raziel into the British armed forces. Now the IZL reformed itself and under the leadership of a refugee from Poland, the hard-line right-winger Menachem Begin, prepared for armed revolt. The IZL rejected the individual terrorism of the LEHI in favour of a protracted campaign of guerrilla warfare intended not to persuade the British to return to the Balfour commitment, as the Jewish Agency intended, but to drive them out of Palestine altogether. The decision to wage war was taken in 1943, but the proclamation of the armed revolt against the British was not made until 1 February 1944.

The declaration, addressed to both the Yishuv and the British, declared:

> Four years have passed since the war began, and all the hopes that beat in your hearts then have evaporated without a trace. We have not been accorded international status, no Jewish Army has been set up, the gates of the country have not been opened. The British regime has sealed its shameful betrayal of the Jewish people and there is no moral basis whatsoever for its presence in Eretz Israel.
>
> We shall fearlessly draw conclusions. There is no longer any armistice between the Jewish people and the British Administration in Eretz Israel which hands our brothers over to Hitler. Our people is at war with this regime – war to the end... We shall fight, every Jew in the Homeland will fight. The God of Israel, the Lord of Hosts will aid us. There will be no retreat. Freedom – or death.[11]

As the year progressed there was a succession of attacks that left an increasing toll of destruction, dead and injured. The British only began to take the revolt seriously after a series of co-ordinated attacks on the police on 23 March when the LEHI shot up police stations in Tel Aviv, killing two policemen, while the IZL made bomb attacks on police stations in Jerusalem, Jaffa and Haifa, killing six more. These attacks were followed by a curfew that lasted for nine days and large-scale searches in the districts affected. On 28 July the High Commissioner, Sir Harold MacMichael, reported to London that, 'The security position may be deteriorating, and the outlook is not encouraging'.[12] Only ten days later, on 8 August, the LEHI narrowly missed assassinating him, machine-gunning his car on the Jerusalem-to-Jaffa road and killing his ADC in the attempt. The attacks continued into September. On 27 August some 150 IZL guerrillas made co-ordinated attacks on four heavily fortified police outposts, leaving two soldiers and two policemen dead. Two days later a CID Assistant Superintendent, Tom Wilkins, regarded as the most dangerous of the group's enemies, was assassinated, shot 11 times by LEHI gunmen in broad daylight in Jerusalem.

The decisive act of this first phase of the revolt, however, occurred on 6 November 1944 when two young LEHI gunmen, Eliahu Hakim and Eliahu Bet-Zouri, assassinated the British Minister Resident in the Middle East, Walter Guinness, Lord Moyne.[13] According to Yellin-Mor, 'We weren't yet in a position to try to hit Churchill in London, so the logical second best was to hit Lord Moyne in Cairo'.[14] This killing of a senior government figure and a personal friend of Churchill's had a shattering effect. Lord Moyne's death broke Churchill's already weakening faith in the reliability of the Yishuv as an ally, and he warned in the House of Commons that if these outrages continued, 'many like myself will have to reconsider the position we have maintained so consistently in the past'.[15]

Lord Moyne's assassination provoked the Jewish Agency into action. The activities of the IZL and LEHI were beginning to compromise the security of the whole Yishuv, undermining its diplomatic position and threatening to bring British reprisals. However spectacular their attacks, the dissident Zionist organisations were still only very small (the LEHI and IZL between them probably had only about a thousand members) and enjoyed the support of only a tiny proportion of the settler population, less than one per cent according to one estimate.[16] By way of contrast, the Jewish Agency commanded the allegiance of virtually the entire Yishuv, had considerable financial resources both in Palestine and abroad, controlled the 60 000-strong Haganah militia together with its elite strike force, the Palmach, and had quantities of weapons hidden throughout the country. The IZL and LEHI were putting all this at risk. Moreover, as far as Ben Gurion was concerned they were politically little better than Nazis; indeed, he condemned the IZL as a 'Nazi gang' and as 'Jewish Nazis' and compared Begin to Hitler.[17]

The 'Saison'

As far as Ben Gurion and the Jewish Agency were concerned, the real enemy was not the British Empire but the Arabs. In the end, the Zionists were going to have to fight the Arabs for control of Palestine and whatever other Arab territory they might eventually be able to seize. For this reason it was absolutely vital to avoid a full-scale confrontation with the British which, even if it ended with their withdrawal, would still leave the Yishuv crippled in the face of Arab attack. The IZL and LEHI threatened to provoke such a confrontation, and indeed this was very much Begin's intention. The British were aware of plans being hatched in New York for an uprising modelled on the Easter Rising in Dublin in 1916, involving the seizure of buildings in Jerusalem, including the General Post Office.[18] While this particular plan was stillborn, Begin still hoped to bring about a full-scale rebellion involving the entire Yishuv, an outcome that Ben Gurion quite correctly regarded as a recipe for disaster. The British, with their overwhelming military superiority, would have been able to inflict a crushing defeat on a full-scale rebellion. Moreover, at the time it still appeared possible that once the war was over the British government would return to its Zionist commitments without the need for conflict in the Mandate. The Jewish Agency therefore resolved to put a stop to the activities of the dissident organisations.

Once it was made clear that the Agency intended to take the necessary physical measures to curb the dissidents, the LEHI promptly agreed to suspend operations. Begin, however, refused to comply, whereupon Ben Gurion launched the 'Saison', a campaign of intimidation and betrayal that saw Palmach volunteers collaborating with the CID in an effort to smash the IZL. The split within Zionism between the followers of Ben Gurion and the followers of Begin was to be one of the decisive factors in Israeli politics for many years.

From the very beginning of the IZL offensive in February 1944, elements within the Haganah had taken action against their rivals, but only towards the end of the year did this become a co-ordinated campaign designed to root them out of the colony once and for all. Palmach volunteers, working together with Haganah intelligence, the Shai, began by seizing suspected or known IZL members, inflicting salutary beatings or holding them for interrogation, which often involved force and sometimes torture. Some IZL cadres were held captive for months in conditions that were intended to break their spirit. The IZL intelligence chief, Eli Tavin, for example, was tortured and then held in solitary confinement for seven months. It quickly became clear that there was a limit to the number of dissidents who could be imprisoned, so the decision was taken to inform on them to the British. Altogether some 700 names were passed over to the CID, which made large-scale arrests, seizing some 300 IZL activists. Sympathisers were intimidated and victimised, sacked from their jobs and even expelled from school.

The 'Saison' was extremely effective, resulting in the removal of virtually the entire IZL leadership with the important exception of Begin himself, driving the organisation deep undercover and preventing the continuation of its guerrilla campaign. It is important to note that this conflict within the Zionist camp took place along a sharp political divide. For the Palmach members involved in combating the IZL, the dissidents were traitors to the Yishuv, refusing to acknowledge its government and putting it at risk by their adventurism. More than that though, the dissidents also rejected, from an extreme right-wing position, the collectivist kibbutz ethos that still informed the Yishuv, and were consequently regarded as little better than Nazis. Even so, many who were prepared to take action against the IZL were very uncomfortable about handing them over to the British, and indeed this policy became untenable once it became clear that the British had no intention of satisfying Zionist ambitions.[19]

What of the IZL? Despite the damage done to it, the organisation survived underground. Much of the credit for this must go to Begin, who insisted that there should be no retaliation against the Jewish Agency, even once it became known that 'third degree' methods were being used against IZL members and that they were being handed over to the police. He presents this as a decision from the heart, that Jew should not fight Jew, but almost certainly the decision was also informed by the knowledge that if the conflict became a shooting affair the IZL would inevitably be destroyed as would any hope that it could ride out the 'Saison'. This would only benefit the British. Instead Begin believed that if the IZL could hold out long enough, then the British government would inevitably disappoint the hopes the Jewish Agency placed on it and the IZL strategy would be recognised as correct. This simple conviction was to be at least partly rewarded.[20]

The 'Saison' had come to an end even before the election of the Labour government in July 1945. The IZL had disappeared underground and the handing over of its members to the police had caused increasing dissatisfaction among Palmach volunteers involved in the operation. Now, however, the whole episode seemed likely to become irrelevant with the election of a Labour government ostensibly committed to abandoning the White Paper policy, establishing a Zionist state and allowing unrestricted immigration. One senior Labour politician, Hugh Dalton, a future Chancellor of the Exchequer, actually advocated paying the Palestinians to vacate the country and expanding its borders.[21] David Horowitz has recalled the 'jubilant atmosphere' that gripped the Yishuv when news of the election result arrived. This joy was short-lived. It soon became clear that whatever its position in opposition, the new Labour government regarded the need to maintain good relations with the Arabs, thereby safeguarding the

British Empire's strategic position in the Middle East, as a more vital interest than any sentimental attachment to Zionist ideals. This turnabout on the part of Labour was, once again, according to Horowitz, 'the greatest disappointment and disillusionment suffered in the history of Zionism'. A wave of bitterness swept through the colony: 'Disappointment, anxiety, despair and restlessness spread through the Yishuv'.[22] This sense of betrayal was to be compounded by the continued refusal of the British to allow the survivors of the death camps into Palestine. The Labour government, it is worth noting, also refused to allow their entry into Britain![23]

The Jewish revolt

In these changed circumstances the Jewish Agency decided that a show of strength was necessary in order to force the British to accede to Zionist demands. They had to demonstrate that the maintenance of the British position required their support and that this would only be possible if the British agreed to honour the Balfour Declaration. Their strategy had three aspects to it. First, there was to be campaign of sabotage and civil disobedience inside Palestine, it was hoped with minimal loss of life. This would demonstrate that security in the Mandate could only be maintained with the co-operation of the Jewish Agency. Secondly, they intended to organise mass illegal immigration, confronting the British with the enormity of forcibly denying entry to survivors of the Holocaust. Thirdly, the Zionist movement in the United States would be used in an attempt to bring pressure from Washington to bear on the British. Given Britain's economic weakness and dependence upon the US, American support was a crucial element in the Jewish Agency's strategy. There was still a fixed determination to avoid a full-scale conflict with the British, the intention being to pressurise them into changing their policy, not to drive them out of Palestine by force of arms. Nevertheless, to achieve this objective the 'Saison' was called off and the Jewish Agency entered into an uneasy secret alliance with the dissident organisations, the LEHI and IZL, both of which were committed to very different strategies. A United Resistance Movement was established in mid-October 1945, bringing all the various armed formations under a unified command.

On the night of 31 October–1 November, 'the Night of the Trains', the United Resistance Movement launched its first joint operation against the British. In an impressive display of co-ordinated action, some 1000 Palmach members paralysed the railway system throughout the Mandate, cutting the track in 242 places, and sunk or damaged police patrol boats used to prevent illegal immigration at Haifa and Jaffa. Simultaneously, the IZL attacked the Lydda railway junction, blowing up buildings, locomotives and rolling stock, and killing one British soldier, while the LEHI bombed the oil refineries at Haifa. This demonstration would, it was hoped, influence the Labour government's forthcoming statement on Palestine. The second phase of revolt had begun.

In retrospect it can be seen that the British seriously underestimated the strength of the Yishuv and its ability to conduct a struggle against them. The war years, while an unprecedented catastrophe for Europe's Jewish population, had paradoxically seen the Jewish colony in Palestine grow in wealth and power. By 1946 the population of the Yishuv numbered some 560 000 and the number of settlements had increased to 348. Agriculture had prospered and, more significantly, industrial development – much of it war production – had increased dramatically. The number of Jewish factory workers rose from 22 000 in 1937 to 46 000 in 1943 and, over the same period, industrial output increased nearly five-fold from £7.9 million to £37.5 million.[24] This, together with the Jewish Agency's increased military capability, made the Yishuv a force to be reckoned with. British protection from the Arabs was no longer regarded as necessary. The Yishuv was beginning to realise that it no longer needed the British Empire.

For the British, the Zionist revolt posed an impossible dilemma which in the end was to force them to abandon the Mandate. In order to secure their position in Palestine and throughout the Middle East they had to try to find a formula that would reconcile the incompatible ambitions of both the Zionists and the Palestinian Arabs and neighbouring Arab states. Concessions to the Arabs were made impossible by a Zionist recalcitrance increasingly endorsed by the United States. Concessions to the Zionists were made impossible by Arab hostility to the colony that had been established in their midst and was taking their land. The British government failed to find a political solution that the security forces could then seek to impose. It was in this difficult context that British counterinsurgency operations were to fail so humiliatingly.

Ernest Bevin, the British Foreign Secretary, was left unmoved by the United Resistance Movement's explosive demonstration of its capabilities on the night of 31 October. He had already been informed by intelligence sources that such an event was planned and had warned Weizmann, a staunch Anglophile, that if 'you want a fight you can have it'. This was not the sort of language that the Zionist leader expected from Labour politicians. Bevin, however, was positively hostile towards Zionism. He had no sympathy whatsoever with the establishing of a Jewish state in Palestine and, more importantly, he was also convinced that such an ambition was a threat to the British Empire's position in the Middle East and so had to be defeated. On 13 November he made his statement on Palestine to the House of Commons. This announced the setting up of an Anglo-American Commission which would report back on the problem and, it was hoped, endorse British government policy. The commission was intended to involve the United States in decision-making in the Middle East and thereby counter Zionist influence in American domestic politics. The struggle for influence in the United States was recognised as a crucial arena of the conflict. At the same time his statement also made quite clear that Labour's commitment to Zionism when in opposition was a thing of the past and that Labour in government was not prepared to antagonise Arab opinion. Bevin followed this up with a press conference at which he warned that if Jewish refugees wanted to get to the head of the queue for resettlement then they risked the 'danger of another anti-Semitic reaction'. This crass and offensive allegation of queue-jumping outraged Jewish opinion, both Zionist and non-Zionist. The honeymoon with the Labour government was over.[25]

The Zionist response to Bevin's statement in Palestine was the calling of a general strike on 14 November. In Tel Aviv this was accompanied by serious rioting. When troops from the 6th Airborne Division arrived to restore order, they were stoned and after repeated warnings responded with directed fire, that is, marksmen shooting individuals identified as ringleaders. This was the traditional method for dealing with crowd disturbance in the colonies. When the rioting came to an end, six Jews had been killed and another 60 injured. This was regarded with some satisfaction by the military, but for the administration it was little short of disastrous. American sympathy for Zionism meant that Jews could not be treated like other natives. Worse was to follow. On 25 November, 50 Haganah men attacked the Sidna Ali coastguard station and then disappeared into two settlements, Hogla and Givat Haim. When troops attempted to carry out searches, they met with fierce resistance from the settlers, who fought them hand-to-hand. Eventually some 10 000 troops were involved in establishing British control over the two settlements, killing eight settlers in the process and arresting more than 300. After this episode the practice of searching settlements involved the assembly of overwhelming force in an effort to deter any attempt at resistance.[26]

The insurgency grows

The six months following the launching of the United Resistance Movement's Campaign saw some 50 serious attacks on police stations, airfields, army bases and installations, government buildings and the railways. The British were confronted by a guerrilla insurgency waged by a well-organised underground, operating with the support of the overwhelming majority of the Yishuv. While the Haganah by and large confined its operations to the destruction of the system of immigration control, the LEHI and IZL attacked what they regarded as the forces of occupation with a ruthlessness that took the British military completely by surprise. They conducted a relentless campaign against the Palestine police, and its CID branch in particular, determined to cripple the British intelligence apparatus. On 27 December the two organisations made a combined attack on the CID offices in Jerusalem and Jaffa. These daring commando-style raids left ten police and soldiers dead and another 11 wounded. The British responded with a curfew, large-scale searches and the screening of the male population in the affected districts. By the time the curfew was lifted on 5 January, some 50 suspects had been detained and a handful of weapons discovered. They had completely failed to inflict any serious damage on the underground.

In his study of the revolt Bowyer Bell provides an excellent account of the situation that confronted the new High Commissioner, Lieutenant General Sir Alan Cunningham:

> By December he had what should have been the means to impose order. All twenty-thousand men of the Sixth Airborne Division had been moved to the Mandate, and British troop strength continued to rise to eighty thousand. There were also thousands of police, units of the Transjordan Arab Legion, and others attached to security duty. There were two cruisers, three destroyers, other naval units off the coast, and naval radar and communication bases on shore. The ratio of British security forces to the Jewish population was approximately one to five. By 1946 the Mandate was an armed camp...Security regulations ran on for over fifty densely-printed paragraphs, including the death penalty for any member of a group whose other members had committed one of several crimes...There were curfews, confiscations, searches in the streets, sweeps through the countryside, collective fines, detentions and arrests...The Mandate became a garrison state under internal siege, and the garrison, despite its size, equipment, and determination, proved ineffectual and self-defeating.[27]

Why was it that despite this large and growing military presence the insurgents were able to operate with comparative impunity? Inevitably operations sometimes miscarried and there were casualties, but this cannot disguise the fact that the security forces failed to cause any serious harm to the underground organisations. There were two reasons for this failure: inappropriate military tactics and a lack of intelligence.

The British response

The only way the British army knew of responding to rebellion was derived from the pre-war doctrine of 'Imperial Policing', a tried and tested way of suppressing tribal insurgency. This involved mobile columns and punitive expeditions marauding through rebel territory, the free use of artillery and bombing, the destruction of villages, crops and livestock and the hanging of large numbers of rebel prisoners. Overwhelming force would be deployed against the insurgents, who would be battered into submission and taught a healthy respect for British power. It was a doctrine that involved straightforward military action in open country against clearly identifiable rebel forces and their supporters without any great need for political considerations to be taken into account. Such a doctrine was completely inappropriate in the politically charged campaign against the mainly urban terrorism of the United Resistance Movement. In Palestine, guerrilla attacks were invariably surprise commando-type raids against carefully reconnoitred targets, usually in urban areas, with the attackers in civilian clothes or even British uniforms. They would disappear without trace into the city streets. There were no rebel forces to bomb or shell into submission. Moreover, while the British had almost no intelligence relating to their opponents, the police force was heavily infiltrated by the Haganah. According to one senior British officer, 'every order of his was in Jewish hands within 24 hours'.[28]

The British response was to carry out large-scale cordon-and-search operations, sealing off the district where the insurgents were believed to have gone to ground, searching every house and screening the civilian population. These affairs inevitably brought the troops into conflict with the population whose homes were invaded and who were manhandled with varying degrees of force and abuse, effectively alienating them. These operations invariably failed to produce results. The troops were not adequately trained in search-and-screening procedures. Furthermore, the special unit which was trained in these procedures, the Police Mobile Force, had to be disbanded because of manpower shortages. The most these cordon-and-search operations achieved was to restrict the guerrillas' freedom of movement. The lesson of British counterinsurgency operations throughout the post-war period, a lesson that had to be learned time after time, was that the most effective way of combating guerrilla forces was the use of small- unit tactics, small patrols, ambush parties and undercover squads. As we shall see, these methods were beginning to be introduced towards the end of the conflict, but too late to have any real effect.[29]

The most significant factor, however, was the lack of intelligence. The security forces had too little information about the underground and most of what they knew concerned the Haganah. They were, to all intents and purposes, fighting blind and this inevitably meant that their operations were clumsy and misdirected. In many ways large- scale cordon-and-search operations were an attempt to compensate for the lack of intelligence. Without effective intelligence, the security forces were always on the defensive, at best responding to guerrilla attacks, but never able to take the initiative to carry the battle to them. This intelligence failure is without any doubt the key to the security forces' inability to defeat the Zionist underground.

The most important component of the intelligence apparatus was the 80-strong political section of the CID. The Jewish Affairs section was headed first by Assistant Superintendent Richard Catling and then by John Briance. This was a comparatively small outfit, totally inadequate to the scale of the problem. Expansion was limited by a lack of Hebrew-speaking British policemen and the known unreliability of Jewish policemen, many of whom were either members of or sympathised with the underground. Moreover, the CID was targeted by the IZL and LEHI, which succeeded in killing or wounding a number of its members and in making survival a high priority for the rest. The army had its own intelligence staff but gave this area of operations a low priority. Also involved in the conflict were both MI5 and the SIS, and the latter's Major Desmond Doran, a former head of station in Bucharest, was assassinated in Tel Aviv in September 1946.[30]

The weaknesses in the intelligence apparatus and the effectiveness of the underground's countermeasures were less important than the fact that the Yishuv was solidly united behind the revolt. This is brought home in R.D. Wilson's history of the 6th Airborne Division in Palestine:

> At no stage during the whole period under review did the Jewish community, either individually or collectively, show any desire to

co-operate with the Security Forces...Moreover, on occasions too numerous to mention they actively assisted the dissidents to escape detection. It is worthy of mention that there was not one case in the Divisional area during the whole period under review in which one member of the Jewish community was prompted by his or her conscience to come forward and give evidence against a known criminal. It need not have been done openly; in fact it was quite possible for information to pass without the least danger to the law-abiding citizen. Herein the greatest factor of all, for it is well known that in all forms of guerrilla or underground warfare, if the partisans have the undivided support of their kinsmen, the work of the occupation forces is increased beyond calculation.[31]

As we shall see, neither of the two methods that could have fractured this unity, intensified repression or concession (or a combination of the two), were politically possible.

The conflict continued in the New Year. On 25 February 1946, the LEHI and IZL mounted simultaneous attacks on RAF airfields at Lydda, Kfar Sirkin and Qastina. Under cover of darkness the raiders destroyed three Halifaxes and seriously damaged another eight, destroyed seven Spitfires, two Ansons and three other light aircraft. The cost of the destruction was estimated at around £2 million. The attackers lost one man killed. These raids were a tremendous blow: not only were they humiliating, but they also displayed a worrying degree of expertise and tied down more troops in static defence duties.

Increased security did bear fruit, however. A daring attack on Sarafand army camp on 7 March miscarried with a number of IZL raiders taken prisoner. On 2 April, IZL sabotage of the railway line between Haifa and Acre ended in disaster when the raiding party was trapped within the cordon that the 6th Airborne Division threw around the area. They lost two of their number killed and another 30 captured. Another raid on Ramat Gan police station saw the IZL attackers escape with a haul of weapons but suffer two of their men killed and another, Dov Gruner, wounded and taken prisoner. Then, on the night of 25 April, the LEHI raided the 6th Airborne car park in Tel Aviv, killing seven paratroopers, some of them unarmed and shot down in cold blood, before escaping with 12 rifles. According to the Divisional history, previous attacks had been for arms or to sabotage installations, but this 'was one of, if not, the first, in which the causing of casualties was an objective'.[32] More than any other, this attack changed the nature of the conflict as far as the troops were concerned. Previously, off-duty soldiers had gone unarmed but, henceforth, they almost always carried their weapons. As one paratroop officer subsequently recalled, after this incident, 'The lord help anyone who even smelled like a terrorist'.[33]

The car park attack provoked minor outbreaks by angry paratroopers in Nathanya and at Beer Tuvya, but officers and NCOs were able to prevent the more serious trouble which threatened to break out in Tel Aviv itself. There was a great increase in the use of anti-Semitic abuse. General Bernard Paget warned that 'if nothing is done there is risk that the troops will take law into their own hands'.[34] The danger of troops going on the rampage sufficiently alarmed the army for it to demand that punitive action be taken against the Yishuv. The 6th Airborne's commander, Major General James Cassells, together with the GOC Palestine, Lieutenant General John D'Arcy, went to see the High Commissioner about the incident. Cassells warned him that the paratroopers were near mutiny and asked for tough action. He wanted a collective fine of £1 million imposed on Tel Aviv, the requisition of buildings in the city for use by the troops, the blowing up of public buildings if the municipality did not hand over the culprits and the closure of all restaurants and places of entertainment from 8 p.m. To his disgust Cunningham only agreed to the last demand.[35] On 30 April the decision was taken in London that any serious reprisals against the Yishuv would first have to be agreed by the Cabinet. Military considerations were not to be allowed to interfere with the overriding political need to maintain good relations with the United States.

That same day the report of the Anglo-American Commission was published. While it rejected the establishment of a Jewish state and recommended the continuation of British control over Palestine, it also called for the entry of 100 000 Jewish refugees. This last proposal was immediately given public endorsement by President Truman. Both Attlee and Bevin were outraged by what they regarded as Truman's undermining of the British position for domestic political reasons. As far as they were concerned, the report was unacceptable because of the impact on the Arabs of allowing in 100 000 Jewish refugees. The Chiefs of Staff, for example, warned that this would provoke an Arab revolt in Palestine and cause trouble for Britain throughout the Middle East; they even thought it might cause unrest in India, perhaps a mutiny in the Indian army.[36]

Was this an opportunity missed? Was the Anglo-American Commission's report a way out of the predicament in which the Labour government found itself? It has been argued that this was indeed the case.[37] If the British had accepted the report, the moderates in the

Jewish Agency would have called off the revolt and ensured that the dissident organisations either did likewise or faced a renewed 'Saison'. This argument is not convincing for two reasons. First, as far as the Zionists were concerned (Ben Gurion as well as Begin, Shamir and Co.), there could be no final settlement short of the establishment of a Jewish state and, moreover, a Jewish state controlling territory still inhabited by Arabs. Once the 100 000 refugees had arrived, the problem would have resurrected itself with the demand for further or unrestricted immigration and also for a Jewish state. And this was at a time when the British would have been involved in suppressing an Arab revolt. Secondly, it neglects the fact that maintaining good relations with the Arabs was by now the prime objective of British policy in the Middle East. This aim would not be sacrificed for the sake of Zionism. Instead the Labour government was to bow to the growing demand that the army should be given a freer hand in the battle against terrorism.

Cracking down

General D'Arcy, the outgoing GOC Palestine, pressed for the forcible disarming of the settler population. This measure would, it was hoped, both intimidate the Yishuv and cripple the underground resistance, leaving only mopping up operations to finish off the revolt. Such a display of British determination would also predispose the Arabs to accept a further measure of Jewish immigration, thus strengthening the hand of the moderates in the Zionist camp. This plan was endorsed by the Chiefs of Staff on D'Arcy's return to London. At the same time, the Jewish Agency was considering making another major demonstration of its military capabilities as a way of putting pressure on the British government and securing the entry of the 100 000 refugees. In a quite unprecedented way, they sought to discover the likely political effect of such a demonstration. Richard Crossman, a Labour MP, staunch Zionist sympathiser and former member of the Anglo-American Commission, was charged with the task and approached John Strachey, a Cabinet member with similar sympathies. Strachey advised that the attack should go ahead.[38] On the night of 16–17 June, 'the Night of the Bridges', the Haganah destroyed eight of the nine bridges connecting Palestine with its neighbours. Despite efforts to avoid British casualties, one soldier was killed. This was followed on 18 June by the IZL kidnapping of five British officers having lunch in a Tel Aviv officers' club. They were taken hostage to prevent the hanging of two IZL members sentenced to death for their part in the Sarafand raid. These two incidents were the last straw for the British.

Montgomery

A crucial figure in the hardening of British attitudes was the incoming Chief of the Imperial General Staff, Field Marshal Bernard Montgomery. He visited the Mandate as part of an overseas tour in June and subsequently confessed himself 'much perturbed by what I heard and saw'. He thought Cunningham completely unsuited to cope with a crisis situation and complained of indecision all down the line, beginning in Whitehall. 'All this', he went on,

> had led to a state of affairs in which British rule existed only in name; the true rulers seemed to me to be the Jews...I made it very clear to the GOC in Palestine that this was no way to carry on. The decision to re-establish effective British authority was a political one; we must press for that decision. If this led to war with the Jews from the Army's point of view it would be a war against a fanatical and cunning enemy...I would then give the troops the fullest support in their difficult job.[39]

Montgomery attended the Cabinet meeting on 20 June and, with Ernest Bevin's support, carried the day. Cunningham was told to put into effect the army's plan to seize the initiative from the Zionist guerrilla forces.

On Saturday 29 June the British carried out Operation Agatha, known to the Zionists as 'Black Sabbath'. Troops occupied the Jewish Agency headquarters and a number of other buildings in Jerusalem and sealed off over 20 settlements. There were mass arrests. By the end of the day 2718 people had been detained, including four members of the Agency executive. The searches of the various settlements met with resistance in which four Jews were killed and many others injured. Altogether, 33 arms caches were discovered, containing nearly 600 weapons, half a million rounds of ammunition and a quarter of a ton of explosives. This apparent success was misleading. The overwhelming weight of the army's searches fell on the Haganah, the most open and vulnerable of the Zionist armed formations. The Haganah undoubtedly suffered a serious blow, but the LEHI and IZL were virtually untouched, their military capability left intact. Chaim Weizmann was so appalled by the escalating conflict that he threatened to resign as head of the World Zionist Organisation if it were not called off.

Less than a month later the failure of the army's crackdown was brought dramatically home on 22 July when the IZL carried out a bomb attack on the King David Hotel, which housed both army headquarters and the offices of the Palestine Secretariat. The explosion completely destroyed one wing of the building, killing 91 people (41 Arabs, 17 Jews, 28 British and five others) and injuring many more. Most of the dead and injured had nothing to do with the British Administration. Body parts were still being discovered three months later. A warning was given too late for the building to be evacuated, although whether this was the fault of the IZL or the British has never been, and probably never will be, definitively established. The attack left the Palestine Administration seriously rattled.[40] Immediately after the bombing, the GOC Palestine, General Evelyn Barker, issued a non-fraternisation order, putting all Jewish establishments out of bounds to the troops. This, as he put it, 'will be punishing the Jews in a way the race dislikes as much as any, by striking at their pockets and showing our contempt for them'. This anti-Semitic outburst soon became public knowledge and caused great embarrassment to the British government, particularly in the United States. Despite calls for his removal, Barker was kept in place. When he finally left Palestine he showed his feelings by pointedly urinating on the ground before boarding his plane. Barker was not the only senior officer or official to show evidence of anti-Semitism. According to Matt Golani, Henry Gurney did not miss any opportunity 'to assail the Jews and the Zionists and their tentacular global intentions' in his diary.[41]

The British response to the bombing of the King David Hotel was Operation Shark. The 6th Airborne Division was ordered to seal off Tel Aviv, a city of 170 000 people, conduct house-to-house searches and screen the entire adult population. This operation, involving over 17 000 troops, lasted four days and resulted in 787 people, most of them perfectly innocent, being detained. Five arms caches were uncovered, one of them in the basement of the Great Synagogue. The only significant success was the arrest of the LEHI leader, Shamir, picked out by CID Sergeant T.G. Martin despite being disguised as a rabbi. Two months later the LEHI assassinated Martin while he was playing tennis. The troops missed Begin, however, hidden inside a secret compartment in a friend's house. Once again a large-scale operation carried out without effective intelligence, a treasure hunt without clues, had failed to inflict any serious damage on the underground. For the Jewish Agency, however, the situation was getting dangerously out of hand.

Operation Agatha, the bombing of the King David Hotel and Operation Shark together broke the Jewish Agency's nerve. Its strategy was not to try and drive the British out of Palestine by force of arms but to pressurise them into conceding the Zionist case. Instead the conflict was escalating, inviting repression on a scale that threatened seriously to damage the Yishuv. While the IZL and LEHI were not really hurt by the British crackdown and were soon able to regroup, the Haganah had suffered serious blows and it was expected that worse was to come. This damage threatened its ability to fight the coming war with the Arabs. The British had actually succeeded in intimidating the Jewish Agency. Fearful of the consequences of an all-out war the Agency called off the struggle and withdrew from the United Resistance Movement.[42] It would, however, continue to smuggle illegal immigrants into Palestine and confront any British attempt to stop them. Much to Montgomery's disgust, Cunningham responded to this by relaxing British repressive measures, such as they were, and over the next few months released most of the detainees taken in Operations Agatha and Shark. This comparative leniency was a mystery to the Arabs who contrasted it with the severity used to crush their rebellion less than ten years earlier.

The failure of repression

It is at this point worth considering the often bitter argument over strategy that took place within the British military and political establishments. Montgomery and others believed that repression consistently and relentlessly applied could crush the revolt, that if the army had not been hampered by weak, indecisive political leadership it would have already defeated the underground. This argument has a number of weaknesses. First, there was a limit to the extent to which the British could use repression against the Zionists. The methods that had been used against the Arabs – collective punishments, the shooting of prisoners, the widespread use of torture and large-scale hangings – were not politically possible. This much was fully realised by the Zionist underground. As Samuel Katz, a member of the IZL High Command made clear:

> Of course, the British could physically crush the Jewish population of Palestine. But we knew...that there were limits of oppression beyond which the British government dared not go. She could not apply the full force of her power against us. Palestine was not a remote hill village in Afghanistan which could be bombed into submission...The British government had discovered in 1945 that their behaviour towards the Jews was an important factor in American attitudes and policies.[43]

What of the repressive measures that were taken? As we have seen, the large-scale operations of June and July 1946, with their mass arrests, certainly damaged the Haganah and the Jewish Agency but they were comparatively ineffective against the organisations most involved in the guerrilla campaign, the IZL and LEHI. Indeed, by weakening the Jewish Agency, these operations arguably undermined its ability to restrain the dissident organisations and increased support within the Yishuv for those advocating all-out war.

One factor which is completely ignored in discussion of this conflict is the possibility of enlisting the Palestinian Arabs against the Zionists. The Zionist settlers were only a minority of the population of Palestine, and their objectives were bitterly opposed by the majority. In these circumstances a divide-and-rule strategy could have powerfully strengthened the British who instead persisted in a supposed attempt at even-handedness. At the very least, large numbers of Arabs could have been enlisted in special police units or in a local militia, which would have provided the security forces with both manpower and a way of intimidating the Yishuv. It was not without precedent. In the late 1930s the British had recruited Jewish police and made use of the Haganah against the Arab revolt. As we shall see, one of the key factors in the defeat of the mainly Chinese Communist guerrillas in Malaya was the enlistment of the Malay population against them (see Chapter 2). This idea was never entertained in Palestine. The political concessions necessary to enlist the support of the Palestinian population were not possible because of the strength of support for Zionism, especially in the United States. And, of course, in the last instance it was not really conceivable to use the Arab population against the Zionists who were, after all, Europeans, even if they were Jews. This inability to use the hostility of the majority of the population of Palestine against the Zionists was without doubt one of the major reasons for the British defeat.

Cunningham, however, was much more aware than the military of the political constraints imposed by the need to maintain good relations with the Americans. His strategy was to enlist the support of the Jewish Agency in suppressing the dissidents. By means of restraint and concession he hoped to persuade the moderate Zionists to carry out another 'Saison'. As Cunningham explained to one of his critics, it was his policy 'to encourage to the greatest extent possible the growing tendency among the Jews to deal with the matter themselves'.[44] The chronic shortage of intelligence that crippled the security forces would be remedied overnight if this could be accomplished and with Jewish help the IZL and LEHI could be eradicated. This policy did enjoy limited success, but it was never fully implemented because it was politically impossible for the British to make sufficient concessions to the Zionists. The hostility of the Palestinian Arabs and of the Arab states stood in the way. The British were to fall inexorably between these two stools of repression and concession, with the argument going first one way and then the other, until both were clearly seen to have failed and withdrawal became inevitable.

Cunningham's attempt to conciliate the Jewish Agency was soon put under strain as the dissident organisations regrouped and struck back. They turned increasingly to the use of bombs and mines – abandoned vehicles were packed with explosives and electronically detonated mines placed by the side of the road. A pram containing a bomb was discovered outside General Barker's residence. This type of warfare put troop morale under considerable pressure. As the 6th Airborne's historian confesses, in this period mines caused 'a high proportion of the army's casualties' and were 'one of their most difficult problems'.[45] A good illustration of the sophistication (or 'devilish ingenuity') of these attacks is provided by the account of an officer in the Argyll and Sutherland Highlanders, Colin Mitchell. He describes an incident that occurred in October 1946:

> We had set up a road block and positioned a number of Jocks in the centre of Jerusalem to enforce a curfew. It was the Sabbath and because this was a very orthodox quarter of the city and all work was forbidden on this day, the metal blinds over the shop windows were opened automatically by electric time-clocks. Knowing where the Jocks would be positioned, sleeping on a certain stretch of pavement, the terrorists had planted plastic explosives inside the rolled-up blinds of the shops at that point and set the time-clocks to unroll the blinds at 8 o'clock that night.
>
> All seemed quiet in the street, deserted except for the Argylls, many of them sleeping on the pavement, when, silently, the blinds began to unroll. Suddenly there was a series of shattering explosions. Nobody knew what was happening. Were we being mortared? Nobody knew how to react. All we knew was that there on the pavement lay a dead Argyll and a wounded officer, a corporal who was to die from his wounds, and six other wounded Jocks.[46]

Increasingly, dissident attacks were mounted with the intention of inflicting casualties on the security forces.

Once again, Montgomery returned to the attack. At the end of November he complained to Attlee that, since 1 October, 76 soldiers and 23 police had been killed or wounded in terrorist attacks. Shootings and bombings had increased since the release of the Operation Agatha detainees, not decreased as the Colonial Office had promised. The army was suffering casualties at the rate of two per day and was increasingly frustrated at not being able to hit back. The only way to stamp out terrorism was to take the offensive, but instead it had surrendered the initiative to the terrorists. This, Montgomery recalls in his memoirs, caused 'the devil of a row'. He then went to visit the Mandate for himself and his worst fears were confirmed:

> At 6.30 p.m. one night a police station was attacked by armed Jews, who had laid mines in certain streets to cordon off the area. The attack was repulsed; troops arrived and picked up the mines; normal life was then resumed. A conference was held the next morning to decide whether to search the area in which the outrage had taken place. If the matter had been properly handled, mobile columns of troops would have been on the scene within ten minutes and few of the terrorists would have escaped. The only firm and quick decision taken in Jerusalem that night was to cancel a dinner-party at Government House because the mines in the streets prevented the guests from getting there.

Inevitably, he clashed with Cunningham, who, according to Montgomery, believed that the Jewish Agency and the Haganah were going to suppress the dissidents. Any repressive action by the security forces would only make matters worse. Montgomery's response was that if Britain could only govern Palestine on Jewish sufferance, then it would be best to get out.[47] Montgomery's pressure once again bore fruit. In January 1947 Operation Polly was put into effect, evacuating families and non-essential personnel from the Mandate. This was accompanied by the concentration of the civilian administration into heavily guarded, wire-enclosed security compounds from which Jewish residents were evicted. These compounds were derisively known as 'Bevingrads' by the Zionists but, as far as Montgomery was concerned, the authorities were at last putting themselves on a war footing.

The security forces became more security-conscious and more aggressive. New tactics were introduced with small parties of troops and police patrolling and raiding in known trouble spots. These had some success. Nevertheless, the Zionist underground still held the initiative, choosing where and when to strike. The security forces were still fighting blind, without effective intelligence. On 1 March, the IZL carried out 16 separate attacks that left 20 soldiers dead and another 30 wounded. The most serious was a daylight raid on the officers' club in Jerusalem in which 12 soldiers were killed. The following day, the new GOC Palestine, Lieutenant General Gordon MacMillan, put into effect Operation Elephant and imposed martial law on Tel Aviv and the Jewish districts of Jerusalem. This was something the army had long demanded and planned for. It took complete control of the proclaimed areas, sealing them off, imposing a punitive curfew and bringing economic activity to a complete halt. Houses were repeatedly searched and the population was screened. Even while the martial law regime was in operation, guerrilla attacks continued, sometimes carried out within the security cordons. After two weeks martial law was lifted, not because it had accomplished anything, but because the army could no longer maintain it. There were just too few troops and police. While the paper strength of the British army in Palestine was 100 000, only a quarter of these were combat troops. The police were also seriously under-strength.

This failure effectively ended the credibility of Montgomery's continued claim that if the army were given a free hand it could crush the revolt. Proposals to place the whole Mandate under martial law could now be seen as impractical unless substantial troop reinforcements were forthcoming, and this was not feasible. It had finally been made clear that a military solution was not a realistic proposition.

On 31 March the IZL provided a spectacular demonstration of British failure by blowing up the Haifa oil refineries, causing a fire which blazed out of control for nearly three weeks. The British had still not abandoned repression, however. On 17 April the first four underground fighters were hanged, and four days later two others blew themselves up with a hand grenade rather than share the same fate. The following day, 22 April, the IZL attacked the Cairo-to-Haifa train, killing five soldiers.

The full extent of the British army's failure was brought home on 4 May when the IZL carried out a daring rescue operation against the Acre fortress. The attackers blew a hole in the wall, allowing 255 prisoners, most of them Arabs, to escape. The IZL guerrillas suffered heavy casualties while making their getaway, losing eight killed and five captured, but nothing could disguise the fact that the dissident underground's military capability was increasing rather than diminishing.

A free hand

There was one last attempt at defeating the underground. An attempt was made to improve the effectiveness of the Palestine Police, with

Sir Charles Wickham, fresh from heading the British Police Mission in Greece, producing a critical report on the force's organisation and morale. As part of an attempt to bring in new ideas, the Inspector General, Nicol Gray, appointed Bernard Fergusson, a former officer with the Chindits and the head of Combined Operations, as Assistant Inspector General with responsibility for Operations and Training. He proposed setting up a special mobile undercover counterterrorist force to operate in Jewish areas and carry the war to the terrorists. Two units were established, one commanded by Roy Farran, a former Special Air Service (SAS) officer and the other by Alistair MacGregor, formerly with the Special Operations Executive. These were not intelligence- gathering units, having no fluent Hebrew speakers, but were ostensibly an executive arm for the CID, acting on its information. According to Farran they were given a free hand:

> In Jerusalem Police Headquarters the brief was explained to us. We would each have full power to operate as we pleased within our own specific areas. We were to advise on defence against terror and to take an active part in hunting the dissidents. We could each select ten volunteers from our districts – mine were to be Tel Aviv and Jerusalem – and train them for a fortnight in our methods. It was to all intents and purposes a carte blanche and the original conception of our part filled me with excitement. A free hand for us against terror when all others were so closely hobbled! I selected ten excellent men from the host of volunteers, including five who had operated with me during the war. I started the regular instructors at the depot by teaching these boys to put six rounds in a playing card at fifteen yards... After a fortnight's preparation under conditions of strict secrecy, by the beginning of April we were ready to commence operations. Ten sun-tanned young men, looking like any party of Jewish youths from a Kibbutz moved off in a converted Citrus truck down the road from Jenin. They were dressed in the shirts, grey caps or panama caps most commonly worn in Jewish Palestine, and the Arabs hissed us as we passed through their villages. Underneath the sacks at the back were tommy-guns, ammunition, rations, and sufficient petrol to maintain our two civilian cars for a week. It was a 'Q' ship going into the heart of the enemy.[48]

The operation had some small successes, and certainly provided an example for later British counterinsurgency campaigns. In Palestine, however, it was a case of too little, too late and smacked of desperation.

Incredibly, Farran's team did not include one Hebrew speaker. The whole operation quickly fell foul of the complex political situation. Farran was accused of having tortured and killed a 17-year-old LEHI prisoner, Alexander Rubowitz, and promptly fled to Syria. As David Cesarani has shown pretty convincingly, he beat the teenager to death with a rock. Farran was eventually persuaded to return to stand trial. A statement that he had earlier prepared for his defending officer, wherein he admitted the offence, was ruled inadmissible and his commanding officer, Fergusson, refused to give evidence on the grounds that he might incriminate himself. Needless to say, Farran was acquitted.[49] Meanwhile the undercover squads had been disbanded. Why was Farran so unceremoniously dispensed with? It seems that his methods were an embarrassment precisely at a time when the Haganah, acting on Ben Gurion's instructions, was beginning to take limited action against the dissidents. On a number of occasions the Haganah interfered with IZL and LEHI attacks and a small-scale 'Saison' of kidnappings and beatings was taking place. The Haganah actually foiled an attempt to blow up the British Army headquarters in Tel Aviv, losing one man dead in the process. This conflict, of course, had more to do with a struggle for power between the Jewish Agency and the dissidents than with helping the British.[50]

The hangings

Three more IZL members were still to be hanged for their part in the Acre rescue, an operation in which no British lives had been lost. To prevent this, on 12 July the IZL kidnapped two British Field Security sergeants in Nathanya and held them hostage. Operation Tiger saw the town sealed off, placed under a punitive curfew and repeatedly searched in a fruitless attempt to find the two men. On 29 July the three IZL prisoners were hanged, whereupon the two sergeants were hanged in reprisal. The ground beneath the bodies was mined so that when soldiers went to cut them down one body was blown to pieces and an officer was wounded. This incident provoked widespread anti-Semitic attacks and rioting in Britain, while in Palestine troops and police took unofficial reprisals against the settler community, leaving five Jews dead and many more injured. The widespread outrage that is still voiced over this admittedly ruthless act seems misplaced. The execution of the three IZL members was every bit as reprehensible as that of the two sergeants and, moreover, provoked the IZL reprisal. The real mistake that Begin and his comrades made was, one suspects, in kidnapping ordinary soldiers rather than officers or someone 'important'. What was the impact of this grim episode? It had a completely disproportionate effect in convincing the British authorities that neither repression nor concession within the limits of what was politically possible could crush the revolt and that the longer it continued the greater the danger of a breakdown of discipline in the security forces.[51]

The conflict was not confined to Palestine. The LEHI struck at the British wherever they could. On 31 October 1946, the British Embassy in Rome was bombed, followed by the British Army HQ in Vienna. British politicians were targeted for assassination with letter bombs being sent to Attlee, Bevin, Sir Stafford Cripps and others. There were a number of bomb attacks in London. The Colonial Club was bombed in March 1947, and the following month an attempt was made to blow up the Colonial Office itself. The timer failed on the Colonial office bomb which consisted of 25 sticks of dynamite wrapped in copies of the Evening Standard and the Daily Telegraph. If it had gone off it would certainly have caused considerable damage and loss of life. One senior policeman thought it would have been as devastating as the King David Hotel bombing. In his memoirs, Yaacov Eliav, the man in charge of this operation, also claimed to have procured concentrated cholera cultures from Zionist sympathisers at the Pasteur Institute in Paris with the intention of infecting London's water supply and causing a mass cholera outbreak. Only the British decision to withdraw prevented an attempt at carrying out this attack. The consequences of such an attack for British Jews does not seem to have concerned the conspirators. As Norman Rose points out, Eliav quite cheerfully recounts this episode in the Hebrew edition of his memoirs, but for some reason it was cut from the English translation. All this was designed to 'beat the dog in his own kennel'.[52]

This account has so far neglected one important aspect of the conflict that is not directly relevant to the counterinsurgency campaign in Palestine but was, nevertheless, a tremendous embarrassment to the British. The Haganah organised a massive illegal immigration operation that was to culminate in July 1947 in the *Exodus* affair. The storming at sea of this immigrant blockade-runner, its capture after a violent hand-to-hand struggle in which three Jews were killed, and the forcible deportation of its 4554 refugee passengers back to camps in Germany, of all places, was a propaganda disaster of the first order. The Palmach responded to the *Exodus* affair by attacking British installations in Cyprus.[53]

According to the historian Ritchie Ovendale, it was the *Exodus* episode, together with the hanging of the two sergeants, that finally convinced the Labour government to surrender the Mandate and withdraw British forces from Palestine. Hugh Dalton, the Chancellor of the Exchequer, who was strongly pro-Zionist in sympathy, complained to Attlee of the cost in 'man-power and money', pointed out that 'you cannot in any case have a secure base on top of a wasp's nest' and warned that the conflict was 'breeding anti-Semites at a most shocking speed'.[54] With the military failing to suppress the insurgency, these arguments prevailed. The final decision was taken on 20 September, despite the objections of the Chiefs of Staff who continued to insist that military bases in Palestine were vital for British security and could not be abandoned.[53] Attacks on British forces continued into 1948 (on 28 February, for example, the LEHI attacked a train, killing 28 soldiers), but once the United Nations had voted for partition, the conflict increasingly became an unequal struggle between the Zionists and the Arabs. The last British troops were evacuated at the end of June 1948.[55]

How was it that the British suffered such a humiliating defeat? It is important not to exaggerate the scale of the conflict despite the violence involved. The security forces were never in danger of military defeat at the hands of the few thousand IZL and LEHI guerrillas, and throughout the entire conflict they suffered only 338 fatalities. Rather it was their failure to crush the Zionist underground that was to be a major factor in Britain's political defeat at the hands of the Jewish Agency and its supporters in the United States, and in this way contributed to Britain's eviction from a territory that the Chiefs of Staff regarded as essential for the security of the Empire. This failure to defeat the IZL and the LEHI is usually put down to either tactical weaknesses or intelligence failure (or a combination of the two), or to the restraints that were imposed on the security forces by their political masters. There is some truth in both these views, but they miss the larger issues – the extent to which the British defeat was the result of political failure. The British government was trapped between the Zionists and the Palestinian Arabs, unable, because of external circumstances and considerations, to enlist the support of either group in the maintenance of British rule in the Mandate. In effect, the government's political failure left the security forces fighting the Zionist underground without any allies or collaborators among the local population and unable to use repression on the scale that had defeated the Arabs a decade earlier. It was this which accounts for the security forces' defeat and suggests that the outcome was inevitable.

2
The Running Dog War: Malaya

While the British had suffered a humiliating defeat in Palestine, the conflict that was developing in Malaya was to later be seen as a model for the conduct of counterinsurgency operations. Indeed, for a while, the Malayan experience was put forward quite explicitly as an example to be emulated by the United States in Vietnam. One leading British counterinsurgency specialist, Sir Robert Thompson, who served in Malaya throughout the Emergency, eventually becoming Secretary for Defence in Kuala Lumpur, argued that 'the countermeasures developed and proved in Malaya...would have succeeded in the early stages in Vietnam if they had been suitably adapted and consistently and intelligently employed.[1] Thompson was to head the British Advisory Mission to Vietnam from September 1961 to March 1965 and later became a special adviser to President Richard Nixon.[2]

Others broadly accepted this view of the Malayan conflict; among them, for example, US Army Colonel J.J. McCuen, who, in his influential *The Art of Counter-Revolutionary Warfare*, argued that Malaya 'was a major counter-revolutionary victory...the British have made important contributions to the art of counter-revolutionary warfare'.[3] How valid is this view?

What will be argued here is that the vaunted British 'model' provides only half the answer to the Communist defeat in Malaya and that the other half is provided by the enormous political difficulties that the Malayan Communist Party (MCP) faced. Despite these difficulties and the overwhelmingly superior forces that the British were eventually able to concentrate against them, the Communists were nevertheless able to sustain their insurgency for ten years, a remarkable tribute to their courage, endurance and dedication. The conflict must not be seen in isolation, however, as if it were some sort of counterinsurgency laboratory experiment. Instead it has to be placed in the context of British Imperial history in the post-war period. This will better enable us to assess the importance of what Winston Churchill described as Britain's 'small but costly preoccupation in Malaya'.[4]

Occupation and resistance

From its very inception, Communism had been associated with the Chinese community in Malaya, having virtually no influence whatever among the overwhelmingly peasant population of native Malays. To begin with, Communism had developed in Malaya as a left-wing faction within the Kuomintang and had achieved some limited success in the organisation of trade unions. In 1930, the Malayan Communist Party (MCP) was itself formally established as a distinct organisation and after some setbacks began to make headway, taking advantage of a strike wave that swept over much of the colony in the mid-1930s. According to one historian:

> the MCP moved in on the growing wave of labour unrest in Malaya. Its influence grew by leaps and bounds, culminating in the strike at the Batu Arang coal mine in Selangor at the end of 1937. Workers under Communist leadership took possession of the mines and set up a Soviet Government. They were put down after an armed clash with the police, but the strike wave continued.[5]

The situation was viewed with considerable, if somewhat exaggerated, alarm by the authorities. One senior police officer reported that in his opinion Malaya had just 'passed through the most serious crisis of its history. It was within an ace of dissolving into temporary chaos as a result of communist intrigue. The evidence is now clear that Batu Arang was to be a trial of strength between the Communist Party and the government. Had the organisation there not been crushed, and crushed quickly, it is almost certain that there would not only have been a general strike, but that this country with its European women and children living in scattered bungalows or estates would have been in very serious danger of being overrun by angry and desperate Chinese mobs'.[6]

It was to this revolutionary conspiracy that the British were forced to turn for help in fighting the Japanese in December 1941. The MCP provided 165 recruits for the British 101 Special Training School (STS) – 'the best material we had ever had at the School', according to one British Officer – where they underwent ten-day courses in jungle warfare, preparatory to operating behind Japanese lines.[7]

While fighting still continued, the various STS classes were infiltrated through the Japanese lines to link up with local MCP groups and establish guerrilla bands. With what local support they could muster, they went into immediate action against the Japanese, conducting raids and ambushes in the confident expectation that Japan's successes would be short-lived, a temporary aberration which the Allies would reverse in months rather than years. The ferocity of the Japanese response nearly swept them away.[8]

The Japanese army responded to Chinese resistance with an exemplary massacre, the *Sook Ching*. Beginning on Singapore, the Chinese population was assembled for screening and then thousands were put to death, often in the most horrible circumstances. This pogrom then spread to the Malayan peninsular, and by the time it had exhausted itself, in the region of 40 000 Chinese had been killed.[9] In these weeks, the guerrillas suffered heavily and found that instead of harrying the Japanese, they were engaged in a desperate struggle to survive. They retreated into the jungle and began organising and training for a protracted war in which they could expect little help from the outside.

By mid-1942, the guerrillas had managed to secure their position, with seven regiments established in jungle camps, forming the Malayan People's Anti-Japanese Army (MPAJA). Guerrilla strength in the camps was to eventually rise to around 4000 men and women. Spencer Chapman, one of a number of British servicemen and civilians sheltered by the MPAJA, provides an interesting view of the guerrillas in his classic war memoir, *The Jungle is Neutral*, a view that is in stark contrast with British propaganda during the Emergency:

> The rank and file were absolutely magnificent. I can hardly find words to express my admiration for their courage, fortitude and consistent cheerfulness in adversity...Although they took their politics, fighting the Japs, and especially themselves very seriously, they were always laughing, and when they played games, they made as much noise as a girls' school. But the greatest recreation was the camp concert...I was very happy in my personal contacts with the guerrillas.[10]

The MPAJA engaged in only limited military action against the Japanese, intent as far as possible on keeping its forces intact, and concentrated instead on political work. To have done otherwise would have invited destruction and massive reprisals against the civilian population. To ensure that the guerrillas retained popular support, the Communists established a front organisation, the Malayan People's Anti-Japanese Union (MPAJU), an underground network of supporters, organising among the civilian population, particularly among the burgeoning Chinese squatter population living on the edges of the jungle. One consequence of Japanese rule had been to drive tens of thousands of Chinese from the towns and cities into the jungle to survive as market gardeners, growing rice and vegetables and keeping pigs and poultry. These people were ideally placed to assist the guerrillas. The MPAJU provided the guerrillas with food, clothing, medicines, funds, weapons, intelligence and recruits. The guerrillas also established good relations with the aboriginal population that lived in the deep jungle. Despite their failure to secure support from the Malays, the Communists had nevertheless successfully built the only effective resistance movement in Malaya, a factor that the British were unable to ignore as they planned to invade.[11]

SOE's Force 136 only established contact with the MCP in August 1943, when one of its agents, Colonel John Davis, after having landed by submarine, finally managed to meet with a senior party official, Chin Peng. The following month Davis began a long trek inland to join up with the MPAJA, meeting up with Spencer Chapman on Christmas Day. Six days later they had a meeting with the MCP general-secretary, Lai Tek, and reached an agreement whereby the MPAJA was placed under the control of the Allied South East Asia Command (SEAC). It was intended that when an invasion eventually took place, the guerrillas would prevent Japanese troop reinforcements from marching to the invasion beaches. Chapman was completely confident that if the MPAJA had actually been called on to play its part and prevent Japanese troops from marching south then 'I do not think many of them would have got through'.[12] The Japanese surrender after the atomic destruction of Hiroshima and Nagasaki made invasion unnecessary.

The British return

Historians have long puzzled over the failure of the MCP to establish a Provisional Government and issue a Declaration of Independence once it became known that Japan had surrendered in August 1945. The party would have been in a strong position to stage an armed revolt against the restoration of British rule. It had a guerrilla army that was high in morale and impatient for the struggle to begin. This force was supported by the MPAJU's extensive political network that was quite capable of coming out into the open to function as a revolutionary administration. Moreover, among the Chinese population, the Communists' wartime activities had won them tremendous popularity and support. The party could also reasonably hope to ally itself with the many former members of the Japanese-controlled Indian National Army who were strongly anti-British.[13] There was also a small radical Malay grouping, the Kesatuan Melayu Muda (KMM), led by Ibrahim Jaacob, that was actively seeking an alliance to oppose the British return. Indeed, after it became clear that the MCP had rejected the path of armed struggle, Jaacob and other KMM leaders decamped for Indonesia to fight in the independence struggle there.[14] In the period between the Japanese surrender and the arrival of the first British troops early in September, the MPAJA was in de facto control in most of the country and could easily have prepared the ground for a full-scale revolt.

There were also external factors strengthening the Communists' position. The British were at this time seriously overcommitted militarily. They faced immense difficulties in India and Burma, countries that were simmering with unrest, and were soon to become involved in shooting wars in both Indochina and Indonesia. A full-scale revolt in Malaya would have constituted a heavy additional burden on an already overstrained military machine.

Other factors argued against revolt. Communist support was negligible among the Malays. How much the KMM would have been able to contribute to a revolutionary struggle must remain doubtful. Moreover, serious clashes between the Communists and Malays were already breaking out in a number of areas of the country. On top of that it is important to recognise how important Malaya was to the British. They were determined to regain control for military, political and economic reasons. While the Indonesian intervention certainly imposed a considerable strain on the British, it also served as a demonstration of British ruthlessness. No one can seriously doubt that a Communist revolt in Malaya would have been met with a similar response. Moreover, the British would certainly have made use of the Japanese forces in Malaya, as they were to do in both Indonesia and Indochina. Having said this, however, the fact remains that, while the success of a revolt in 1945 could certainly not be guaranteed, it can be said with some confidence that the conditions for revolt at that time were considerably more favourable than they were to be in 1948. A protracted guerrilla war launched against the British in 1945 would have had at least some prospect of eventual victory; by 1948 this was no longer to be the case.

Why then did the MCP leadership decide to accept the return of the British and undertake to work within the framework of the British Military Administration (BMA)? The decision was certainly the cause of much debate and argument. Within the ranks of the MPAJA there was considerable support for an armed struggle against the British.[15] The party leadership, however, was dominated by Lai Tek and he carried the day. It was decided that armed struggle was not the way forward and that the party should follow a constitutional road, concentrating on trade union activity and the establishment of legal front organisations through which it could build up its political influence. On 27 August the Central Committee formally endorsed Lai Tek's position and this decision was subsequently, with great reluctance in some cases, endorsed by the party apparatus throughout the rest of the country.[16]

Discussion of this fateful decision is complicated by the personality of Lai Tek, one of the most remarkable figures in Communist history. It now seems established beyond any serious doubt that he was an agent of the British before the outbreak of the Second World War and that during the Japanese occupation he had only remained alive by performing the same role for the Japanese secret police, the Kempeitai. He handed over an unknown number of party members to execution at the hands of the Japanese, most notoriously the rest of the Central Committee assembled at the Batu Caves in August 1942, protecting himself from discovery by a carefully fostered 'cult of the personality'. It is difficult to conceive of such a man willingly entering into an armed struggle.[17]

In the period between the Japanese surrender and the arrival of British troops, the Communists came out of the jungle and quickly established themselves as the dominant political force among the Malayan peoples. They appeared as liberators, and were enthusiastically welcomed by the Chinese population. Collaborators and traitors were ruthlessly eliminated, and people's committees were appointed to take over the local administration. As has already been noticed, however, the MPAJA takeover in some areas met with fierce resistance from the Malays, most notably in parts of Perak and Johore, where many Chinese were killed. These clashes continued to flare up into March 1946.[18] They highlighted the failure of the MCP to make any significant headway among the Malays, to become a genuinely multi-ethnic party rather than an overwhelmingly Chinese one that merely preached unity. The political implications of this in a country (excluding Singapore) where 49 per cent of the population were Malay and only 38 per cent Chinese were obvious. Meanwhile, as British troops and officials began arriving throughout the country, the MPAJA offered no resistance, despite some provocation, but withdrew and handed over control.

While the MCP leadership endeavoured to co-operate with the British, disbanding the MPAJA and surrendering much of its weaponry, nominating members for the Governor's Advisory Council, even sending a detachment to take part in the Victory Parade in London, most of the rank and file remained bitterly opposed to the restoration of British rule. The situation was exacerbated by seriously deteriorating social and economic conditions which produced increasing social unrest. This unrest provided the setting for a struggle between the BMA and Communist militants. Having decided against armed struggle, the party directed its energies into political work. The Communists provided the drive and initiative behind the establishment of a number of broadly-based front organisations that were intended to ally it with various nationalist groupings: the Malay Nationalist Party, the Malayan Indian Congress and the Malayan Democratic Union. Crucial to this strategy, however, was the establishment of a powerful trade union movement; it was this that would provide the industrial muscle capable of forcing the political concessions that would make possible a constitutional takeover of power.

The constitutional road

In Singapore and throughout Malaya, the Communists set up General Labour Unions (GLUs) that were immediately involved in strike action and demonstrations. Singapore was gripped by a strike wave throughout December 1945, involving hospital workers, taxi and bus drivers, engineering workers, brewery workers, municipal and rubber workers, and others. The unrest culminated in a one-day transport strike on 27 December, involving 18 000 workers. As well as fighting on the economic front, the unions also posed a political challenge to the British. At the end of January 1946 a general strike was called in protest against the imprisonment of Soong Kwong, a MPAJA leader and war hero. He was released a few days later. Particularly ominous was the fact that some 700 British troops at Bukit Timah were reported to have joined the general strike. By now, though, the BMA had decided to take a stand against the unions. As a deliberate challenge to the authorities a general strike was called for 15 February, the anniversary of the surrender of Singapore. The strike was banned, troops and police were mobilised to deal with any disorder, and a number of Communist activists were arrested and later deported. The strike failed and demonstrations were broken up with considerable violence that left some 20 people dead in Singapore and Johore. It was now clear that the British preferred repression to concession and so steps were taken for a partial return to clandestine activity. Party offices were closed everywhere, except in Kuala Lumpur and Singapore, and the Communists now worked entirely through front organisations.[19]

The Communists' organising efforts, together with continued working-class unrest, soon enabled the recovery of lost ground. By mid-February, they were able to establish a national trade union organisation, the Pan-Malayan General Labour Union, soon to become the Pan-Malayan Federation of Trade Unions (PMFTU). Alongside their trade union work, the Communists also tried to construct a political alliance, uniting progressive Chinese, Malays and Indians, strong enough to demand democratic reforms from the British. In July 1946, proposals for a Federation of Malaya were put forward, safeguarding the position of the Malay Sultans and severely restricting the citizenship rights of non-Malays. These proposals were strenuously opposed by a broad alliance of organisations. A Pan-Malayan Council of Joint Action (PMCJA) was established, largely on the initiative of the MCP. It was supported by the Malayan Democratic Union, the Malayan Indian Congress, the MPAJA Comrades Association, the Indian Chamber of Commerce, the trade unions, and later the Chinese Chamber of Commerce. The Malay National Party (MNP), which was very much influenced by the MCP (its President Moktaruddin Lasso was a former MPAJA guerrilla), established a parallel Council of Joint Action (PUTERA) and the two bodies joined together to oppose the Federation and to demand the democratisation of the state. The PMCJA–PUTERA conducted a campaign of meetings and demonstrations against the Federation proposals, culminating in a one-day general strike on 20 October 1947. The British ignored their protests and on 1 February 1948 inaugurated the Federation of Malaya.[20]

The Cold War interpretation of the eventual outbreak of Communist insurrection in Malaya in 1948 was that the MCP had been ordered to revolt by Moscow and was faithfully following orders. It was believed that these instructions had been transmitted via a conference held in Calcutta in February 1948 and that subsequently the Malay, Indonesian, Burmese and Filipino Communists had all taken up arms. This interpretation is now completely discredited. While it is recognised that at this time relations between the Soviet Union and the United States and its allies were deteriorating, the increase in international tension is seen as only part of the context in which national party leaderships took their decisions rather than the sole determinant. The domestic situation decided whether or not the Communists took the road of armed struggle. In Malaya this was one of increasing desperation.[21]

The Federation scheme was a massive setback for the MCP, closing off, as it did, any prospect of their coming to power constitutionally. The British, it seemed, had decided to return Malaya to its pre-war condition and all the optimism and hopes of 1945 had been turned to ashes. Inevitably this undermined the position of the moderates in the party leadership and strengthened the arguments of those who advocated armed struggle. Then in March 1947, just before his role as a police agent was exposed, Lai Tek disappeared, taking most of the party's funds with him. This completed the rout of the hard-pressed moderates. Lai Tek was replaced as general-secretary by Chin Peng.

The final element in preparing the way for armed revolt was the developing offensive against the trade unions. With the full support of the government, the employers had combined together to launch a concerted attack on trade union organisation, cutting wages, victimising militants and engaging in the mass dismissal and eviction of strikers. The government backed up this offensive with increased legal harassment of the unions and the liberal use of police and troops as strike-breakers. Whereas in 1946 and early 1947 the unions had been on the offensive and strikes had generally ended in victory, now the tide was running the other way. According to one account, 'by the beginning of 1948 employers had recovered to a considerable extent the position they had lost in the immediate post-war years'.[22]

With prospects for constitutional advance closed off and with the trade union movement under sustained attack, the MCP leadership decided to prepare for an armed struggle. The decision was taken some time between March and November 1947. This, as Stenson points out, was long before the Calcutta Conference.[23] No actual timetable for revolution was laid down, however. Rather, it seems that the intention was to reactivate elements of the MPAJA and establish camps in the jungle, at the same time as increasing the momentum of the industrial struggle. As class conflict intensified, so the conditions for launching an armed struggle would materialise; it would be the responsibility of the party leadership to choose the correct moment. This was not to be. The MCP was proposing to go on the offensive at a time when the trade unions and the broader left were suffering defeats, a situation that almost guaranteed failure. Moreover, while the party leadership was thinking in terms of launching an armed revolt sometime in the near future, Communist militants were increasingly resorting to terrorist methods in their conduct of industrial disputes. These spontaneous acts of violence were to provide the British with a pretext for unleashing massive repression against both the Communists and the rest of the Malayan left. Even more damaging to the prospects for a successful revolt was the MCP's failure to recruit Malays. As late as February 1947 its membership consisted of 11 000 Chinese, 760 Indians and only 40 Malays. While many more were involved in party front organisations, this was still a terrible weakness that the British were to take full advantage of.[24]

In May and June 1948 there was an upsurge in the industrial struggle which the British subsequently claimed was in fact the first stage of a Communist revolt. This was provoked by the employers' offensive. It was largely confined to south Perak, Malacca, Johore and Selangor and did not involve other areas with a strong union presence. The workers involved had ample economic justification for taking strike action and there is no need to see them as part of any 'Communist conspiracy'. The strikes were, it is true, characterised by considerable violence, but this violence was by no means one-sided. The worst, but by no means the only, incident of police violence occurred on the Chang Kang Swee estate at Segamat in north Johore, where the police beat eight strikers to death. At this time it was very much the government and the employers who were making the running, who were engaged in battering the trade unions into submission. Some Communist militants responded by shooting strike-breakers and anti-union estate or mine managers. The government decided to take even more determined action to maintain law and order and smash the Communist menace. On 12 June a decisive step was taken with the banning of the PMFTU. Then, following the fatal shooting of three British estate managers, the High Commissioner, Sir Edward Gent, declared a State of Emergency on 19 June 1948. The MCP was taken completely by surprise.

State of Emergency

The British were committed to holding on to Malaya for vital economic reasons. The war had virtually bankrupted the British economy, dramatically increasing the importance of rubber and tin production in Malaya as dollar earners for the Empire. By 1947, for example, rubber was the Empire's principal dollar earner, bringing in $200 million, compared with the $180 million earned by Britain's own exports of manufactured goods. The point was emphasised in the Federation's Annual Report for 1948: of the world's total output of rubber and tin in 1948 this country produced 45.8 per cent of the former and 28.1 per cent of the latter. This achievement afforded more assistance to the UK and Commonwealth in terms of gold and dollars earned than was afforded by the total export drive of Great Britain over the same period.[25]

In 1950, Malaya earned $350 million out of the sterling area's total dollar earnings of $2385 million.[26] Moreover, both the tin and rubber industries were dominated by British companies: in 1953, 83 per cent of the acreage under rubber cultivation was European-owned and 60 per cent of the tin output was from British-owned mines.[27]

Paradoxically, it was under a Labour government that the British Empire was to be most ruthlessly and effectively exploited in the interests of the metropolitan centre. Whereas between 1946 and 1951 the colonies received £40.5 million under the Colonial Development and Welfare Act, the colonies' sterling balances held in London and used to support the British economy rose from £760 million to £920 million. There was a massive transfer of funds so that, in effect, the colonies were subsidising Britain.[28] While the Labour government had pulled out of India and Burma, this was, in the words of one historian, 'only to reveal an expanded appetite for African and South-East Asian exploitation'.[29]

Originally, the British had planned to prepare Malaya for independence sometime in the future: the process was expected to take at least 25 years. Even then, power would only be handed over to a government that accepted a subordinate, client position in what was regarded as a British sphere of influence, that was prepared to remain within Britain's 'informal' Empire. It would also have to be able to maintain law and order and protect private property. A secret Foreign Office memorandum of 2 April 1949 demonstrated a clear appreciation of the dangers that threatened the British position:

> It would clearly be disastrous if Malaya were ever to meet the same fate as Burma. We should of course lose one of our principal dollar-earning sources. Worse than this, we should also lose one of the principal sources of vital raw materials, as a result of which the economy not only of the UK, but also of the US would suffer severely... It seems to me that in the foreseeable future we shall be met with strong demands for constitutional developments in Malaya which we would be very rash to grant if there was the remotest risk of things developing badly.[30]

At this time even the most gradual progress towards independence was made dependent upon the crushing of the Communists.

With the declaration of the Emergency, the British launched a massive wave of repression against not just the Communists, but the whole left. Within a matter of days over 600 people had been detained as the police picked up known Communists, socialists and trade union activists. The number of those detained was to grow week by week. By the end of August, 4500 people had been arrested. The Malay left, in particular, was effectively broken by the eventual arrest and detention of over a thousand people, testimony to the government's fear of the Communists influencing Malay opinion. According to one account, the facts concerning the number of Malay leftists detained were deliberately suppressed by the government which was determined to present Communism in Malaya as a wholly Chinese affair. Many MNP activists fled into the jungle with the Communists to escape arrest and take up the armed struggle.[31] The brunt of the repression fell on the trade unions, however. By September 1948 nearly 200 leading trade unionists had been detained, and the following year, in May, the former President of the PMFTU, S.A. Ganapathy, was to be hanged for the possession of a firearm. There was some concern in Malaya about how the Labour government would react to this execution, especially as Nehru had made a plea for clemency, but, as Sir Robert Thompson observed, 'there was no comeback from Attlee'.[32] The militant trade union movement was altogether destroyed by bans, arrests, mass deportations and sackings. Between April and September 1948, union membership plummeted from 154 434 to 75 504. Union membership fell by an astonishing 78 per cent between December 1947 and December 1949. This was a crushing defeat.[33]

As has already been remarked, the declaration of the Emergency took the MCP by surprise. Many of its members were picked up by the police before they had any opportunity of disappearing underground. Gerald de Cruz, himself a party member at this time, argues that the fact that the police were able to arrest all the people working on the party's daily newspaper, *Min Sheng Pau*, many of them key militants, including Lau Yit Fan, a Central Committee member, shows how unprepared they were. Even Lau Yiu, President of the MPAJA ex-Comrades Association, only narrowly escaped capture. Police raided his home in Cheras, just outside Kuala Lumpur, but he escaped out of a back window while they broke down the front door.[34]

Driven precipitately into the jungle, with its numbers already seriously depleted by arrests, the MCP was forced to launch its armed struggle piecemeal and in circumstances not of its choosing. Whereas the party had planned, if and when it began its guerrilla war, to make co-ordinated attacks throughout the country that would paralyse the administration and cripple industry, 'a hundred or two hundred in the first week or so – the incidents in June and July were numbered in dozens'.[35] This gave the British time to take countermeasures.

Essentially, the MCP guerrilla strategy involved widespread and continuing attacks on police, officials and estate and mine managers in order to drive them out of the interior. This would have the effect of leaving the local population under Communist control. As these attacks forced the British to concentrate their forces in order to protect their communications and supply lines, and the towns, so the guerrillas would be able to establish liberated areas. Here they would establish their own revolutionary administration and be able to build up their forces. As they increased in strength, so they would be able to expand the liberated areas, launching large-scale attacks, until at last the British position became untenable and they were forced to surrender. No decision had been made as to when to launch this campaign, but now the British had effectively thrust it upon them.[36]

Before going on to discuss the first phase of the war, one often neglected aspect of the Communist strategy needs to be considered. The MCP withdrew into the jungle to mount its revolutionary challenge and subsequently never again, at least on the mainland, posed a problem for the British in the big towns and cities. The British themselves found this quite inexplicable. J.B. Perry Thompson, a psychological warfare expert in Malaya wrote that

> It is one of the remarkable features of the Emergency that, except for a few bombs in Ipoh in 1950 and one or two killings in Penang, the big towns have been relatively undisturbed. The absence of security precautions in Kuala Lumpur was startling to anyone who had been in Jerusalem... had the terrorists been so minded, they could have blown up any Government office or major institution in the country with the exercise of the minimum determination and audacity.[37]

Without any doubt an urban guerrilla campaign would have constituted a significant additional security problem for the British and they were duly relieved that one never developed.

This failure is all the more striking in view of the relatively high level of urbanisation in Malaya. In 1947, 27 per cent of the population of the Federation were classified as urban dwellers and 80 per cent of the population in Singapore. Even more striking is the fact that 43 per cent of the Chinese living in the Federation were urban dwellers, making up a majority of the population in ten of the 15 largest cities and constituting the largest ethnic group in three of the others. In Singapore, of course, the situation was even more marked, with 81 per cent of Chinese classified as urban dwellers.[38] Given this, the MCP's withdrawal into the jungle can be seen as effectively surrendering a large proportion of the sympathetic Chinese population to British control and, instead, directing its efforts on terrain where the generally hostile Malays predominated.

The British success in mobilising the rural Malay population against the Communists was to be a crucial factor in the MCP's eventual defeat.[39]

The guerrilla army, the Malayan People's Anti-British Army (MPABA), that assembled in its jungle camps during the second half of 1948 had a strength of only 5000 men and women. It was poorly armed (most of its weapons were of Japanese origin). According to one British account, it faced considerable problems in the initial stages of the revolt:

> the newly formed MPABA was in no fit state to mount company-sized assaults. It had in fact extreme difficulty in completing the fairly straightforward job of assembling the units in camps in the jungle and supplying them. There were few competent officers, the men were untrained, few knew how to handle their weapons, their knowledge of tactics was nil, their discipline poor and morale even worse at times. In short, command, organization and ability in the MPABA were either bad or non-existent.[40]

Communist successes in this first phase were few. On 1 July a guerrilla force occupied the small town of Gua Musang and remained in possession for five days before withdrawing in the face of strong British relief forces; on 13 July another Communist unit seized Batu Arang for 24 hours. The British themselves were convinced that an attempt by another guerrilla force to seize Kajang, south of Kuala Lumpur, was foiled only when, on 16 July, police clashed with a party of guerrillas, killing a number. Among the dead was Lau Yiu, the intended military commander of the insurrection.[41] Nowhere did it prove possible to establish liberated areas that could be held against the British, although the Communists were able to gain some degree of control over perhaps as many as a hundred rubber plantations. The war was an affair of sporadic incidents: raids on police stations, ambushes and the shooting of collaborators and informers. It did not, as of yet, amount to a serious threat.

By the end of 1948, according to official figures, the guerrillas had killed 149 troops and police and wounded another 211. They had also killed over 300 civilians, mostly Chinese collaborators. Their own losses were estimated at 374 killed and another 319 surrendered or captured. By the end of the year, facing up to their difficulties, the guerrillas decided to withdraw their main forces into deep jungle camps for a period of training and reorganisation. They also set about re-establishing the underground network of supporters among the Chinese squatter population that they had maintained during the Japanese Occupation. Now known as the Min Yuen, this network was developed into a powerful secret movement, estimated by the British to be some 60 000 strong. The number of incidents fell dramatically from an average of 200 a month to less than 100 a month by the spring of 1949. The British authorities were confident that they had the insurgency firmly under control and that by the end of 1949 all that would remain to be done was to mop up the defeated remnants of the guerrilla army.[42] The Communists were soon to prove them wrong when the renamed Malayan Races' Liberation Army (MRLA) launched a new offensive. By the end of 1949 the number of incidents was averaging 400 a month and British confidence in the outcome of the struggle was no longer so sure.

The Briggs Plan

The declaration of the State of Emergency saw the British impose a veritable police state on the people of Malaya. Sweeping Emergency regulations were introduced which gave the police wide powers of search, arrest and detention, and made possible the imposition of curfews, bans, collective punishments and rigorous food controls. The regulations were to eventually cover 149 pages. Large numbers of people were placed in detention: at the end of 1949 there were 5362 people in detention camps and by the end of the following year the number had risen to 8508. Altogether between 1948 and 1957, when Malaya finally became independent, nearly 34 000 people had been detained without trial, and this figure does not include those held for less than 28 days.[43] Along with detention, a large number of the regime's opponents, overwhelmingly Chinese, were deported: over 600 in 1948 and over 10 000 in 1949. By 1955, 31,245 people had been deported.[44] Moreover, the government introduced a battery of legal sanctions, including the death penalty for a wide range of offences, including the possession of firearms and explosives. In the course of the Emergency, 226 Communists were to be actually hanged, a figure only exceeded in British post-war counterinsurgency operations by the judicial slaughter that was practised in Kenya.[45] These draconian measures were, as Thompson observes, all introduced 'with the full consent of the Labour government in London'.[46]

The government dramatically increased the size of the security forces, expanding the regular police from some 10 000 to over 40 000 by the end of 1949. The police were stiffened by the arrival of some 500 British ex-Palestinian Police, veterans of the Zionist insurgency against British rule, who were enlisted as sergeants for the war against the Communists. The number of troops was increased from 10 to 22 battalions. Of crucial importance were the overwhelmingly Malay special constabulary and auxiliary police, which effectively enlisted the Malay population in the war against the Communists. Eventually the special constabulary was to number over 40 000, while the auxiliaries reached a peak strength of almost 100 000 in late 1951.

With the administration continuing to function and a strong security apparatus, equipped with extensive powers, put into place, the government still failed to bring the revolt to an early end. According to Anthony Short, one reason for this was that when the MRLA returned to the offensive, their organised support among the population, particularly among the Chinese squatters, was easily equal to that of the government 'in the matter of supplies and superior in the matter of intelligence'. From the middle of 1949, the number of incidents rose to over 400 a month. Major incidents reached their peak during the first week of September 1950, with a total of 65, which was 17 more than the previous peak. On the whole, road ambushes offered the guerrillas the greatest possibilities both of inflicting casualties and of securing weapons, and while, from September 1949 to February 1950, road and occasional rail ambushes averaged about 17 per month, the figure rose to an average of 56 a month between March and September 1950, with a peak of over 100 in the latter month. Features of the renewed guerrilla offensive were the attention that was now being paid to the railways – 25 attacks on trains and rail jeeps in the first seven months of 1950 compared with four in the whole of 1949.[47]

A number of factors are crucial to understanding the initial failure of the government to defeat this offensive, an offensive which for a while threatened to break British morale. First was the fact that much of the Chinese rural population, particularly the squatters, were more under the control of the Communists than they were under that of the government. Very few Chinese rallied to the government: most willingly, some not so willingly, supported the guerrillas. The Min Yuen provided the guerrillas with food, money, medicines, clothing, all kinds of supplies, as well as intelligence and fresh recruits. There was no way that the security forces could effectively police the widely dispersed Chinese squatters; indeed, it is arguable as to whether government control over these people had ever been restored after the Japanese occupation.[48] As long as the connection between the MRLA and the Chinese rural population remained intact, so the Communists would be able to continue the revolt.

Another factor was the terrain in which the guerrillas were operating. The dense tropical rain forest which covered four-fifths of Malaya was ideally suited to guerrilla warfare, providing excellent concealment.

Moreover, the British Army responded to the guerrilla challenge, at least initially, with the traditional methods of 'Imperial Policing', that is, with a series of large-scale sweeps through areas of jungle believed to be hiding guerrilla camps accompanied by reprisals against the civilian population. These operations were invariably failures with any guerrillas in the vicinity slipping away as the troops got into position and the civilian population successfully alienated. Only gradually did the army introduce the more painstaking approach of small jungle patrols and jungle ambushes which were to bear fruit as intelligence improved.[49]

The British response to the guerrilla challenge has been described as one of 'counter-terror'. In the first phase of the conflict, according to Huw Bennett, the 'security forces deliberately aimed to coerce the population into supporting the government with mass arrests, property destruction and forced population movements, including deportation. At the same time lethal force was controlled in a loose manner.'[50] With the MRLA offensive beginning to achieve some success, the troops and police treated the Chinese population with increasing levels of brutality and violence. As long as the guerrillas appeared able to strike at will and then melt away into the jungle, so the security forces turned on the uncooperative Chinese. Harry Miller, a journalist totally opposed to the Communists, described how the ex-Palestinian Police, in particular, resorted to violence as a matter of routine:

> To many of these sergeants every Chinese was a bandit or a potential bandit, and there was only one treatment for them, they were to be 'bashed around'. If they would not talk a sock on the jaw or a kick in the guts might have the desired result. I myself once saw a British sergeant encouraging a heavy-booted policeman to treat a suspect like a football. The young Chinese was kicked all round the room until a threat to report this treatment to headquarters brought the game to a stop.[51]

Troops and police 'infuriated by the squatters' stubborn silence... dismissed them all as "f- Reds" and were liable to knock them about'.[52] On occasion the violence used went considerably further than beatings. There were numerous shootings where the victims were reported as having been 'shot while trying to escape'. Bennett records the first such fatal shooting as taking place on 20 July 1948, to be followed by the shooting of two more men the following day. On 7 November 1948, south of Lenga, no less than 11 men were shot dead while trying to escape, with three more killed in similar circumstances over the next two days. And on 10 November, another six men were shot dead while trying to escape in the Kuala Kubu area.[53]

The worst *known* incident occurred in December 1948 when British troops massacred 24 Chinese civilians at Batang Kali in Selangor; the knowledge of this incident was successfully suppressed by the authorities for 22 years, and no one has ever been prosecuted.[54] A few days after this episode, the High Commissioner, Sir Henry Gurney, wrote to the Colonial Secretary, Arthur Creech-Jones, that the Chinese 'are as you know notoriously inclined to lean towards whichever side frightens them more and at the moment that seems to be the government'.[55] In January the following year, Gurney admitted that it was 'impossible to maintain the rule of law and to fight terrorism effectively at the same time', that the government itself was breaking the law and that 'the Police and Army are breaking the law every day'.[56] On 28 April 1952 the Daily Worker carried a photograph of a smiling Royal Marine holding up the severed head of a dead guerrilla. The government expected a storm of protest, 'but no other British newspaper replicated the photographs or even commented adversely on the practice of severing heads'.[57] Houses, sometimes whole villages, were destroyed in reprisal after Communist attacks: after the guerrillas' brief occupation of Batu Arang in October 1948, over 5000 people were summarily expelled from the area as a punishment, and early the following month, the village of Kachau in Selangor was destroyed leaving some 400 people destitute and homeless. According to Stubbs, the authorities were following a 'coercion and enforcement' policy, an attempt to bully the Chinese into supporting the government and turning against the Communists. It was counterproductive, only increasing support for the Communists among those it affected.[58]

What became clear as the insurgency continued was that urgent measures had to be taken to bring the Chinese squatter population fully under government control, to root out the Communists' organisational infrastructure, the Min Yuen, and to deprive the guerrillas of their sources of food and recruits. Without this, the Communists would be able to continue the struggle indefinitely.

In April 1950, General Sir Harold Briggs was appointed Director of Operations in Malaya and, with the support of the High Commissioner, set about developing a comprehensive long-term strategy for the defeat of the MRLA. The following month Briggs produced his 'Federation Plan for the Elimination of the Communist Organisation and Armed Forces in Malaya'. The so-called Briggs Plan is generally remembered for its proposed resettlement of the Chinese squatter population, but, as Clutterbuck insists, 'it looked far deeper than that'. Briggs recognised that the struggle was, in effect, 'a competition in government' and that the victor would be the side best able to control the population and hopefully win their consent.[59] In this respect it represented 'a milestone in British counterinsurgency policy'.[60]

The thinking behind the Plan was subsequently codified by Robert Thompson in his influential *Defeating Communist Insurgency*:

> An insurgent movement is a war for the people. It stands to reason that government measures must be directed to restoring government authority and law and order throughout the country, so that control over the population can be regained and its support won. This cannot be done unless a high priority is given to the administrative structure of government itself, to its institutions and to the training of its personnel. Without a reasonably efficient government machine, no programmes or projects, in the context of counterinsurgency, will produce the desired results.

He continues:

> The battle in the populated areas represents a straight fight between the government and the insurgents for the control of the rural population. The main method required to restore government authority and control is the strategic hamlet programme, supported by 'clear and hold' operations. The purpose of the programme, supported by these operations, is not just to kill insurgents in the populated areas but to destroy the insurgent subversive organisation and infrastructure there.[61]

Despite later rhetoric about a war for the 'hearts and minds' of the people, the struggle has to be regarded, as one commentator puts it, as a competition in authority rather than in popularity.[62]

The first step in the implementation of the 'Briggs Plan' involved the reorganisation of the machinery of government so as to place it on a war-footing. Briggs established a small Federal War Council to plan and co-ordinate the campaign at national level and War Executive Committees at State and District level to carry out policy. There is little doubt that this administrative shake-up greatly increased operational efficiency and was an essential preliminary to the forced resettlement of the Chinese squatter population into 'New Villages' (NVs).[63]

The resettlement programme was launched in June 1950 and carried out with remarkable speed and urgency: by the beginning of 1952, over 400 000 people had been resettled in some 400 new villages. The programme continued at a slower pace thereafter; but by the time the Emergency finally ended in 1960 a total of some half a million people had been resettled. Resettlement was not accomplished freely, but by the application of overwhelming force in order to prevent any attempt at escape or resistance. It was an emergency measure in a war that the British believed they were in serious danger of losing, and was carried out with little regard for the feelings of the Chinese. Squatter settlements were encircled by large numbers of troops and police before first light, then occupied at dawn without any warning. The squatters were rounded up and allowed to take with them only what they could carry. Their homes and standing crops were fired, their agricultural implements were smashed and their livestock either killed or turned loose. Some were subsequently to receive compensation, but most never did. They were then transported by lorry to the site of their 'new village' which was often little more than a prison camp, surrounded by a barbed wire fence, illuminated by searchlights. The villages were heavily policed, with the inhabitants effectively deprived of all civil rights. They were only allowed out to work and were subjected to rigorous personal search when both leaving and entering the camps. As Malcolm Caldwell observes, in its early phases, at the height of the revolt, resettlement had 'the aspect of an all-out assault on a whole people'.[64]

An account by a Gurkha officer, wholly committed to the policy of resettlement, nevertheless bears witness to

> the human suffering and the emotions of the squatters as they faced the combined forces of police and soldiers who had descended on their homes, without warning, during the hours of darkness...A few cursed, some wept, but the majority of the squatters moved like automata in a dream, without visibly expressing their emotions. For those who watched as part of the cordon force it was a very moving experience; the flotsam of humanity being carried away by the Government as a step, a vital step, in this struggle against Chin Peng and his followers.[65]

A parallel security measure to resettlement was the regrouping of estate and mine labour. This is sometimes neglected in the literature dealing with the Emergency, although it affected 650 000 people. The government ordered that all the workers and their families had to be concentrated in barbed wire–enclosed compounds where they could be effectively controlled and policed. The miners, in particular, were regarded as 'unregenerate bandit-sympathisers'.[66] One study sums up the resettlement and regrouping exercises that in the end involved the compulsory movement of one-seventh of the country's entire population:

> Keeping in mind the economic distress villagers faced, the deterioration in conditions in the NV's and the restrictions which circumscribed everyday life, one is nevertheless forced to conclude that they were indeed pacified. But this is very different from saying that their hearts and minds had been won. At most a small group of elites came to identify with the British cause'.[67]

Briggs also reorganised the intelligence system, establishing a Special Branch in August 1950 with responsibility for all Emergency-related intelligence gathering. He also strengthened the Information and Psychological Warfare services, bringing in Hugh Carlton Greene, a future Director General of the BBC, as head of Emergency Information Services.[68]

In retrospect, resettlement and regroupment can be seen as the measures that broke the back of the Communist revolt, that by isolating the MRLA from the Chinese population, made its defeat inevitable. At the time, however, this seemed far from being the case. MRLA strength reached its peak during 1951 with some 8000 men and women under arms. The number of casualties they inflicted continued to rise: in 1950 the guerrillas killed 70 soldiers and 323 police, and in 1951 killed 124 soldiers and 380 police. They achieved their most spectacular success on 6 October 1951 when the High Commissioner, Sir Henry Gurney, was killed in an ambush. Moreover, large-scale operations to clear the Communists from the southern states of Johore, Negri Sembilan and south Pahang, as a first stage in rolling them back up the peninsular, ended in failure. The situation appeared desperate.

Templer

The death of Gurney was followed soon after by the retirement of Briggs in December 1951, and the incoming Conservative government took the decision to replace them with one man who would combine both civil and military responsibilities. The government considered a number of soldiers for the new post, among them Field Marshal Montgomery, but, in the end, General Sir Gerald Templer was appointed High

Commissioner and Director of Operations. He arrived in Malaya in early February 1952. Templer was well-qualified for his new post, having had considerable experience of intelligence work and civil administration as well as of actual combat. Before the Second World War, he had fought in the counterinsurgency campaign to suppress the Arab revolt in Palestine; during the War itself he had for a time served in the Special Operations Executive and, since the War, had been Director of Civil and Military Government in the British Zone in Germany and later Director of Military Intelligence. Moreover, despite the low level of morale and the administrative infighting that he inherited, he took over in Malaya at a time when the foundations for a British victory had already been laid by the Briggs Plan.

While the fact that the tide had turned was not apparent to the British, it was very much apparent to the MCP. As Anthony Short emphasises, 1951 might have been a bad year for the government, but it was a worse year for the Communists, culminating in a dramatic change of policy in October. The Central Committee recognised that military victory was not possible in the foreseeable future and consequently downgraded military operations. Political agitation and organisation among the people became the priority, while MRLA units were ordered to withdraw deeper into the jungle, to retrain and regroup, to try and achieve a degree of self-sufficiency. It was considered of the utmost importance that any future guerrilla operations should be conducted so as not to alienate the population. This was a major strategic retreat and provided ample testimony to the efficacy of the Briggs Plan. It did not, however, indicate that the war was over or that the MCP had altogether abandoned the military struggle. Instead, they had been forced on the defensive.[69] Interestingly, Chin Peng himself was to acknowledge the decisive importance of the Briggs Plan 'in isolating us so dramatically from our mass support' and thereby accomplishing 'the CPM's defeat on the battlefield'.[70]

What then was Templer's contribution to the British counterinsurgency effort? He brought new energy and vigour, putting an end to the administrative infighting that had characterised the early years of the Emergency and placing the governmental machine on an effective war-footing. His combining of the offices of High Commissioner *and* Director of Operations gave him a degree of authority that Briggs had lacked, and he made decisive use of it. From now on, everything was subordinated to the task of defeating the Communists and he was publicly scathing about those sections of the European community who did not pull their weight. Considerable effort was put into raising morale, with Templer himself playing a significant role as the symbol of British resolve and determination. This high profile led to an exaggeration of his part in the Communist defeat. Essentially, what he did was to provide the leadership necessary to carry the Briggs Plan through to success, but the job was more than half done by the time he arrived.[71] Despite his commitment to a 'hearts and minds' approach and to Malayan independence, Templer was certainly not a liberal in the Mountbatten mould. As Chief of the Imperial General Staff he was enthusiastically to support the Suez Invasion in 1956 and advocated the invasion of Iraq in 1958. Templer was an 'ardent Imperialist' who conceived of Malayan independence as a way of strengthening, not liquidating, the British Empire.[72]

Under Templer, the police and the military continued to exploit the strategic advantage that resettlement had given them. The security framework that Briggs had established, with its grid of police stations and outposts and their supporting army units, was improved. There were more police with better equipment and communications. The army increasingly abandoned large-scale sweeps in favour of more productive small-scale patrols and ambushes. A great deal of effort was put into the study of jungle warfare, producing a handbook for officers, *The Conduct of Anti-Terrorist Operations in Malaya*, soon after Templer's arrival, and leading to the establishment of the Jungle Warfare School at Kota Tinngi in 1953. Food denial operations greatly increased the pressure on the MRLA, forcing them to take greater risks in order to get supplies from their supporters, and making them more vulnerable to ambush in the process.[73]

Templer abandoned Briggs' intention of systematically rolling the Communists up from the south and instead resolved to provide the resources for intensive framework operations wherever they appeared vulnerable and results were achieved, effectively clearing the areas where they were weakest first and then working outwards. This enabled him to introduce a policy of declaring areas 'white' once the Communists had been destroyed or driven out, relaxing the unpopular Emergency regulations in them and thereby, it was hoped, consolidating support for the government.[74] This policy was to have most success in central Malaya, and from it came the strategy, later developed by General Sir Geoffrey Bourne, of cutting the peninsula in half by creating a band of 'white' areas across it, effectively severing communications between the Communists in the north and south of the country. From this 'white' band the security forces would then work outwards, crumbling away the Communist districts to both the north and south.[75]

To protect the Malay Kampongs and Chinese 'New Villages', the Home Guard was dramatically increased until, by mid-1953, it was 250

000 strong. Most were Malay, but Templer was insistent that Chinese also be recruited, trained and armed in order to help protect themselves against the Communists: eventually some 50 000 Chinese were enrolled in the Home Guard. The successful establishment of this militia force, whatever its military deficiencies, was a serious blow for the MRLA. The government was all the time increasing in strength, while the MRLA were in an apparently irreversible decline. As areas were cleared of guerrillas and the Min Yuen organisation was uprooted, so the election of representative village councils was allowed, introducing an element of local government and helping with the emergence of political alternatives to the MCP.

Templer gave the highest priority to intelligence. Soon after his arrival in Malaya, he told one newspaper correspondent that the Emergency 'will be won by our intelligence system'.[76] The main problem that faced the security forces was how to identify the Min Yuen operatives in the New Villages and how to find the MRLA guerrillas in the jungle. Under Templer, Special Branch was built up and played the decisive part in breaking the Min Yuen organisation, tearing it up by the roots. Even in the pursuit of the MRLA, Special Branch had an important contribution to make. It was not so much the countless hours of exhausting jungle patrols and ambushes, important though they were, as the intelligence gathered by Special Branch from its growing network of informers and agents and from the interrogation and turning of prisoners that made possible the successful hunting down of the elusive guerrillas. By May 1953, some 180 captured or surrendered guerrilla fighters had been successfully 'turned' and formed into 12 Special Operations Volunteer Force platoons and sent back into the jungle to help hunt down their former comrades.[77]

What part did torture play in all of this? According to Calder Walton, there can be no doubt that torture took place, but there is no evidence that it was 'institutionalised'. Instead, he argues that 'Gestapo methods' were sometimes used in front-line questioning, as much as punishment as for information, but that it was eventually realised that other methods were necessary if reliable intelligence was to be obtained and prisoners even 'turned'. Nevertheless, he still recounts the case of an Australian Communist sympathiser who, in 1951, was beaten, kicked, punched and caned, threatened with execution and had a needle inserted under his fingernails by the police. By 1954, there was apparently, according to one senior police officer, 'less beating up'.[78]

Another important element in the defeat of the MRLA was psychological warfare. The dropping of huge quantities of leaflets on the jungle and the use of 'voice' aircraft to broadcast to the guerrillas, sometimes referring to them individually, urging them to surrender, had an inevitable effect once it became clear that the MRLA was in retreat. In 1953 alone the RAF dropped 54 million leaflets on the jungle.[79]

One factor that was of little importance in the conflict was air power. The MRLA never presented a good enough target for attack by aircraft to be effective, although, of course, this did not stop bombing missions taking place. According to one account, between 1950 and 1958 one of the Lincoln heavy bomber squadrons stationed in Malaya dropped 17 500 tons of bombs and was credited with killing a derisory 16 guerrillas.[80] More recently it has been argued that aerial bombardment was more successful, with the dropping of 35 000 tons of bombs during the course of the fighting which accounted for nearly 700 guerrilla fatalities. This claimed casualty level seems wildly inflated but, even if true, still meant that it took 5 tons of bombs to kill one guerrilla.[81] The sceptical observation of one police officer to the effect that carpet bombing the jungle was 'like dropping bombs in the sea in the hope of hitting a passing submarine' seems eminently realistic.[82] Such operations continued throughout the Emergency regardless.

Breakthrough

By September 1952, Templer was already writing to the Colonial Secretary Oliver Lyttelton with cautious optimism: 'Though I hardly dare admit it to myself...I sometimes feel that, in a small way, we have to some extent got the initiative at last...I think I can say to you privately that the situation is improving a bit.' In fact, of course, the Briggs Plan had already driven the MCP on the defensive, and with their change of policy in October 1951, the security forces were able to seize the initiative much more quickly than Templer expected. In February 1953, while still wary, he nevertheless wrote with more confidence: 'For the last couple of months...all the incidents, practically speaking have been staged by us. The balance of arms and ammunition recovered over arms and ammunition lost is extremely satisfactory – as is the reduction of our own casualties which today are practically nil. What puzzles me is how they are going to keep up their morale unless they are more offensive than they are at present.'[83] His confidence was justified: 1953 was, for the British, to be the 'breakthrough year', with September seeing the declaration of the first 'white' area.[84]

The MRLA's retreat into deep jungle created fresh problems for the security forces. The Communists succeeded in allying themselves with the aboriginal tribes of the interior who provided them with food and acted as an effective 'radar screen', warning of the approach of troops or police. Initially, attempts were made to resettle the aborigines in new villages, but this policy was abandoned as between a third and a quarter of those captured died of disease or despair. According to one account 'literally thousands died' as a result of this disastrous policy.[85] An attempt was made to starve the Communists out by spraying jungle gardens and cultivations from the air with trichlorophenoxyacetic acid (245T), something which the British 'have remained rather shy about', but this only further alienated the aborigines.[86] Eventually it was decided to establish jungle forts in the interior with strong police garrisons who would drive away the Communists and establish good relations with the aborigines, providing medical and trading facilities. The recently re-formed Special Air Service (SAS) was to play an important part in deep jungle operations.[87]

Templer's military successes were, however, underpinned by social and political reforms which provided the essential framework within which the MRLA's defeat was accomplished. He was the great exponent of the 'hearts and minds' approach, of attempting to secure the allegiance of the better off Chinese and to make sure of retaining the allegiance of the Malays. This was to be achieved by a combination of material rewards and political advance. Templer saw the Emergency very much as a process of 'nation-building', of creating a strong Malayan State that was accepted as legitimate by a majority of the population and remained loyal to the Empire. His success in this regard was, as Richard Stubbs has emphasised, due in good part to the Korean War:

> Prices for the two pillars of the Malayan economy – rubber and tin – were catapulted to record heights. The resulting boost had important consequences for the financial position of the Malayan Government as well as for the prosperity of Malayans in general. If not for the Korean War boom, the course of the Emergency would have been very different.[88]

Unemployment fell and living standards rose, inevitably undermining the appeal of revolutionary politics. And for those foolish enough to remain obdurate there were the Special Branch and the Gurkhas.

Templer actively sought to encourage the development of 'moderate' political groupings, the United Malays National Organisation (UMNO) and the Malayan Chinese Association (MCA). The MCA, in particular, was regarded as a crucial factor in combating Communist influence within the Chinese community. Moreover, as the British moved in the direction of independence, so inevitably the prestige and influence of these two inheritor parties increased and the raison d'être for the Communist rebellion accordingly diminished.[89] This political strategy was really the key to victory. The point was fully acknowledged by one of the foremost exponents of jungle warfare, John Cross, a Gurkha officer in Malaya and later Commandant of the Jungle Warfare School: regardless of the tactical victories achieved through jungle craft, the British won the conflict because 'their political base proved stronger than the Communists', whereas the Dutch, French and Americans all lost in similar conflicts 'because the political bases from which they operated were not as strong as those of their adversaries'.[90]

The Communist defeat

By the time Templer stepped down as High Commissioner in June 1954, the Alliance Party that had been formed between UMNO and the MCA was already beginning to demand more rapid progress towards representative government and independence. In July 1955 the first federal elections were held, with the Alliance obtaining 81 per cent of the vote and winning 51 out of 52 seats. The Alliance leader, the Tunku Abdul Rahman, became chief minister and set about extracting an early declaration of independence from a reluctant British government that predictably favoured a more leisurely pace.[91]

The changed situation with an elected Malayan government, and independence clearly imminent, did not go unnoticed by the MCP. Chin Peng made secret approaches for peace talks and, to the consternation of the British, the Tunku agreed. The talks took place at Baling near the Thai border over two days in December 1955. They broke down when it became clear that the MCP was required, in effect, to surrender and would remain proscribed even once the fighting stopped.[92] When independence was finally granted to Malaya on 31 August 1957, the counterinsurgency campaign continued.

This last phase of the Emergency saw the British using overwhelming force to relentlessly hunt down the last surviving MRLA units. The campaign still involved immense, painstaking effort against a brave and determined enemy, but the final outcome was never really in doubt. By the time of the Baling talks, guerrilla strength had been reduced to some 3000 hard-pressed men and women effectively isolated from their popular base. Unable to make good their losses, they were being remorselessly ground down by a process of attrition: in 1956 over 300 were killed, 52 were captured and 134 surrendered, and the following year a further 240 were killed, 32 captured and 209 surrendered. The extent to which the Communists had been forced on the defensive is shown by the fact that in these two years they killed only 47 and 11 members of the security forces.

Under General Bourne, a band of 'white' areas was established across the country, effectively cutting off Chin Peng, hiding out on the Thai border, from the MRLA units under Hor Lung in Johore. Bourne's successor as Director of Operations, General Sir Roger Bower, began operations to both the north and south of this band in the summer of 1956. Operations Cobble, Shoe and Tiger effectively destroyed the MRLA in Johore, with the formidable Hor Lung himself surrendering in April 1958. He was successfully turned and brought out another 160 guerrillas for which he was paid $247 000. To the north, Operations Chieftain, Bintang and Ginger accomplished the same task in Perak, with the last surviving guerrillas escaping into Thailand. The MRLA effectively ceased to exist as a fighting force in the course of 1958. During that year, 153 guerrillas were killed and 22 captured, but most significantly 502 surrendered; the security forces suffered ten fatalities. The MCP itself recognised defeat and that year took the decision to 'fold up the banner and silence the drums'. The war was over and the Emergency was finally ended on 31 July 1960.[93]

What factors then account for the Communists' defeat and for the successful establishment of a stable conservative pro-Western regime? There are three essential elements. First of all, the MCP failed to win any significant support among the majority Malay population and yet still launched their rebellion regardless. While some Malay leftists took to the jungle to fight with the guerrillas, their number was always relatively small. According to one account, of the 3791 guerrillas killed between June 1948 and January 1953, only 281 were Malays or Indians, the rest Chinese.[94] The only real success that the MRLA had in recruiting Malays into its ranks was in Pahang, where its Tenth Regiment had a multi-racial character, but this unit was destroyed by early 1950. As Short observes, 'with the elimination of the Tenth Regiment...the threat of a multi-racial "People's War" dwindled away and the MCP was again subject to its racial limitations'.[95] Elsewhere, the reality was always that the Malays and their leaders rallied to the government, providing it with home guards, police and, increasingly, regular soldiers. It was the British success in keeping the loyalty of the Malays, in dividing the population, that was the key to their victory. If, at any time, the British had lost Malay support, then without question their position would have quickly become untenable. The commitment to independence was vital in this regard.

Second, the British were able to bring to bear overwhelming force which was applied with increasing sophistication. The Briggs Plan and the manner of its implementation can be seen as crucial in this respect. If, however, the MRLA had had the support of a significant section of the Malay rural population, rather than just of the Chinese squatters, then it is difficult to see how the British would have found the resources to implement it. Instead, the British were able effectively to isolate the guerrillas from their popular base and then subject them to a remorseless process of attrition, both physical and psychological. The effectiveness of Special Branch together with the Army's improving jungle warfare skills resulted in the Communists being relentlessly hunted down. At no time in the campaign did the MRLA possess either the numbers or the weaponry to be able to think realistically of wresting the initiative from the British and, once the Briggs Plan was put into operation, their eventual defeat was assured.

Lastly, the MCP received no outside help. There were no bases in neighbouring friendly countries, no Ho Chi Minh trails, no supplies of modern weapons. They relied completely on their own resources, fighting on with weapons that had been captured from the Japanese or from the British. This last factor is not necessarily of decisive importance in a guerrilla war, but taken together with the first two factors it accounts for the completeness of the Communist defeat. They lost first of all because of the scale of the difficulties they faced and secondly because of the success with which the British made use of overwhelming force to exploit those difficulties.

3
The Mau Mau Revolt

The 'Mau Mau' revolt in Kenya was for many years an almost forgotten incident in British colonial history. At the time it was portrayed as a barbaric tribal response to the pressures of modernisation, as a reversion to primitive superstition and blood-crazed savagery caused by the inability of the African to cope with the modern world. This racist caricature disguised the grim reality of a revolt against oppression, exploitation and injustice that was to be crushed with incredible brutality and ruthlessness. The scale of the repression unleashed during the Kenya Emergency remains unprecedented in the history of the post-war British counterinsurgency campaigns. Whereas this reality was once routinely denied, now, it is fair to say, it is accepted as fact with the actual dimensions of the repression still in the process of being uncovered. David Anderson, for example, has described the conflict as 'the great horror story of the British empire in the 1950s'.[1] This is not an exaggeration.

There seems little doubt that if African protest in Kenya had been opposed only by the British government and its colonial administration, then concessions would have been made. The British, however reluctantly, would have initiated the process of seeking a neo-colonial resolution of African demands and thereby avoided the large-scale bloodletting that was to come. This was to be accomplished elsewhere, in Ghana and Nigeria, for example. In Kenya, the Africans confronted not just the British government, but a white settler community that had interests distinct and separate from those of the Imperial homeland and that was prepared, in defence of those interests, to unleash repression on a scale that the British themselves would not have regarded as productive. Whereas at the start of the 1950s the British still perceived their interests as identical with those of the settlers, by the end of the 1950s they had separated out their interests and were prepared to sacrifice the settlers in order to safeguard them. The settlers in Kenya, unlike their 'kith and kin' in Rhodesia, did not have the necessary social weight to attempt going it alone. In the last instance, they were dependent on the British government and could be 'betrayed' if a deal with moderate African nationalists proved necessary. It was the 'Mau Mau' revolt that, even in defeat, forced the British down this road.

The Kikuyu and revolution

The 'Mau Mau' revolt was largely confined to the Kikuyu tribe, which had borne the brunt of the socially disruptive impact of European rule and settlement. For the Kikuyu, the white settlement was an unqualified disaster. As well as occupying part of their tribal lands, it also occupied lands into which they would have eventually spilled over had the Europeans never come. Now the settlers penned them in. By 1948, one and a quarter million Kikuyu were restricted to landholding in 2000 square miles of tribal lands, while 30 000 settlers occupied 12 000 square miles, including most of the land worth cultivating.

On the Kikuyu reserves there was widespread poverty, unemployment and under-employment, and chronic overpopulation. There was bitter resentment among the great mass of the Kikuyu against those who were prepared to collaborate under the status quo. In the 1947 Kiambu District Annual Report, E.H. Windley wrote of a 'tendency to create a landlord class' in the reserves, and many other observers commented on the increasing differentiation among the Kikuyu peasantry, the mass of whom were sinking deeper into poverty and economic insecurity, while at the same time a *'kulak'* gentry class was emerging that supported the government.[2] By 1953 almost half the population of the Kikuyu reserves was without land. This process of differentiation was to provide the basis for the civil war within the Kikuyu that became an important aspect of the 'Mau Mau' revolt.

Over the years of colonial settlement, some 120 000 Kikuyu had been forced off the reserves and had settled as squatters on European farms, with a patch of land for themselves in return for their labour. They were, in effect, tenant farmers. Increasingly, their position as independent producers came under attack from their European landlords, who sought to transform them into agricultural labourers without viable landholdings of their own. Whereas before the Second World War a labour rent of 90 days a year had served as payment for five or six acres of land, by 1946 a labour rent of 240–70 days was being demanded for one and a half acres of land. Frank Furedi has estimated that the real income of the

Kikuyu squatter population may have fallen by as much as 30 to 40 per cent and that this deterioration was accelerating during the late 1940s. A bitter hatred of the white settlers and a fierce determination to retain their stake in the land made the squatters the backbone of the revolt in the countryside.[3]

Thousands of Kikuyu were forced off the land altogether and driven to seek work in the towns. Between 1938 and 1952 the African population of Nairobi more than doubled, increasing from 40 000 to 95 000. Times were hard. In 1955 the East Africa Royal Commission reported that 'the conditions of life of the poorer Asian and the majority of Africans in the towns have been deteriorating over a considerable period'. The commission found that the majority of African workers were paid too little to obtain accommodation that was adequate 'by any standard', and cited instances of working men sleeping 14 to a room while others, of necessity, slept outdoors. Half the workers in private employment and a quarter in public employment earned less than was necessary to provide for their essential needs as single persons: wages were altogether inadequate to support a family. The African worker was usually hungry, poorly clothed and either badly housed or altogether homeless.[4] It was in these deteriorating conditions, highlighted by racial discrimination and gross inequality, that the spirit of revolt was kindled and that desperate men and women were ready to turn to desperate remedies. Nairobi was to become the centre of the 'Mau Mau' revolt.

The accumulation of resentments and grievances among the Kikuyu in the early post-war years coincided with the closing off of any possibility for peaceful reform or political advance. When the Labour government's Colonial Secretary, James Griffiths, visited Kenya in May 1951, the constitutional Kenya African Union (KAU) presented him with a memorandum demanding 12 elected representatives on the Legislative Council, the abolition of discriminatory legislation, greater freedom for trade unions and financial aid for African farmers. Independence was not a demand. In the best traditions of British social democracy, Griffiths offered to increase African representation on the Legislative Council from four to five nominees. The proposals that he put forward gave the 30 000 settlers 14 elected representatives, the 100 000 Asians six, the 24 000 Arabs one, and the five million Africans five nominated representatives. The Labour government's position was that the Africans should, for a long time to come, remain in the paternal care of the colonial administration and the white settlers.

Even the settlers were astonished at this sell-out of African hopes; they had been fully prepared to make greater concessions to the Labour government. There was no opposition from the Labour left in Parliament, although, outside Parliament, Fenner Brockway attempted to rally support for reform in Kenya. Griffiths' proposals effectively crushed African hopes of peaceful advance. It is worth noting that the Labour Party only officially came out in favour of 'one man, one vote' in the colonies as late as 1956, in its policy statement 'The Plural Society'.[5]

The development of the revolutionary movement in Kenya in these years is still shrouded in secrecy and uncertainty. The exact delineations of the movement have still not been satisfactorily laid bare and some doubt must exist as to whether they ever will be. However, we can say with some certainty that it was the General Council of the banned Kikuyu Central Association (KCA) that in the late 1940s decided to launch a recruitment campaign intended to enrol the whole of the Kikuyu in a movement of civil disobedience against the British. Land was the central question that concerned the KCA. Certainly the time was ripe for such an initiative and, using the legal activities of the KAU as a cover, the movement made great headway. It was bound together by the oathing rituals traditionally important in Kikuyu life. This was the movement that was to become known to the white settlers, and has since become generally known, as 'Mau Mau'. 'Mau Mau' was not its Kikuyu name. To them it was known variously as 'Muingi' or 'The Movement', 'Muigwithania' or 'The Unifier', 'Muma wa Uiguano' or 'The Oath of Unity', or simply as the KCA. It is a tribute to the effectiveness of British propaganda that a revolt in which thousands of Africans were killed still bears the bastardised name coined for it by the British. Indeed, the rebels themselves eventually came to embrace the name as a mark of honour.[6]

While the KCA General Council carried on the oathing campaign and the establishment of secret committees throughout the reserves and the White Highlands, the centre of gravity of the movement began to shift towards a more radical leadership in Nairobi. Here the nascent trade union movement, in particular the Transport and Allied Workers Union led by Fred Kubai, and the Clerks and Commercial Workers Union led by Bildad Kaggia, were the backbone of resistance to the colonial authorities. The important part played by the semi-proletarianised urban Kikuyu and their unions in the 'Mau Mau' revolt is still often unrecognised but, in fact, their participation was crucial. It is most unlikely that any sustained revolt would have taken place without it.[7]

On 1 May, 1949 six trade unions came together in Nairobi to form the East African Trades Union Congress (EATUC). Kubai was elected president and Makhan Singh, an Asian socialist, was elected general-secretary.

Early in 1950 the EATUC launched a campaign against the granting of a Royal Charter to Nairobi because of the city's undemocratic white-controlled council. Africans were urged to boycott the celebrations. The campaign was a great success and caused the colonial authorities considerable embarrassment. Presaging the future, the campaign led to violent clashes between African radicals and loyalists, with unsuccessful attempts to assassinate Tom Mboteli, the vice president of the KAU who had opposed the boycott, and Muchohi Gikonyo, a prominent Kikuyu loyalist. Soon afterwards, at a rally on 1 May, the EATUC issued a demand for Kenyan independence. This was too much for the authorities; both Fred Kubai and Makhan Singh were arrested.

On 16 May those EATUC officials still at large called a general strike in Nairobi. The strike paralysed the city for nine days and was broken only after more than 300 workers had been arrested and a massive show of strength involving heavily armed troops, armoured cars and overhead demonstrations by RAF aircraft had been made. The strike spread elsewhere and, according to Makhan Singh, at its height involved more than 100 000 workers. Mombasa was paralysed for two days. Despite this display of militancy and solidarity, the strike failed, and over 2000 workers were victimised.[8] Makhan Singh was placed in detention, where he remained without trial for the next 11 years, while Kubai was held in custody charged with complicity in the attempted murder of Gikonyo. He was eventually acquitted and released eight months later. This repression effectively smashed the EATUC. The Kenya Labour Department, in its annual report at the end of the year, ascribed the authorities' victory to 'the careful preliminary planning of those concerned with law and order' and reaffirmed its belief 'that the trade union movement should be encouraged to develop slowly'.[9]

After the defeat of the general strike and the collapse of the EATUC, the leaders of the trade union movement threw themselves into the KCA oathing campaign. They constituted a new radical leadership that gave the oathing movement in Nairobi an altogether different complexion from what it had in the reserves or in the White Highlands. In Nairobi it was a revolutionary movement committed to the overthrow of colonial rule by militant mass action, by strikes, demonstrations and armed conflict, rather than to the KCA General Council's timid and ineffective adherence to civil disobedience.[10]

Whereas the radicals had previously ignored the Nairobi branch of the KAU, they now proceeded to capture control of it, packing meetings with trade union members. In the branch elections in June 1951 Kubai was elected branch chairman, John Mungai, another

Transport Union leader, was elected vice-chairman and Kaggia was elected general-secretary. They had effective control of the organisation. As John Spencer, the KAU's historian has argued: 'KAU was the only nationalist party of its time in British Africa to fall under the control of a radicalized worker movement'.[11] This did not involve any moderation of their politics. Soon after, they established a secret Central Committee to co-ordinate and control the activities of the oathing movement throughout the city. Both Kubai and Kaggia were also members of this body. It was the effective leadership of the revolutionary movement in Nairobi. Armed squads were formed to enforce its edicts, protect oath administrators from the police, and eliminate informers and collaborators. Kaggia has described how he took part in the trial of an informer in the back of a taxi, found him guilty and immediately had him executed.[12]

While its influence was growing in the KAU, the Nairobi Central Committee was also extending its influence throughout the oathing movement outside of the city. The Nairobi radicals were contemptuous of the KCA General Council's strategy of civil disobedience. Their militancy and advocacy of active resistance won them the allegiance of many local committees in the reserves and in the White Highlands, where younger elements were coming to the fore. By the time of the declaration of the Emergency the General Council's authority was virtually confined to Kiambu District and was being eroded even there.

The movement continued to grow and increase in strength and determination. Its activists, following the lead of the Nairobi Central Committee, became increasingly aggressive: opponents were attacked and sometimes killed in broad daylight, Europeans' property was fired and their livestock were hamstrung. The Governor, Sir Philip Mitchell, only months away from retirement, refused to heed reports of a deteriorating security situation, so the movement's activities went unchallenged. In June 1952, he retired and was succeeded by Henry Potter, who took over as Acting Governor. The following month the Commissioner of Police reported that he considered a plan of rebellion to be already under way. Reluctantly, Potter agreed to limited steps to restore the situation. Collective fines and punishments were imposed in particularly disturbed areas, arrests for illegal oathing were stepped up and an attempt was made to rally moderate and loyalist Kikuyu against the movement. Loyalist chiefs publicly condemned 'Mau Mau' and great pressure was put on prominent KAU leaders, particularly Jomo Kenyatta, to repeat and endorse these condemnations. On a number of occasions Kenyatta gave way to this pressure. At a rally at Nyeri on 26 July he condemned

'Mau Mau' in front of 30 000 people and on 24 August he repeated this condemnation at Kiambu.[13]

This highlights the crucial ambiguity of Kenyatta's position. He was the undisputed idol of the Kikuyu peasantry; despite his lack of sympathy with the radicals they were forced to acknowledge him as their figurehead. His public condemnations sufficiently alarmed the Nairobi Central Committee for them to arrange a meeting with him. Kaggia recalls that up until this time Kenyatta was completely ignorant of the composition of the Central Committee and was surprised to find that it included two members of the KAU National Executive, Kubai and himself.[14] After much argument Kenyatta reluctantly agreed not to continue with his condemnations of the movement. According to Josiah Kariuki, even after this meeting, Kenyatta's relationship with the Central Committee was stormy, and he writes of plans being made to assassinate him on two occasions: at a meeting in Nairobi and at the funeral of Chief Waruhiu, himself a victim of radical gunmen.[15] It is arguable that only Kenyatta's arrest saved him from a collaborator's fate and restored his position as unchallenged leader of the national movement. This evidence that Kenyatta, far from being the leader of the movement, was in fact its opponent, contrasts sharply with the conviction, shared by the colonial authorities and the settlers, that he was virtually its sole instigator, the origin of all the country's problems, and consequently someone whom they had to destroy.

On 17 August the Colonial Office in London received its first indication of the gravity of the situation in Kenya in a report from Acting Governor Potter, who warned of imminent revolution:

> The covert organization is the proscribed Mau Mau secret society, the terms of whose illegal oath include the killing of Europeans 'when the war horn blows,' and the rescue of Kenyatta should he ever be arrested and there is little doubt, though no proof, that he controls this revolutionary organization in so far as it is susceptible to control... In brief, public opinion of all races is greatly disturbed and the Kikuyu are sullen, mutinous and organising for mischief.[16]

On 6 October Sir Evelyn Baring arrived in Kenya to take over as Governor of the colony. The day after his arrival radical gunmen stopped the car of the loyalist Chief Waruhiu on the outskirts of Nairobi and in broad daylight shot him dead. This provided Baring with a dramatic demonstration of the threat the movement posed to British rule. He informed London that 'we are facing a planned revolutionary movement' and on

20 October declared a State of Emergency.[17] That same day troops and police swooped down on known Kikuyu political leaders in what they called Operation Jock Scott. By the end of the day nearly a hundred people had been arrested, including Kenyatta. This sweep, it was hoped, would behead and overawe the Kikuyu resistance and permit a quick return to normality. Baring himself envisaged the Emergency as lasting only a few weeks. Instead a bloody revolution was precipitated. Two weeks after the declaration of the Emergency the first European was killed.

State of Emergency

Operation Jock Scott effectively eliminated the first rank leadership of the Nairobi Central Committee, with both Kubai and Kaggia among those arrested, but it failed altogether as an attempt to crush the movement. That was too deeply rooted to be more than shaken by the mass arrests. According to one account there were over 8000 arrests in the 25 days following the declaration of the Emergency.[18] The destruction of European property and attacks on loyalists increased in number in succeeding weeks as the local committees took individual decisions to fight back.

It was not until January 1953 that the reconstituted Nairobi Central Committee, now called the Council of Freedom, met under the chairmanship of Lawrence Karugo Kihuria and decided to launch a war of liberation. The network of secret underground committees was reorganised into the Passive Wing, which assumed responsibility for supplying the Active Wing, the Land and Freedom Armies, with weapons, ammunition, food, money, intelligence and recruits. The Council appointed Stanley Mathenge to command the movement's armed forces, the Land and Freedom Armies, which were already beginning to assemble in the forests. The revolutionary struggle to drive the British out had begun.

Donald Barnett, in the indispensable book that he co-authored with Mau Mau veteran Karari Njama, *Mau Mau from Within*, has made a number of pertinent points concerning the declaration of the Emergency. He argues that the movement may well have had long-range intentions of engaging in armed struggle against the Europeans but that, at the time the Emergency was declared, it was totally unprepared. Ill-timed action by the more restive of the movement's activists precipitated the Emergency, with its attendant repression, long before the movement was at all ready for an insurrection. There was no prepared strategy to guide a protracted guerrilla war, there were no trained guerrilla cadres, there were pitifully few modern weapons and no channels for smuggling them in from outside the colony, and the movement was, as yet, limited to the Kikuyu and the related Embu and Meru. As Barnett sees it, far from heading off a Kikuyu uprising, the Emergency effectively provoked one before the movement was ready. A section of the settler community saw the Emergency as an opportunity for declaring open season on the Kikuyu to eradicate their political and national consciousness. Beatings, forced confessions and summary executions were common enough to arouse fear among the Kikuyu that the Europeans intended the physical destruction of the tribe. Within six months of the declaration of the Emergency, an incredible 430 men had been officially shot dead while trying to escape! Indeed, the police were actually joking that *simama* (halt) really meant goodbye. Confronted with this repression, the Kikuyu rebelled. This point has been powerfully endorsed by military historian Huw Bennett in his recent account of the conflict where he writes of how 'settler and government action accelerated the onset of the rebellion by radicalizing a large proportion of undecided Kikuyu'. For Barnett the revolt only really began in early 1953, when the first of the Land and Freedom Armies began to assemble in the forests.[19]

The revolt did not extend to the whole of Kenya. Largely confined to the Kikuyu, Embu and Meru, it was geographically restricted to the Central Province, which included Nairobi and the Kikuyu, Embu and Meru reserves, and to the four white settler districts of Nanyuki, Laikipia, Naivasha and Nakaru in the adjoining Rift Valley Province – all in all, ten districts covering an area of 14 000 square miles at the very heart of the country. Topographically, the area was dominated by the heavily forested Aberdare mountain range and by Mount Kenya. It was here that the Land and Freedom Armies established their camps.

The rebel cause had the overwhelming support of the Kikuyu people. According to General Sir George Erskine, over 90 per cent of the Kikuyu gave the rebels their moral support.[20] This tremendous tide of popular sympathy, together with the authorities' initial shortage of troops and lack of an effective intelligence system, gave the Land and Freedom Armies the initiative in the first half of 1953. Large bands were able to move across open country to exact vengeance on collaborators and to attack isolated police and home guard posts. Casualties were heavy, but they were easily replaced by fresh enthusiastic recruits. Only a chronic shortage of firearms prevented the rebels from inflicting serious losses on the police and the settler community. If supplies of modern weapons had been available in these early days, the revolt would have developed very differently from the way it did.

From the beginning the colonial authorities set out to rally the loyalist Kikuyu against the rebels. This local application of the old divide-and-rule tactic was seen as important if the police and troops were to dominate the reserves and successfully uproot the movement's underground organisation. The Kikuyu home guard was intended to play an important part in this process, but it never performed satisfactorily, being, from the beginning, heavily infiltrated by rebel sympathisers. The rebels concentrated considerable effort on the intimidation and elimination of loyalists so that, to some extent, the revolt assumed the characteristics of a civil war between the haves and the have-nots among the Kikuyu.[21] During the course of the fighting over 2000 loyalists were killed. It is perhaps worth making the point that this is a feature of all wars of national liberation, including the American War of Independence.

The most notorious incident in this 'civil war' was the Lari massacre of 26–27 March 1953, when nearly 3000 rebels overran the village of the loyalist Chief Wakahangara. This attack had its origin in a protracted pre-war land dispute in which Wakahangara had collaborated with the authorities at the expense of other Kikuyu.[22] Now his village was destroyed and, together with 70 others, including women and children, he was hacked to death. This raid, with its mutilated corpses and burned-out huts, became the linchpin of British propaganda to discredit the rebels and their cause. What were not publicised were the reprisals that followed, in which hundreds of suspects were killed out of hand by the police and loyalist home guards. At public meetings in the settler districts in subsequent weeks, settler leaders, when asked what was being done to hit back, boasted that so far 400 rebels had been shot out of hand.[23]

In these conditions of rebellion, civil war and government repression, Kenyatta was brought to trial and charged, together with Kubai, Kaggia and others, with managing 'Mau Mau'. The trial lasted five months. There was no evidence of any substance against him, but his conviction was assured. He was found guilty by Mr Justice Thacker and sentenced to seven years' hard labour, to be followed by restricted residence in the remote north of the country for life. The others all received similar sentences. Thacker subsequently received a secret *ex gratia* payment of £20 000 from the Kenya government for his exemplary services.[24]

Only with the arrival in June 1953 of General Erskine to take up the post of Director of Operations did the security forces begin serious efforts to regain the initiative. Troop reinforcements were drafted, bringing their strength up to 20 000 men. They were placed on an offensive footing. The Kikuyu reserves were declared Special Areas, where anyone failing to halt when challenged could be shot. The shooting of suspects on this pretext soon became commonplace. The Aberdares and Mount Kenya were declared Prohibited Areas where Africans were to be shot on sight. The army carried out large-scale sweeps in an attempt to bring the elusive rebel bands to battle where they could be destroyed by superior firepower. All these measures failed to stem the tide of revolt.

The gravity of the situation from the point of view of the authorities was evidenced by the sombre report of the Parliamentary Delegation to Kenya in January 1954:

> It is our view based upon all the evidence available to us, both official and responsible unofficial sources, that the influence of Mau Mau in the Kikuyu area, except in certain localities, has not declined; it has, on the contrary, increased; in this respect the situation has deteriorated and the danger of infection outside the Kikuyu area is now greater, not less than it was at the beginning of the State of Emergency .... In Nairobi, which is one of the most important centres in Africa, the situation is both grave and acute. Mau Mau orders are carried out in the heart of the city. Mau Mau 'courts' sit in judgement and their sentences are carried out by gangsters.[25]

The alarm registered in this report was certainly justified. A settler account of the Emergency published that same year describes the 'Mau Mau' as 'beginning to dominate the city: they forbid Africans to travel on buses, and buses are taken off the road; they forbid Africans to smoke in Nairobi, or to frequent Asian cafes, and their orders are obeyed'. This author believed that 'ninety per cent of the Kikuyu in the city are secretly engaged in Mau Mau activities'.[26]

The inability of the security forces to defeat the rebels was attracting men and women from other tribal groups to the path of armed struggle. Already the authorities had uncovered a secret Kamba Central Committee in Nairobi, which was allowed one representative on the all-Nairobi Central Committee that had been established after the arrest of the Council of Freedom in April 1953, and had ascertained that thousands of Nairobi Kamba had been enrolled in the movement. The leadership of the rebel Kamba were all railwaymen and they effectively dominated the railway workforce, using the railway system as their own lines of supply and communication. This development boded ill for the British since the Kamba were the backbone of the African units in the Army and of the African police. As the Corfield Report on the 'Mau Mau' observes, for the rebels to have enlisted the Kamba in their revolt 'would have been a resounding triumph'.[27] Similarly, rebel Masai bands were becoming active in the Narok district of the Southern Province and this necessitated the despatch of troops and police to hunt them down before the revolt caught hold there. The message of rebellion was being carried into Tanganyika by migrant workers from Kenya. It was no wonder that the settler leader, Sir Michael Blundell, could subsequently recall how in March and April 1954, he feared that the colonialists 'were going to lose the battle for the mind of the African everywhere'.[28]

In Nairobi the movement remained inextricably involved with, and heavily dependent on, the trade unions. A number of union leaders were members of the Council of Freedom, which had established a special committee to supervise trade union work. When the Special Branch temporarily disrupted the Council in April 1953, among those arrested were the general-secretary, the treasurer and three executive members of the Transport and Allied Workers Union and the chairman of the Domestic and Hotel Workers Union. Even after this setback, union involvement in the revolt continued, organising and co-ordinating the activities of the Passive Wing and providing the armed squads that enforced the movement's edicts in the city. It was in Nairobi that the weapons, the supplies, the funds and the recruits were raised to keep the revolt going. Without access to this source, the Land and Freedom Armies would have soon withered and died.

The backbone of the rebellion in Nairobi and consequently throughout the rest of Kenya was provided by the nascent labour movement. The urban petty bourgeoisie, the white-collar workers and intelligentsia, which have predominated in the leadership of national liberation movements in many other countries, were nowhere in evidence. They were either altogether opposed to the revolt or were only reluctantly forced by fear of reprisals to go along with it. What is particularly remarkable, given this situation, is that the revolt lacked any socialist dimension. The rebels demanded the expropriation of the white settlers' land, an end to racial discrimination, freedom for the trade unions, and political independence, but did not challenge the capitalist system. They were against white ownership of industry, trade and commerce, rather than against private ownership. The Kenyan working class was still in the process of formation, and most workers were only semi-proletarianised in that they still had roots in the countryside. In addition, the movement was totally isolated from contacts outside the colony.[29]

In an effort to combat rebel influence in the trade unions, the Kenya Labour Department adopted a policy of encouraging moderate trade unionism. In March 1953 the Kenya Federation of Registered Trade

Unions (KFRTU) was established under the auspices of the Labour Department and an attempt was made to build it into a rival focus against the more militant unions controlled by the Nairobi Central Committee. The Federation had its main base among white-collar unions, such as the Kenya Local Government Workers' Union and the Kenya African Civil Servants' Association. Towards the end of 1953 the ambitious Tom Mboya, a Luo, became general-secretary of the Federation and converted it into a platform for constitutional nationalism. He was completely opposed to the revolt, but blamed it on the injustices perpetrated by the authorities and the settlers. While the Labour Department encouraged this development as the best way to defeat the rebels in Nairobi, the settlers and the military were barely capable of distinguishing Mboya from a hardened 'Mau Mau'.

Despite this myopia on their part, the KFRTU was soon in conflict with the Central Committee. Early in 1954, the KFRTU opposed the boycott of the bus service called by the Central Committee, but was completely ignored. Soon after, when the Committee prepared to call a general strike that would have constituted a major challenge and embarrassment to the British, the authorities, in Mboya's own words, 'sought the assistance of the Federation to stamp out this threat'. The KFRTU played a large part in undermining the Committee's plans and forcing a postponement. In Mboya's own words once again, though many of its officers were 'threatened by the terrorists...fearlessly they went on to stamp out the strike threat'.[30] This development had serious implications for the future, but, in the short term, the whole trade union movement was to feel the full weight of military repression.

Operation Anvil

Only after some time did the British become aware of the extent of the rebel organisation and of the part played by Nairobi. Once this was realised, the security forces achieved their first tangible success, marking the turning point of the Emergency. On Saturday 24 April 1954, Operation Anvil began. It was, as David French points out, 'probably the largest cordon and search and mass detention operation in the history of the British Empire'.[31] Some 25 000 troops and police cordoned off the city and proceeded to round up the entire African population for identification and screening. Among those arrested was Mboya. He noticed that many of those rounded up had white paint splashed on their faces to indicate that they had tried to escape or were picked up in suspicious circumstances.[32] The haphazard nature of the operation was offset by the sheer numbers that were subsequently detained without trial: 27 000 men and women, almost all Kikuyu. According to Huw Bennett, the police actually had targets for the number of people to be detained.[33] Those detained lost everything, taken away, leaving their possessions and property left to be looted by the police and the home guard. Another 20 000 people were deported from the city and returned to the reserve.

The repression struck the trade unions a heavy blow: Mboya reported that detentions and deportations reduced membership of his own union, the Kenya Local Government Workers' Union, from 1300 to 500. However, the main weight of the repression fell on the Transport and Allied Workers' Union and the Domestic and Hotel Workers' Union, both of which were known to Special Branch as organising centres for the revolutionary movement. Nineteen of the officers of these two unions were detained. An interesting commentary on the attitude of the military was provided when a Labour Department official attempted to secure the release of a number of moderate trade union leaders only to be told at the Manyani detention camp that everyone carrying a union card was automatically placed in detention.[34]

Operation Anvil dealt the movement a blow from which it never recovered. It was, according to Michael Carver, at the time a senior staff officer in East Africa, 'the turning point of the campaign'.[35] The attempt to enlist other tribes in the revolt came to an abrupt halt as the whole Nairobi organisation was simply swept away into the detention camps. The Nairobi Central Committee, which had provided the political leadership in the struggle, was gone, and although attempts were made to reconstitute a leadership in the forests, none was successful. The freedom fighters had their most important source of supplies and recruits eliminated almost overnight. From that point on they became an increasingly heavy burden on the already hard-pressed people in the reserves. As a corollary, militant trade unionism in Kenya was decisively crushed and the way was left clear for Mboya's KFRTU, which, although itself battered, was still intact.

The tide was turning decisively against the revolutionary movement. Having successfully cleared Nairobi, the military now carried out similar operations in other areas, until by the end of the year, there were 77 000 Kikuyu in detention. There were thousands of women among those detained; indeed, women's support for the movement was of particular concern to the British. According to one police officer it was 'remarkable how strongly Mau Mau appealed to the women who were consistently more wholehearted in their support of it than the men'.[36] Children as young as 12 were interned. Some 100 000 Kikuyu squatters were forcibly uprooted from the White Highlands and deported back to the reserves. In June 1954, the authorities decided on a massive programme of compulsory 'villagisation' throughout the reserves. According to one account, this was 'the most punitive measure of all'.[37] It would enable the Kikuyu to be effectively policed and kept under close surveillance. The programme was modelled on the resettlement of the Chinese squatters in Malaya, but was on a much larger scale and was carried out with considerably more brutality. Poverty and starvation were to haunt the new villages as thousands of Kikuyu were rounded up, forced to abandon their possessions, herded into the villages where they were left without work, without land, without hope. Surrounded by barbed wire, deprived of all civil rights, they were left at the mercy of a rapacious home guard. The programme was carried out with incredible speed and was completed in October 1955, by which time 1 077 500 people had been resettled in 854 villages. By the end of the conflict, brutality, hunger and disease 'would claim the lives of thousands of these rural people'.[38] During the Emergency, the Kikuyu were to be subject to 'a degree of direct administration...unparalleled among any other people in the history of British colonial Africa'. It was not a happy experience.[39]

The inability of the rebels to prevent or seriously disrupt this resettlement programme signalled the beginning of the end. The Passive Wing throughout the White Highlands and the reserves was completely disrupted, and the Land and Freedom Armies were penned into the forests and isolated from their popular base. They were cut off from their supplies of food and increasingly found their existence dominated by the mere effort to stay alive, leaving no energy to fight the British. There was now no way for losses to be made up and the ranks of the rebel forces were soon depleted. From an estimated strength of 15 000 at the end of 1953, the number of rebels in the field fell to an estimated 2000 at the end of 1955. According to the account of one freedom fighter, by this time the rebels were in such dire straits that they were forced to raid their own impoverished people for food. 'After this it became evident that people from the Reserves were forsaking the forest fighters...their sympathy for the warriors was alienated as they saw forest people come and take away the little that had been left by imperialist denudation'.[40] The resettlement programme was the second crushing blow that won the war for the British and brought the Emergency to an end.

Throughout 1955, massive sweeps involving thousands of troops and auxiliaries were carried out in the forests in an attempt to comb out the remaining rebel bands. The effort involved in these operations was out of all proportion to the results obtained. Peter Hewitt's recent memoir of the Emergency provides a graphic account of one such operation, Operation Bullrush, that began at the end of 1955 and continued into the new year. Some 50 Mau Mau were trapped in a swamp on the shore of Lake Naivasha. Altogether some 3000 troops and police, together with thousands of home guards, were employed in surrounding and searching the swamp, which was subjected to a relentless bombardment night after night. 'Seldom', Hewitt wrote, 'had so many soldiers enjoyed such a one way shooting match ... it was an unparalleled military extravaganza'. He could not understand how the Mau Mau, starving, poorly armed and surrounded by overwhelming numbers, could possibly hold out. Eventually, half of them broke out of the trap, leaving behind 19 of their number killed and six captured, together with one rifle.[41]

More effective was the pseudo-gang technique. This technique had already been employed in Palestine and Malaya and was first introduced into Kenya by the then Captain Frank Kitson.[42] It involved the use of bands of renegades, of captured rebels who were prepared to change sides, pretending to be still loyal to the revolutionary movement in order to make contact with the surviving rebel bands so that they could be broken up and eliminated. Kitson believed this to be the most effective way to kill rebels. By September 1956 it was estimated that there were only 500 rebels still at large. Then the following month pseudo-gangs captured the almost legendary guerrilla leader, Dedan Kimathi, commander of the remaining Land and Freedom Armies. He was subsequently hanged.[43] This success marked the end of the campaign. At the end of the year the army was withdrawn from active service. The fighting was over, although the Emergency remained in effect until January 1960.

One last point worth considering here is the recent attempt to give the RAF and aerial bombardment a central role in the defeat of Mau Mau. According to a recent discussion, between June 1953 and October 1955 the RAF made 'a significant contribution to the conflict' because only air power was 'capable of both psychologically influencing and inflicting considerable casualties on the Mau Mau in Kenya's vast, inaccessible forests'. Indeed, air power was the government's 'chief weapon'. Huge numbers of leaflets were dropped from the air: some 5 million in June 1955 alone. And the RAF bombed the forests. During the Emergency, Lincoln heavy bombers apparently dropped nearly 6 million bombs (!), inflicting heavy casualties, with 900 rebels killed or wounded 'between November 1953 and June 1954 alone'.[44] On 5 December 1953, Baring wrote to the Colonial Secretary justifying the use of heavy bombers against fighters armed with home-made rifles and the occasional precision firearm on the grounds 'that casualties have been caused on a number of occasions' and 'that air bombing has had a detrimental effect on the morale of gangs'. He assured Lyttelton that the Lincolns were carrying out their attacks with 'pin point accuracy'. Erskine himself was more circumspect, describing the Lincoln's military contribution as 'not vital', but expressing concern that their removal would have a bad effect on morale.[45] Claims of the importance of air power have not been treated with enough scepticism. The RAF was, in fact, bombing the forests in the hope of hitting someone. How casualties were assessed is unclear. The claims of success were much more likely a way of ensuring that the bombers were not withdrawn than an accurate assessment of their contribution.

Reform

So far this account has concentrated on the military side of the Emergency, but this is only half the story. The repression was accompanied by political and social reforms that played an equally important part in containing the revolt. The political developments will be dealt with separately, but here we shall look at the social policies the colonial authorities pursued. The government introduced a programme of land reform, the Swynnerton Plan, intended to consolidate the fragmented landholdings of the Kikuyu into single holdings. The intention was to speed up the process of differentiation of the Kikuyu into a gentry Kulak class on the one hand and a mass of landless labourers on the other, to expand the social base of loyalism. In June 1956, C.M. Johnston, Special Commissioner for Central Province, told an audience that the authorities had embarked on what amounts to 'an agrarian revolution in the Kikuyu, Embu and Meru Districts – its nearest equivalent is the 18th and 19th century enclosures in England... it will have the effect of creating a solid middle-class Kikuyu population anchored to the land who has too much to lose by reviving Mau Mau'.[46]

While just over 3500 rebels had their land confiscated, a growing number of other Kikuyu were given a stake in the status quo. The land reform programme, which was completed by the end of the 1950s, was accompanied by a relaxation of the ban that had forbidden Africans to grow coffee, a profitable cash crop. This had long been a bitter grievance of the African farmers and they profited greatly from its removal. Between 1955 and 1964 the recorded value of output from African smallholdings rose from £5.2 to £14 million. The Kikuyu gentry were the main beneficiaries of this remarkable increase.[47]

A somewhat similar picture is seen in the towns where the authorities recognised that the revolutionary politics of the labour movement could most effectively be undermined by combining repression with reform. After Operation Anvil had crushed the movement in Nairobi, the way was clear for concessions. The Report of the Carpenter Committee on African Wages in 1954 prepared the way for substantial rises in African wage rates. Between 1955 and 1964 the annual average wage for African workers doubled from £52 to £107. These rises greatly strengthened the position and standing of the moderate KFRTU and its leader, Tom Mboya. Sharon Stichter argues that the whole character of the labour movement changed in this period and that it was finally constituted as a labour aristocracy – a junior partner of the petty-bourgeois politicians who were eventually to negotiate the neo-colonial settlement in Kenya.[48] While the notion that the whole African working class is to be viewed as a labour aristocracy must be rejected, it has to be acknowledged that the revolutionary nationalism, so evident in the early 1950s, had by the end of the decade turned into political quiescence.

The scale of the repression

According to Wunyabari Maloba, 'the chief characteristic of the war against Mau Mau was brutality'.[49] There was always overwhelming evidence to support this claim, although for many years the accusation was still denied in many accounts. D.H. Rawcliffe, in a book, *The Struggle for Kenya*, published as early as 1954 and promptly banned in the colony, described how during the first months of the Emergency the beating of prisoners and suspects became almost a routine measure if it was thought that information was being withheld. One young man told the author:

> 'It's no use beating the beggars; I've beaten them until I was tired of it!' Every European in the security forces knew about these beatings, talked about them and very often had ordered them or participated in them...There was a tacit conspiracy involving the Kenya government, the police and the press not to reveal or even hint at anything which the outside world would term acts of brutality or callous behavior towards the Kikuyu...However, a report of one appalling case, out of several similar ones, involving a Kikuyu who had been flogged to death, did reach the British press months after its occurrence. It was so well substantiated that the authorities could no longer ignore it; two Europeans were charged with manslaughter and

were later fined. In Kenya white men are never convicted of murder if the victim is black.[50]

British methods, he argued, were 'often reminiscent of Nazi methods'. At the time, Rawcliffe's allegations were either ignored or dismissed as malicious and exaggerated. Such claims were completely overwhelmed by the weight of propaganda that portrayed Mau Mau as a savage reversion to barbarism, detailed the movement's atrocities and celebrated the struggle against it. Over the years, however, it has become clear that, if anything, Rawcliffe's account understated the brutality of the security forces in Kenya.[51]

Beating, torture, mutilation and the shooting of prisoners out of hand were everyday occurrences. A bitter opponent of Mau Mau, Carey Francis, a British headmaster, complained to the authorities that the police were to his certain knowledge 'involved in many acts of brutality to prisoners (sometimes amounting to deliberate and despicable torture) and of looting and destruction of private property'. This behaviour was so widespread 'as to be regarded as the normal policy of the Security Forces'. The police 'are feared and loathed, and never trusted, by the great bulk of Africans, not least by those who are well-disposed'.[52] Anthony Clayton, in his study of the Emergency, places most of the blame for security force excesses on the Kenya Police Reserve (KPR), which seems to have behaved on occasion as a settler vigilante force. He details a number of incidents of torture with British police officers being fined for setting prisoners on fire, beating and flogging them (including beating one man to death), setting dogs on them and roasting one prisoner over a fire. And these cases were, Clayton acknowledges, merely 'the tip of the iceberg of unrecorded but widespread roughing up and the frequent kickings or beatings of prisoners practised by the KPR'.[53]

Robert Edgerton's 1990 account of the rebellion goes even further. Not only were suspects routinely beaten and tortured, but there were also a large number of summary executions being carried out. He describes how

> if a question was not being answered to the interrogator's satisfaction, the suspect was beaten and kicked. If that did not lead to the desired confession, and it rarely did, more force was applied. Electric shock was widely used, and so was fire. Women were choked and held under water; gun barrels, beer bottles, and even knives were thrust into their vaginas. Men had beer bottles thrust up their rectums, were dragged behind Land Rovers, whipped, burned, and bayoneted.

Their fingers were chopped off, and sometimes their testicles were crushed with pliers...Some police officers did not bother with more time-consuming forms of torture; they simply shot any suspect who refused to answer, then told the next suspect who had been forced to watch the cold-blooded execution, to dig his own grave. When the grave was finished, the man was asked if he would now be willing to talk. Sometimes suspects were forced to watch while others were killed, often slowly, with knives instead of bullets.

Edgerton includes in his horrific catalogue of atrocities extracts from some revealing interviews with settlers and former members of the security forces. One man described how a group of settlers dragged two young Kikuyu they suspected of being Mau Mau to death behind a Land Rover, all the time laughing and joking about it: 'the nigger wasn't much more than pulp. He didn't have any face left at all.' A former police officer told how he shot out of hand three Mau Mau suspects who refused to talk and reported them as shot while trying to escape: 'I stuck my revolver right in his grinning mouth...His brains went all over the side of the police station.' Another former police officer described beating prisoners to death as part of the screening process in the detention camps: 'At the end of the day my hands would be bruised and arms would ache from smashing the black bastards.'[54]

William Baldwin, an American who served in the KPR, provides justification for these methods in his first-hand account of the Emergency, *Mau Mau Man-hunt*. After a graphic description of how he shot two wounded Mau Mau prisoners out of hand, he explains his lack of remorse: 'They had lived foully and by their actions had forfeited all rights to be treated as human beings...I looked upon them as diseased animals...Only in death was a cure possible.' He goes on to describe a relentless succession of summary executions of Mau Mau suspects and prisoners, both men and women, shot, bayoneted, throats cut and beaten to death. His account is accompanied by a macabre gallows humour: after he beats a woman to death with his rifle butt, another policeman tells him, 'You might make a good cricketer...Is the bitch dead?' All this is justified on the grounds that the African 'understands and respects summary justice far more than legal pronouncements'. 'Mau Mau', he goes on, 'is like a cancer...and no one ever used an aspirin to cure cancer.'[55]

A more recent memoir by Leonard Gill, cheerfully subtitled 'The anecdotal adventures of a Kenya lad fighting terrorists', recounts the exploits of one officer who 'liked to take prisoners into the forest from which they never returned'. Indeed, on a number of occasions, he took 'an officer from Battalion HQ with him, so that officer could notch the grip of his revolver'. Gill goes on to tell the story of a Captain Harris, who set about killing three prisoners, stabbing one and watching him die, shooting another in the stomach and setting the third on fire with a phosphorous grenade. A Sergeant Rick complained about these sadistic killings, 'but was deemed to have gone off his head and was taken away for psychiatric treatment. We never saw Rick again.'[56]

Nevertheless it was not until the publication of David Anderson's *Histories of the Hanged* and Caroline Elkins' *Britain's Gulag*, both in 2005, that the question of the extent of the repression was decisively settled. Anderson's book is a tremendously impressive account of the conflict and of the part played by capital punishment in bringing it to an end, while Elkins, despite accusations of exaggeration, successfully chronicled the assault on the Kikuyu population through internment, villagisation and imprisonment.[57] More recently the 'discovery' of the Hanslope Park archive has surely put the severity of the repression completely beyond reasonable dispute. As David Anderson has written: 'Many of the documents provide copious detail on the administration of torture and substantive allegations of abuse...our listing of individual notified cases now stands at close to 500 examples...This included the burning alive of detainees.'[58] Another choice revelation from the archive was a letter that the Attorney-General in Kenya, Eric Griffiths-Jones wrote to Baring in June 1957. Here he recommended that when Mau Mau suspects were beaten, the 'vulnerable parts of the body should not be struck' and that those who carried out the beatings 'should remain collected, balanced and dispassionate'. He sagely advised the Governor that 'if we are going to sin we must sin quietly'.[59]

In the past, most accounts of the Emergency, when they admitted to the beatings, torture and summary executions, blamed them on the police and the home guard, and argued that the British troops involved in the campaign were, by and large, well behaved. Certainly after Erskine's arrival an attempt was made to tighten up army discipline, but he still felt obliged to issue a quite remarkable order in June 1953 to the effect that he 'would not tolerate breaches of discipline leading to unfair treatment of anybody...I most strongly disapprove of beating up the inhabitants of this country just because they are the inhabitants'.[60] Nevertheless there were serious incidents involving the army, most notably the summary execution of some 20 captured home guards mistaken for Mau Mau, an affair that was successfully covered up.[61] One officer later recalled that before one operation he received official instructions to take prisoners but unofficial instructions to shoot-to-kill. Who, he wondered, would 'take responsibility' for this order. At what point in the military hierarchy was the order 'subtly transformed'? This, one suspects, is a pertinent question in every counterinsurgency campaign. He is assured that there would be no trouble with 'pinko' magistrates because the intelligence officer had a collection of Mau Mau weapons 'with which to rig the tableau if necessary'.[62] Insofar as the army was less involved in the excesses that characterised security force conduct during this Emergency, this was primarily because the brunt of the fighting was born by others, notably the police. Army casualties were very light, with only 12 British soldiers killed by Mau Mau. Moreover, according to one recent account, by January 1954, Erskine had actually given up trying to impose tighter discipline on some units.[63]

The scale of the official repression was also without precedent in postwar conflicts. As well as the tens of thousands interned without trial, even more people, men and women, were imprisoned for violating the Emergency laws. Between 1952 and 1958, over 34 000 women were sentenced to terms of imprisonment for Mau Mau offences. The number of men sentenced was probably ten times that figure. The government also presided over the most drastic and cruel implementation of capital punishment in modern British history. Between the declaration of the Emergency and early November 1954, no less than 756 rebels were hanged, most for offences less than murder, including 45 for administering illegal oaths and 290 for possessing arms or ammunition. By the end of 1954 the number executed had risen to over 900, and by the end of the Emergency was 1090. This was nothing less than a judicial massacre, justified on the grounds that punishments had to be exemplary to stop the settlers taking the law into their own hands.[64] The Public Works Department built a mobile gallows so that prisoners could be hanged in their home districts as an example to others. At one point, prisoners were being hanged at the rate of 50 a month after what the *Daily Telegraph*'s correspondent subsequently described as 'drumhead trials' that 'made a mockery of British justice'.[65] The scale of the hangings even caused concern in London, where Prime Minister Winston Churchill advised 'that care should be taken to avoid the simultaneous execution of any large number of persons'. It would not do to have public opinion in Britain disturbed by 'anything resembling mass executions'. Churchill actually intervened to prevent Baring from adding the possession of incendiary materials to the list of capital offences on the quite reasonable grounds that men would be hanged for the possession of a box of matches.[66] One has to go back to the suppression of the Great Indian Revolt of the 1850s to encounter such murderous methods.

Despite this slaughter, Frank Kitson could still complain that the security forces in Kenya 'had firmly fastened one of their hands behind their back with the cord of legal difficulties'.[67] Why, one has to ask, was the Mau Mau Rebellion suppressed with such savagery? Racism is the only possible answer. The beatings and the torture, the summary executions and the judicial massacre were only possible because the victims were black. This conclusion is inescapable.

The number of rebels killed in action during the Emergency was officially put at 11 503, but the actual number was considerably higher. Many must have died of wounds in the forests, unknown to the authorities, while others must have been disposed of quietly by the loyalists or the police. Estimates go as high as 50 000, and this is certainly nearer the truth than the official figures. The number of civilians who died takes the total much higher. The casualties suffered by the security forces were considerably lower: only 63 European soldiers and police were killed, 3 Asians and 524 Africans. This disparity emphasises the overwhelming superiority in terms of firepower that the military had over the rebels. One typical British infantry regiment, the Buffs, during their tours of operation in Kenya, killed 290 rebels and captured 194, while suffering only one fatal casualty themselves. Among the weapons they captured were a mere nine precision firearms.[68] Despite the popular image of the revolt as a massacre of the settler community, only 32 settlers were killed, fewer than the number of those who died from traffic accidents in Nairobi over the same period.

One question remains to be considered: did the rebels have any prospect of victory? Realistically the revolt was doomed to defeat despite its tremendous support among the Kikuyu, despite the extent of the revolutionary movement's underground organisation, which could be destroyed only by massive repression, and despite the courage of its fighters. In the first 18 months of the Emergency the rebels had the initiative, the security forces appeared unable to stem the tide of revolt, panic seized hold of the settlers and other tribes were beginning to stir. But they were unable to translate these opportunities into military successes. Why? Their problem was not courage, motivation or skill, but firepower. Bill Woodley, an officer in the Kenya Regiment described how a 30-strong KR patrol had cornered a lone Mau Mau armed only with a pistol in a hut. He shot the first two men who went into the hut after him and then hid in the roof while it was raked with bren gun fire and a grenade was thrown in through the door. Before the smoke cleared, he burst from the hut shooting the bren gunner and two more soldiers before disappearing into the bush. The patrol retreated in disarray whereupon he returned to collect the weapons, ammunition and uniforms of the four men he had killed.[69] Despite such heroism, without modern weapons the rebels were doomed to defeat. They were virtually unarmed and received no outside aid whatsoever. In these circumstances the overwhelming superiority of the security forces was bound to prevail in the end. But while the movement suffered military defeat, it still managed to inflict a major political defeat on the settler community by revealing the fragility of their position, and by demonstrating the complete reliance of the settlers on the support of the British government. Once the British government perceived the settlers as an obstacle to a secure political settlement in Kenya, their fate was sealed.

Not yet Uhuru

Both the Conservative government and the Labour opposition at Westminster were united in the conviction that the revolt had to be suppressed. They were divided over how this was to be accomplished. Labour was critical of the scale of the repression and favoured immediate concessions as the way to strengthen the hand of the moderate African nationalists and undermine the rebels. This, of course, was its opposition position. Its earlier behaviour, when in government, suggests that its practice would have been little different from that of the Tories. The Conservative leaders, on the other hand, wholeheartedly endorsed the repression and were only reluctantly compelled to accept the need for reform and concession. Oliver Lyttelton, later Lord Chandos, recalled that when dealing with Kenyan affairs as Colonial Secretary he felt the close presence of the forces of evil. On occasions, while reading documents relating to the Emergency, a horned shadow fell across the page – the shadow of the devil himself reading over his shoulder. But devil or no devil, even Lyttelton eventually recognised that Africans would have to be given a 'share' in the government. The only alternative was the indefinite continuation of rule by force, and this was not a practical proposition. First of all, Britain no longer had the necessary force, and secondly, the shifting balance of world power made such a policy untenable.[70] The suppression of the revolt, moreover, imposed a severe financial strain on the British government, costing some £55 million. A renewal of the fighting after 1956, especially with the prospect of the rebels receiving aid from abroad, was not appealing, and there was every likelihood of this.[71]

Direct election of African members of the Legislative Assembly was conceded before the 1956/57 elections; the Lennox-Boyd Constitution increased the number of African members to 14 and the Lancaster House Conference of January 1960 pointed out the way to majority rule. What these political concessions involved was the sacrifice of the white settler community in order to facilitate the establishment of a stable neo-colonial regime in Kenya. The rebels had not been strong enough to defeat British Imperialism, but they had determined the fate of the white settlers. This was a major achievement, although it was certainly not a predetermined development, as some accounts seem to suggest.[72] Rather it was accomplished only by armed struggle involving the self-sacrifice of tens of thousands of heroic men and women. During the immediate post-war years in Kenya white supremacy reached its apogee, with the settlers increasingly looking towards the examples of southern Rhodesia and South Africa. Their ambitions were shattered by the revolt. What the rebels accomplished was the separation of the interests of the British state from those of the settlers.

Colin Leys has cogently shown the economic basis for this separation of interests. While the settlers dominated Kenya politically, this was by no means true economically. The settlers probably owned no more than 15–20 per cent of the foreign assets invested in Kenya by 1958, the remainder being owned by British and foreign companies that were quite prepared to accommodate themselves to Africans. The settlers were essentially an 'epiphenomenon': they were marginal to the more fundamental relationship that existed between foreign capital and the Africans. When the intransigence of the settlers was seen to endanger foreign capital, they were abandoned in favour of an alliance with African leaders prepared to safeguard foreign investments.[73]

Nevertheless, while reform and even some form of eventual self-government was accepted as inevitable, this was envisaged as taking place over a considerable period. In January 1959, Lennox-Boyd, Lyttelton's successor as Colonial Secretary, warned that Kenya could not expect independence until after 1975.[74] Later that year, Sir Evelyn Baring told a settler audience that Kenya would never get more than some form of limited home rule because of its strategic importance.[75] This dilatory strategy was swiftly overturned.

Iain Macleod, who became Colonial Secretary in October 1959, was fearful of a fresh outbreak of fighting after the fatal beating of 11 detainees by guards at the Hola internment camp earlier that year. There was evidence that Kikuyu militants were stockpiling weapons and that rebel bands were reforming in the forests. Supported by Prime Minister Macmillan, Macleod greatly speeded up the process of British withdrawal, disregarding the protests of the settlers. Macleod even allowed a certain Peter Poole to become the first European in Kenyan history to be hanged for killing an African. This was a crucial sign of the times, demonstrating Macleod's lack of concern for settler susceptibilities if they stood in the way of negotiating a settlement.[76] He proceeded to negotiate an agreement with the moderate nationalist leaders, including Kenyatta, that effectively abandoned the white settlers but secured the position of foreign capital, which was the overriding concern of the British government. The final handover of power to the Kenyatta government took place on 12 December 1963. The regime that emerged has since proven to be a classic instance of neo-colonialism. The fruits of the revolt were reaped by others.

4
Cyprus and EOKA

The outbreak of the EOKA rebellion on 1 April 1955 came as a complete shock to the British; in the somewhat understated words of the then Minister of Defence, Harold Macmillan, the 'Colonial Office seemed surprised'.[1] As one Conservative MP commented only six months earlier: 'It seems inconceivable that the Cypriots should become vicious like the Egyptians.'[2] The British had convinced themselves over the years that the Greek Cypriot population were not capable of armed resistance and had grown accustomed to ignoring their grievances and wishes with comparative impunity. The interests of the British Empire always came first as far as Cyprus was concerned. What resulted was a guerrilla insurgency that the security forces signally failed to defeat, but where a political success of sorts was nevertheless finally achieved by the mobilisation of the Turkish Cypriot population and with the support of the Turkish government. The military successes that the British were having in Malaya and Kenya were not to be repeated in Cyprus, the counter-insurgency lessons learned in these campaigns were not to produce the same result in the very different context of the Cyprus problem.

Fortress colony

Cyprus was a 'strategic' or 'fortress' colony, a colony whose retention was regarded as essential for the security of the British Empire. The long-standing Greek Cypriot demand for *'enosis'*, union with Greece, was of little consequence compared with Britain's strategic requirements. Moreover, it appeared that Greek Cypriot wishes could be safely ignored. The island had, over the years since Britain had acquired it, been routinely neglected; indeed, as late as 1927, the British had actually been taxing it to pay off old debts incurred by the Turkish government! For many

Greek Cypriots, Turkish rule had actually been preferable to that of the British.[3] Resentment against British rule only came to the surface in the autumn of 1931 when the Governor, Sir Ronald Storrs, introduced stringent economy measures and increased the island's taxation. The Greek Cypriot members of the Legislative Council resigned in protest and Nicodemus, the Bishop of Kitium, issued a manifesto demanding *enosis*. This precipitated a week of rioting and disorder in which Government House was burned down. British reinforcements quickly arrived and suppressed the outbreak, killing 11 people and injuring many more in the process. A number of clerical and political leaders were expelled from the island, a large collective fine was imposed, the constitution was suspended indefinitely and it was made illegal to advocate union with Greece. The flying of Greek flags was banned, and for a while the ringing of church bells was prohibited.[4] This dictatorial regime was, to all intents and purposes, to remain intact until the British finally surrendered sovereignty in August 1960. Attempts at liberalisation were inevitably to come up against the demand for *enosis* on the one hand and Britain's strategic concerns on the other, and so came to nothing.

While constitutionally the situation in Cyprus was one of stalemate, nevertheless the island did undergo considerable change, especially during the war years. There was a dramatic increase in the level of urbanisation, and this together with the failure of wages to keep up with prices combined to increase support for the Communists. The first Communist Party of Cyprus (KKK) had been established in the 1920s, only to be banned in the aftermath of the 1931 rebellion. The party survived underground, continuing its political activities that included despatching some 60 volunteers to fight with the International Brigades in Spain. It finally came back out into the open in October 1941 when it re-formed itself as the Progressive Party of the Working Class (AKEL), enthusiastically supporting the British war effort and urging Cypriots to enlist in the British armed forces. In the municipal elections of 1943 the party captured control of two of the island's six town councils with its leader, Plautas Servas, becoming mayor of Limassol. Both the British and the Greek Cypriot middle class were alarmed by this development.[5]

At the end of the war, the British were worried that AKEL intended to mount a challenge to their rule, perhaps even an armed rebellion. Increasing agitation and conflict seemed to support this view. In March 1945, police had fired on an AKEL demonstration at Lefkonico, killing two people, and then in October a Cypriot army unit mutinied at Famagusta and was forced to surrender only after Indian troops had opened fire on them, killing one man and wounding a number of others. There were a number of other protests within Cypriot units and the British saw the hand of AKEL in all of them.[6] This unrest was accompanied by increasing industrial conflict. In December 1945 the British cracked down and 18 leading trade unionists and Communists, among them Stelios Paulides, Secretary-General of the Pancyprian Trade Union Committee (PTUC), were arrested and charged with sedition. Twelve of the accused were jailed for 18 months and another two for a year. The trial was defended by the Labour Colonial Secretary, Arthur Creech Jones, on the grounds that they had encouraged subversion and advocated revolution. At the same time, the PTUC was banned.[7] This attack did nothing to weaken AKEL, which was by now the strongest political force in Cyprus. The party quickly established a new trade union federation, the Pancyprian Federation of Labour (PEO) and, in May 1946, improved its electoral position when it won control of four of the island's town councils including Nicosia. At this time AKEL was campaigning for self-government for Cyprus rather than *enosis*.

As well as confronting the British, AKEL also came into conflict with the forces of the Greek Cypriot right. This conflict took place on the streets as well as at the ballot box, with violent clashes taking place with increasing regularity. This was partly a reflection of the civil war in Greece, even to the extent of George Grivas's anti-communist organisation, 'Khi', making an appearance. According to Costas Kyrris, the conflict between left and right came near to spilling over into 'a mini-civil war'.[8]

Three factors turned the tide against AKEL. First, the right reorganised with the establishment of the Cyprus National Party and the Cyprus Farmers' Union (PEK). Second, the Church threw its weight into the scales against AKEL, condemning Communism and using its organisation to mobilise for the right. Indeed, the Church quickly became the dominant partner in this alliance. Third, the right and the Church joined together to take up the issue of *enosis* as the way to rally popular support and out-manoeuvre the left. *Enosis* became the key to political supremacy.[9] AKEL found itself on the defensive as middle-class politicians and clergy joined in making nationalism the central political issue. This loss of the political initiative was accompanied by industrial and electoral setbacks. When miners employed by the Cyprus Mines Corporation went on strike in January 1948, taking on the police, the company and the British administration, it was the Church that broke the strike, providing scab labour to replace the strikers in May.

With the tide beginning to turn against it, AKEL changed its position on the national question and came out in support of *enosis*. The party attempted to make the nationalist cause its own. One celebrated incident occurred when the Limassol council changed the name of Palmer Street (named after an unpopular former Governor) to 28 October Street, the date of the Greek stand against Mussolini in 1941. Despite British pressure, the council refused to back down, and so the mayor and other councillors were imprisoned, provoking a general strike in protest. The then Governor, Sir Andrew Barkworth Wright, seriously considered banning AKEL. Despite this, the Communists failed to recover the initiative. When AKEL proposed a united front with the Church and suggested the organisation of an unofficial plebiscite on the *enosis* issue, its approaches were ignored and, instead, the Church decided to organise the plebiscite itself. On 15 January 1950, the plebiscite took place in churches throughout the island, continuing for a week. According to the bishops, 215 108 Greek Cypriot adults, an overwhelming majority, voted in favour of *enosis*. The man behind this plebiscite was the new Bishop of Kition, Michael Mouskos.[10]

Makarios and *enosis*

Before the year was over, Mouskos, aged only 37, was elected Archbishop of Cyprus, taking the name Makarios III. His commitment to the defeat of the left and the achievement of *enosis*, both closely related as far as he was concerned, was total. To achieve these objectives, he first of all set about consolidating the position of the nationalist right with himself as Ethnarch, in place as both the political and religious leader of the Greek Cypriot population. The substantial wealth of the Church was to be used to help mobilise the people against the British and to increase the Church's own political influence. By 1954, according to one account, under Makarios's charismatic leadership, 'the Church had grown more powerful, more militant, more politically pervasive than it had ever been before'.[11] At the same time, he recognised that Britain was too powerful to be defeated by the Greek Cypriots on their own, so he set out to internationalise the issue of *enosis*, looking towards the Greek government and the United Nations for support. At this time, there was no intention as far as Makarios was concerned of organising a full-blown guerrilla insurgency against the British. What he did consider acceptable, however, was a campaign of sabotage, civil disobedience and public disorder. This was being discussed as a possibility as early as 1951, and then in July 1952, while on a visit to Greece, Makarios chaired a clandestine committee of liberation that was set up to plan and prepare for this subversive dimension of the struggle for *enosis*. It was this body that turned to the notorious Colonel George Grivas, a retired Greek army officer of Cypriot origins and extreme right-wing politics. Makarios always intended that this aspect of the struggle should be primarily symbolic and very much subordinate to his diplomatic efforts which, he believed, would in the end prove decisive. Grivas had his own ideas.

The British response to the *enosis* campaign was uncompromising. When confronted with the plebiscite result in 1950, Governor Wright had dismissed it as an irrelevance because the question of sovereignty was already settled and not open to negotiation. This intransigent stance was actually strengthened over succeeding years for both strategic and domestic reasons. As the British were reluctantly forced to withdraw their armed forces from their Suez bases, so Cyprus became increasingly important as a military base, vital, as far as the Chiefs of Staff were concerned, for the defence of the Middle East.[12] At the same time, many Conservative MPs, dismayed at the retreat from Egypt, were determined to make a stand for the Empire somewhere. Cyprus seemed weak enough for Britain to be able to ignore the wishes of the majority of the population without too much inconvenience. This was not just a backbench sentiment, but was also strongly represented in the Cabinet, not least by the Foreign Secretary and future Prime Minister, Sir Anthony Eden. On an informal visit to Greece in September 1953, Eden was challenged over the Cyprus question by the Greek Prime Minister, General Alexandros Papagos. He tried to assure Eden that *enosis* would not affect British military bases on the island. Eden angrily rejected any Greek claim to Cyprus, remarking that New York had a large Greek population so why not claim that, and emphasising that the question of sovereignty was not open to discussion. Papagos, a staunch anglophile, was outraged at this treatment.[13]

Worse was to follow. Under pressure from Conservative rebels in the House of Commons over the withdrawal from Suez, the government attempted to disarm its critics with a strong statement on Cyprus. On 28 July 1954, Henry Hopkinson, a junior minister at the Colonial Office, told the Commons that 'there are certain territories in the Commonwealth which, owing to their particular circumstances, can never expect to be fully independent'. Subsequent attempts to qualify the word 'never' were at best half-hearted.[14] With the transfer of Middle East Headquarters to the island in December 1954, it seemed clear that Britain intended to hold on to Cyprus no matter what. This British intransigence combined with the refusal of the United Nations General Assembly to discuss the issue finally decided Makarios that the time had come for a demonstration of Greek Cypriot determination and, in January 1955, he authorised Grivas to initiate a campaign of confrontation and sabotage.

Grivas and EOKA

Grivas was born in Nicosia in May 1898 but left the island in 1916 to enlist as an officer cadet in the Greek army. He fought against the Turks in Greece's disastrous campaign in Asia Minor in the early 1920s, established himself as an authority on infantry tactics in the 1930s and fought against the Italians in 1940–41. During the German occupation, he established his own underground organisation, 'Khi', not to fight against the Axis forces, but to counter the Communist threat. The politics of his organisation were extreme right-wing, anti-democratic and fanatically nationalist, and it conducted a terrorist campaign against the left, both Communist and non-Communist. In Athens in December 1944, he was only saved from death at Communist hands by the intervention of British troops.[15] This in no way lessened his determination to expel the British from Cyprus. He had first met Makarios in Athens during this turbulent period, and the young priest had written a number of articles for the Khi newspaper. Subsequently he attempted to enter Greek politics, founding his own political party, but his efforts were unsuccessful. It was at this point that he became involved in preparations for a revolt against British rule.

Grivas carried out a first reconnaissance of Cyprus as early as July 1951 and then, with the authorisation of the committee of liberation, he returned to the island for a five-month stay in October 1952. At the end of this second visit, he drew up his plan of campaign. Whereas Makarios was thinking in terms of a short campaign of sabotage and public disorder lasting a matter of months as a way of pressurising the British, Grivas planned for a protracted guerrilla insurgency, for a shooting war, that would take years before victory could be accomplished. To begin with, he accepted Makarios's strategy but set about establishing an underground organisation, the National Organisation of Cypriot Fighters, EOKA, that could carry out his strategy if Makarios's failed. He was certainly not in a position as of yet to challenge the Archbishop's domination of the nationalist movement, but theirs was always an uneasy relationship characterised by tension and distrust.

The circumstances for rebellion were not promising. Grivas was intending to take on the British Empire in an island with an area of only 3572 square miles, about half the size of Wales, and a Greek Cypriot population of only some 419 000. The island had good communications which would be a great advantage for the security forces and could easily be cut off from any outside assistance by British naval units. On top of this there was a question mark over whether the Greek Cypriot population would actually support a guerrilla campaign and the hardship and suffering it would inevitably bring. Makarios was certainly sceptical, telling Grivas on one occasion that he would not find 50 men to follow him. Interestingly enough the British shared this view.[16]

Grivas finally arrived on the island in early November 1954 and set about establishing his underground organisation. He recruited from the Cyprus Farmers' Union (PEK) in the villages and from the two main youth movements, the Church-controlled Christian Youth Movement (OHEN) and the nationalist Pancyprian Youth Movement (PEON) in the towns. By the time EOKA was to go into action for the first time, he had only established groups in the five main towns and seven villages with perhaps 80 members. At its strongest, however, the organisation was to muster seven mountain groups, 47 town groups and 75 village groups, with a total strength of just over a thousand men. The backbone of EOKA were the mountain groups, a conventional guerrilla force, living in hidden camps in the forests, and the town groups, assassination squads, living among the civilian population and often continuing with their civilian jobs or their schooling. Together these numbered some 300. The village groups, about 700 strong, were generally little more than a local militia, armed with shotguns and hunting rifles, and not capable of independent action against the British. Even at its strongest EOKA remained a small force.

Supporting this armed wing was the much broader National Liberation Front of Cyprus (EMAK), which organised the guerrilla movement's sympathisers. EMAK provided EOKA with intelligence, supplies, weapons, medicines, recruits and safe houses, confronted the British on the streets with demonstrations and riots and conducted the propaganda offensive. Grivas was particularly concerned with mobilising the young, schoolchildren and juveniles, behind the struggle and was later to identify this as one of the distinctive features of EOKA: 'I know of no other movement, organisation or army which has so actively employed boys and girls of school age in the front line.' He intended 'to turn the youth of Cyprus into the seedbed of EOKA'.[17]

For EOKA, Greek nationalism was always a confessional affair. As Doros Alastos points out, 'EOKA was a deeply religious body...they considered nation and religion as one.' Phrases such as 'In the name of the Holy Trinity', 'with the help of God' and 'God will help us in our work' regularly appear in EOKA statements and proclamations.[18] Members had to swear 'in the name of the Holy Trinity' to remain steadfastly loyal to the organisation, to carry out its instructions without question and to reveal nothing about it even to other members on pain of 'punishment as a traitor and may eternal contempt cover me'.[19]

The campaign suffered an early setback on 25 January 1955 when the British captured a Greek vessel, the *Aghios Georghios*, carrying munitions, together with the reception party waiting on shore. Initially Grivas assumed that the organisation had been compromised and that he himself was in imminent danger of arrest. In fact, far from alerting the British, the authorities concluded that the threat came from Greece rather than from within Cyprus itself and that it had been nipped in the bud. This complacency was soon to be shattered. While Grivas argued that operations were planned, his sabotage groups were ready and that there should be an immediate start to operations as the best way to build EOKA, Makarios prevaricated. At last, at a meeting on 29 March, the Archbishop told Grivas to begin operations on the night of 31 March–1 April.

The revolt begins

That night there was a series of bomb attacks across the island, 18 altogether, the most successful destroying the Cyprus Broadcasting Station's transmitter. The attacks were accompanied by a revolutionary proclamation:

> With the help of God, with faith in our honourable struggle, with the backing of all Hellenism and the help of the Cypriots. WE HAVE TAKEN UP THE STRUGGLE TO THROW OFF THE ENGLISH YOKE, our banners high, bearing the slogan which our ancestors have handed down to us as a holy trust – DEATH OR VICTORY... Our struggle will be hard. The ruler has the means and he is strong in numbers. We have the heart, and we have RIGHT on our side and that is why we WILL WIN... Greeks, wherever you may be, hear our call: FORWARD ALL TOGETHER FOR THE FREEDOM OF OUR CYPRUS.

The proclamation was signed 'The Leader, Dighenis'; Grivas having decided to keep his involvement secret instead used the name of a Byzantine general who had defended Cyprus in the past.[20]

A number of these first attacks miscarried with sabotage groups in Famagusta, Larnaca and Limassol being captured by the police. This was due to the inexperience and bad luck of the attackers rather than to the effectiveness of the police response. In fact, the attacks took the authorities by surprise and this intelligence failure was in many ways more disturbing than the damage they caused. Why were the police not forewarned of the attacks? Looking back on this period, the Police Commissioner's Report of 1956 concluded that 'a vicious circle developed in that the government neglected the police force because there was no evidence of unrest...and the force failed to get any inkling of unrest because the government neglected it'.[21]

In the weeks that followed, sporadic attacks continued against what Grivas described as 'targets of opportunity', including an unsuccessful attempt on 24 May 'Empire Day' to blow up the Governor, Sir Robert Armitage, at a film show (the bomb exploded after he had left). These operations were accompanied by demonstrations in favour of *enosis*, often involving schoolchildren and increasingly erupting into violent attacks on the police and government property. All the time, Grivas continued building up EOKA, making ready for a second big push and beginning to put into operation his own strategy for a guerrilla victory. Essentially his strategy involved two overlapping phases: the first, an offensive against the police and those Greek Cypriots opposed to *enosis*. The police, in particular Special Branch, were the eyes and ears of the British on the island. To intimidate or eliminate them would leave the British blind, without intelligence, and ensure that EOKA would operate with comparative impunity. As for EOKA's Greek Cypriot opponents, Grivas was determined to ensure their silence by terror if necessary. He was particularly concerned with AKEL, a powerful political force on the island, and was worried that the Communists would launch their own liberation struggle. Instead, AKEL condemned the resort to arms and was to find itself increasingly marginalised as the struggle developed. They were eventually forced to turn to Makarios for protection against EOKA. As far as informers were concerned, they would be executed. Once the objectives of this first phase had been achieved, attention then would be turned to the British presence on the island with a stepping up of attacks on military installations and on the troops. Of course, these two phases continued alongside each other, but they served different purposes, the first to create the environment for guerrilla action, the second to exploit that environment.

While Grivas always rejected Makarios's attempt to limit the campaign to acts of sabotage, avoiding loss of life, nevertheless he did share the Archbishop's recognition that victory would in the end be won not in Cyprus but in the international arena. Grivas had no illusions that his small band of guerrilla fighters would be able to defeat the British militarily, to physically drive them off the island. Instead, EOKA would subject the British to continued, relentless harassment, making clear that continued occupation carried a price, but more importantly, keeping *enosis* on the international agenda. The British response to the EOKA campaign was crucial in this regard: repression would on the one hand alienate the Greek Cypriot population from British rule, and on the other hand provide Makarios and the Greek government with a stick to beat the British with before the United Nations. EOKA would ensure that there was a 'Cyprus problem' and demonstrate to the world that the British could not resolve it.

Grivas launched his second offensive on the night of 19 June with co-ordinated bomb and grenade attacks against police stations, military installations and the homes of army officers and senior officials. One bomb planted inside Famagusta Police Headquarters by an EOKA policeman demolished the building. A few days later an arms raid on Amiandos police station left a police sergeant dead and the armoury stripped of weapons. Once again the first wave of attacks was followed by sporadic incidents, shootings and bombings, and increasing public disorder. There were attacks on the police, with two Special Branch members being assassinated in separate incidents in August. One of them, Herodotus Poullis, was shot at an AKEL rally in front of hundreds of people, none of whom would admit to having seen the attack. According to Grivas, these attacks 'struck a fatal blow against police morale...shattered opposition to EOKA among the Greek police'.[22] There were street clashes between demonstrators and police and troops which were easily precipitated by the simple expedient of raising the Greek flag which the British then felt obliged to remove by force if necessary. The final straw, however, was the escape from Kyrenia Castle prison of 16 EOKA members including a number of key figures, such as Markos Drakos and Grigoris Afxentiou, who were to go on to play prominent parts in the guerrilla campaign. As Nancy Crawshaw puts it, 'Public confidence in the administration was shattered.'[23] The situation seemed to be deteriorating out of control.

Harding

The British attempted to safeguard their position in Cyprus by diplomatic manoeuvring and a counterinsurgency offensive. The first involved playing the Greek and Turkish governments off against each other. Eden saw the Turkish government as 'the key to protecting British interests' in Cyprus. The British were to do everything possible to fuel Turkish fears with what were to be disastrous consequences for Greek–Turkish relations.[24] The second saw the new Prime Minister, Sir Anthony Eden, replace Armitage as Governor with a military man, Field Marshal Sir John Harding, until then Chief of the Imperial General Staff (CIGS) and Britain's most distinguished serving soldier. He was charged by Eden with showing the Greek Cypriots 'steadily and firmly rather than harshly that we mean to carry out our responsibility'.[25] This appointment was both an indication of the seriousness with which the government regarded the situation on the island and of their determination to crush EOKA. Harding, who as Commander-in-Chief Far East Land Forces and later as CIGS had been involved in both the Malayan and Kenyan Emergencies, was believed to be the ideal man to defeat Grivas. The experience of counterinsurgency that the British had gained in these two campaigns would, it was hoped, provide the methods whereby EOKA would be defeated. More particularly, Harding was concerned with laying the ghost of the Palestine defeat, a defeat that he blamed on the failure of the politicians in London to back the soldiers on the spot.[26]

Harding arrived in Cyprus on 3 October. He had three immediate objectives: to put the British administration on a war-footing, to open negotiations with Makarios, and to take the offensive against EOKA. The first he achieved by integrating the administration, the police and the military into a co-ordinated security machine on the model established in Malaya.[27] This was comparatively straightforward in a small island like Cyprus. Negotiations with Makarios were less productive. Harding was prepared to offer a degree of Cypriot control over domestic affairs, a form of home rule, and a £38 million development programme. The hope was that a deal could be made with Greek Cypriot moderates, thereby isolating EOKA. Makarios would not accept this role. Meanwhile, troop and police reinforcements were drafted in to begin operations against the guerrillas. On 26 November, Harding proclaimed a State of Emergency. That same night the first attempt was made to assassinate him at a ball at the Ledra Palace Hotel.

The State of Emergency greatly increased the powers available to the security forces. The death penalty was extended to cover the use of firearms and the planting of bombs. Life imprisonment was introduced for the possession of firearms, ammunition or explosives. The courts were allowed to sentence prisoners under 18 years old to corporal punishment. Collective punishments, fines and curfews were introduced; censorship and banishment were implemented, and strikes were made illegal. Altogether there were 76 new regulations. Ironically, the first to feel the weight of this repressive apparatus were the Communists. On 13 December, Harding, who saw Cyprus very much as a pawn in the Cold War, banned AKEL and detained 128 of its leading members, effectively crippling the only political force in the Greek Cypriot community opposed to EOKA.[28]

Repressive legislation and troop reinforcements were not the answer, however. What was needed to combat EOKA was intelligence, information about its members, its organisation, its safe houses and forest hides, and this was not available. The Greek Cypriot population was hostile and the Special Branch had been neutered. This problem was to hamstring the security forces for most of 1956. The British response was large-scale cordon-and-search operations that rarely resulted in arrests or the discovery of arms caches, but which invariably alienated those whose houses were searched or who were roughed up and dragged off to be screened. Collective punishments, far from undermining support for EOKA, only succeeded in making the Greek Cypriots more hostile to British rule. Charles Foley, the editor of *The Times of Cyprus* newspaper during the Emergency describes how, following the shooting of a policeman in Nicosia, troops wired off the area, set up gunposts on rooftops and searched every house. After a 72-hour curfew the families caught inside the barbed wire net were taken out and addressed by the Commissioner of Nicosia, Mr Martin Clemens.

'Tonight', he said, 'a policeman will visit every home in the curfewed area with envelopes and paper. Every householder will write on the paper everything he knows about EOKA, then seal it in the envelopes. All the envelopes will be given to me tomorrow and I will open them myself in private. Here is your chance to help the Police without fear of any consequence.'

Next day the envelopes were collected: the papers were all blank.

Clemens responded by closing that area of the city, 31 houses and 20 shops, for three months, evicting the inhabitants with what they could carry, leaving them homeless, unemployed and bankrupt.[29]

Harding himself had a 'no-nonsense' attitude. He later made clear that, as far as he was concerned, the 'rough treatment' of prisoners on capture was something that 'inevitably does happen'. There was nothing that you could do about it, and anyway, he thought it, 'perfectly natural and to my mind, acceptable'.[30] The problem was, however, that in a guerrilla conflict, the troops could not distinguish between the gunmen and the civilian population who were, moreover, known to be sympathetic to the gunmen. The consequence was that the rough handling, often extremely rough handling, was inflicted, without too much discrimination, on civilians uninvolved in the war but who often merely happened to be in the wrong place, at the wrong time. No matter how understandable the troops' behaviour might have been, given their fear, frustration and fury (the three f's), the inevitable result was to increase sympathy for EOKA and to assist its recruitment efforts.

The problem was that the Greek Cypriot community was overwhelmingly in favour of *enosis*. Far from moderates emerging with whom Britain could do a deal, repression actually increased support for the extremists, for EOKA. It was this popular support, enabling Grivas and his small band of guerrillas to take on the growing security apparatus that Harding was marshalling against him, that sustained the armed struggle. No matter how many troops and police the British were able to put on the streets and into the forests, without effective intelligence they were fighting blind and were consequently either ineffective or counterproductive. Worse than that, it became clear that EOKA did have an effective intelligence apparatus and that the guerrillas were often forewarned of security force intentions. The experience is described by an officer in the Parachute Regiment:

> The pursuit of EOKA by the security forces resembled a display of shadow-boxing. Most of the British hammer-blows landed on air, as their targets vanished into the forests, the farms, or the dark, twisting alleyways of the towns. For the essential element of surprise was usually denied them. Great cordon-and-search operations, involving thousands of troops and great movements of trucks, inevitably sent out vibrations which were picked up by the sensitive antennae of EOKA, and messages of warning could often be sent off ahead of the darkened convoys twisting through the night.
>
> It was the extreme efficiency with which EOKA had permeated every organisation on the island which made this possible. Postmen, telephone operators, contractors, foresters, policemen, all passed on what was required of them in the way of information.[31]

Support for *enosis* was so strong and widespread that EOKA was able to penetrate every area of Greek Cypriot activity, organising a network of informants that invisibly surrounded the British. Schoolchildren, domestic servants, civilian personnel on the military bases, the police, all were enlisted by Grivas in the intelligence war. While the security forces were operating in the dark, their every move was observed.

The police were the most serious problem. Not only had Greek Cypriot personnel been successfully intimidated by EOKA, they had also been thoroughly infiltrated. One of Grivas's agents, Polycarpos Georgadjis, successfully established a secret network of some 20 informers within the police. They warned of security force operations, targeted colleagues for assassination, betrayed informers, provided safehouses and, on occasion, even carried out EOKA attacks themselves.[32] One Special Branch Sergeant, George Lagoudontis, actually tape-recorded high-level British security conferences for EOKA. One such recording revealed the names of three informers, all of whom were subsequently executed on Grivas's orders.[33] The British were never to succeed completely in eliminating EOKA agents from the police force.

The virtual collapse of the police in the face of EOKA did bring some important changes, however. Many Greek Cypriot policemen resigned and those that remained were increasingly distrusted, so new recruits were sought in Britain and among the Turkish Cypriot community. A large number of volunteers were recruited from police forces in Britain, 600 of them by 1958, and they increasingly provided the backbone of the force. Interestingly enough, Harding vetoed recruits from the Royal Ulster Constabulary because of their 'heavy-handed reputation'.[34] More important, however, was the dramatically increased recruitment of Turkish Cypriots. By the start of 1956 they had come to dominate the force, numbering over 4000 compared with less than 1000 Greek Cypriots. This was a complete reversal of the position before the insurgency began, when Greek Cypriots had been in a large majority. The Turkish Cypriot police were very much in the front line against EOKA. They were one of the mainstays of the British counterinsurgency effort, and without them the British would have been hard-pressed to contain the rebellion let alone defeat it. Inevitably, however, the use of Turkish Cypriot police against the Greek Cypriot community exacerbated relations between the two communities. The spectacle of Turkish Cypriot riot police clubbing Greek Cypriot schoolchildren caused outrage, while the occasional killing of Turkish Cypriot policemen by EOKA inevitably provoked reprisals. In retrospect, there can be no serious doubt that the British made a calculated, deliberate decision to enlist the Turkish Cypriot community in the campaign against EOKA.[35]

EOKA offensive

1956 came without any let-up in EOKA attacks and street disorders. The security forces were involved in suppressing a veritable schoolchildren's revolt that, by the end of February, had left one boy shot dead by troops and the island's school system almost completely closed down.[36]

Without any signs of progress in the struggle against EOKA, Harding became increasingly incensed with Makarios's failure to accept what he regarded as Britain's generous terms and refusal to condemn terrorism. With the agreement of London, he decided to remove the Archbishop in the hope that moderates within the Greek Cypriot community would then come forward. On 9 March, Makarios was arrested and, together with the Bishop of Kyrenia, was deported to the Seychelles. This provoked a week-long general strike followed by a dramatic increase in EOKA activity. There were 246 EOKA attacks in the last three weeks of March, including another unsuccessful attempt to assassinate Harding (a servant planted a bomb under his bed but it failed to explode). The offensive continued through April and into May with security force casualties averaging about two killed every week. The British were 'forced on to the defensive with the safeguarding of life and property taking priority'.[37] On 10 May the first two EOKA prisoners were hanged by the British, and Grivas responded by ordering the execution of two British soldiers who were being held by his men. Only with the arrival of further troop reinforcements was Harding in a position to strike back.

The British were increasingly concerned at the build-up of EOKA's mountain groups, the conventional guerrilla forces hiding out in the forests. These were seen as a potential threat to communications on the island. It was known that Grivas was with them and they were a target that the army felt it could deal with, unlike the elusive assassins and bomb throwers in the towns. A large-scale exercise, Operation Pepperpot, involving some 2000 troops, was planned to comb some 400 square miles of the Troodos mountains. The British had identified the area around the Kykko monastery and the village of Kambos as the likely site for EOKA headquarters and Grivas's hideout. The area was incident-free while surrounded by a suspicious periphery of incidents. Inevitably Grivas received warning of the operation and had given orders for diversionary attacks in the towns. He divided his band into smaller groups and was slipping out of the area when the troops arrived. He only escaped by a night march over the most difficult and dangerous terrain, a march in which he very nearly fell to his death.

This was a remarkable feat for a 58-year-old. Operation Pepperpot ended on 28 May, but after a brief respite it was followed by Operation Lucky Alphonse. This second operation in the Troodos mountains started on 8 June and continued until 23 June. Once again, Grivas only narrowly escaped his pursuers. He was nearly taken by a paratroop patrol, escaping under fire and leaving behind his belt, beret and diary. His diary provided the British with '250,000 words of the leader's verbose musings' that had to be translated, an astonishing security lapse on Grivas's part.[38] After another forced march, without food for 30 hours and without water for 18, he finally found temporary sanctuary at Trooditissa Monastery. At this point, Grivas decided to abandon the mountains and instead go to ground in Limassol. He was driven into the town by a Greek Cypriot police inspector and established himself in an underground hide in the house of a local businessman who had made himself known to be hostile to EOKA.[39]

While Grivas himself had escaped, the Troodos operations were still a success. Some 20 EOKA guerrillas and 50 weapons were captured, a number of hides discovered and EOKA's Troodos mountain groups effectively eliminated. Arguably more important, however, thousands of documents were captured in an amazing lapse of security on Grivas's part. These formed the intelligence breakthrough the British had been seeking. Now, for the first time, they were able to gain an insight into the EOKA organisation as well as details of the troubled relationship between Grivas and Makarios, and the names of many members and sympathisers. This was a real success and the British were to build on it in the coming months.[40] The Troodos operations were crowned with disaster, however. No less than seven British soldiers were killed in shooting or traffic accidents; then, on 17 June, a mortar bombardment of an area of forest where it was thought EOKA were hiding started a forest fire that quickly blazed out of control with the flames reaching speeds of 30 mph in places. Twenty-one soldiers were burned to death, another 16 injured and a number of vehicles and considerable equipment was destroyed. This disaster completely overshadowed the first real success the security forces had achieved.

Although EOKA had been dealt a serious blow in the mountains, its attacks continued in the towns with the security forces apparently impotent. Grivas himself describes one such attack that took place in Limassol while he was still being hunted in the mountains. Two men were detailed to attack a bar, 'The King's Arms', that was regularly used by off-duty soldiers and police. On Saturday night when the place was packed, they 'burst open the doors and emptied their guns into the crowd of soldiers, killing two and vanished before anyone could fire back. They ran...along a prearranged escape route, to a house where they hid the guns and then left for the mountains, to hide out during the three-day curfew and search of Limassol that followed the attack.'[41] The guerrillas always had a choice of targets and the advantage of surprise, so that such attacks carried out with preparation and determination were difficult, if not impossible, to counter.

On 9 August three more EOKA prisoners were hanged. Grivas had ordered that hostages be taken. An RAF man was killed resisting capture but a retired British civil servant was successfully seized. When the three condemned men called for his release, Grivas complied. The hangings went ahead without reprisals. There were widespread strikes held in protest, however. Soon after, on 16 August, acting on the advice of the Greek government, Grivas announced a ceasefire. The hope seems to have been that the British would take the opportunity to open negotiations with Makarios. The British, however, were pinning their hopes on Lord Radcliffe. He had visited Cyprus on behalf of the British government in July and was now drawing up a constitution that the British intended to impose. Moreover, Harding assumed that the ceasefire meant that EOKA was beaten and that Grivas had admitted defeat. On 22 August, Harding invited the guerrillas to surrender, with the option of either leaving for Greece or remaining in Cyprus and standing trial for any crimes they had committed. The following day Grivas called the ceasefire off and EOKA resumed operations.

On the run

The Suez invasion of November 1956 was a serious setback as far as Harding was concerned. He told London: 'I have little doubt that if it had been possible to continue active operations against them on that scale for several months, their defeat would have been completed.'[42] The invasion removed large numbers of combat troops from the island and directed attention elsewhere, allowing Grivas to launch a fresh offensive. On 2 November, EOKA made 21 separate attacks, inaugurating what became for the British 'Black November'. That month there were 416 attacks that left 39 people dead, 21 of them British. Harding was forced on the defensive once again, but only temporarily. The tide was already turning in the intelligence war. When the troops returned at the end of the Suez debacle, bringing his military strength up to 20 000 men, Harding was able once again to seize the initiative and bring EOKA close to defeat.

British success in the intelligence war derived from the efforts of the new interrogation teams that Harding introduced into Cyprus. With little hope of winning over the Greek Cypriot population, the security forces resorted to the use of torture to secure intelligence. According to Charles Foley this was common knowledge among journalists covering the conflict on the island, who jocularly referred to the interrogators as 'HMTs', 'Her Majesty's Torturers'. Prisoners were subjected to conveyor belt interrogation methods with relays of interrogators so that questioning could be sustained for extended periods. This was accompanied by physical assault. Once again, according to Foley,

> You might be beaten on the stomach with a flat board, you might have your testicles twisted, you might be half-suffocated with a wet cloth which forced you to drink with every breath you took, you might have a steel band tightened round your head. Techniques were backward for the twentieth century; there were, for instance, no proven reports of treatment by electric shock. No more than six people died under interrogation during the whole Emergency.[43]

These methods of interrogation produced an increasing flow of intelligence. The use of torture was, of course, denied at the time, and as David French has pointed out, when dealing with this question, the historian inevitably finds his or herself 'walking through a hall of mirrors'. Nevertheless, he goes on to quote an Intelligence Corps veteran to the effect that in Cyprus, 'torture of suspects was endemic'.[44]

To exploit this intelligence, the security forces replaced the cumbersome cordon-and-search operations with snatch squads. These were small parties of troops and police who would drive into a Greek Cypriot area in civilian vehicles to raid specific houses where suspects were believed to be hiding. The security forces were no longer operating in the dark. Increasing use was also made of Q patrols, heavily armed undercover squads that operated in the Greek Cypriot villages and towns, gathering intelligence, carrying out raids and killing or capturing EOKA. The Q patrols, which were similar to the pseudo-gangs used in Kenya, consisted of Greek Cypriots, sometimes turned EOKA members, more often criminals, recruited from the Greek Cypriot community in Britain, Turkish Cypriots and British personnel. They had the advantage of personal knowledge both of the areas they operated in and of the men they were hunting. An added advantage was that they were only loosely bound by the constraints of police or military discipline and so behaved with much greater ruthlessness. While Grivas dismisses the Q patrols as completely ineffective, there is no doubt that they successfully carried the war to the guerrillas and played an important part in forcing EOKA on the defensive.[45]

Starting in December 1956 the security forces dealt EOKA a series of damaging blows. The first big success was the breaking up of the organisation's arms smuggling set-up in Limassol, with 44 EOKA members detained, including a number of customs officials. In the New Year this was followed up with successes against the town groups. In Nicosia one of the organisation's most effective assassins, Nicos Sampson, was captured and this was followed by the arrest of a number of other members, most notably the town leader, Andreas Chartas. The same time the town organisations were being broken up, the British also achieved considerable success against the mountain groups. On 19 January 1957, Markos Drakos was ambushed and killed by troops from the Suffolk Regiment. Even more successful were 2nd Battalion, the Parachute Regiment who, in the course of the month, captured 21 EOKA and 46 weapons, effectively eliminating the organisation in their area. Their success was due in good part to 'the Special Branch use of agents and to the Q men'.[46] Then, on 3 March, an informer led troops to a hide containing Grivas's second-in-command, Grigoris Afxentiou, and his group. His four men surrendered, but Afxentiou fought to the death, killing one soldier before the hide was filled with 50 gallons of petrol and set alight. He perished in the flames. By now 15 EOKA had been killed that year and there were another 60 in prison facing capital charges with every likelihood that they would be hanged. The insurgency seemed close to defeat and, as if in recognition of this, on 17 March, Grivas announced another ceasefire.

According to one fervently pro-British account

> EOKA was virtually crushed. It was practically stripped clean of its organization in the towns and villages. The worst of the assassins had been captured... The mountain gangs had been broken up, and deprived of their leaders... If the operations had been continued rather longer, and Grivas himself could have been taken at that time in the mountains, the whole Cyprus rebellion would have collapsed and peace would have returned to the island.[47]

From this point of view, the ceasefire saved EOKA from certain defeat and gave the organisation a breathing space to recover and reorganise. How valid is this view? A number of points can be made. First of all, Grivas did not order a ceasefire in order to save EOKA from destruction. He was determined to carry on the fight but was persuaded, only very reluctantly, by the Greek government that a ceasefire was a diplomatic necessity. His condition that Makarios should be freed was also promptly met by Britain, although the Archbishop was not allowed to return to Cyprus. Second, while British successes had certainly hurt the insurgents, they still had considerable popular support, especially among the young, and would certainly have been able to replace the fighters they had lost. Rebuilding the organisation was necessary, but this could have been accomplished while operating at a lower level, without a ceasefire. Moreover, it is important to remember that the British did not observe the ceasefire but continued with their efforts to destroy EOKA and to capture Grivas. This is not to say, however, that the ceasefire, by reducing the level of conflict, did not make EOKA's recovery easier, only that it would probably have been accomplished anyway. The important point, something that many commentators do not take sufficiently into account, is the extent to which guerrilla organisations that have a popular base are capable of recovering from setbacks, of making good their losses and rebuilding their organisation.

The ceasefire lasted from March 1957 until March the following year, although physical attacks on security force personnel were not to restart until May. In the interim, communal tension increased with the British openly tolerating the paramilitary preparations of the Turkish Cypriot organisation, Volkan/TMT, as a counterweight to EOKA. This threat was of increasing concern to Grivas. He was also concerned at continuing Communist activity and on a number of occasions ordered action against them. In January 1958, EOKA shot a number of leading trade unionists, threatening to start a civil war within the Greek Cypriot community. The PEO called a 48-hour general strike in protest at the shootings and appealed to Makarios to intervene.[48]

Foot arrives

Meanwhile, in November 1957 Harding had retired and been replaced as Governor by Sir Hugh Foot, an experienced colonial official, who was thought better able to achieve a political settlement than another soldier. Although generally considered a liberal, Foot had first-hand experience of suppressing rebellion. He had been an Assistant District Commissioner in Palestine during the Arab Revolt, and in his own words, 'once it was clear that we had to fight a rebellion we entered into our task with a will'. For two years, 'I never moved without a gun in my hand...it was useless to have a gun in a holster'; the whole experience 'was exhilarating'.[49] Whatever his supposed liberal inclinations, however, Foot was still charged with resisting *enosis*. Even though the Macmillan government's determination to hold Cyprus was weakened in the aftermath of the Suez debacle, nevertheless any settlement was still required to exclude union with Greece and recognise continued British sovereignty at least in the short term. In these circumstances it was only a matter of time before the ceasefire came to an end.

The last phase of the conflict began in March 1958 when Grivas launched a 'campaign of "passive resistance"...This was to take the form of widespread minor sabotage backed by a boycott of everything British.'[50] The boycott campaign met with a mixed response and brought EOKA into conflict with many Greek Cypriots, leading to an appeal from Makarios for more flexibility. By now, however, Grivas was himself under pressure from his followers to restart the armed struggle. At the end of April he ordered his guerrillas into action once again, and on 4 May two military policemen were shot dead in Famagusta.

This time the conflict between EOKA and the British was overlaid by the outbreak of the most serious communal violence so far. On 7 June, Turkish Cypriots attacked the Greek Cypriot community in Nicosia, precipitating a wave of violence that spread over the island. British intervention on the side of the Turkish Cypriots seemed proven on 12 June when troops disarmed 35 Greeks and then left them near the Turkish village of Geunyeli to make their way home on foot across country. Once the troops were out of sight, the Turks attacked and killed eight of them. Across the island, people were driven from their homes and a grim pattern of atrocity and reprisal was established. While communal violence was still continuing, another incident was taken as a demonstration of British partiality. On 5 July in the Greek Cypriot village of Avgorou a British armoured car detachment came across a cardboard poster bearing a pro-*enosis* slogan. A boy was ordered to take it down and when he refused the troops tried to arrest him. Some 200 villagers came to the rescue, attacking the armoured cars with bottles, bricks and chairs. One man who climbed up on one of the armoured cars was machine-gunned, and a young woman, the mother of six children, was also killed. By the time the troops had control another 50 villagers had been injured. The boy escaped. This brutal incident over a cardboard sign took place at a time when the nearby Turkish quarter of Famagusta 'was plastered with Volkan and TMT proclamations' that the British ignored. As a reprisal for this incident EOKA gunmen killed two soldiers in a shop in Famagusta three days later.[51]

Foot responded to the crisis with a massive clampdown. On 22 July he proscribed the TMT and ordered large-scale arrests. Some 50 Turks suspected of involvement in the violence were detained along with 1500 Greeks. The clampdown was decisively one-sided and was clearly intended to reassure Turkish Cypriots that the British would protect their interests, that there would be no surrender. This is not to say that the British had inspired or organised the outbreak; indeed, British troops had contained it and prevented many more people losing their lives.

Nevertheless, the British had deliberately set out to use the Turkish Cypriot community on the island and the Turkish government as a means of blocking the demand for *enosis*. They had effectively allied themselves with the Turkish minority, an overwhelming majority in the police force, and tolerated opposition to union with Greece while repressing advocacy of it. This had now got out of control as far as the British were concerned, but nevertheless they still managed to exploit the situation. Turkish opposition to *enosis* was in the end to prove the decisive factor in defeating it. The communal violence of June and July left 56 Greek Cypriots and 53 Turkish Cypriots dead and was a grim warning of what was to come.

Once the riots were at an end, EOKA returned to its war against the British. The organisation was stronger, more determined and better armed than ever before and, moreover, had gained considerably from coming forward as the defender of the Greek Cypriot community against the Turks. The British found themselves once again confronting a guerrilla offensive and were once more forced on the defensive. The intelligence effort that had dealt EOKA such heavy blows in the winter of 1956–57 had to begin all over again. This time they were taking on a tougher organisation that was more decentralised, operated more on local initiative and was increasingly ruthless. According to Byford Jones, Grivas had by now lost control of the guerilla bands.[52] The conflict became increasingly bitter. By now, the British had one armed man for every Greek Cypriot household.[53]

On 2 September, acting on information extracted from a prisoner by torture, troops discovered four EOKA men hidden in a barn near Liopetri. Instead of surrendering in the face of superior numbers, they resisted, fighting a three-hour battle with the troops. They repulsed an assault, withstood a rocket bombardment and then the two survivors came out shooting when the barn was successfully set on fire. One soldier was killed and a number of others were wounded; all four EOKA men died. This was a new kind of sacrificial determination. The informer threw himself on Grivas's mercy and was executed. Later that month, on 26 September, EOKA only narrowly missed blowing up the British Director of Operations, Major General Kendrew. His car went over a mine but it exploded too late and caught the escort vehicle, killing one soldier.

Unable to retaliate effectively against the elusive gunmen and bombers who struck and then disappeared, the troops became increasingly brutal towards the Greek Cypriot population. This was wholeheartedly endorsed by some officers. There was already in existence a secret vigilante organisation, the Cromwell Society, that originated within the Military Police and threatened unofficial reprisals.[54] Frustration finally exploded in Famagusta on 3 October when an EOKA gunman shot two British service wives, killing Mrs Catherine Cutliffe. In less than two hours troops had rounded up a thousand Greek Cypriot men and taken them off for screening and interrogation. Over 250 required medical treatment, 16 were seriously injured and three were killed, one a 12-year-old boy. While they were being rounded up, a 12-year-old girl had collapsed and died of shock. One soldier wrote home that the dead boy had been strangled by a sergeant major in the Military Police and that the dead girl had been raped. He wrote of 'wholesale rape, looting and murder', including four more men killed in reprisal in Varosha. Everything had got 'particularly bloody and disgusting'.[55] EOKA denied the shooting, but there seems little doubt that it was carried out by their men, although probably without Grivas's sanction.

The EOKA campaign continued with increasing effectiveness throughout the rest of October and into November, causing 'more damage...than in any period since November 1956'.[56] And yet while EOKA was still posing an apparently insoluble problem for the security forces, Grivas had in fact been defeated politically. While he was eager to continue the fight, Makarios agreed to give up *enosis* and to accept in its place independence for Cyprus on terms acceptable to the Turkish government. The Turks proved to be the British trump card. With great reluctance on 24 December 1958 Grivas ordered his last ceasefire. The struggle with Britain was over.

A victory of sorts?

According to some accounts, EOKA was once again near defeat when the conflict ended, Grivas was going to be eliminated any day and the rebellion would have been finally crushed. There is little evidence to support this. Whatever setbacks and losses EOKA suffered, and some were inevitable when they were sustaining such a high level of activity, they would have been made good. Even the loss of Grivas himself would not have destroyed the organisation at this stage. Rather, this is just so much wishful thinking. The reality is that the British, with overwhelming strength, 40 000 men at one point, signally failed to eradicate a guerrilla force a few hundred strong led by a 60-year-old man on an island half the size of Wales. The lessons learned in Malaya and Kenya had been unsuccessful against a primarily urban guerrilla movement that organised and retained a high level of popular support throughout. This is not to say that EOKA could not have been defeated, but it would have taken considerably more brutal methods than the British could use in the prevailing political circumstances. With regard to the question of minimum force, Christopher Soames, the secretary of State for Defence, made the point that minimum force could often involve 'quite a lot of force'.[57] Even so, there were limits beyond which the British could not trespass without inviting serious political embarrassment and damage. As it was, the conflict had cost the lives of 104 soldiers and 51 police, 26 British civilians and at least 90 EOKA. Over 200 Greek Cypriot civilians were killed, the majority by EOKA. While they failed to defeat EOKA militarily, nevertheless the British did succeed in inflicting a political defeat on it. In the end, they were able to use the Turkish Cypriot minority and the Turkish government as the means to prevent *enosis*. It was the threat from this quarter that forced first Makarios and then the Greek government to accept an independent Cyprus. According to John Reddaway, administrative secretary under both Harding and Foot, the conflict 'ended on a very satisfactory note'.[58] This was acceptable to the Macmillan government because, in the aftermath of the Suez debacle, the retention of Cyprus as a 'fortress colony' was no longer regarded as a necessity. The British were happy to bring the conflict to an end and retain two sovereign bases at Akrotiri and Dhekelia. Interestingly, in 1974, the British actually proposed to give up these bases, but were persuaded, indeed 'told', not to by the United States, because of the crucial importance of the 'sigint' stations they housed.[59]

5
The Struggle for South Yemen

Aden had long been regarded as an important strategic asset in the maintenance of Britain's position as a world power. As late as May 1956, a junior minister, Lord Lloyd, had made clear that 'for the foreseeable future it would not be reasonable or sensible or in the interests of the Colony's inhabitants for them to aspire to any aim beyond that of a considerable degree of internal self-government'. The colony's strategic importance was such that the government could not 'foresee the possibility of any fundamental relaxation of their responsibilities for the Colony'.[1] Paradoxically, as British power declined, this importance actually increased. Evicted from Egypt and Iraq, with Cyprus and Kenya uncertain, the Aden base became increasingly important. In 1960 Aden replaced Cyprus as headquarters of Middle East Command and it was described in the 1962 Defence White Paper, along with Singapore and Britain itself, as one of three vital permanent military bases. It was regarded as the key to the defence of British interests in the Middle East, the Gulf and the Indian Ocean. The problem was, however, that the British position was coming under increasing challenge from Arab nationalism, both in the colony itself and in its hinterland, the Arab protectorates that made up the Federation of South Arabia. There was every confidence, however, that by force and fraud this challenge could be contained and that, in the words of a former Governor, Sir Tom Hickinbotham, the security of Aden would be 'maintained as long as Britain remains great'.[2]

The challenge to the British position came from two different directions. In the colony of Aden itself it came from the increasingly powerful trade union movement with its left-wing nationalist leadership. This threat, it was believed, could be contained by a combination of repression and improving living standards. The Arab working class would be reconciled to the frustration of their national ambitions by prosperity, and more accommodating, moderate trade union leaders would emerge. This Fabian policy was soon recognised as having failed and some other means of containing popular agitation had to be found. The other challenge came from neighbouring North Yemen whose autocratic ruler, the Imam Ahmed, had long had designs on the protectorate states. His policy of confrontation with Britain involved periodic border incidents and the active encouragement of subversion and insurgency. These backward, semi-feudal regimes were regarded as particularly vulnerable and liable to collapse without British support.

Trouble in the protectorates had broken out as early as 1954, beginning what Gregory Blaxland calls 'the Border War', which continued into 1958. This conflict involved sporadic border incidents and uprisings that were dealt with by the traditional British methods of punitive expeditions and bombing. The trouble came to a head in 1957–58 when there were serious border clashes between British and Yemeni troops; Azraqi rebels ambushed and killed British soldiers before being subjected to punitive air strikes. Trouble continued with exchanges of artillery fire across the border. Then in April 1958 the Assistant British Adviser in Dhala was besieged by rebels in al-Sarir fort. A strong British relief column with air support drove the rebels across the border and air strikes were launched against Yemeni positions, destroying the Qataba barracks.[3] After this demonstration of British power, the Imam decided that his confrontationist policy had proven too expensive and unproductive and an uneasy truce came into effect.

Aden and the Federation

At the same time as the Border War was successfully concluded, the British consolidated their position in the protectorates by establishing the Federation of South Arabia in February 1959. Initially six of the states of the Western Protectorate, Beihan, Fahdli, Aulaqi, Dhala, Lower Yafa and Upper Aulaqi, joined together in what was always a ramshackle affair, completely dependent upon Britain. None of the individual rulers would accept any of their number being given precedence, so all became members of the Federation government, the Federal Supreme Council, with a rotating chairman. Other states joined later: Lahej in September 1959, and Dathinah, Lower Aulaqi and Agrabi in February 1960. The Federation served as a useful buffer against North Yemeni influence, but was also regarded as a way to contain the Adeni working class. The various petty emirs, sheikhs and sultans were completely dependent upon British support and so could be relied upon to oppose the nationalism that flourished in Aden. Any that were reluctant or unwilling could be replaced without too much trouble. The British decided to incorporate Aden into the Federation, regardless of the wishes of the colony's population. The intention was that the sultans, supported by Britain, would be able to outweigh the influence of the urban nationalists. This would in itself be a significant defeat for the nationalists with the backward hinterland states being brought in to dominate the modern colony. Moreover, British repression would no longer be the work of British imperialism, but would instead be British support for a compliant Arab ally.

The cynical nature of the exercise was quite transparent and was acknowledged as such, in private, by those responsible. Prime Minister Harold Macmillan, for example, confided to his diary that the intention was to make use of 'the Sultans to help us keep the Colony and its essential defence facilities', and that when Aden merged with the Federation we should 'give as much power as we can to the Sultans who are on our side'.[4] With British force to back it up, it was believed that the Federation would be able to dominate Aden and contain the nationalist challenge.

What was the nature of this challenge? According to Fred Halliday, the rise of the trade union movement, 'the most militant of its kind the Arab world has yet seen', was at its centre. This was a product of the expansion of the colony's economy, led by the development of British Petroleum's refinery facilities, established in 1954 and employing 2000 people, as well as the success of the port. The average yearly number of ships stopping off in the late 1950s and early 1960s was 5450, so that by 1964 Aden had the fourth largest bunkering trade in the world after London, Liverpool and New York. Other industries included soft drinks factories, ship-building and ship-repair, and construction that boomed during the building of the British military base. This economic expansion provided work for a growing number of migrants from the protectorate states and from North Yemen. The population of the colony rose from 80 516 in 1945 to 138 400 in 1955 and an estimated 250 000 by 1967.[5]

Trade unions had been legal in Aden since 1942. There had been a serious dock strike in 1948 but no stable organisations for the mass of workers were established until the mid-1950s. Not until 1956 with the formation of the Aden Trades Union Congress (ATUC) did the trade union movement become a force to be reckoned with. The strike wave of that year was 'the turning point between the old society and the new':

On this occasion, the work stoppage was on a far larger scale than in 1948. The disputes spread from the port to practically all the major employers of labour in Aden. At the peak, in March and April 1956, more than 7000 men were involved, and during the course of the trouble there were two serious clashes between workers and police... At the beginning of 1956 there were eight workers' unions; at the end of the same year there were twenty-four involving some 4000 men... The trade union movement went from strength to strength; by 1959 more than 15 000 men were unionised, by 1963 trade union membership exceeded 22 000.[6]

The ATUC was the undisputed leader of this nascent labour movement, putting forward trade union, democratic and nationalist demands: 'one people, one Yemen, one struggle'.[7] The authorities retreated and made concessions on working hours and wages, but there was a steadfast refusal to make any political concessions.

Indeed, far from making political concessions, the British were actually taking steps preparatory to the colony joining the Federation. They proposed to give the Legislative Council an elected majority for the first time (12 out of 23 members), but its powers were not increased and the franchise remained restricted. Only 21 500 people had the vote out of a total population of 180 000. This was achieved quite simply by excluding North Yemeni immigrants who could not prove they had lived in the colony for seven out of the last ten years. In this way a third of the population was disenfranchised. The ATUC led a militant aggressive campaign against both the franchise and the Legislative Council.

In April 1958 there was a successful two-day general strike and unrest continued into May when the British finally declared a State of Emergency. In October, after two days of rioting in Crater, there were mass arrests and 240 workers were deported to North Yemen. At the same time, the ATUC newspaper, The *Worker*, was banned and its general-secretary, Abdullah al-Asnag, was arrested. Unrest continued throughout 1959 with the port paralysed by a 48-day strike and the oil refineries by a 34-day strike. According to the Aden government, by the end of the year there had been 84 strikes in the colony. Meanwhile, the elections to the Legislative Council went ahead. The ATUC campaign for a boycott had a significant impact with only 27 per cent of those eligible voting. Once the elections were over a barrage of condemnation of the Council was kept up, condemning it as undemocratic and calling for its overthrow. When strikes continued into 1960, the Legislative Council passed a new Industrial Relations Ordinance in August. This imposed compulsory mediation in industrial disputes and effectively made strikes illegal. The ATUC responded with go-slow tactics in the work place and turned increasingly to politics.

As the British proceeded towards the incorporation of Aden into the Federation, so opposition mounted. The ATUC was instrumental in establishing the People's Socialist Party (PSP) to lead the resistance to this measure. A successful general strike against the proposed merger was called in July in defiance of the law. When the Legislative Council met on 24 September to vote on the proposition, the ATUC called another general strike. There were large demonstrations that erupted into serious rioting that required the deployment of British troops to assist the police. Tear gas was used and the troops opened fire, leaving one man dead and five wounded, before order was restored. Inside the Legislative Council a majority of the elected members walked out of the debate in protest against the merger leaving the colony's constitutional future to be settled on 26 September by the unelected members and a rump of collaborators. The whole affair was a quite blatant exercise in vote-rigging and gerrymandering carried out without even the most nominal pretence of consulting the wishes of Aden's inhabitants. Indeed the whole exercise was expressly designed to thwart their wishes under a camouflage of constitutional propriety. The safeguarding of the colony as a military base was an absolute priority.

Revolution in North Yemen

On the same day as this shabby disreputable manoeuvre was accomplished, radical army officers, sympathetic to Egypt's President Nasser, staged a coup d'état in Sanaa, overthrew the Imam and proclaimed the Yemen Arab Republic (YAR). The news was received with tremendous celebration in Aden. Thousands of North Yemenis, in exile from the Imam's rule, crossed the border to rally to the new regime. No less than four leading members of the ATUC left to take up cabinet posts in the republican government of Abdullah as-Sallal. This revolution brought Britain's bastard Federation face to face with the forces of Arab nationalism.[8] Macmillan subsequently recalled being 'gravely concerned about our position in Aden' and on 5 and 6 October held important meetings with ministers from the Colonial Office, Foreign Office and Ministry of Defence. They agreed to authorise defensive precautions in case the Federation 'was openly attacked and meanwhile to take such other action as might seem justifiable'. This 'other action' was eventually to include covert intervention in the YAR, assisting royalist rebels against the Sallal regime. For the time being, Macmillan confessed to being 'very concerned about Aden, where the position may easily get out of hand'.[9]

The British response to these developments was two-fold. Steps were taken to ascertain the strength of royalist opposition to Sallal. Towards the end of October, Neil McLean, a Conservative MP and former SOE agent, crossed into the YAR to establish contact with the royalists and report back to London on their prospects for either overthrowing the republicans or at least harassing them. This was to be the preliminary step of an important covert operation to assist the rebel forces with both weapons and mercenaries, an operation carried out in collaboration with the Saudis. Among those involved were McLean himself, his old friend from SOE, David Smiley, and a number of SAS veterans, among them John Cooper and Peter de la Billiere.[10]

At the same time as embarking on a destabilising operation in the YAR, the British cracked down on the opposition in Aden. A tough new police chief was appointed, Nigel Morris, a veteran of the Malayan Emergency, charged with curbing enthusiasm for the Sallal regime. Both the PSP and the ATUC were subjected to continual legal harassment with members being arrested or deported. This was effective in driving the opposition underground and, out of desperation, the PSP leadership determined on a demonstrative act of terrorism. They took the decision to assassinate the High Commissioner, Sir Kennedy Trevaskis, the principal architect of the Federation and the man they held most responsible for the situation in Aden. On 10 December a supervisor at the Aden airport, Khalifa Abdullah Hasan Khalifa, threw a grenade at Trevaskis as he was boarding a plane for London. He was carrying proposals to further restrict the franchise in Aden. The grenade only slightly wounded Trevaskis, but it killed his aide, George Henderson, and a woman bystander. The British responded with the immediate declaration of a State of Emergency accompanied by large-scale arrests. Some 280 people were deported to the YAR and another 50, virtually the entire PSP and ATUC leaderships, were placed in detention. The franchise reform cutting the electorate to only 10 per cent of the population was also put into effect. These measures seemed effective, but only because there was not yet a guerrilla movement established in Aden. The attempt on Trevaskis had been a one-off attack. The PSP remained committed to a campaign of strikes and demonstrations and had not yet embraced the armed struggle as the way forward. Others had.

Across the border, in the YAR, a number of activists and organisations from Aden and the Federation came together to establish the National

Liberation Front for Occupied South Yemen (NLF). The leaders were 'middle class...clerks, teachers, officers' and the most prominent figure among them was Qatan al-Shaabi.[11] They had rallied to the Republican cause in September 1962 and now proposed to carry the revolution to the Federation. Initially, this new revolutionary organisation was barely tolerated by Sallal, who still hoped that it might be possible to reach some sort of accommodation with Britain. Once it became clear that the British had no intention of recognising his government and were continuing to encourage and assist the royalists, Sallal decided to sponsor rebellion in the South Arabian Federation. With the PSP rejecting armed struggle, Sallal together with his Egyptian advisers gave their support to the NLF. The new organisation's ambitions embraced the whole of the Federation, not just Aden as was the case with the PSP. It was committed to destroying the Federation, overthrowing the feudal rulers, evicting the British and establishing a Communist-style People's Democracy.[12] Now it became the recipient of large-scale Yemeni and Egyptian aid: weapons, training, finance and the tremendously effective propaganda support of Cairo radio.

The Radfan campaign

The NLF's first challenge to the British was a guerrilla insurgency in the Radfan mountains to the south of Dhala. Armed groups crossed into the area from the YAR and rallied and organised the tribesmen for rebellion. They had successfully cut the Dhala road by the end of 1963. The British response was Operation Nutcracker, an expedition carried out by three battalions of the Federal Regular Army (FRA) supported by British artillery, tanks and airpower. The operation began in early January 1964 with the FRA advancing on the Bakri ridge which commanded the Dhala road, and bringing Wadis Rabua and Misrah under their control. Having accomplished this against negligible opposition, the FRA felt confident that it 'had subdued most of Radfan' and at a cost of only five killed and 12 wounded.[13] A road was constructed through the area to ensure continued domination. Rising tension on the frontier with the YAR necessitated the withdrawal of the FRA troops in March, however, whereupon the NLF reappeared, destroying the strategic road just laid down and once again threatening the Dhala road. Meanwhile on the frontier, YAR cross-border raids in Beihan were countered on 28 March by an RAF attack by eight Hunter jets on a Yemeni fort at Harib, reducing it to rubble and destroying a number of vehicles.

The Federation and the Republic seemed close to war and FRA troops could not be spared for further operations in the Radfan. Instead it was decided to commit British troops. This decision was the subject of much debate with some arguing against the use of troops and in favour of subduing the insurgents by the traditional method of aerial bombardment.[14] Certainly the NLF's intention was to pull British troops into the Radfan and the army, for its part, was very keen to oblige; indeed, it was positively enthusiastic about what was regarded as a straightforward old-fashioned colonial campaign against primitive tribesmen. Intelligence sources had as yet not identified the role of the NLF in the insurgency.

The British assembled a thousand-strong expedition, Radforce, and prepared for another incursion into the mountains. The objective was to prevent the spread of the revolt, to reassert British authority and to end the attacks on the Dhala road. The hope was that the insurgents would stand and fight so that they could be destroyed by superior firepower, but failing that the area would become a war zone and the local population, some 50 000 people, would be driven out. It was not intended to establish a permanent occupation.

The plan was to seize two towering features, known as Cap Badge and Rice Bowl, north of Bakri ridge. This would be accomplished by a surprise night march on 30 April–1 May which would then be reinforced at daylight by a parachute drop. On the evening of 29 April a nine-man SAS patrol was helicoptered in to mark out a dropping zone for the paratroopers at the foot of Cap Badge. This aspect of the operation quickly miscarried. The patrol was discovered, surrounded and came under heavy attack. Only continuous air support kept the rebels at bay and gave the seven survivors of the fiasco a chance to break out under cover of darkness. Hunter jets supporting the patrol fired 127 rockets and 7131 cannon rounds. The GOC Land Forces Middle East later complained that the heads of the two SAS killed had been paraded in Taiz in the YAR. While this has never been confirmed, both corpses were found to have been beheaded when they were eventually recovered. With this setback, the plan had to be changed and instead of being seized with the advantage of surprise, Cap Badge now had to be taken by assault with the Paras losing two men killed and six wounded.

The NLF fought a classic guerrilla war. They refused to stand and fight, except on rare occasions, and instead melted away into the landscape, subjecting the British to continual sniping and laying fresh mines every night. Julian Paget pays tribute to their prowess:

> The Radfan tribesmen made excellent guerrillas. They had been born to warfare, and had been brought up to regard possession of a rifle as a normal sign of maturity. They were normally good natural shots with wonderful powers of observation; they thus made fine snipers, for they knew just where to look for targets. They could conceal themselves perfectly, and also used to place marks on the ground, so as to know the range exactly. Being accustomed to carrying out lightning raids and ambushes, they could move far and fast across mountains and were thus an elusive enemy. They were also extremely courageous, as was shown by their capacity to fight on in the face of heavy artillery and air attack.[15]

Against this opponent the British decided they needed reinforcements so operations were briefly suspended while another 2000 troops were brought in. The campaign recommenced on 19 May with the British occupying Bakri ridge and then proceeding to take a number of other features commanding the surrounding terrain. The 'decisive battle' occurred in early June when troops advanced up the Wadi Misra only to find some 50 members of NLF in entrenched positions before the village of Shaab Sharah on the slopes of the Jebel Huriyah. The rebels were shelled and strafed throughout the day but when a dawn attack went in the next morning they had vanished.[16]

How serious a setback this was for the insurgents is difficult to assess. It was certainly not the end of the fighting in the Radfan which, with peaks and troughs, continued until the British finally pulled out. Rather it seems to have fulfilled the British requirement for something approximating a conventional victory so that the operation could be officially called off and proclaimed a success. There is a distinct feel of fraud about the whole affair. It seems a victory comparable with the many American victories in Vietnam where the guerrillas slipped away and the full force of the military machine's considerable firepower fell on the local population. Certainly this was an important feature of the 1964 Radfan campaign that is not given enough emphasis in most accounts.

What of the role of air power in the campaign? While it was important for greatly increasing the mobility of the troops (the use of helicopters and air-dropped supplies, especially water) and for reconnaissance purposes, nevertheless its two main roles were close support and interdicting the proscribed areas. The troops relied on air strikes to deal with even individual snipers, let alone more serious opposition. This was an absolutely crucial feature of the campaign without which British casualties would have been considerably higher and much larger numbers of troops would have been required. The other role involved the terrorising of the local population. The British proclaimed that insurgent areas were proscribed zones and dropped leaflets telling the inhabitants to leave. Once this formality was completed the RAF was free to roam over these areas, attacking targets of opportunity, strafing and rocketing any sign of human activity. The local people either fled the area or abandoned their homes to take shelter in caves. This was a deliberate, calculated attempt to terrorise and starve them into surrender. Their crops were destroyed, their livestock seized and their homes blown up. So much is admitted quite openly in the Commons by Peter Thorneycroft, the Minister of Defence. He confessed that it was 'inevitable that crops should suffer and food stocks be destroyed in the process of excluding the rebels from the settled area' but, he went on, once the people had agreed to 'submit to authority' they would, of course, be fed by the Federation government.[17]

The importance of air power is indicated by the scale of attacks made on the rebel areas. Between the end of April and the end of June 1964 Hunter jets fired 2508 rockets and nearly 200 000 cannon rounds, while the four-engined Shackleton bombers dropped 3504 20-lb anti-personnel bombs and 14 1000-lb bombs and fired nearly 20 000 cannon rounds. This bombardment was decisive in driving the NLF underground or out of the area. And it did not stop at the end of June. Throughout July, August and September air attacks on the proscribed areas continued. As one account gleefully notes:

> as the time for harvesting the crops approached it became apparent that the air control was so effective that the tribes began to emerge at night to work in their fields, a move which was countered by the Shackletons dropping flares and a number of bombs at irregular intervals to add to the general discomfort.[18]

By the middle of November the last of the Radfan tribes finally submitted to the Federal government and surrendered hostages who were held in a special camp. This was not the end of the fighting, however. By early 1965, attacks were already beginning again and continued with varying degrees of intensity until the British abandoned the interior to the NLF in April–June 1967.

In assessing the Radfan campaign there seems considerable justice to Fred Halliday's judgement that the British had 'all along misunderstood the situation, thinking they were up against an old-style tribal resistance' that could be suppressed by punitive columns, bombing and the taking of hostages. Instead, in the NLF they were encountering an increasingly well-armed guerrilla force that was conducting not a particularist tribal rebellion, but a revolutionary war.[19] The British victory in Radfan was, from this point of view, illusory, more to do with the categories in which the military thought than with what was actually happening on the ground. While the guerrillas without any doubt sustained losses, nevertheless they avoided defeat and were to return to the attack within a matter of months. For the NLF, war was a political activity and even while the British were occupying the Radfan they were establishing bases in other Federation states. In the summer of 1967 these were to deliver the interior into their hands. The British not only failed to prevent this, they were largely unaware that it was happening. A good example of the security forces' lack of intelligence is provided by the experience of John Watts of 22 SAS. When assigned to the Mishwara area he asked the District Officer for one or two reliable Arabs to act as guides and was told much to his disgust that there was none.[20] One recent study has commented on 'the absence of anything like a hearts and minds campaign' in the Radfan or anywhere else.[21] The NLF's final victory was, of course, made considerably easier by the British withdrawal into Aden, but there is absolutely no doubt that if the British had tried to prop up the Federation, they would have been confronted by an insurgency throughout the interior on a scale that it is most unlikely they would have had the resources to withstand. While attention was now to shift to the urban guerrilla struggle in Aden itself, the final outcome of the conflict was decided in the interior. The states that the British had hoped would contain Adeni radicalism were the first to fall to the revolution.[22]

Rebellion in Aden

The struggle in Aden was complicated by deep divisions within the nationalist camp. The dominant political force was still the PSP–ATUC alliance, but now this began to come under a challenge from the NLF. The new organisation succeeded in recruiting the more militant trade unionists and activists, who were prepared for armed struggle, into its underground cells. They set about establishing a secret urban guerrilla force, ready to wage war on the British. For the time being, however, the political scene was dominated by the PSP's campaign of strikes, demonstrations and rallies. The Party achieved a notable success in the elections to the Legislative Council in October 1964. Despite Trevaskis's new franchise, which reduced the electorate to some 10 000 people, a number of

PSP members were elected. Among them was Khalifa, who was still being held for the grenade attack on Trevaskis the previous year but received 98 per cent of the votes in the Crater North constituency. This showed beyond any shadow of a doubt that the Federation regime, in which the British had invested so much effort, had no significant popular support in Aden whatsoever. It was a stunning repudiation of British policy despite their having changed the rules in an attempt to rig the game in their favour. All the claims that the opposition were an unrepresentative minority of troublemakers were now shown up as empty propaganda. Some kind of new British initiative was inevitable.[23]

That same October, a general election in Britain brought Harold Wilson and the Labour Party to power. This, according to some commentators, was a disaster as far as the Federation was concerned. The Labour government's weak mishandling of affairs was to result in the Federation's destruction and the loss of the Aden base. One critic, J.B. Kelley, goes so far as to blame Labour's 'doctrinal convictions about the evils of Western imperialism'. Presumably the belief is that a Conservative government would have continued with its policy unchanged, disregarding its repudiation in the Legislative Council elections. This would have required an indefinite commitment to direct rule or perhaps, as Kelley suggests, the government should have allowed the FRA to carry out an exemplary massacre in Aden, 'an Arab solution in a night of the long knives'.[24] This is so much nonsense and tells us considerably more about the political prejudices of the writer concerned than it does about what it was politically possible for any British government to do at this time. More recently, the historian Aaron Edwards has similarly identified Labour politicians as the problem, singling out Denis Healey: 'It is difficult to think of a Labour politician more decidedly anti-colonialist than Denis Healey.' This is most unfair. In fact there were many Labour MPs more anti-colonialist than Healey, who was, very much on the right of the party and was, moreover, a staunch supporter of NATO. He was quite coincidentally credited by Air Vice-Marshal Menaul with ensuring the survival of the Royal United Service Institute. According to Menaul, Healy helped raise funds by 'writing to more than 100 friends in important positions', indeed, without his help it 'would not have existed'.[25] Blaming the situation on the supposed anti-colonialism of Labour politicians is just not credible.

What Anthony Greenwood, the new Labour Colonial Secretary, found on taking office was that the outgoing government's policy was in ruins. He realised that unless a policy that could command broad enough support was found, Britain would find itself embroiled in another Cyprus-style Emergency. This appreciation was absolutely sound. The problem was that Greenwood and his colleagues were not prepared to abandon the sultans and emirs and embrace Arab nationalism. They certainly, at this time, had no intention of giving up the Aden base.

Greenwood's arrival in Aden on 26 November 1964 was the occasion for the NLF to launch its urban guerrilla war in Aden. A weekend of violence left five people dead and 35 injured. This outbreak was accompanied by demonstrations and clashes with the police. Essentially what Greenwood offered the PSP was power and position in return for accepting the Federation and the continuing British military presence. Instead of being treated with contempt by the authorities and subjected to continual harassment, they were now invited to take over in the run up to independence. This might well have been acceptable earlier on, but by now the state of popular feeling was such that al-Asnag and his comrades were not in a position to abandon their principles for the fruits of office. This was something that Greenwood, coming from the traditions of British Labourism, had considerable difficulty in coming to terms with. With the rise of the NLF, the PSP leaders were under increasing pressure from the left and felt obliged to maintain a position of uncompromising hostility to British imperialism. While Greenwood was certainly right in believing that the only way to avoid the situation getting out of hand was to come to an arrangement with the nationalist opposition, something that had been accomplished in many other former colonies, he was wrong in believing that this could be done on the basis of a continued British military presence. The other side of the coin was the PSP belief that if it continued its pressure, in the end the Labour government would come round to accepting the need for a complete British withdrawal and the dismantling of the Federation. The failure of the two sides to agree terms was to see the initiative pass to the NLF.

Greenwood pressed on regardless, dismissing Trevaskis, who was regarded as a reactionary hardliner, too committed to the sultans, and replacing him with Sir Richard Turnbull. The new High Commissioner had a reputation for toughness, acquired in Kenya where 'he had played a major role in crushing Mau Mau', but more recently in December 1961 he had successfully carried through the granting of independence to Tanganyika.[26] Turnbull appointed a PSP member, Abdul al-Makkawi, as Chief Minister. A few years earlier this would have been a master stroke. Makkawi was on the right of the Party and would in normal circumstances have certainly been amenable to an accommodation with the

British. Now, however, he presided over a colony in turmoil, where any compromise would have been repudiated on the streets.

Instead of coming to an agreement with the British, Makkawi and his fellow ministers called for an end to the Federation, immediate independence and a British withdrawal. They refused to condemn the increasing level of guerrilla activity, opposed British security measures and condemned the behaviour of the security forces. The British ploy had backfired, but was nevertheless sustained until September 1965 when the deteriorating security situation finally led Turnbull to dismiss Makkawi and return Aden to direct colonial rule. This provoked a general strike on 2 October that was accompanied by two days of rioting in which over 700 people were arrested. It was this British constitutional coup d'état that finally determined the PSP to take up the armed struggle.

The NLF campaign has many similarities with that of EOKA in Cyprus. The insurgents made the police and the Special Branch their priority target, seeking to blind the security forces. They achieved this in the course of 1965, effectively eliminating the Arab members of Special Branch, while the police were either intimidated into passivity or in increasing numbers were actually enlisted in the rebel cause. Unlike Cyprus, there was no ethnic minority hostile to the nationalist cause for the British to recruit a police force from. According to Julian Paget the guerrillas

> employed all the traditional methods against the authorities, the Security Forces and the civil population, ranging from subversion and propaganda to intimidation and violence; their tactics and techniques were remarkably similar in most respects to those adopted by EOKA in the Cyprus Emergency. They employed all the customary weapons, such as grenades, mines, bazookas, mortars and small arms. They resorted to booby traps and sabotage attacks, and they carried out a series of murders and assassinations, all of which bore the mark of cold-blooded professionals. Finally, they made skilful use of constant strikes, riots, and demonstrations, both to cause trouble and to provide useful propaganda material.[27]

Attacks on the security forces became increasingly frequent and although there was never any danger of a military defeat, nevertheless they imposed a tremendous strain. In 1965, six soldiers were killed and another 83 were wounded, and the following year, 1966, only five were killed, but 218 were wounded.

The British responded to this insurgency with the establishment in the summer of 1965 of an integrated repressive apparatus combining police, army and civil administration along the lines pioneered in Malaya. Troop reinforcements were brought in. The problem, however, was lack of intelligence. Not enough was known about the NLF, its cellular structure or its guerrilla fighters, and the destruction of the Special Branch closed off the most promising means of remedying this situation. At one point there were no less than ten separate intelligence agencies operating in Aden without any overall direction. This was compounded by the fact that the local people were overwhelmingly hostile to the British and sympathetic to the nationalist rebels. A vital element for successful counterinsurgency, allies and collaborators among the population of the occupied territory, was missing.[28] Later, when it became known that the British were intent on withdrawal, any slight hope of winning over any support disappeared altogether. Without effective intelligence the British were forced to rely on other methods. Search operations were carried out on a large scale in a routine attempt to restrict the movement of men and weapons by the NLF and in the hope of arrests that might subsequently prove a source of information. The results were not promising. One unit operating in Crater between February and September 1965 searched 35 000 people and 8000 vehicles, and found only 12 grenades and six pistols.[29] Inevitably these searches, accompanied by racist abuse and physical manhandling, further alienated the population. Stephen Harper, *Daily Express* correspondent in Aden, wrote fondly of the troops that 'There's a lot of boot, gun-butt and fist thumping', but this wasn't brutality but rather 'righteous anger'. An officer recalled how, when troops were banned from calling the Arabs 'wog', they wittily responded by calling them 'gollies' instead.[30] This was most unlikely to win over any 'hearts and minds' among a people rebelling against foreign domination.

More effective was the use of small mobile patrols, sometimes operating disguised as Arabs. These were known as 'Special Branch Sections' and were usually eight to ten strong with an officer in command. They carried out raids, searches and surveillance under Special Branch direction. The Anglian Regiment provided a number of such squads: they 'operated with speed and surprise, mostly at night'. One squad in particular was responsible for the capture of 14 guerrillas and the seizure of 105 grenades, five automatic weapons, three pistols, two rocket launchers and a quantity of explosives.[31] The SAS, in what was its first deployment against urban guerrillas, also operated in small, mobile 'Keeni-Meeni' squads. They functioned 'like the "Q" squads of the Palestine Police...started by Roy Farran' and were made up of men thought most likely to pass for Arabs. Sometimes they staked out lone soldiers in uniform in an attempt to lure gunmen and grenade-throwers into an attack whereupon the squad would capture or kill them. The intention was to take prisoners if possible in the hope that they would break under interrogation and provide a gap in the 'total, silent security surrounding Nationalist operations'. On one occasion, they shot it out with an Anglian undercover squad, having mistaken them for rebels, and seriously wounded two of them.[32]

Without intelligence sources within the Arab population, the security forces came to rely on the interrogation of prisoners for information. Inevitably this involved the use of torture, usually beatings of one kind or another, but also the use of sensory deprivation techniques that were to be later used in Northern Ireland. The British refused to cooperate with any independent inquiry into the allegations that were made about this at the time and successfully rode out the furore. According to Edwards, the Fort Morbut Interrogation Centre was known to the local population as 'the fingernail factory'. The preferred torture technique, he goes on, was apparently, 'to place a detainee on a chair, walk behind him in a menacing way and then slap both his eardrums...medical records frequently noted "Characteristic Traumatic perforation to Tympanic Membrane" (commonly known as burst eardrums)'.[33]

The decision to withdraw

Regardless of these continuing efforts to crush the insurgency, in February 1966 the Labour government's Defence White Paper announced its intention to abandon the Aden base and withdraw from South Yemen when the Federation became independent in 1968. This decision involved the sudden abandonment of the traditional rulers of the interior, the sultans and sheikhs, leaving them defenceless against their nationalist enemies. The decision was regarded as a betrayal of trust by many colonial officials, army officers and Conservative MPs. The Labour government, as far as these people were concerned, was selling out British interests and Britain's allies to appease the cowards, reds and traitors on the Labour benches. This was, of course, very much a right-wing fantasy, one of the streams that later fed into attempts to destabilise the Labour government in the early 1970s, the so-called Wilson Plot.[34] The reality was very different. Two factors lay behind the decision. First, there was the influence of economic considerations, of the need for cutbacks in defence expenditure. This necessarily involved a hard-nosed reassessment of Britain's strategic commitments and was to culminate in the abandonment of an east of Suez presence, 'the most far-reaching change in Britain's world position to occur since the withdrawal from India twenty years before'.[35] Second, there was also a recognition that the Federation was a completely artificial creation without any popular support. It would require propping up indefinitely and the military effort this would involve negated Aden's usefulness as a base. The troops who should have been available for redeployment to trouble-spots elsewhere were in fact fully engaged containing the insurgency. The Aden base had become a liability rather than an asset and was increasingly regarded as a potential 'Vietnam'. The decision to withdraw involved a facing up to the realities of Britain's position in the world, a strategic readjustment that recognised Britain's economic weakness. Whatever the complexion of the government in power, Labour or Conservative, the decision was inevitable. Unfortunately for the sheikhs and sultans, they were not sitting on any oil reserves which would, of course, have completely changed the situation. Instead, once withdrawal was announced, the struggle in South Yemen became increasingly a struggle over who was to take over from the British.

The nationalist movement was bitterly divided between the NLF and a rival organisation deriving from the PSP–ATUC connection, the Organisation for the Liberation of the Occupied South (OLOS). OLOS had a shrinking base in South Yemen, even in Aden where al-Asnaj's influence had by now been eclipsed by the NLF, but it was sponsored by the Egyptians. They were increasingly suspicious of the NLF's independence and radicalism and attempted to bring it under control by forcing a union between the two organisations. In January 1966 the Egyptians were instrumental in persuading the NLF leadership to join with OLOS in establishing the Front for the Liberation of South Yemen (FLOSY). This union was not acceptable to the NLF organisation in the South and in June they expelled those leaders, including Qahtan al-Shaabi (he was later re-admitted), held responsible for the decision. A new General Command consisting of the leaders of the armed struggle was elected to replace the discredited Politburo which was regarded as being in the hands of the Egyptians. This led to an irretrievable break with FLOSY in November 1966 and to the beginning of armed hostilities between the two organisations. The struggle against the British was from now on accompanied by fighting between rival supporters of the NLF and FLOSY.[36]

War on the streets

1967 saw the insurgency enter its final phase with a considerable increase in both the level and sophistication of guerrilla activity in Aden and the interior. Whereas in the whole of 1966 there had been 480 incidents, in 1967 up until November there were 2900. The guerrillas became more aggressive and determined in their challenge to the security forces. The NLF staged its first major confrontation in February, proclaiming the 11th, the eighth anniversary of the establishment of the Federation, 'the day of the Volcano'. The British responded with a curfew enforced by the large-scale deployment of troops on the streets of Sheikh Othman, Crater and Maala. This successfully kept the lid on the situation but, when the curfew was lifted the following day, there was serious rioting and the troops came under fire. The popular uprising that the NLF had envisaged never materialised.

This was followed by a protracted struggle for control of the town of Sheikh Othman, just inside Aden state. The NLF launched a guerrilla offensive to coincide with the arrival of a UN mission on 2 April. They intended to drive the security forces off the streets. For the first time, the British lost effective control over an urban area. By the time the 1st Battalion, the Parachute Regiment were deployed in the town at the end of May, 'law and order had virtually completely broken down'.[37] On 1 June, the NLF attempted to resist the Paras' deployment. A general strike was called. The Paras moved in to occupy eight observation posts in the heart of the town under cover of darkness and came under attack at first light. A grenade attack outside the main mosque 'signalled the start of hostilities, and all OPs came under heavy and well co-ordinated fire, some at only 50 yards range'.[38] Armoured cars were brought in to support the embattled troops, engaging NLF positions and resupplying the observation posts which were running short of ammunition. By the end of this first day the Paras had lost one man killed and four wounded while they claimed to have killed 16 of their attackers. Attacks with small arms, grenades and rocket launchers continued virtually every day until the Paras were relieved, by which time there had been nearly 800 incidents recorded in Sheikh Othman alone.[39]

While this battle continued, the Labour government came under increasing pressure from the Saudis and the United States to change its policy. In March it had been announced that the withdrawal of British forces had been brought forward to November 1967, and the following month British troops began to pull out of the interior, handing over to the Federal Regular Army. In May, Turnbull was replaced as High

Commissioner by Sir Humphrey Trevelyan who was charged with managing the withdrawal. He arrived to find the situation 'bleak' and a revolution 'in full swing'.[40] Now, however, with Egypt defeated by Israel in the June 1967 'Six Day War', it seemed possible that something might be salvaged from the debacle. On 20 June the Labour Foreign Secretary, George Brown, put back the date of withdrawal to January 1968, promised another £10 million in military aid and announced that British air and naval forces would continue to support the Federation for another six months after independence. If the insurgency had collapsed in the aftermath of the Egyptian defeat, then it is certain that more determined efforts to prop up the Federation would have followed. The rebellion had a momentum all of its own, however, and was certainly not the creation of the Egyptians as some on the British side still thought. All the Egyptian defeat accomplished was to further undermine FLOSY and to increase Arab hostility towards Britain, which was regarded as an ally of the Israelis. At the same time as Brown made his announcement, the NLF emerged into the open and began to take over the hinterland, while in Aden itself the British confronted the most serious crisis of the conflict.

Mutiny

On 20 June the South Arabian Army (the newly renamed FRA) and the South Arabian and Aden Police all mutinied. This was not something that came out of the blue. It had been known for some time that both the army and the police were infiltrated by the NLF and that on occasions they had been actively assisting the insurgents, even carrying out attacks on the British.[41] Moreover, in May fighting had nearly broken out at a funeral between British and Arab troops, some of them carrying NLF placards and, for a while, 'the entire British garrison stood to general alert'.[42] This incident had been contained. Now, however, violence was to erupt and put an end to Brown's manoeuvring.

The outbreak began with a mutiny within the South Arabian Army, following the suspension of four senior officers for protesting against the appointment of a new commanding officer known to be loyal to the Federation. This affair was short-lived, with troops at Lake Lines rioting, setting fire to some buildings and firing off a few shots before their own officers restored order. The noise of the disturbance was heard by the South Arabian Police at Champion Lines a mile away and, fearing a British attack, they prepared to defend themselves. They shot dead two Aden police coming to find out what was going on and a British Public

Works official driving past the Lines. Then a truck came along the road carrying British troops back from the firing range and was promptly shot up. Eight soldiers were killed and another eight were wounded. A burst of fire into the Radfan Camp across the road killed a British Army subaltern. British troops, supported by armoured cars were sent to put down the mutiny but with orders to use the absolute minimum of force in order to avoid the crisis escalating. The last thing the British wanted was a shooting war with the forces to whom they were supposed to be transferring responsibility for security. As it was, the troops successfully took the Lines against only slight resistance, killing four policemen and themselves losing one man killed and eight wounded. While this outbreak had been successfully overcome, the mutiny spread to the Police Barracks in Crater.

Here, once again, the police were fearful of a British attack and took steps to defend themselves. They opened fire on vehicles out looking for an army platoon that had been ordered out of the area precisely to avoid any such clashes. Among those killed were two British officers and four soldiers. The lone survivor of this incident was taken prisoner and later released to the British unharmed. Having seen the wrecked vehicles and dead bodies, the officer commanding the missing platoon went to investigate with three of his men. They were all killed, although in what circumstances has never been made clear. A helicopter flying over the area was fired on and brought down but without any loss of life. Rather than risk escalating the conflict, the British withdrew from the area. They surrendered control of Crater, considered by the Arab population to be the true capital of Aden, to the NLF. Jubilant crowds took to the streets celebrating the victory. They abused the bodies of the British soldiers, hanging two of them in Maidan Square, burned down the Legislative Council building, opened the local jail and looted shops and businesses. The police distributed weapons to the local people to help defend the area.

The day had ended with 22 soldiers killed and 31 wounded. The loss of life, however, was overshadowed by the scale of the political disaster. The army and police, to whom the British proposed to hand over as they withdrew, had demonstrated beyond any doubt that they were at best unreliable and at worst pro-insurgent. And the town of Crater, with its 80 000 inhabitants, was in the hands of the NLF.

There was considerable criticism of the High Commissioner and Army Command for not sending in troops to crush the Crater mutiny immediately. It was widely believed that a number of the British dead had in fact been captured alive and were only killed later, lynched by the crowd.

The authorities were condemned for not mounting a rescue attempt, for sacrificing soldiers' lives to political considerations. Certainly as far as the Commanding Officer of the Argyll and Sutherland Highlanders, Colin Mitchell, was concerned the affair confirmed him in his 'complete lack of confidence in the military management of Aden'.[43] He was in the process of taking over responsibility for Crater when the mutiny occurred and had lost three men killed. As far as the authorities were concerned, however, to have intervened in force, with the inevitable loss of life on both sides, would have been to risk precipitating a mutiny throughout the rest of the South Arabian Army and the Police. This would have involved the British in a far more dangerous situation and would have cost them even more casualties. That this was not a vain fear was shown by the disturbances that did occur among a number of Arab army units but were resolved by diplomacy and persuasion. An armed incursion into Crater, which would have involved taking on the NLF guerrillas and armed civilians as well as the police, would have certainly tipped the balance.[44] Instead, the town was surrounded by troops who engaged in continued exchanges with the guerrillas but were ordered not to fire on the police. The crisis had been contained, but the spectacle of Crater in rebel hands was an immensely damaging blow to British prestige. George Brown's brief flirtation with the notion of extending the British commitment to the Federation was over.

The British eventually re-occupied Crater on the evening of 3 July. The Argylls, accompanied by armoured cars, entered the town and secured a number of strong points without meeting any opposition. The police had agreed to return to discipline and the nationalist guerrillas declined to make a stand. Indeed, for the past two weeks FLOSY and the NLF had been busy fighting each other for control of the town. Once installed, the Argylls proceeded to establish their domination over the area with what Mitchell described as 'tolerant toughness'. Any incident involved the immediate establishment of roadblocks and the rounding up of 'all terrorist suspects – usually males between the ages of 15 and 35'. They were held for interrogation and then driven off to another part of Aden, dumped and told to make their own way home. As Mitchell himself notes, there were some 'who felt that we were alienating the civil population', but he disregarded such considerations. The NLF attempted to challenge the Argylls in August with a series of attacks, but by the end of the month they had admitted defeat and thereafter Crater remained quiescent until the middle of October. As far as Mitchell and his admirers were concerned, this was a vindication of his tough, no-nonsense methods and showed what could have been achieved throughout Aden and the Federation if the political will had been present.[45]

Accusations of brutality were made against the Argylls at the time but only subsequently did soldiers themselves come forward and admit what had gone on. The conviction of members of the regiment in January 1981 for the brutal murder of two Catholic farmers in Northern Ireland in the autumn of 1972, the so-called Pitchfork Murders, led to revelations with regard to events in Aden.[46] According to David Ledger, who served as a Political Officer in Aden, in the weeks following the trial, the Glasgow *Sunday Mail* conducted a careful and comprehensive investigation. Scores of former soldiers were interviewed and many maintained that no impropriety took place. Eventually a dozen men signed sworn statements detailing robbery and murder by officers and men. One soldier admitted personally shooting down five unarmed Arabs in different incidents. Several alleged murder of men by morphine injections and shooting. Others claimed to be the distressed witnesses to the brutal killing of a teenager found in a café after curfew and bayonetted to death on the orders of an officer. Roadblock duty, they claimed, was the opportunity for wholesale theft. All this and more was published by the *Sunday Mail* in their editions of 26 April and 10 May 1981. In the days following publication the newspaper kept two telephone lines open for reaction from the public. A lot of calls were abusive but a significant number were from former soldiers supporting the allegations, including some of those who had formerly denied them.[47]

The Argylls were not, of course, the only troops involved in such conduct. Inevitably, the Parachute Regiment worked along similar lines. One senior Para officer subsequently complained of the squeamishness of 'those in high places' who did not approve of what he described as 'vigorous interrogation'. 'Word came down', he recalled, 'that if any more prisoners were "shot trying to escape" or "fell downstairs", there would be a full investigation and dire consequences.'[48]

Meanwhile, the withdrawal from the hinterland had been accomplished. Ostensibly the British handed over to the Federal rulers and the SAA but, in fact, as they withdrew the NLF came out into the open and took control. The Radfan guerrillas finally triumphed, occupying Dhala on 20 June and imprisoning the Amir in his own jail. After Dhala they took Lower Yafai, Audhali, Lahej, Dathina and Fahdli. By the end of August they controlled 12 of the Federal states and in early September they established a revolutionary government in Zinjibar, just 25 miles from Aden. The only serious fighting to accompany this astonishing success was between the NLF and FLOSY, and this was decided when the South Arabian Army finally declared their support for the NLF.[49]

With fighting between the rival guerrilla forces continuing, the British withdrew into Aden and then began to abandon the colony district by district. On 13 September troops pulled out of Little Aden, and on 24 September Sheikh Othman was abandoned as the British retreated towards Steamer Point. Only on 13 November did the High Commissioner acknowledge the NLF government, finally bringing attacks on British troops to an end. The last British personnel were helicoptered out on 29 November. The struggle to free South Yemen from British rule was over.

British defeat was complete, a humiliating withdrawal, leaving the country in the hands of self-proclaimed Marxist revolutionaries who promptly proclaimed the People's Republic of South Yemen. The conflict had cost the lives of 92 British soldiers with another 500 wounded.[50] Subsequently most commentators have put the responsibility for the debacle on the Labour government. It has been argued that the security forces could have put down the insurgency without too much difficulty if only they had been freed from political restraints and the government had made clear its determination to support the Federation until victory was complete.[51] What this neglects is the complete absence of any popular support for the Federation either in Aden or in the interior. The Federation was a transparent attempt to make use of the traditional rulers of the hinterland states in order to defeat the forces of Arab nationalism, but unfortunately these men themselves were completely dependent on British support. They were not allies, they were puppets. In these circumstances, the British, using the counterinsurgency methods they had developed in Malaya and Cyprus, might well have been able to contain the insurgency but only for a while. Even this would have involved an open-ended commitment and the certainty that the conflict would intensify over time. The continuing cost and casualties, together with the international political embarrassment of sustaining a puppet regime, was too much. As the Labour Secretary of State for Defence, Denis Healy, subsequently observed: 'The cost of trying to stay in Aden...was out of all proportion to the gain.'[52] This, combined with the strategic reassessment forced by Britain's economic problems, made defeat inevitable. From this point of view, claims that the army could have defeated the rebels, kept the sultans in power and saved the Federation are simplistic. Guy Arnold supplies what is the best summing up of the experience:

> Aden represents a classic example of a colonial possession treated by the imperial power solely as an imperial convenience. Not only were few if any efforts made to improve the conditions of the people, but

by and large they were treated with contempt, and even when nationalism was sweeping through the Arab world in the 1950s the British still behaved as though they only had to manipulate a few backward Arab tribes. They learnt their lesson in one of the most humiliating 'end of empire' defeats which they were to suffer.[53]

6
The Unknown Wars: Oman and Dhofar

The two wars fought on behalf of the Sultans of Oman, Said bin Taimur and his son, Qaboos, were both small affairs that involved only small numbers of British military personnel. Nevertheless, they were both important, first of all for maintaining a British presence and British influence in the Middle East and, secondly, for the part they played in the fortunes of the Special Air Service (SAS). The Jebel Akhdar campaign of 1958–59 arguably saved the SAS from disbandment once the Malayan Emergency came to an end, while the later, more protracted war in Dhofar has been generally regarded as a triumphant success for British counterinsurgency methods comparable with the success in Malaya. Moreover, the success in Dhofar indicated that British counterinsurgency specialists had a post-colonial future as, in effect, mercenaries hired out by the British government to friendly foreign governments to advise and assist in the suppression of unrest and rebellion.

A medieval tyranny

The Sultanate occupies 82 000 square miles between South Yemen and the Gulf and had a population estimated at 750 000. It is made up of two distinct territories: in the northeast Muscat and Oman, a fertile coastal region and a mountainous interior dominated by 'the Green Mountain', Jebel Akhdar. Southwest, across 500 miles of desert is the province of Dhofar, an Omani colony that was even worse governed than the rest of the Sultanate.

Since the 1870s the Sultanate had been a British protectorate, 'a de facto British colony' in Fred Halliday's phrase, ruled by the Sultan but under the effective control of his British advisers.[1] They presided over a backwards poverty- and disease-ridden society where the infant mortality rate was 75 per cent and the literacy rate was 5 per cent, where slavery was still practised quite openly (the Sultan himself owned some 500 black slaves) and where mistreatment, mutilation and torture were routinely used to intimidate the population into quiescence and passivity. As Halliday insists, however, Said bin Taimur's regime was not that of an ignorant feudal reactionary who knew no better, but of a man who had been educated by the British at Mayo College, 'the Eton of India', who regularly spent his summers living in the best hotels in London and who diverted his country's oil revenues into his personal Swiss bank accounts. He was a despot 'very much of the Duvalier and Somoza kind', but relying on Britain rather than the United States for support.[2] It is wrong to regard Said as ruling by 'naked terror', however. According to John Townsend, who went out to Oman as an adviser in early 1969, his was more 'a tyranny of indifference to want and suffering backed up by a very genuine threat of punishment if people complained'.[3] He quite deliberately and calculatedly kept his people impoverished and uneducated as a means of political and social control. As he told David Smiley, the commander-in-chief of his army in the late 1950s, if he provided hospitals and clinics to cut the infant mortality rate this would only cause social unrest by increasing the numbers of the poor and, as for schools and education, 'That is why you lost India.'[4]

Some of the British soldiers in Said's service did have doubts about his regime. In his account of his service with the Muscat Regiment, Ranulph Fiennes, later to achieve fame as an explorer and adventurer, confessed as much:

> The evidence of my own eyes suggested the British were bolstering a corrupt regime where the Sultan and his chosen few lived sumptuously, enjoying the first fruits of oil wealth whilst the mass of Omanis lived out their narrow lives in squalor and illness benefiting not at all from the culling of their country's riches...Content that the age-old conservatism of the Ibadhi system would continue to strangle all strivings for change, to smother all revolutionary mutterings, Sultan Said bin Taimur seemed determined to perpetuate the medieval gloom of Oman. And here I was volunteering my services to the military machine that upheld the old man in denying eight hundred thousand Omanis their rightful inheritance; the benefits of human progress, hospitals and schools.

Although he considered resigning on a number of occasions, Fiennes convinced himself that the threat of Communist subversion necessitated propping up the Sultanate and that the Sultan's son, Qaboos, was a proponent of modernisation who would bring reform if given time.[5] According to Peter Thwaites, the commander of the Muscat Regiment, the Dhofari guerrillas' shift to the left 'came as a relief...as balm to the troubled conscience'. It was much easier fighting *against* Communism than *for* the Sultan.[6]

Another British officer in the Muscat Regiment, P.S. Allfree, described a visit to the Muscat prison, the Jellali: 'I had no wish to repeat my excursion; I felt physically depressed and mentally sick. The ordinary prisoners were permanently shackled with ponderous iron bars between their ankles. The tiny water ration, in that steaming furnace, must have been a tantalising mockery. More important prisoners were kept in perpetual solitary confinement.' He was shown a massive block of wood that held prisoners' legs absolutely rigid unable so much as to flex a muscle; after a while 'the joints would set hard as in the most extreme arthritis' and if continued long enough the torture resulted in permanent injury, leaving its victims crippled. This unpleasant experience did not prevent Allfree serving as the Sultan's chief intelligence officer, actually consigning suspected dissidents to the Jellali.[7]

Other British officers in the Sultan's service were not so sensitive and had no reservations about their employer and his regime; indeed, royal autocracy was a perfectly legitimate form of government with which they felt completely at home. Corran Purdon, another later commander of the Sultan's army, wrote enthusiastically of Said that you 'could almost touch his royal dignity and presence'.

> He cared not one whit for world or public opinion. He thought he was doing what was right for his people and he was determined that there would be no sudden change to modernity and to possible decadent ways...On the few occasions when the Sultan did go out among his people they cheered him to the echo...I think he also could shut his mind to unpleasant things as well as being very hard and tough, and he had little time for the inmates of Jellali.

This is a really quite remarkable apology for a brutal tyrant who regarded his subjects as his enemies. Purdon obviously saw monarchs as a special breed to be respected and admired precisely because they were monarchs without any regard for the nature of their rule. The reason Said did not go among his subjects was, of course, his quite justified fear that if he did he would be assassinated.[8]

Even more extreme was the endorsement that John Akehurst, the commander of the Dhofar Brigade in the closing stages of the Dhofar war, was to give to Said:

I respect the old man's motives and am not so appalled as some by the cruelty and viciousness of his methods. These should not be judged by Western standards; indeed I often found myself trying to explain to foreign journalists that many aspects of life in the country which were anathema to them were accepted as normal by the inhabitants. Crime deserved punishment, no matter how inhuman. Lopping off the hands of thieves or stoning adulterers did not lead to an orgy of bloodletting. It meant no stealing and precious little adultery.[9]

This support for Said's regime even extended to the institution of slavery. James Morris, who visited Oman at the end of 1955, described the country as 'a little backward Paradise on the sea-shore'. The Sultan was a benign despot who even treated his slaves 'kindly'; indeed, they 'had all the advantages of the welfare state, with one exception: they had to work'. It is perhaps something of a surprise to find such a well-known writer expressing a coded preference for slavery as opposed to the welfare state, but Morris was not alone.[10] David Smiley also considered that slaves 'were well-treated – unless they ran away and were caught, in which case they might well be whipped or put in shackles'. He recalls a quaint custom whereby 'if a runaway slave could reach the British Consulate and clasp the flagpole in the courtyard, he became free. My most accomplished bugler, whom we named Sambo, was one of these.'[11] A somewhat less favourable view was presented by a reporter from *The Times* newspaper who visited the royal palace in Salalah after Said had been deposed in July 1970:

Among twelve slaves presented to foreign journalists some had been forced, under pain of beating, not to speak. As a result they had become mutes. Others stood with their heads bowed and eyes fixed on the ground, their necks now paralysed. The slightest glance sideways resulted in a severe beating or imprisonment. Others had incurred physical deformity from similar cruelty.[12]

British support for this despotism, which continued under successive governments, both Conservative and Labour, and without which it could not have survived, remains one of the most unsavoury episodes in post-war British foreign policy.

Jebel Akhdar

Ever since the conclusion of the Treaty of Sib in 1920 the Sultanate had controlled Muscat but exercised only nominal control over the interior of

Oman, where the tribes had instead given their allegiance to the Imam. This situation continued until the 1950s with Sultan Said showing no interest whatsoever in trying to regain control of the area. Only when exploration for oil began to get underway did the British decide that it was necessary to secure the interior, something that became increasingly urgent once it became clear that the Imam Ghalib bin Ali had ambitions to establish an independent state. He was encouraged and supported by Saudi Arabia and the powerful American oil company, Aramco. They hoped to exclude the British from the exploitation of any oil reserves discovered in the area.

In September 1955 the Sultan's forces began what James Morris light-heartedly described as 'a healthy old-fashioned little war', invading the interior and marching on Nizwa, the Imam's capital. They occupied the town on 15 December without having met any resistance. Ghalib surrendered, but his brother Talib attempted to rally opposition and put up a fight, before being forced to flee. He took sanctuary in Saudi Arabia. While the operation had been a great success, Talib began training and equipping a rebel army with the intention of returning to drive the Sultan's forces out of the interior. In mid-June 1957, Talib and his men landed on the Batinah coast, bringing with them weapons and large quantities of American-made mines that were to play a crucial part in their rebellion. Moving in small groups, they made their way up country and raised the standard of revolt. Ghalib rejoined his brother in the struggle. The rebel forces occupied a number of fortified strongholds and carried out a series of harassing attacks and ambushes that culminated in the destruction of the Oman Regiment in July. Ghalib reoccupied Nizwa and drove the Sultan's forces out of the interior. The British responded with a series of air attacks on rebel strongholds carried out by rocket-firing Venom jets, a demonstration of air power intended to intimidate the rebel tribes. They imposed an air blockade on rebel areas which were subjected to regular air patrols in search of targets of opportunity. At the same time, the Sultan's forces were reinforced and counter-attacked in two columns, advancing on and re-taking Nizwa. The Imam and his brother, with some 600 followers, withdrew to the comparative security of the Jebel Akhdar.

The Jebel Akhdar is a sheer limestone massif some 50 miles in length and 20 miles wide with peaks rising to nearly 10 000 feet. On the massif is a fertile plateau at 6000 feet with villages and crops that could feed and house the rebel forces and caves in which they could take shelter from bombing. The only approaches were through narrow ravines that were easily defended by machine gun and mortar. It was, as Michael Dewar points out, 'one of the greatest natural fortresses in the world'.[13]

Early attempts to break on to the plateau were repulsed. Indeed, the rebels proved much more effective raiding down from the Jebel and laying mines that caused the Sultan's forces considerable problems. According to Allfree, the mines were 'an imperial headache...at the height of the plague, we lost two and sometimes three trucks blown up in one day. We had no wealth of lorries and certainly none to spare, so this was developing for us into something like the U-boat blockade was to Britain.'[14] Another British officer, Anthony Shepherd, complained of how the rebels had come down one night to lay mines 'within a few yards of the camp. The Hussars' water-truck went up on one just beyond the gates, and the camp began to look like a scrapyard for crashed vehicles.'[15] Mines continued to be a problem throughout the campaign. David Smiley bemoans the fact that he was not 'able to use the German – or Russian – methods of reprisals against the nearest villages whenever there was an incident'. If he had 'we should have had no trouble'. As it was, even when captured, mine-layers were only imprisoned: 'I felt they should have been shot.' Nevertheless, he admits that there were reprisals. After a British soldier was killed outside the village of Muti, he had the place destroyed: 'We went systematically from house to house, setting each alight with paraffin until nothing remained but smouldering ruins.'[16]

The British responded with a relentless air and artillery bombardment of the plateau and the plateau villages that steadily intensified over the course of 1958. According to Air Chief Marshal Sir David Lees, both Venom jets and four-engined Shackleton heavy bombers 'carried out a heavy programme of attacks on cultivation and water supplies...So effective was this form of harassment that cultivation and movement by daylight in the villages under attack came virtually to a standstill.' In order to sustain the pressure, night-time bombing and shelling were introduced.[17] Despite this bombardment, by the middle of the year, support for the Imam seemed to be increasing among the tribes of the interior and it became clear that the army was going to have to take action to drive him off the plateau.

Enter the SAS

David Smiley was sent to Oman to take command of the reorganised Sultan's Armed Forces (SAF), as his army was now known, charged with the reduction of the Jebel Akhdar. It was clear that the SAF was in no state to attempt the operation and so he submitted a plan that required the commitment of British forces: an infantry battalion plus supporting arms. The Jebel would be stormed by a conventional assault accompanied by a small diversionary airborne landing. This was turned down by the British government as too expensive and politically inconvenient. Instead, Frank Kitson, by now a staff officer at the War Office, put forward a proposal for a pseudo-gang operation which would require only 40-odd British soldiers, who, together with a contingent of 'turned' rebel prisoners, would be able to infiltrate the Jebel. While the use of pseudo-gangs was considered impractical, Kitson's plan did suggest a method that perhaps the SAS, at that time employed in Malaya, could put into effect. It is doubtful whether the SAS would have survived the ending of the Malayan Emergency being regarded as a deep jungle penetration unit. Now they were provided with an opportunity to demonstrate their versatility. There is some justice to Kitson's judgement that the most important effect of the Jebel Akhdar campaign was to be 'that it ensured the continued existence of the Special Air Service.'[18]

Meanwhile the air bombardment was stepped up and at last began to have some effect. Lees gives some idea of the 'weight of this attack':

> [D]uring the week ending 12 September, Shackletons dropped 148 × 1.000lb bombs; 40 rockets were fired by Venoms and a large quantity of 20 millimetre ammunition expended. During the latter part of this month HMS Bulwark arrived in the Gulf of Oman and her full complement of Sea Venoms and Seahawks joined in the air attack. In one week, forty-three offensive sorties against plateau targets were flown from the ships as well as ten reconnaissance sorties. Within the confines of a relatively small target area, air attacks continuing for week after week against simple agricultural tribes was a terrifying experience...There were increasing numbers of reports that villagers were pleading with their Imam Ghalib to go down the mountain and surrender because of the miserable conditions they were being forced to endure resulting from the destruction of cultivation and livestock.[19]

According to David French, between July and December 1958, the RAF bombarded the Jebel with 'more than twice the weight of bombs that the Luftwaffe dropped on Coventry in November 1940'.[20] This was, of course, hardly minimum force.

D Squadron of 22 SAS, about 60 strong, arrived in Oman on 18 November. They were, according to Allfree, 'the coolest and most frightening body of professional killers I have ever seen'.[21] They immediately set about aggressive patrolling to clear the lower slopes of the Jebel and identifying possible routes on to the plateau. December saw the first incursions from both the north and the south sides of the plateau, where they encountered fierce resistance. This decided the SAS commander, Colonel Tony Deane Drummond, that reinforcements were needed for the final assault, and so, on 9 January 1959, A Squadron was flown in. Morale, Peter de la Billière, recalled, was

> soaring. Even by our own high standards we were incredibly fit:... we rejoiced at the challenge of the hard climbing with which the jebel presented us. In every way this was an ideal operation for the SAS. Unlike in Malaya, where we hardly ever set eyes on the enemy, here we saw adoo every day: once we were up in the mountain, pretty well any Arab was fair game.[22]

The plan of attack involved the SAS breaking on to the plateau in strength on its southwest side while diversionary measures directed Talib's attention elsewhere. It worked without a hitch. The rebels left a strong detachment watching the Tanuf track on to the plateau and reinforced the Aquabat al Dhafar position. Only two men were watching the approach the SAS attackers actually used and they were killed in a grenade attack. Once they were on the plateau in strength the rebels either surrendered or melted away. They quite correctly recognised that they had no chance of defeating well-trained, well-armed troops with strong air support in a stand-up fight for control of territory. Their guerrilla tactics that had proven so effective in harassing the Sultan's Armed Forces were of no use once the SAS had got on to the plateau. It would have taken conventional infantry attacks to have driven them off, and these the rebel forces were not organised, trained or equipped to make. The Imam had lost his stronghold (both he and his brother escaped to Saudi Arabia) and all that remained was for the defeated rebels to be mopped up. The SAS had successfully broken the back of the rebellion with the loss of only three men killed and one wounded.[23]

Smiley was subsequently to complain about the way 'the SAS received the entire credit for our success' while the Sultan's Armed Forces 'were totally ignored, although they had suffered the highest casualties'.[24] This was to become a regular feature of operations involving the SAS. For the SAS, however, the Jebel Akhdar operation was 'a turning-point'. In de la Billière's words, 'We had shown that we were a flexible force capable of adapting quickly to new conditions. We had demonstrated that a small number of men could be flown into a trouble spot rapidly and discreetly, and operate in a remote area without publicity – a capability much valued by the Conservative Government of the day.'[25]

As for the Sultan, in the aftermath of the revolt, he was not in a forgiving mood. He reneged on all promises of aid to help reconstruction in the areas devastated by the conflict. The town of Tanuf was destroyed, a revenge carried out by the rockets of the RAF at the request of the Sultan![26] He cancelled the amnesty he had promised the surrendered rebels, and, when David Smiley interceded with him on behalf of the political prisoners in the Jellali who were dying from ill-treatment and neglect, he dismissed his concerns. As far as he was concerned, 'he preferred they die in prison and that they die sooner rather than later so that he would have more room at the fort to imprison others'.[27]

The Dhofar war

Dhofar is the southern-most province of the Omani Sultanate, a distinct tropical region, about the same size as Wales, adjacent to South Yemen and separated from the rest of Oman by 500 miles of desert. The province has relatively heavy monsoon rainfall (30 inches a year) which creates a 40-mile wide strip of green along the coast. Within this strip, the coastal plain is dominated by the mountainous hinterland, the Jebel, which is ideal terrain for guerrilla activity. Beyond this tropical strip of plain and mountain lies the desert stretching to Saudi Arabia. In the 1970s Dhofar had a population estimated at 30 000–50 000. According to Fred Halliday, while Oman was a British colony, Dhofar was an Omani colony, ruled even more oppressively than the rest of the sultanate.[28] The Sultan himself had taken up residence in the Dhofari capital, Salalah, in 1958 and was consequently able to satisfy his great dislike for the Dhofari people at first hand. As he told Corran Purdon on a number of occasions: 'If you are out walking and meet a Dhofari and a snake, tread on the Dhofari.'[29]

The Dhofar Liberation Front (DLF) was founded in 1962 by Dhofaris living and working in exile. Before the end of that year, the first small-scale attacks had begun. The guerrilla campaign only developed slowly, but the Sultan failed to take any effective countermeasures. Said's dislike of the Dhofaris precluded any concessions and his army, such as it was, had not the strength to successfully intimidate the Jebel tribesmen. After members of his bodyguard attempted to assassinate him on 28 April 1966, Said imposed a virtual blockade on the Jebel in retaliation and placed Salalah under effective martial law so that anyone 'trying to enter or leave, was shot'.[30] This repression only succeeded in driving the population into the hands of the DLF. By the end of 1967 the rebels were strong enough to dominate the Jebel but not to pose any serious threat to Jelalah with its RAF base. At the same time, the Sultan's forces could mount operations into the Jebel but were not strong enough to remain there and pacify it. The situation was one of stalemate.

This changed in November 1967 when the British were expelled from South Yemen and a revolutionary government took power committed to liberating the Gulf from the control of the British and their Arab allies. The new People's Republic of South Yemen not only supplied the rebels with military assistance (weapons, training, safe bases) but also brought about a radicalisation of the DLF. The humiliating defeat inflicted on the British in the struggle for South Yemen strengthened the revolutionary nationalists within the DLF.[31] In August 1968 the DLF became the People's Front for the Liberation of the Occupied Arabian Gulf (PFLOAG) under the control of a radical faction led by Muhammad Ahmad al-Ghassani. The rebels went on the offensive.

Ranulph Fiennes, an officer in the Muscat Regiment, writes of how:

> newly trained adoo bands with modern weapons had arrived in many regions of the Jebel. Their tactics were imaginative, their shooting accurate. Weapons such as heavy 81mm mortars and Russian machine-guns were now in adoo hands. It was no longer safe for Army units to travel in the Jebel at less than half-company strength, some sixty men... As the last monsoon mists lingered over the Jebel, four Land Rovers of the Northern Frontier Recce Platoon were ambushed in a gulley between three adoo machine-guns. The leading two vehicles and their crews were shredded. Total slaughter was averted only by a shift in the mist cover.[32]

By the summer of 1970 the guerrillas 'were in control of roughly two-thirds of Dhofar'.[33] The Sultan's forces were penned into a coastal enclave around Salalah which was effectively under siege. A further blow was a rebel attempt in June to open a new front in Oman with attempts to seize the towns of Izki and Nizwa. These failed, but they seriously worried the British. What seems to have finally decided the British that Said had to go, however, was his awarding of an oil exploration contract to a US company![34] On 23 July 1970 the Sultan was forcibly deposed in an almost bloodless coup and the British installed his son, Qaboos bin Said, in his place. The new Sultan, a product of Sandhurst and a former British army officer, who was very much under the influence of a British intelligence officer, Captain Tim Landon, was thought a better figurehead for the reconquest of Dhofar and the safeguarding of British oil interests.[35] His father was flown into exile in Britain, kept in secluded luxury at the Dorchester, where he died in 1972. The newly installed Sultan Qaboos was to himself provide problems for the British. His extravagance and toleration of corruption created serious difficulties. According to one account, in 1971 some 20 per cent of the country's oil revenues were spent on royal palaces alone, with millions more squandered on the Sultan's luxury, jet-set lifestyle.[36]

Shortly before this 'palace revolution', an SAS team headed by Colonel John Watts had visited Dhofar and drawn up plans for a sustained counterinsurgency campaign. Rebel control of the Jebel had to be contested and broken by determined military action and rebel lines of communication with South Yemen had to be severed. Instead of this bringing reprisals in its train against the local people, Watts recommended a 'hearts and minds' effort to be conducted on 'five fronts' and spearheaded by the SAS. The five fronts campaign would involve the establishment of an effective intelligence apparatus, the provision of medical treatment, the provision of veterinary assistance and a programme of agricultural development, the establishment of a psychological warfare capability, and the raising of local militia forces, the firqats, to help fight the PFLOAG.[37] Literally within hours of Said's removal, an SAS team was on its way by air to Dhofar, ready to begin the implementation of Watts's plan.

A model counterinsurgency campaign

In his memoirs, Peter de la Billière, who commanded 22 SAS for part of the Dhofar conflict, describes it as 'the most important and far-reaching ever fought by the SAS. Our involvement...rolled back and finally dissipated the tide of Communism which threatened to overwhelm Southern Arabia.'[38] Tony Jeapes, an SAS squadron commander in Dhofar, in his account of the war describes it as 'a model campaign...one of the most successful campaigns of modern years'. He emphasises, however, that it was a very small-scale war: 'an infantry brigade with a strong air force and some naval support on the one side, and about two thousand guerrillas on the other' and the casualties 'were few, measured in hundreds rather than thousands'. Moreover, it was 'a war in which both sides concentrated upon winning the support of the civilians of the Jebel Dhofar and which was won in the end by civil development, with military action merely a means to that end'. The role of the SAS was, he insists, 'critical' and 'it is fair to say that without the SAS the war would not have been won'. This is not to say that the SAS won the war on their own, far from it, but, rather, that they made the victory of the Sultan's Armed Forces possible.[39] Even leaving aside the SAS tendency towards exaggeration and self-advertisement there is some justice in these claims, but, it has to be insisted, only because of the small scale of the war.

The reconquest of the Jebel had two interrelated components: first, the establishment of a military presence, the ending of PFLOAG domination and the severing of rebel lines of communication with neighbouring Yemen; and, second, the consolidation of military success through civic action, through a 'hearts and minds' programme that was intended to win the local people over to the Sultanate. These two aspects of the campaign against the PFLOAG went hand in hand, each making the success of the other possible. From this point of view it does seem legitimate to characterise it as a model counterinsurgency campaign. One vital development made the waging of such a campaign possible: the increasing revenues that Qaboos was receiving from the exploitation of the Sultanate's oil reserves. This made possible the modernisation of the SAF, the dramatic increase in spending on welfare and development projects and the regular payments to large numbers of surrendered rebels. Whereas in 1971 the government spent $144 million on the military, by 1975 this expenditure had risen to almost $645 million. There was also a dramatic increase in expenditure on development.[40] Without such massive resources, Qaboos would have been forced to rely on repression carried out by a badly equipped army with every likelihood that the war would have been lost. It must also be said that as far as the British government was concerned it was only the need to safeguard the Sultanate's oil reserves that made the prospect of the overthrow of the regime unacceptable, that prevented the British from cutting their losses and abandoning Qaboos as they had the sultans and sheikhs of South Yemen. It was only the oil that made the Dhofar worth fighting for.

Early in 1971 the SAF launched Operation Hornet, an incursion into the central region of the Jebel that achieved some success when the rebels attempted to stand and fight rather than slip away. Other operations were carried out in the western and eastern regions. These attacks certainly shook the rebels, but the SAF was not yet confident or strong enough to establish permanent military bases. With the onset of the monsoon in June, SAF units withdrew back to the coastal plain and the PFLOAG quickly reasserted its control, eliminating anyone who had collaborated with their enemy. The monsoon brought rain, mist and cloud that closed down air support and left the SAF vulnerable to attack.

Clearly, if the Jebel was to be pacified, some way had to be found to overcome this problem. Only once this was accomplished could the Civil Action Teams that were to win the allegiance of the local population get to work.

Crucial in this respect were the activities of the SAS, usually no more than a hundred strong, operating as a British Army Training Team (BATT). They were responsible for raising the firqats, a local militia cum pseudo-gang that enlisted surrendered or defecting rebels. As early as February 1970, the increasing radicalisation of the revolutionary movement had seen some defections with one group led by Salim Mubarak deciding to throw in its lot with the new Sultan rather than remain with the PFLOAG. A crucial factor here was the PFLOAG's hostility to Islam. This particular defection not only provided vital intelligence that had hitherto been in short supply but also provided the core of the first firqat, the Firqat Salahadin, that went into action for the first time in February 1971. The firqats were to play an important role in the defeat of the PFLOAG. They proved a continual source of intelligence and local knowledge, fought the rebels using their own methods against them and, moreover, offered any rebels whose commitment might be weakening a permanent reminder that surrender could be both safe and profitable.

'Hearts and minds' campaigns are not soft-hearted exercises in sentimentality carried out by social workers in uniform. Alongside the reforms and concessions, the material advantages, that are intended to win over the 'hearts' of the local population, there is the use of force to focus their 'minds'. The population have to be convinced of the power of the government and of the ability of the security forces to inflict punishment if support and assistance is extended to the rebels. Only in this way would their 'minds' be won over. In Dhofar, this use of force involved a war waged against the civilian population in those areas of the country under PFLOAG control, a war carried out primarily from the air. Fred Halliday, who paid a number of clandestine visits to the liberated areas, later wrote of

> the suffering inflicted on the population. In the border area I went through the civilian population were forced to live in the deeper caves...Everybody one met had lost animals in the recent fighting; and many had lost members of their family. A growing number of refugees from the west and the central region had moved out of the combat zones and on to the Yemeni side of the border. In addition the economic blockade had led to intense malnutrition, especially

in the east and the centre as a result of the cutting off of imports from the coast and the systematic SOAF (Sultan of Oman's Air Force) burning of crops at harvest-time. Among the population as a whole, the consequences of malnutrition, tuberculosis and anaemia were increasing.

He goes on:

> By bombing and shelling the liberated areas the British forced the population to move out and to flee to safer areas. The British poisoned and blew up the wells, burnt villages, set crops and food stores on fire, shot herds and cut off food supplies. This policy, already consistently applied in the Radfan, was one of all-out attack on the population who supported the revolution.[41]

Another point worth making is that while the Jebel has been described as 'ideal country for insurgents', this was not altogether true.[42] As Abdel Razzaq Takriti has pointed out, while 'the fastness of the highlands, the spread of caves, the thickness of wild fig and tamarind forests, and the cloak of the monsoon mist, all afforded perfect cover for the revolutionaries', there was also a downside. The area 'was not sufficiently productive to support a long-term war effort. Water was available but not abundant. Livestock herds were profuse but vulnerable to attack.' More generally, 'the low density of the population and the smallness of settlements rendered the revolutionaries vulnerable'. They comprised 'a substantial percentage of a tiny population', so that there was really no mass of people for them to hide among.[43]

The battle of Mirbat

In October 1971 a determined effort, Operation Jaguar, was made to establish permanent bases on the Jebel. A strong force composed of two SAF companies, two SAS squadrons, five firqats and supporting arms (nearly 800 men) and commanded by Colonel John Watts moved on to the eastern Jebel. After some skirmishing they occupied the village of Jibjat and established a stronghold known as 'White City' at Medinat Al Haq. The consolidation of this military success by the activation of civil action programmes was slow, much to the disgust of John Watts. Nevertheless, this was a first significant success.[44] Other operations were carried out to disrupt rebel supply lines. Much further to the west on the Yemeni border, Operation Simba saw the SAF establish a stronghold at Sarfait in April 1972. The garrison was not strong enough to dominate the surrounding area and remained under virtual siege. Sarfait was subjected to continuous shelling by both the rebels and the Yemeni artillery and had to be resupplied by air. It had been hoped that the stronghold would provide a base from which rebel supply lines across the border could be threatened, but this proved to be too ambitious an objective at this time. Instead, all that was achieved was to tie down troops holding a fixed position which could not be exploited, when they could have been better employed elsewhere. Nevertheless, despite setbacks and difficulties, as the monsoon season approached in 1972 the military situation had been successfully transformed with the SAF taking the offensive.

The PFLOAG leadership responded with a daring counter-attack. In mid-July a force of heavily armed guerrillas, perhaps 300 strong, equipped with two 75mm recoilless rifles, a Carl Gustav rocket launcher and a number of mortars, attempted to overrun the seaside town of Mirbat, some 40 miles from Salalah. Taking advantage of monsoon cloud cover that would prevent air support, they hoped to capture the town before reinforcements could arrive. They did not intend to try and hold it, but were going to execute the local collaborators, before retreating back to the safety of the Jebel. This would be a humiliating setback for the Sultan's regime, effectively deterring any Dhofaris from rallying to his cause and possibly even forcing the SAF to withdraw from the Jebel in order to defend against any further rebel attacks.

Mirbat's defences consisted of two mud-walled forts, one held by a force of 25 gendarmes and the other by 30 askars, the local governor's personal bodyguard, and a fortified BATT-house occupied by Captain Mike Kealy and eight SAS soldiers. There was also a 60-strong firqat whose members lived with their families in the town itself. The heaviest weapon available to the defenders was a 25-pound howitzer outside the gendarme fort. A barbed wire fence surrounded both the town and the two forts. Earlier, rebel movements had been reported in the nearby Jebel that came down near to the coast and 30 firqa had been sent to investigate. The likelihood is that the guerrillas believed the SAS would have gone with them.

In the early hours of 19 July the guerrillas launched an assault on the gendarme fort, advancing under a barrage of artillery and mortar fire from off the Jebel. The attacking force was broken up by machine-gun fire from the BATT-house and their attempts to knock out the howitzer and storm the fort failed. Even after this initial assault was thwarted, the rebels still seemed to have victory in their grasp given their superior numbers and firepower. The weather then let them down: the cloud cleared enough for Strikemaster jets to provide air support, pounding them with cannon and rocket fire, and for helicopters to fly in SAS reinforcements. The guerrillas were caught out in the open, badly hurt and forced to retreat. They were under continual air attack and pursued by the SAS. They had suffered a serious defeat in a battle that had lasted only five hours.[45] Two SAS troopers and two gendarmes had been killed in the fighting, but rebel losses were considerably heavier. Thirty-eight bodies were recovered, but most estimates place their fatalities at double that number at least, with some going as high as 200 dead! Another 12 rebels were captured. The rebel dead were flown back to Salalah and 'put on public display in the main square for several days...so the local people could see for themselves that the law was being carried out and that the Sultan and his forces were winning the war'.[46]

According to most accounts, the battle of Mirbat was the turning point in the Dhofar war. John Watts described it as 'the beginning of the end' for the PFLOAG; Tony Jeapes considered it 'a milestone'; for Peter de la Billière the battle was 'a shattering reverse' for the rebels and 'the turning point'.[47] In a recent popular history of the SAS, Anthony Kemp argues that 'the successful defence of Mirbat broke the back of the adoo resistance...the rebels had been decisively beaten'. He writes of the war being 'destined to linger on'.[48] These claims are exaggerated. Undoubtedly the PFLOAG had suffered a serious setback, but one from which they certainly could have recovered if they had not already lost the strategic initiative in the war. Decisive in this respect was the establishment of permanent SAF strongholds on the Jebel and the beginning of its effective pacification. There was still to be considerable fighting, in which the SAS was to play only a minor role, before the rebels were finally defeated. Moreover, a good case can be made that the PFLOAG suffered an even more serious, if much less well-known, reverse in December 1972 when the Sultan's intelligence service broke up a network of underground revolutionary cells and recovered ten tons of weapons and munitions in Oman. Both the SAF and the Oman Intelligence Service (OIS) had been penetrated; indeed, OIS director Malcolm Dennison's driver was among the conspirators. There were 77 arrests, followed by the execution of ten of those involved at the Sultan's personal insistence, and long prison sentences for the rest, including 32 life sentences. This was a more serious blow even than the defeat at Mirbat.[49]

Why then has the battle of Mirbat, a brief five-hour engagement involving at most 500 men, come to be seen as so important, been celebrated as the moment of decision? The answer is quite simple: the battle has a useful ideological function, in general terms as a celebration of the British soldier hero and in more particular terms as part of the myth of the SAS. It has become another Rorke's Drift. The best of British manhood demonstrated their courage and prowess against overwhelming odds in an exotic setting. In Michael Dewar's words, it 'is a wonderful tale of derring-do'.[50] The romance of Empire is combined with the excitement of a heroic stand against the menace of Communism. The British are triumphantly shown to be still the same people who had in earlier years ruled much of the globe. As well as this validation of British masculinity, focus on the battle of Mirbat also serves to invert the reality of the war whereby Goliath is able successfully to pass himself off as David. Instead of hard-pressed guerrillas being remorselessly ground down by superior forces with complete air superiority, the dominant image of the war is one of the outnumbered SAS holding off waves of Arab fanatics. The wonder is that the battle has not yet been made into a feature film.[51]

Pacification and defeat

Even after the victory at Mirbat, the SAF remained too weak to press home its advantage. The war continued, but more troops were required for offensive operations to secure the Jebel. With the British unwilling to increase their commitment (at its height this amounted to around a thousand military personnel including officers serving with the SAF, the SAS and a RAF contingent), the Sultan turned elsewhere. Abu Dhabi sent troops to garrison northern Oman, releasing Omani forces for service in Dhofar. Jordan provided the Sultan with Hunter jets and 800 troops. Both India and Pakistan seconded officers to serve with the SAF and provided military equipment. And towards the end of 1973, the Sultan received welcome reinforcements in the form of a 1500 strong Iranian battle group despatched by the Shah. This well-equipped American-trained force was used to open the Midway Road from Salalah through the Jebel to Thumrait in the north. The rebels made a determined effort to prevent this and successfully ambushed Iranian troops on a number of occasions, inflicting heavy losses, but the road was kept open. Indeed, it was converted into a modern made-up motorway. This was a major success, opening up the central Jebel and greatly strengthening the government's position. Most British accounts of the war, it should be noted, seriously downplay, indeed sometime denigrate, the Iranian contribution to the Sultan's eventual victory. There can be little doubt that if it had been British troops who had opened the road, it would be regarded as a crucial episode in the winning of the war. Iranian troop strength was eventually increased to 3000 men. By 1974, over a third of the troops fighting for the Sultan in Dhofar were from Jordan and Iran. Oman and its allies had 'amassed overwhelming forces in Dhofar'.[52] The regime also received considerable financial assistance, particularly from Saudi Arabia.

While operations continued on the Jebel in the central and eastern regions of Dhofar, a major effort was made to cut rebel supply lines. To this end, in March 1974 British and Jordanian engineers were brought in to construct a 35-mile long barrier, the Hornbeam Line, inland from the coast near Mugsayl. This was intended to cut the central and eastern regions off from the western region, making it much more difficult for the rebels to send in weapons, supplies and reinforcements. The barrier consisted of a barbed wire fence reinforced with mines and ground sensors, and with the high ground dominated by SAF outposts. Construction was completed by the summer of 1974. This never completely stopped supplies getting through, but considerably reduced the quantities: instead of camel trains making the journey, now only small groups of guerrillas on foot and with what they could carry got through. Later, the Hornbeam Line was backed up by another barrier, the Hammer Line, built as a long-stop further to the east. Once these were in place, the successful pacification of the central and eastern regions became only a matter of time.

A key part in the pacification of the Jebel was played by the Civil Aid Teams (CATs) that followed after the SAF. Very much the brainchild of the SAS, these were meant to provide the local population with tangible, material benefits that would win them over to the Sultan's cause. Once an area was considered secure, a CAT would move in and establish a centre. A well would be dug, a school and a clinic would be established, a market would be set up and a mosque would be built. Various longer-term projects would be initiated, such as road-building schemes and programmes for the improvement of livestock. According to Tony Jeapes, 'Civil Aid was...one of the success stories' of the war. By June 1975, 35 wells had been drilled and 155 miles of road opened up on the Jebel.[53] A measure of their success was the growing number of defectors from the rebel army and the growth of the firqat force that by the end of the war had increased to around 3000 men. The 'hearts and minds' dimension to the campaign secured the rear, ensuring that the guerrillas never returned. What made this possible, of course, was the oil wealth to which the Sultan now had access and financial assistance from the Saudis and others.

Religion also played a vital role in all this, with the government proclaiming its devotion to Islam and condemning the rebels as atheists and the enemies of God. 'Islam is Our Way, Freedom is Our Aim' became the campaign's slogan. It was 'used to conclude Radio Dhofar's daily broadcasts and adorn propaganda leaflets'. The British even persuaded the senior Qadi of Dhofar to declare the counterinsurgency campaign 'a holy war'.[54] This Islamist propaganda campaign even saw the insurgency condemned as a Zionist plot as laid out in The Protocols of Zion. The insurgents' support for women's liberation and recruitment of women as guerrilla fighters (the numbers are variously estimated as between 5 and 30 per cent of rebel strength) was also used against them.[55] The successful dressing up of the counterinsurgency campaign in Islamic garb is all the more impressive given that Qaboos was generally believed to be gay, consorting with long-haired youths 'of exquisite countenance' and given to extravagant expenditure on his own pleasures.[56]

At the end of 1974 the new British commander of the Dhofar Brigade, John Akehurst, was in a position to turn his attention towards the western region. By now rebel strength had been reduced to around 800 guerrilla fighters with perhaps another thousand men in their home guard. They were still to put up a determined resistance. At last, in December Akehurst launched a two-pronged attack towards Rakhuyt, the last settlement of any importance still in rebel hands, and towards Sherishitti with its heavily defended complex of caves. Rakhuyt fell to the Iranians but resistance was unexpectedly fierce and Sherishitti could not be taken. Enough had been achieved, however, for the Iranians with Jordanian help to begin the construction of another barrier, the Demavand Line. This would cut off the contested border area from the rest of the western region so that supplies and reinforcements could no longer get through. While the western region was being cleared, preparations were made for a final offensive to secure the border. The final defeat of what had by now become the Popular Front for the Liberation of Oman (PFLO) was only a matter of time.

The last offensive was launched in October 1975. By now the guerrillas had been reinforced by 300 to 400 regular troops from the People's Republic of South Yemen. Akehurst ordered air strikes against guerrilla bases and artillery positions across the border, much to the consternation of the British government. At the same time, the strengthened garrison on the border at Sarfait at last broke out to join up with forces advancing from Rakhuyt. After heavy fighting the Sherishitti caves were cleared and the Yemeni forces, together with the remnants of the rebel forces, retreated across the border. Defeat was complete. In November,

94 guerrillas surrendered, and the following month another 36, among them a number of senior guerrilla leaders. On 4 December Akehurst informed Qaboos that victory was his.[57]

Artillery exchanges and air strikes across the border continued into the new year until an agreement was finally reached with the People's Republic in March 1976. Also there were many isolated groups of guerrillas still at large and scattered throughout Dhofar. How dangerous they could still be was demonstrated on Christmas Day 1975 when, only a couple of weeks after he had announced victory, Akehurst was visiting troops in the eastern region. He was flying by helicopter to Tawa Atair when below him he saw a lone guerrilla who 'began to fire his AK47 at us'. Much to Akehurst's discomfort the helicopter was hit seven times and forced to crash land, although without any casualties. Six months later when the man finally came in to surrender, he was, Akehurst somewhat ruefully remarks, 'rightly very proud of himself'.[58] All that remained, however, were mopping-up operations and the activities of the Civil Aid Teams, consolidating the military victory into a political one. The SAS were finally pulled out in September 1976.[59]

One last point worth making concerns the outside assistance that the PFLO received. The war is often presented as an episode in the Cold War, and as we have seen, this was a more comfortable proposition than fighting in defence of a corrupt feudal autocracy in order to get one's hands on its oil. According to Ian Gardiner, for example, on one side in the conflict were troops from Oman, Britain, India, Pakistan, Iran and Jordan and on the other were 'men and women from Yemen, Russia, China, Cuba and Libya'. Interestingly, other than this observation on page 1 of his memoir, the men and women from these countries do not put in another appearance.[60] The reason for this is quite simple: the PFLO was a home-grown revolutionary movement that was certainly given every assistance possible by their fellow revolutionaries in Yemen, but that only received limited, some would say half-hearted, help from Russia and China. Chinese assistance, for example, ended when the Chinese government reached a rapprochement with Iran in 1973.[61] The Cold War dimension to the war was largely the creation of British propaganda. Yemeni support was certainly vital, however. The British responded to this Yemeni support for the PFLO by providing covert assistance and encouragement for a nomadic insurgency inside the People's Republic. The Mahra nomads were provided with modern weapons and vehicles. On one occasion, with the assistance of former SAS mercenaries, they destroyed a fort 80 miles inside Yemen.[62]

The British had, according to one counterinsurgency expert, produced a textbook counterinsurgency campaign to add to their renowned victory in Malaya.[63] How valid is this assessment? In reality, the Dhofar war was a very small-scale conflict in which the Sultan was eventually able to bring overwhelmingly superior force to bear on the PFLO insurgents. This military superiority, together with the ability, courtesy of his oil revenues, to finance development in the Jebel and to buy loyalty, gave him a decisive advantage. The guerrillas' courage, self-sacrifice, skill and endurance were in the end not enough to overcome this. While Dhofar was certainly a victory, it was a victory achieved in particularly favourable circumstances and to which other countries contributed.

7
The Long War: Northern Ireland

The conflict in Northern Ireland has been the most protracted of British counterinsurgency campaigns, with the retreat from Empire ending up in what is still part of the United Kingdom. The consequences have been devastating. Nearly 2 per cent of the province's population have been killed or injured since fighting began. If the ratio of fatalities to population were to be reproduced for the United Kingdom as a whole there would by now have been some 111 000 people killed, considerably more than were killed by German bombing during the Second World War, and 1.4 million injured. More people have died as a result of political violence in Northern Ireland since 1969 than in the rest of the European Community put together over the same period.[1] Moreover, the conflict on a number of occasions extended into England. Only sheer luck saved Prime Minister Margaret Thatcher and her Cabinet from death in the bombing of the Grand Hotel in Brighton on 12 October 1984.

What we shall examine here is the conduct in this conflict of the security forces and, in particular, the transformation in strategy from a counterinsurgency model, that served only to exacerbate the situation, to an internal security model that successfully contained it. A process of attrition subsequently saw Sinn Fein and the Provisional IRA come to terms with the Unionists. Both sides were so worn down by the years of conflict as to accept terms that would once have been completely unthinkable. For the British, the inability to comprehensively defeat the IRA was substituted by diplomatic success that was trumpeted as if it were a victory.

The Troubles begin

Northern Ireland was established in conflict. The creation of the new devolved state involved the denial of national rights to a third of its population and was accompanied by violence and disorder that approached the level of civil war. Over 550 people, mainly Catholics, were killed between July 1920 and July 1922. In Belfast alone, 23 000 people, a quarter of the city's Catholic population, were driven from their homes by Protestant vigilantes carrying out a series of bloody pogroms. In September 1921 the Unionist government had begun raising a Protestant militia, the Special Constabulary, that was to be in the forefront of repressing the minority. This was followed in March 1922 by the passing of the Special Powers Act that endowed the new state with draconian emergency powers. And, in May 1922, internment was introduced, leading to the imprisonment without trial of some 500 Catholics (and a handful of Protestants). They were not released until the end of 1924. To all intents and purposes, the Catholic minority was beaten into submission.[2]

This Protestant victory was consolidated by the establishment of the new Northern Ireland state as a sectarian Orange state that relied on discrimination, gerrymandering and intimidation for its survival. From the very beginning, the Stormont regime relied on emergency measures and did not function as a conventional bourgeois democracy on Westminster lines, although it adopted the trappings. Given the manner of its birth and the way in which, by its very nature, it rested on the continued suppression of a third of its population, the eventual breakdown of the Northern Ireland state seems inevitable. All that was in doubt was the timing.

What factors were to lead to the Catholic working-class revolt of 1969 and the subsequent rise of the Provisional IRA? Why was it that a protracted guerrilla war began at this time and not earlier as a result of the IRA campaigns of 1938–44 and 1956–62? These campaigns had been defeated by lack of support among the Catholic minority that, no matter how sympathetic it might have been to the republican cause, nevertheless had no confidence in the IRA's ability to bring about change. They confronted a Unionist government supported by a united Protestant community, with the full backing of the British government and the co-operation of the Irish government.[3] By the end of the 1960s the situation had changed.

A number of factors combined to create the circumstances for a successful challenge to the Stormont regime. The election of Harold Wilson's Labour government at Westminster in 1964 installed an administration that favoured reform in Northern Ireland and was unsympathetic to the use of repression against Catholics seeking the redress of legitimate grievances. The Unionists themselves were divided between those who favoured reform, admittedly a largely cosmetic exercise as far as they were concerned, and the growing band of hardliners who opposed any concessions to the Catholics. While Prime Minister Terence O'Neill offered little of tangible benefit to the Catholic minority, he did propose moving away from the standpoint of unashamed Protestant Ascendancy. Even this was to arouse considerable hostility both within the Unionist Party, even in his own Cabinet, and also among the Protestant population at large where the Reverend Ian Paisley was already warning of betrayal.[4] These two factors, a sympathetic Labour government and a divided Unionist Party, interacted to create a situation where change seemed possible, where it seemed that Catholic demands for the reform of the Orange state might actually have some prospect of success. Instead of confronting a united intransigent Protestant majority backed up by the British government, O'Neill's government looked as if it could be pressed into introducing reform. At the same time as Unionist domination over Northern Ireland seemed to be weakening, there had emerged within the Catholic community an increasingly confident middle class that was prepared to campaign for reform, to take advantage of the situation and challenge O'Neill to satisfy the expectations he had raised. Inspired by the example of the civil rights movement in the United States and by the student radicalism that had spread from America to Europe, the Catholic middle class was unwittingly to precipitate a Catholic working-class revolt, a revolt that was to change everything.

The key event was the civil rights march that was held in Derry on 5 October 1968. The moving force behind this mobilisation was the left-wing Derry Housing Action Committee, but it was supported by the more moderate Civil Rights Association. The march was banned from the city centre by the Minister for Home Affairs, William Craig, a Unionist hardliner, but went ahead anyway. In the event attendance was disappointing (only about 2000 demonstrators), but among them was Gerry Fitt, Republican Labour MP at Westminster and three Labour MPs. In full view of the television cameras the Royal Ulster Constabulary (RUC) attacked the marchers. One of the organisers, Eamonn McCann, later described the scene:

> [T]wo police cordons moved simultaneously on the crowd. Men, women and children were clubbed to the ground. People were fleeing down the street from the front cordon and up the street from the rear cordon, crashing into one another, stumbling over one another, huddling in doorways, some screaming...Most people ran the gauntlet of batons and reached Craigavon Bridge, at the head of

Duke Street. A water cannon – the first we had ever seen – appeared and hosed them across the bridge. The rest of the crowd went back down Duke Street, crouched and heads covered for protection from the police, ran through side streets and made a roundabout way back home. About a hundred had to go to hospital for treatment.[5]

Among those clubbed to the ground was Gerry Fitt. The police pursued the marchers into the Catholic Bogside where they were opposed by working-class youths who had taken no part in the march, but who came on to the streets to defend their community against the police incursion. Barricades were erected and petrol bombs were thrown.

This episode transformed the situation. Catholic demonstrators demanding elementary civil rights had been brutally attacked by the RUC, but to general international condemnation and much to the embarrassment of the Labour government in London. If the challenge was maintained and the Unionists responded with further repression this would only serve to undermine their position even more and make Westminster's intervention more certain. This was certainly the belief of the more radical elements within the civil rights movement, drawing on the American experience. As far as an increasing number of Protestants were concerned, however, the events of 5 October were part of a conspiracy to overthrow Protestant rule and only strengthened the determination of the hardliners to stand fast and oppose any concessions. The problem for O'Neill was that the more the Catholics mobilised to demand reform, the more Protestant hostility to reform built up. This gave him very little room to manoeuvre. His predicament was made worse by the Labour government's support for reform and opposition to the use of repressive measures to suppress the civil rights movement. In the circumstances further confrontation was inevitable.[6]

While the Civil Rights Association called for restraint and a breathing space, the radical student group the People's Democracy decided to carry out a civil rights march across country from Belfast to Derry. Starting out on 1 January 1969 the marchers were subject to continual loyalist harassment that culminated on 4 January in the ambush at Burntollet Bridge near Derry. Here several hundred loyalists armed with clubs studded with nails, iron bars, bottles and chains attacked the marchers while their RUC escort either stood passively by or even joined in. The attackers included a large number of off-duty members of the Special Constabulary, the 'B' Specials. Quite by luck no one was killed.

When the battered remnants of the march reached Derry, fighting broke out between the RUC and Catholic youths once again. This had died down when, in the early hours of 5 January, a strong force of RUC invaded the Bogside, breaking windows and beating anyone unfortunate enough to get in their way. Later that day barricades were put up at the main entrances to the Bogside and groups of hastily raised vigilantes patrolled the streets to meet any fresh RUC incursion. On a gable-end in St Columb's Street the words YOU ARE NOW ENTERING FREE DERRY were painted up. The barricades remained in place for five days.[7]

The Catholic revolt

What was important about the Burntollet ambush was that it demonstrated beyond any doubt that the RUC was a sectarian force that would not enforce the law impartially. Even when supposedly protecting civil rights marchers they had deliberately led them into an ambush and had collaborated and fraternised with their attackers. The police riot in the Bogside in the early hours of 5 January only provided further confirmation that the Catholic community would have to protect itself.

The situation continued to polarise in the months following Burntollet. The civil rights movement kept the pressure up and there were further clashes between the Catholics and the RUC. Meanwhile, the Unionist government began to disintegrate as the hardliners made clear their opposition to any reform. O'Neill called a general election on 24 February which saw the return of 27 Unionist MPs supporting the government (although how reliable they were was most doubtful) and ten Unionist MPs opposing his policies. Despite this apparent victory, two months later, on 28 April, O'Neill resigned. He was brought down by a series of bomb attacks on water and electricity installations that took place between 30 March and 25 April. In his own words, he was 'quite literally blown...out of office'.[8] At the time these explosions were blamed on the Irish Republican Army (IRA) and effectively destroyed O'Neill's credibility by apparently proving the reality of the Republican conspiracy behind the civil rights movement. In fact, they were the work of Protestant paramilitaries who hoped to bring O'Neill down. They were triumphantly successful. O'Neill was replaced as Prime Minister by James Chichester-Clark.

What precipitated the final plunge over the precipice into revolt was the decision by Chichester-Clark's government to allow the traditional Orange parades to go ahead in July and August. While the civil rights movement decided to scale down its activities in an attempt to calm a situation that was getting out of hand, the Orange celebrations of Protestant supremacy took place regardless. Chichester-Clark adopted a tough stance: not only would the marches go ahead, but any opposition to them would be decisively put down. The Catholics were to be put in their place. On 12 July there was serious rioting in Belfast, Derry and elsewhere when Catholic youths stoned the parades and fought with the RUC. In Dungiven, a 67-year-old man, Francis McClosky was killed in an RUC baton charge. On 2 August another Orange parade in Belfast provoked rioting in which another Catholic, Patrick Corry, was killed by the RUC. These disturbances were successfully contained and the RUC felt that it was in control. On 12 August when the annual Apprentice Boys' parade in Derry was attacked by Catholic youths, the RUC responded with a full-scale invasion of the Bogside. The Bogsiders were to be taught a lesson. Once again barricades went up and the police retreated under a barrage of stones and petrol bombs. Eamonn McCann describes the scene:

> The battle lasted about forty-eight hours. Barricades went up all around the area, open-air petrol-bomb factories were established, dumpers hijacked from a building site were used to carry stones to the front. Teenagers went on to the roof of the block of High Flats which dominates Rossville Street, the main entrance to the Bogside, and began lobbing petrol bombs at the police below. This was a brilliant tactical move... As long as the lads stayed up there and as long as we managed to keep them supplied with petrol bombs there was no way – short of shooting them off the roof – that the police could get past the High Flats. Every time they tried it rained petrol bombs.[9]

It was the Unionist government's decision to continue the attack on the Bogside that led to the conflict spreading elsewhere. The Civil Rights Association and People's Democracy threatened to hold protest meetings throughout the province if the RUC were not withdrawn from the Bogside. When this was refused, the meetings went ahead and resulted in widespread rioting, most seriously in Dungannon and Belfast. Chichester-Clark mobilised the 'B' Specials. By now, however, the government had lost control and was forced to turn to the Labour government in London for support. The Labour Home Secretary, James Callaghan, ordered the deployment of British troops in Derry: the RUC had failed to take the Bogside.

While the fighting came to an end in Derry, elsewhere it still continued with even greater ferocity. In Belfast there were 'B' Specials and RUC armoured cars on the streets, leading Protestant mobs in the attack on the Catholic community. The police machine-gunned the Divis Flats, killing a nine-year-old boy, Patrick Rooney. Hundreds of Catholic families were burned out of their homes as barricades went up to protect the Falls Road and Ardoyne. British troops began to deploy in Belfast on 15 August.

The events of July and August 1969, a direct result of the decision to allow the Orange parades to go ahead, left ten people dead and nearly 900 injured. Nearly 200 houses had been destroyed and over 400 had been damaged; 16 factories had been burned out. In Belfast alone 1820 families had been forced from their homes, over 1500 of them Catholics. This was the start of 'the Long War'.

What part had the IRA played in these events? Had they been successfully manipulating the civil rights movement all along, with the intention of bringing about just such a confrontation as occurred in August 1969? Certainly this was what many Unionists and some British Conservatives believed. In fact, the IRA had, in the course of the 1960s, taken the decision to abandon the armed struggle in favour of political action. After the failure of the 1956–62 campaign, a re-evaluation of republican strategy was carried out and, under the influence of Roy Johnston and others, a socialist strategy was adopted. This was very much a reformist strategy that involved attempting to unite Protestant and Catholic workers on social and economic issues as the first stage on the road to a united socialist Ireland. While this became the official policy of the Cathal Goulding leadership in Dublin there remained many more traditionalist republicans who rejected the shift to the left and were still convinced that the armed struggle was the only way forward. For the time being these conservatives were comparatively isolated and the republican movement threw its weight behind the civil rights campaign. When the revolt of August 1969 broke out and the Catholic minority found itself under attack from the RUC, the 'B' Specials and Protestant mobs, the IRA was taken completely by surprise. The organisation was unarmed and unprepared at a time when the Catholic community looked to them for protection. Despite the intervention of a handful of poorly armed IRA men in Belfast, for many working-class Catholics the initials IRA now derisively stood for I RAN AWAY. Even after these events, the Dublin leadership of the movement refused to change direction; indeed, they were appalled by developments in the North and certainly did not regard them as an opportunity to be exploited. The conservative opposition to the Goulding leadership was arguably more in touch with the fears and worries of the Catholic minority. On 28 December 1969, with the covert support of Fianna Fáil and the Dublin government, Sean MacStiofain, Ruairi O'Bradaigh, Daithi O'Connaill and others established a right-wing traditionalist breakaway group that reasserted militarism and the armed struggle, the Provisional IRA.[10]

The road to war

The deployment of British troops in Derry on 14 August and in Belfast the following day provided Northern Ireland with a breathing space, but one that was to be only short-lived. As far as the Labour government in London was concerned, the Stormont regime had not only failed to remedy Catholic grievances in time to prevent an explosion, but had also failed to contain the explosion when it occurred. There had seemed a real danger of Northern Ireland collapsing into civil war with Protestant vigilantes initiating an old-fashioned pogrom against the Catholic minority in an attempt to cow and intimidate them into submission. The troops were sent in not to protect the Catholic population, although this is what they found themselves doing, but to prevent the situation getting out of hand altogether. This involved them interposing themselves between the Protestant mobs and their Catholic victims and on a number of occasions brought them into conflict with the Protestants, but it also involved the longer-term objective of eventually returning the Catholic 'no-go' areas to Stormont rule. There was absolutely no ambiguity about this.

As far as Harold Wilson, James Callaghan and those other Labour ministers involved with developments in Northern Ireland were concerned, what was needed was democratic reform and impartial policing. It was hoped that this would conciliate the Catholics without alienating the Protestants. It failed to recognise the sectarian nature of the Northern Ireland state, that it rested on an artificially created Protestant majority that rejected concessions to the Catholic minority. Moreover, the events of August 1969 had convinced many Catholics that the democratic reforms the civil rights movement had been demanding were no longer sufficient, that the Northern Ireland state was fundamentally flawed and would have to be overthrown or abolished. They were no longer prepared to be ruled by even a reformed Stormont. The consequence of this for the Labour government was that its attempts at reform invariably proved too little too late for the Catholics and too much too soon for the Protestants. This was to be the problem confronting successive British governments. Arguably, the Labour government missed an opportunity in not suspending Stormont and introducing direct rule in August 1969, something that would have satisfied the Catholics and might have prevented the Provisional IRA getting off the ground. Such a step would certainly have involved serious conflict with the Protestants, but whether this would have been worse than what was to come seems unlikely. Instead, Labour remained committed to reforming Stormont and eventually returning the Catholic 'no-go' areas to Stormont rule. Further conflict was inevitable.

Looking back on events of August 1969, James Callaghan recalled his amazement at the weakness of the RUC. Their failure to contain disorder exposed a basic weakness:

> [T]here were simply not enough of them to handle hooliganism and disorder on such a scale. Their total strength throughout Ulster and Belfast was no more than 3000 to control a province of over 5000 square miles and to protect a million and a half people. Making allowances for the fact that they needed rest periods and were working in three shifts round the clock, there were usually less than 1000 police available for duty during any normal shift, and unlike the English police they could not be reinforced by neighbouring Forces. On the Sunday and Monday evenings in Belfast, only a few hundred policemen were on duty. By contrast a large demonstration on a Sunday afternoon in London may be covered by 3000 to 4000 policemen, and at the Vietnam demonstration in Grosvenor Square in October 1968 there were over 9000 policemen on duty along the route. There was a pathetic inadequacy about the number of RUC men available.[11]

Instead of a repressive police state holding down an oppressed Catholic minority, Callaghan saw a seriously under-policed society where the government could not guarantee the maintenance of public order. His comments on the weakness of the RUC as a factor in August 1969 are quite instructive but also seriously misleading. The fact is that Unionist governments in Northern Ireland had never relied on conventional methods of policing but on the use of emergency measures. Catholic unrest was not contained by the RUC acting alone but by the mobilisation of the Protestant militia, the 'B' Specials, and by the use of the Special Powers legislation. The reason the civil rights movement and the Catholic working-class resistance it encouraged were not suppressed in this way was quite simply that the Labour government in London would not countenance such methods being used against people demanding democratic reform. Unable to use emergency methods to suppress the Catholic revolt, the Unionist government could not contain the situation which went out of control and necessitated British involvement.

It was Callaghan's belief that British intervention had brought the situation back under control and he hoped to be able to establish a 'new contract...between the two communities'. What was needed were 'political proposals that would have improved the prospects of Catholic co-operation'. Indeed, he believed that at this time it was even possible that 'the IRA might have broken fresh ground with an entirely new policy of recognizing Stormont and working through the civil rights association'. This was much too optimistic an assessment. First of all, Labour's political proposals were not radical enough to conciliate the Catholics and, second, the establishment of the Provisional IRA, of an underground organisation determined to launch a military campaign for a united Ireland, made war inevitable. What was certainly not inevitable was the scale, intensity and duration of that war. Here Callaghan is on surer ground in laying responsibility at the door of Edward Heath's Conservative government that took office in June 1970. Heath's general election victory was, according to Callaghan, 'a disaster for Northern Ireland...the break in continuity came at the very worst time for the success of the struggle to prevent the Provisional IRA from capturing the sympathy of the majority.'[12]

Cracking down

The new Conservative government was considerably less inclined to force reform on the Unionists and considerably more inclined to support its efforts at regaining control over the Catholic working-class areas of Belfast and Derry. As far as Chichester-Clark and his colleagues were concerned, their friends were now back in power at Westminster and they expected their support in restoring Stormont control over the whole province. A first indication of the tougher line towards the Catholic minority was the decision, quite incredible in the circumstances, to allow the 1970 Orange parades to go ahead. On 27 June, Orange marches in Belfast led to fierce inter-communal fighting with the Provisional IRA going into action against Protestant vigilantes. By the end of the day five Protestants and one IRA member had been killed. This provided clear evidence, as far as the Unionists were concerned, that the IRA was using the no-go areas as sanctuaries in which it could organise and prepare for war. The Protestants demanded that the troops should be sent in to root them out. The result was to be the first serious confrontation between the British army and the Catholic working class.

On 1 July, Reginald Maudling, the Conservative Home Secretary, paid a brief visit to Northern Ireland. He found the place and the people pretty appalling and had already decided to have as little to do with it as possible. The Unionists should be left to put their own house in order. Whereas Callaghan had always insisted on a tight political control over security policy exercised from Westminster, Maudling was content to leave decision-making to the men on the ground, to the Joint Security Committee. This body consisted of army, RUC and Unionist government representatives, including the Prime Minister. Whereas Callaghan had always insisted that the army should try to appear impartial, now the army was to find itself increasingly acting as the strong arm of the Stormont regime.

On the same day as Maudling's visit, the Joint Security Committee met to discuss the previous week's violence. The decision was taken that the next time trouble seemed likely in Belfast, the army should go in and put it down with 'maximum force'.[13] This decision was endorsed the next day by a junior Defence minister at Westminster, Lord Balneil. The necessary incident occurred on 3 July when troops raided a house in Balkan Street, off the Falls Road. A riot broke out and the army went in to teach the Catholic working class a lesson.

The outcome of this high-level decision to get tough was the quite illegal Falls Road curfew that lasted 34 hours from 3 to 5 July. Some 3000 troops sealed off an area covering 50 streets which were then subjected to a house-to-house search. The operation ended with five Catholics dead (four shot by the troops and one crushed by an armoured vehicle). The whole area was deluged with CS gas and the troops wrecked and looted many of the houses they had searched. According to one journalist, the army behaved 'as if this were the rebellious Crater District of Aden colony'.[14] Two jubilant Unionist ministers, William Long and John Brooke, were taken on a guided tour of the area by the army. Any pretence of impartiality had been abandoned.

Paddy Devlin, a Stormont MP at the time, remains convinced that this was 'a punitive raid'. He describes how the troops:

> axed doors down that could easily have been opened, ripped up floorboards, broke furniture unnecessarily and tipped the contents of drawers and cupboards all over the place. Residents later complained bitterly about the Black Watch, a Scottish regiment which seemed to give most of its attention to breaking religious objects and symbols of the Glasgow Celtic football club.

He was arrested himself, threatened with having his brains blown out and placed on the floor of an armoured troop carrier with soldiers resting their feet on him. Only the intervention of senior RUC officers who recognised him secured his release.[15]

This was, in the words of Kevin Kelley, one of the historians of the war, 'the first of many pyrrhic victories for the British army in Northern Ireland'.[16] According to Michael Dewar, a former Lieutenant Colonel who served in the province, the disastrous events of June and July 1970 were a decisive turning point:

> It can be argued that the failure to ban the 1970 Orange parades, and the massive arms searches and curfew in the Lower Falls area which followed was the last chance to avoid the catastrophe that has since engulfed Ulster. The previous August was the watershed, the spring of 1970 the last opportunity for a settlement. Until the spring of 1970, most Catholics regarded the troops as their protectors. The Lower Falls operation changed everything.[17]

As James Callaghan, by now Opposition spokesman, observed, the 'adverse impact' of the episode 'on the Catholic community was out of all proportion to the success of the Army's haul'. It looked to many Catholics as if 'the Army had changed sides...was the servant of the Ulster Unionist Government and of the Protestants'.[18] Certainly this was how it seemed to Paddy Devlin. In the weeks that followed the Falls Road curfew the army were 'cock-a-hoop' and 'proceeded to put the boot in with a vengeance'. They succeeded almost overnight in turning the Catholic working class 'from neutral or even sympathetic support for the military to outright hatred'. Even his own supporters and party workers began to turn their backs on constitutional politics and rallied to the Provisional IRA.[19]

The Provisional offensive

The Provisional IRA launched their military campaign in the summer of 1970. Initially their's was a destabilising strategy, carrying out something like a hundred bombings by mid-September. This offensive put the British army under increasing pressure from the Unionist government to crack down on the Catholic communities that were sheltering the gunmen and the bombers. British efforts in this direction only succeeded in bringing the troops into conflict with the Catholic working class. In these circumstances, the British found themselves acting as recruiting officers for the Provisional IRA. Whereas the Provisionals had begun their campaign with less than a hundred members, by the end of the year they had increased their number to around 800. The campaign built up slowly and not until 6 February 1971 was the first British soldier to be killed. This was followed soon after, on 10 March, by the brutal shooting of three off-duty soldiers, one of them only 17 years old. There can be little doubt that this episode considerably hardened the soldiers' attitude towards the Catholic community. The Provisional IRA's war had begun.

How did the British army respond to this deteriorating situation? An attempt was made to implement a counterinsurgency strategy in Northern Ireland, drawing on the experience gained in earlier colonial wars. This was to come up against three particular problems: first of all, a lack of consistent political direction; second, the fact that such a strategy had not proven particularly successful in dealing with urban-based insurgencies elsewhere; and third, the impossibility of actually introducing the necessary Emergency measures in what was still part of the United Kingdom. What resulted was a security policy that was to be undermined by contradictory political initiatives and that was to prove repressive enough to complete the process of alienating the Catholic working class but not repressive enough actually to defeat the Provisional IRA. Instead of creating 'a culture of fear' that would have successfully intimidated the Catholic working class and reduced it to sullen passivity, the army succeeded only in creating what can best be described as 'a culture of antagonism' that provoked and sustained opposition and resistance. This culture of antagonism produced a Catholic working class that was prepared to support and condone the Provisional IRA's military campaign even on those occasions when it was to involve horrifying civilian casualties and callous murderous brutality.[20]

The army found itself operating in an unstable political situation, trying to wage a counterinsurgency campaign against an increasingly effective and confident opponent without recourse to the emergency measures that had been the cornerstones of other campaigns. Curfews, bans, internment, collective punishments and reprisals, identity cards, compulsory resettlement, deportation, torture and in-depth interrogation, a relaxed attitude towards the shooting of suspects and capital punishment have either not been used or, when they have, quickly proved to be counterproductive. One example demonstrates the kind of repressive measures not available to the army in Northern Ireland: if South Armagh were a province in Malaya many of its Catholic inhabitants would have had their homes burned down and have been either forcibly resettled in heavily policed 'new villages' or deported across the border. Obviously such draconian measures were not politically possible in the context of contemporary Britain and of the European Community. Moreover, where colonial-style repressive measures were used, they proved at best counterproductive and at worst disastrous. The Falls Road curfew was an early example of this, but the most important was the introduction of internment on 9 August 1971.

Internment and 'Bloody Sunday'

The army's failure to curb IRA activity had already led, as we have seen, to the fall of Prime Minister Chichester-Clark on 20 March and his replacement by Brian Faulkner. The new Prime Minister was determined to secure tougher security measures. He actually approached Field Marshal Templer for his advice on how to defeat the Provisional IRA, but Templer pleaded age and the very different circumstances that existed in Northern Ireland. According to one senior civil servant at Stormont, as far as Templer was concerned 'the role of the news media and the political climate at Westminster... made the measures he had employed to such good effect in Malaya totally unacceptable in the UK in 1971'.[21] Nevertheless, Faulkner pressed for the introduction of internment. This was partly to satisfy his own supporters who were demanding repression, but Faulkner also really believed internment was the key to defeating the Provisional IRA. He had been Minister for Home Affairs during the IRA's 1956–62 campaign when over 300 men had been interned and was convinced that it had played a major role in their defeat then just as it had in the early 1920s and during the Second World War. Of course, on these earlier occasions similar measures had been introduced in the South, most recently by Faulkner's friend (they rode to hounds together), Charles Haughey.[22] In the early 1920s, the Irish government had interned over 11 000 men and women, during the Second World War it had interned some 1100, of whom three died on hunger strike, and during the 1950s it interned some 150.[23] However, no Dublin government could contemplate such repressive measures when it was the Catholic minority that was under attack rather than an isolated band of republican intransigents. Moreover, the British army was opposed to the introduction of internment, although it seems that this was a disagreement over timing rather than over strategy.[24] The Heath government in London gave the go-ahead. The result was catastrophic.

The dawn raids of 9 August, Operation Demetrius, picked up 342 people, very few of whom were Provisional IRA members and no less than 116 of whom were released within 48 hours. Special Branch intelligence was hopelessly out of date, with the troops even looking for one man who had been dead for four years. Those arrested were routinely beaten, abused and humiliated. Far from smashing the Provisional IRA, the Operation provoked fierce popular resistance that they were able to use in order to intensify their campaign dramatically. The army found itself involved in serious fighting that by the end of the day left 12 people dead (two soldiers, three Protestants and seven Catholics). The whole episode has a dreadful similarity to the events of August 1969, only two years earlier, when the troops had first been sent in, but now it was the army that was attacking the Catholic working-class districts in Belfast and Derry instead of the RUC. In the weeks that followed, the conflict was to reach a new level of intensity that marked the introduction of internment as a decisive turning point in the war. Whereas before internment only five soldiers had been killed, in just the four months after, 30 soldiers, 11 policemen and members of the Ulster Defence Regiment (UDR) and 73 civilians were killed. The conflict escalated out of control. Internment, according to one commentator, had blown away 'the last shreds of support for the army within the Catholic population, uniting the whole community in angry solidarity with "the men behind the wire"'.[25] According to the GOC in Northern Ireland, General Sir Harry Tuzo, after internment, 'half the Catholic population sympathises with the IRA, and up to a quarter – that is about 120 000 people – is ready to give the organization active support'.[26] Reginald Maudling, in a quite amazing instance of wishful thinking, was later to argue that 'while resentment in the Catholic community was extreme...the security situation had been improved.'[27]

The disastrous consequences of internment were compounded when it became known that a group of internees had been singled out and subjected to in-depth interrogation techniques. The techniques had been approved for use in earlier colonial conflicts, but in Northern Ireland their use was a propaganda disaster, further alienating the Catholic minority and seriously damaging the British government's international standing.[28]

Why was Operation Demetrius such a disaster? On one level this can be put down to faulty intelligence, to the fact that Special Branch just did not know who the Provisionals were. This explains why they were not seriously hurt by internment but not why they were so dramatically strengthened! Here two factors seem crucial: first, internment had been able to play the part it did in the 1956–62 campaign because at that time the IRA did not have any significant popular support. When internment was introduced in August 1971 the Catholic working class was in revolt against the Stormont regime and regarded both the Official and Provisional IRAs as their defenders. Internment was consequently perceived as an attack on the whole community. This was reinforced by the fact that no loyalist paramilitaries were interned. The second factor was that, as we have seen in earlier IRA campaigns, internment had been introduced south of the border as well. This was not politically possible now and, indeed, the Irish Prime Minister, Jack Lynch, had warned the British ambassador to Dublin that the consequences of internment would be 'catastrophic; for every man put behind the wire, a hundred more would volunteer'.[29] One other reason for the failure of internment is that, to be blunt, it was used remarkably little in Northern Ireland. By the time it was phased out in December 1975, 1981 men and women had been interned. This compares with 77 000 in Kenya and 34 000 in Malaya. The relatively low number in Northern Ireland once again reflects the inability to fully implement a counterinsurgency strategy.

The next major episode in this catalogue of catastrophe was the 'Bloody Sunday' massacre of 30 January 1972. A 20 000-strong march in Derry protesting against internment was attacked by British paratroopers who shot 42 unarmed demonstrators (13 died immediately and one later). Those arrested were beaten, with many forced to run a gauntlet of paratroopers, hitting them with batons and rifle butts, and boasting of how many people they had killed. The turning loose of the British army's 'shock' troops on a peaceful, unarmed demonstration had wholly predictable results in terms of the number of casualties, but the political consequences were another matter. Far from restoring order, this exemplary massacre made the situation worse, contributing significantly to the protracted nature of the war. The Derry coroner later accused the Paras of having 'ran amok...it was sheer unadulterated murder.'[30] The British government set up the Widgery Tribunal in an unsuccessful attempt to vindicate the army. Its findings were comprehensively demolished at the time by Eamonn McCann and others.[31] It is worth noticing that years later some British accounts were still proclaiming 'Bloody Sunday' a great success. Popular military histories still claimed that the Paras inflicted a serious defeat on the Provisionals, with perhaps another 15 bodies being smuggled across the border and buried in secret to conceal the fact.[32] In fact 'Bloody Sunday' was a disaster for the British government, bringing down on it widespread international condemnation, while in Dublin a large protest march ended with the British embassy being burned down.

Internment and 'Bloody Sunday' together fuelled the Provisional offensive that was to bring Stormont down. The final death toll for 1971 was to be 174 people (the previous year it had been 25). The following year 467 people were killed and the year after that 250. The number of explosions in the province dramatically increased from about 150 in 1970 to just over a thousand in 1971, to 1382 in 1972 and 978 in 1973. Moreover, the size and power of IRA bombs was also considerably increased. The British were forced to retreat before this offensive.

Counterinsurgency in Northern Ireland

At the same time as internment was being introduced, the army also found itself coming into conflict with the Catholic working class on a routine day-to-day basis. This was inevitable in the circumstances. The Catholic revolt had seen the collapse of local government in Catholic areas and the expulsion of the RUC with the result that the army found itself having to take on a policing, intelligence-gathering and even a local government role. In many areas, the army had reluctantly become 'the de facto civil authority'.[33]

According to Robin Evelegh, a former army officer who served in Belfast, the British had lost the crucial 'competition in government' in this period. He writes:

> From August 1969 when the Army took over the policing of the Republican areas of Northern Ireland, until November 1972, the people of Republican districts were effectively left to conduct the business of civil government on their own. After much pressing by Brigadier F.E. Kitson, at that time commanding the Army Brigade in Belfast, a single civil servant was appointed in September 1971 as civil representative to the Army in Belfast.

The Catholics, Evelegh recognised, considered themselves Irish rather than British and it followed from this that 'they would only acquiesce in British rule if they were offered something in return that would reconcile them to a situation which contradicted their natural patriotism'. The reality was that in his battalion area of the Upper Falls with perhaps 70 000 inhabitants 'there was not a single generally available municipal playing area...with nothing else to amuse them, the bored and unemployed youth of the area found their recreation in throwing stones at soldiers'. Contact between the government and the Catholic communities was minimal: as late as January 1975 the points of contact between the government and the 250 000 Catholic inhabitants of West Belfast amounted to six sub-post offices, two Police Stations, four Civil Affairs Advisers (two in an army fort and two in the Springfield Road Police Station), a public cleansing yard in the Whiterock Road, a welfare office in the Iveagh School, and a Housing Executive Repair Yard in Turf

Lodge. It is therefore not surprising that the Republican citizens of West Belfast felt out of contact with civil government which, it sensed, had no interest in them, if this was the sum total of its representation in their areas.[34]

Another prerequisite for successful counterinsurgency is an effective intelligence apparatus, normally a Special Branch. The army found itself without intelligence in Northern Ireland with the RUC Special Branch having been discredited by the internment fiasco. To overcome this they tried to develop their own intelligence-gathering methods. A crucial part in this was played by Brigadier Frank Kitson, commanding 39 Brigade in Belfast. While serving in Malaya against the Communists, he had argued that the army should not rely only on Special Branch, but should make the collection of intelligence part of its own routine.[35] He had later incorporated this into his attempted theorisation of a British National Security State, *Low Intensity Operations*.[36] He was given the go-ahead to introduce these methods into Northern Ireland. According to the then Chief of the General Staff, Michael Carver, 'there was no alternative'.[37]

The most important development was the use of foot patrols to gather 'contact-information', to build up a detailed, comprehensive profile of their area of operations and its inhabitants. This was achieved by the regular stopping and questioning of the population, vehicle checks and house searches. The mass of information gathered was collated by the army's own intelligence officers in an attempt to uncover the Provisional IRA's organisation, membership and operations. The scale of the effort is shown by the number of house searches carried out which increased from 17 000 in 1971 to 36 000 in 1972 and 75 000 in 1973 and 1974. Between 1971 and 1976 some 250 000 house searches were carried out.[38] On any given day up to 5000 vehicles would be stopped, the driver questioned and the vehicle searched. According to one account between 1 April 1973 and 1 April 1974 an astonishing four million vehicles were stopped and searched.[39]

Whatever intelligence was gathered, whatever arms and explosives were found, however many arrests were made, has to be balanced against the conflict and antagonism that such methods generated. Street questioning and house searches had a guaranteed capacity to produce confrontation to which the troops were trained to respond aggressively, sometimes brutally.[40] Gerry Adams described the impact British troops had on Ballymurphy:

> No one could look on and passively accept having their doors kicked in, their houses wrecked, their family members beaten up. As military

intervention in the neighbourhood increased in frequency and intensity so the local people, out of their own feelings of self-respect, outrage and resistance, organised more and more their own response to the military presence. The attitude and presence of British troops was also a reminder that we were Irish, and there was an instant resurgence of national consciousness and an almost immediate politicisation of the local populace.[41]

The Provisional IRA were the immediate beneficiaries of this. While this sort of harassment of the Catholic working class was regarded as a necessary feature of the policy of repression in the early days of the conflict, it was increasingly to be seen as counterproductive. The intelligence acquired by these methods was, moreover, no substitute for that gathered by an effective Special Branch, through interrogation, the recruitment of informers and the running of agents. Another drawback was that intensive patrolling was actually found to be providing the Provisionals with more opportunities for carrying out attacks on the security forces.

Kitson was also responsible for developing the use of covert operations in Northern Ireland. This was hardly a new development but was a feature of every British post-war counterinsurgency campaign. Certainly the activities of the Military Reconnaissance Force (MRF) and other similar detachments were effective at fighting the IRA with its own methods. Robin Evelegh actually laments the fact that during his tours in Northern Ireland he was not allowed to put more than 20 per cent of his battalion into plain clothes and argues that 50 soldiers in civilian dress were more effective than 400 in battledress.[42] Nevertheless, covert operations have their own inherent drawbacks. As historian Charles Townshend has pointed out, this 'mimetic process' holds considerable dangers with an inevitable tendency for the army's counter- or pseudo-gangs to run out of control and resort to assassination.[43] Indeed, according to one well-informed account, army undercover squads attempted 'to draw the Provisionals into a shooting war with the loyalists in order to distract the IRA from its objective of attacking the army'. They carried out random attacks on Catholic civilians in order to provoke a cycle of sectarian retaliation, a strategy of what 'can only be described as "State-sponsored murder"'.[44] This might not create too many problems in Kenya where pseudo-gangs certainly on occasions behaved as murder squads, but in Northern Ireland it was to provide another propaganda triumph for the IRA and prove a continual embarrassment to the British government.

At this point it is worth briefly considering the Kitson furore of the 1970s. A veteran of counterinsurgency campaigns in Kenya, Malaya and the Oman, Kitson became for many Catholics and for much of the British Left the symbol of repression in Northern Ireland and of the danger of military intervention in Britain. According to Sean MacStiofain, Kitson was 'our deadliest enemy in the North'.[45] The fullest statement of the case against him was Roger Faligot's controversial *Britain's Military Strategy in Ireland: The Kitson Experiment*. This identified him as the architect of a new and comprehensive counterinsurgency strategy that was supposedly being implemented in Northern Ireland. The main problem with this account was that it regarded the war as an opportunity for the British to put into effect new methods, to carry out a controlled experiment, rather than recognising what went on as desperate attempts to grapple with a situation that was escalating out of control and in which everything the army tried only seemed to make things worse.[46] Certainly Kitson had well-thought-out ideas on how to conduct a counterinsurgency campaign in an advanced industrial society, but he was never in control of security policy (he was a brigadier and, for example, had his vehement opposition to the introduction of internment overruled) and only some of his ideas were ever put into effect. Moreover, they proved counterproductive and only contributed to the deteriorating situation. There is much to be said for Paddy Devlin's judgement that Kitson 'probably did more than any other individual to sour relations between the Catholic community and the security forces'.[47]

The fall of Stormont

The Provisional IRA's great victory was the British government's decision to suspend Stormont on 24 March 1972 and impose direct rule. The Protestant state had been brought down by the Provisionals' unrelenting offensive and the British had taken the first major step in distancing themselves from the Unionists. This was followed on 26 June by the first IRA ceasefire and, soon after, by a secret meeting between British ministers and the IRA leadership. On 7 July, William Whitelaw, the new Secretary of State for Northern Ireland, met with an IRA delegation made up of Seamus Twomey, Sean MacStiofain, Daithi O'Connaill, Ivor Bell, Martin McGuinness and Gerry Adams. It seems that the British believed that the Provisionals would be prepared to negotiate a settlement now that Stormont was gone, while, for their part, the Provisionals believed that a British withdrawal was being contemplated. Both sides were mistaken and the discussions came to nothing. The ceasefire ended in fighting in which three soldiers were killed on 13 July. Once the talks became public knowledge, Whitelaw found himself engulfed by a political storm that threatened to end his career. He was to restore his political fortunes with the decision to end the no-go areas in Belfast and Derry, to occupy the Catholic working-class areas militarily.

An important factor in taking this decision was a fall-off in Catholic support for the Provisionals. The suspension of Stormont had satisfied many Catholics who no longer believed the Provisionals' campaign to be justified. This war-weariness was compounded on 21 July, 'Bloody Friday', when the Provisionals blitzed the centre of Belfast with 26 bombs that killed two soldiers and nine civilians and injured another 130 people, many of them horribly mutilated. Whatever excuses the Provisionals made, the fact is that this episode showed an appalling disregard for civilian casualties. Looking back, Brendon Hughes, who commanded the Bloody Friday operation, remarked that 'if I could do it over again I wouldn't do it'.[48] The British took advantage of the backlash that followed to stage a massive offensive that had been in preparation for some time. On 31 July, Operation Motorman, 'one of the most significant events of the Northern Ireland conflict', saw some regular 22 000 troops and 5000 UDR soldiers take part in the biggest British military operation since the Suez invasion of 1956: the occupation of the no-go areas. In Derry, Centurion tanks were actually landed from four landing craft that had been escorted up the Foyle estuary by a minesweeper. It was intended 'to alter the dynamics of the conflict'.[49] While determined to act tough, Whitelaw was also fully aware of the need to avoid another 'Bloody Sunday'. In his memoirs, he recalls awaiting news of the operation 'in considerable suspense' at Army Headquarters in Lisburn. He was worried 'that the population as a whole would be instructed to obstruct the entry of troops by mass demonstrations and even by lying down in the streets in front of armoured vehicles'. In fact, there was only minimal resistance to what was the use of overwhelming force (two young men shot dead in Derry). The operation 'succeeded beyond our wildest dreams' and successfully 'removed the blot of the no-go areas – so long a major source of irritation'.[50] That same day the Provisionals exploded three car bombs in the village of Claudy, killing nine civilians, another reckless act that further undermined support for their cause.

Operation Motorman was undoubtedly a significant success for the British.[51] According to Adams, it had more of an impact in Derry, where the no-go areas were still intact, than in Belfast where the British were already sending patrols into Catholic areas. He argues that it launched a new British offensive which saw the physical occupation of Catholic areas with the establishment of strongly defended forts, nine in the Andersonstown area alone. The Provisionals were placed on the defensive.[52] Certainly in the aftermath of the operation a number of senior IRA members were arrested, including Adams himself. It will not do to describe Operation Motorman as 'decisive', however.[53] The Provisional IRA, as we shall see, possessed great recuperative qualities and an impressive ability to adapt to changing circumstances. Nevertheless, the conflict had entered a new phase. Meanwhile, Whitelaw's main concern was to put in place a political solution that would continue to undermine the Provisionals' popular support and, it was hoped, build up the moderate Social Democratic and Labour Party (SDLP) as a constitutional alternative. The counterinsurgency strategy had failed to deliver military victory, a return to one-party Stormont rule was impossible and so the Conservative government attempted a political initiative. This was inevitably to come up against the fact that any attempt to conciliate the Catholic minority alienated the Protestants.

Power-sharing

Whitelaw established the Northern Ireland Assembly in the summer of 1973 and then proceeded to the more difficult task of constructing a power-sharing executive from among its Unionist and SDLP members. Agreement was finally reached at a four-day conference at Sunningdale in Berkshire in December. The executive, headed by the leader of the Official Unionists, Brian Faulkner, took office on 1 January 1974. From the very beginning it met with considerable Protestant hostility. Even in the Assembly itself, Faulkner could only command the support of a minority of the Unionist members, with a significant proportion of his own Official Unionists aligning with Ian Paisley's Democratic Unionists and William Craig's Vanguard Unionists. He was reliant for his majority on the support of the Catholic SDLP and the Alliance Party. Within a matter of days, the Ulster Unionist Council met to reject the Sunningdale Agreement, whereupon Faulkner resigned as leader of the Official Unionists and formed his own pro-Sunningdale Unionist Party of Northern Ireland. He still had his Assembly majority and hoped to be able to win over Protestant opinion if given enough time. This was not to be.

At the end of February 1974, Prime Minister Heath, embroiled in his second national miners' strike, called a general election and Faulkner found himself somewhat prematurely compelled to test Protestant support for Sunningdale at the polls, albeit for seats at Westminster.

He faced the combined and co-ordinated opposition of all three rival Unionist parties (Official, Democratic, Vanguard), now joined together in the United Ulster Unionist Council (UUUC). In the general election, UUUC candidates received 366 703 votes (51 per cent), capturing 11 of the province's 12 Westminster seats. The pro-Sunningdale Unionists polled only 94 301 votes (13.1 per cent). This was a massive blow to Faulkner, even though he still retained his Assembly majority and was able, as late as 14 May, to comfortably defeat an anti-Sunningdale resolution there by 44 votes to 28. His Unionist enemies were now confident that they had enough support to wreck the power-sharing executive. Their hand was strengthened by the emergence of a new force, the Ulster Workers' Council (UWC). They confronted a new Labour government at Westminster, headed by Harold Wilson, and a new Secretary of State for Northern Ireland, Merlyn Rees.

Rees took office pledging full support for Sunningdale and the power-sharing executive but, in private, the general election result had convinced him the experiment was doomed. Sunningdale was, he later wrote, 'the keystone of our policy in Northern Ireland, but keystone or not...I soon found that there was little support for Sunningdale in the majority community'.[54]

The UWC called for strike action against the executive on 14 May, the day Faulkner won the Sunningdale vote in the Assembly. The following day, there were limited strikes in the power stations, cutting output to 60 per cent of normal, and the Protestant paramilitaries began attempting to enforce a stay-at-home campaign, blocking streets, hijacking vehicles and erecting barricades. According to the army, there were 37 roadblocks in Belfast and the suburbs by the next day. Quite incredibly, neither the army nor the RUC took any serious steps to put a stop to these illegal and intimidatory activities. Rees seemed to have decided not to confront the UWC and its paramilitary allies, but to let the strike take its course in the hope that it would run into the ground. The security forces were ordered not to interfere with the barricades and effectively surrendered the streets to the Protestant paramilitaries. The failure to intervene immediately and decisively to dismantle the barricades and clear the streets can be seen in retrospect to have been fatal for the executive. As Paddy Devlin, SDLP Minister of Health and Social Services, subsequently complained, failure to take action 'created the impression in the minds of the loyalists that the police, the military and Merlyn Rees acquiesced in their illegal actions'. It was this that 'caused thousands of law-abiding people who had earlier given support to the Executive to switch sides'.[55]

The UWC was, at the start of the strike, far from confident that it could carry through a full-scale confrontation successfully and decisive action might well have resulted in the strike assuming a 'token' character. The failure of the security forces to intervene gave the UWC increased confidence and indicated that the British intended to let the executive sink or swim unaided. On Monday, 20 May, the strike dramatically gathered momentum with nearly 200 barricades being erected unhindered in the Belfast area alone, effectively cutting the city off from the rest of the province. Similar action by the republicans would, of course, have brought an immediate forceful response. Robert Fisk provides a superb first-hand account of the situation:

> From ten miles away it was possible to see long columns of brown and jet-black smoke twisting wearily into the dawn sky over Belfast as UDA men set fire to stolen lorries, cars and even bicycles on makeshift barricades...Masked UDA men told the driver of a grain lorry in Great Victoria Street to leave his cab, then they swung the vehicle and its trailer across the road – normally one of the busiest in Belfast – between a motor showroom and the regional office of the AA. Beside York Road railway station in north Belfast, where trains normally left for Coleraine, Derry and the towns of western Ulster, Protestants set fire to overturned cars and effectively cut off the Shore Road and part of the docks. Every one of these incidents was watched, sometimes from only a few yards away, by policemen and soldiers. But the people of Belfast found that they did little or nothing to stop the demonstrations of Protestant lawlessness. Perhaps worse (from the government's point of view) they actually went through the ghostly routine of their ordinary security duties as if nothing untoward was happening or as if they were silently acquiescing with the UWC. The army in their dark green landrovers drove slowly through the streets, discreetly avoiding the human barricades and gingerly squeezing through the gaps in the roadblocks. Soldiers on foot patrol walked the pavements of east Belfast and Sandy Row but made no attempt to interfere with the uniformed UDA men. Sometimes they even stopped and talked to youths on the barricades and on at least two occasions, once in Albion Street in Sandy Row and again in the east of the city near Dee Street, they were seen offering round cigarettes. When confrontation seemed almost inevitable, it was the army who withdrew.[56]

Throughout the strike, only 74 people were charged with any offence by the police, and 31 of these were involved in a Protestant paramilitary attack on a public house near Ballymena in which two Catholics were killed. To all intents and purposes, the barricades, the hijackings, the physical assaults and intimidation were officially tolerated, apparently condoned by the authorities.

In his account of the strike, Brian Faulkner complains bitterly of 'the army making excuses for doing nothing' and of Rees just going 'into a flap'. He describes how on Monday, 20 May:

> I was told by the police that there were so many barricades on roads between my home and Stormont that I would have to be flown in by helicopter...As we travelled across County Down I could see beneath me the evidence of paramilitary activity. Near Moneyrea the road was blocked by a sawn-down telegraph pole and a long queue of vehicles was waiting in front of it. I asked the pilot to hover for a few minutes and watched as the gang manning the barricade turned away the cars...Even at Stormont as we came in to land I could see a barricade within sight of Merlyn Rees' office. I went straight in to the Secretary of State's office and demanded angrily that something be done to remove all the barricades, but he insisted at first that the security forces had the problem under control and that roads were in general clear. I ended the argument by taking him to the window and pointing to the barricade at Dundonald House, and in some agitation he hurried to instruct his officials to have it cleared.[57]

The key to the success or failure of the strike lay not in the streets, however, but in the power stations. As their confidence increased, bolstered by the inactivity of the security forces, the UWC began increasing pressure at this point, turning the screw that was to bring down the executive. Rees was authorised by the Cabinet in London to use troops to work the power stations, but was advised by the GOC, Sir Frank King, that this was not possible, that the Army did not have the technical resources for such a complex operation, particularly when management had made it clear that they would walk out if troops were brought in. On Monday, 27 May, the UWC ordered the complete shut-down of the power stations and, denied army assistance, Faulkner and the executive resigned on the following day. Sunningdale was dead.

Why did the army fail so dramatically even to attempt the maintenance of 'law and order'? According to one sympathetic account, army headquarters at Lisburn had been giving the strike some considerable thought. One matter which touched on all their calculations was the experience of many other campaigns which told them that they could not do their job properly unless they had the broad support of at least one section of the community. Their prime job was to defeat IRA terrorists, and they did not have the support of the Catholic population; now they were being asked to go against the rest of the community.[58]

The army believed that the executive was, in any case, doomed in the long run because of lack of Protestant support; consequently, there was no advantage to be gained from a major confrontation with the Protestants in support of it. Rees more or less shared this view.

As far as Rees was concerned, the RUC 'in their heart of hearts' actually supported the strike, which left him with the army as 'my only firm base'. He faithfully followed King's advice and recalls that they were 'beaten technically...the army also advised me that even if this were not the case, it could not guarantee to protect the power stations or pylons'. When he met with the Cabinet on 21 May, it was to tell them of 'the impossibility of the task', that the strike could not be broken.[59] There was no question during this crisis of the army actually refusing to obey orders as is sometimes suggested. This misunderstands completely the relationship between Rees and the army at this time: he asked their advice and then did as he was told. Staff officers at Lisburn were quite open about this and freely confided to friendly journalists that this was 'the week Merlyn Rees came of age'. It was 'just a lack of training', one officer condescendingly observed. 'He improved a lot as time went on.'[60]

In retrospect, it does seem that the hostility of most Protestants doomed the power-sharing experiment to failure in the long run, but that certainly does not mean that the UWC strike was bound to succeed. Decisive action to keep control of the streets in the first few days of the strike would have prevented it gathering momentum and have undermined the somewhat shaky resolve of the UWC. Nothing was done. Could the power workers' strike have been broken? One counterinsurgency expert has argued very strongly that:

> there was a certain lack of political will to stand up to the strikers. The army's reluctance to take over the operation of key services was natural enough, but it should have been overridden. Emergency powers should have been used to conscript certain key workers and public utilities for the duration of the Emergency. The leaders of the strike could have been arrested and detained quite legitimately under the existing powers.[61]

It is indeed inconceivable that such a challenge would have been refused in any other circumstances. The inescapable conclusion is that it was the army that took the political decision not to support the executive and that Rees tamely went along with it. Even senior army officers were later to express their surprise at how precipitately the Labour government had capitulated to the UWC.[62]

While the UWC general strike was still underway, on 14 May, Protestant paramilitaries carried out bomb attacks across the border in the south: three car bombs exploded in Dublin and another in Monaghan, killing 33 people and injuring another 130.[63] This attack highlighted the rise of Protestant paramilitary organisations: the Ulster Defence Association (UDA) with its terrorist wing, the Ulster Freedom Fighters (UFF) and the Ulster Volunteer Force (UVF). Since the start of the conflict, loyalist vigilantes had been involved in pogrom-style attacks on the Catholic minority, indeed this had been one of the precipitators of the conflict. Towards the end of 1971, however, Protestant murder gangs began to operate. These carried out the random assassination of Catholics, many of them horribly tortured before being killed. On 14 December 1971, loyalist paramilitaries had bombed McGurk's Bar in Belfast, killing 16 Catholics, and then the following year the number of sectarian killings dramatically increased. Loyalist paramilitaries killed 193 people in 1972, 81 in 1973, 93 in 1974, 114 in 1975 and 113 in 1976. Taking the years from 1972 to 1976, the republicans killed 727 people and the loyalist paramilitaries with far less publicity killed 504 overwhelmingly Catholic civilians selected at random and often horrifically tortured and mutilated.[64] While the security forces waged war on the republicans, the loyalist paramilitaries were left relatively unhindered.

The activities of the Protestant murder gangs were in part a response to the Provisionals' continuing offensive and to the resulting Protestant casualties, but this was only in part. Arguably even more important was Protestant hostility to any concessions the British government made towards the Catholic minority. The suspension of Stormont, the power-sharing executive and later the Anglo-Irish Agreement were all developments that provoked an increase in the number of loyalist paramilitary attacks.[65]

Another important factor was the degree of collusion between elements within the security forces and the loyalists. There is a strong suspicion that the Dublin and Monaghan bombers received assistance from a covert British agency in mounting their attack. At a lower level there was a clear overlap between the UDR and the loyalist paramilitaries, an overlap that was condoned by the British despite the terrible toll that was being taken in Catholic lives. The fact is that the British and loyalist campaigns were symmetrical. There is no doubt that the loyalist paramilitaries' murderous war against the Catholic minority was regarded as reinforcing rather than undermining the security forces' war against the Provisional IRA. The Protestant murder gangs helped wear the Catholic working class down and distracted attention from the army and the RUC. The extent to which they legitimised the Provisionals as defenders of the minority was not given enough weight by the British.[66]

Ulsterisation

In the aftermath of the UWC general strike, the Provisionals once again entered into negotiations with the British government. They believed that the Labour government in London was looking for an opportunity to withdraw from Northern Ireland now that power-sharing had failed. On 20 December 1974 the Provisionals declared a temporary ceasefire that continued until 2 January. During this time, secret talks took place between government officials and Sinn Fein and the ceasefire was extended until 17 January. After a temporary breakdown, on 9 February the IRA announced an indefinite ceasefire. This was to continue until late September 1975, although with many violations and a continuing death toll that at times made it indistinguishable from war. Some British accounts have rather optimistically suggested that at the time of the ceasefire, the Provisionals were facing imminent defeat, that the army's counterinsurgency strategy was within sight of victory, but that Rees mistakenly gave them time to recover.[67] It is worth remembering that similar claims were made in Aden and Cyprus. Certainly the Provisionals were under considerable pressure, but there is no evidence that they faced defeat. Moreover, the dominant republican perception of the ceasefire was that it was a serious mistake that actually weakened the IRA. They certainly did not regard it as having saved them. According to Gerry Adams the ceasefire brought the British 'nearer at that time to defeating the republican struggle' than any time since it had begun.[68] In any event, once it became clear that the Labour government had no intention of withdrawing, the ceasefire came to an end.

As far as the British were concerned the Provisional ceasefire can be seen as having provided them with a breathing space during which Rees presided over the initial stages in the most important shift in security policy during the course of the war. This involved a change from the counterinsurgency policy favoured by the army to what can most usefully be described as an 'internal security' strategy, the strategy of 'Ulsterisation'. Those accounts that compare this with the American Vietnamisation of the Vietnam war completely mistake the nature of the change.[69] This consisted of two central related policies: police primacy and criminalisation. The army was to be relieved of overall responsibility for the war against the IRA which would instead become a law and order matter to be handled by the RUC, with the support of the army. A counterinsurgency strategy derived from colonial experience was abandoned in favour of an internal security strategy that was believed to be more appropriate and effective in an advanced liberal democracy. The high profile army presence, together with internment, were recognised as factors exacerbating the situation rather than helping to end it. The problem was, as we have already seen, that the full arsenal of counterinsurgency measures could not, for political reasons, be deployed in Northern Ireland. The result was that the army did enough to alienate the Catholic working class, but not enough to successfully intimidate them. Instead it was hoped that the turn to policing and the judicial process would allow the IRA to be eliminated, at the same time without providing them with fresh recruits in the process. The policy was formalised in the report of a working party set up by Rees and headed by a senior civil servant at the Home Office, John Bourn: 'The Way Ahead'.[70]

The internal security strategy owed more to the European experience combating urban terrorist groups than it did to colonial experience. Both the West German success against Baader-Meinhof and, more particularly, the Italian success against the Red Brigades were influential in this respect.[71] The strategy was not, however, to achieve a similar degree of success in Northern Ireland for the simple reason that, unlike the much smaller organisations on the Continent, the Provisional IRA had a significant degree of popular support and was firmly rooted in the Catholic working class. The continued alienation of the Catholic working class and their refusal to help the security forces against the IRA was crucial in this regard. This community support meant that the RUC inevitably came into conflict with sections of the Catholic working class, thereby maintaining the cycle in which state repression created more recruits for the Provisionals than it actually eliminated. Only a political settlement that effectively conciliated the Catholic community could have broken this cycle, and this was not forthcoming because of Protestant intransigence. Another factor in the strategy's failure was the sectarian dimension to the conflict in Northern Ireland and the fact that the RUC did not respond to UFF or UVF attacks on the Catholic working class with the same determination as they responded to the IRA. Moreover, in some areas such as South Armagh, the level of IRA activity was such that police primacy was never implemented and the counterinsurgency strategy was continued.[72]

Nevertheless, while the new strategy did not bring about the defeat of the IRA, it did successfully contain them. Rees himself subsequently recalled that at no time was he 'advised even remotely, that the paramilitaries of any hue could be defeated. There was no Luneburg Heath on the horizon to be followed by a victory parade.'[73] Containment was the objective, reducing the level of violence, lowering tension, restoring normality as much as was possible.

Rees took office committed to phasing out internment and, despite opposition from the army, this had been accomplished by December 1975. This was followed by an end to special category status for all new prisoners convicted of 'terrorist' offences in March 1976. As Rees subsequently made clear: 'I wished that I might have gone further and ended it for those already sentenced...but quite apart from the lack of prison cells, there were legal difficulties.'[74] But for these legal difficulties, it would have been the Labour government that confronted the hunger strikes that were to face Margaret Thatcher. As it was, the 'blanket' and 'dirty' protests got underway. With the end of internment, the Diplock no-jury courts came into their own. In practice, this amounted to the replacement of internment by trial by confession.[75]

The reorganised RUC under the new Chief Constable, Kenneth Newman, a former member of the Palestine Police, became increasingly effective and this, together with the army's increasingly sophisticated use of covert and undercover operations, began to have some success in breaking up the IRA's organisation, eliminating its cadres, curtailing its level of activity and forcing it on the defensive. According to Kevin Kelley, the Provisionals were at this time: 'slowly losing the war...the British surveillance web was ensnaring many volunteers and making operations more difficult than ever...supply lines for weapons and explosives were under unprecedented strain...Provos today admit that there were fewer than 250 active guerrillas at the end of 1977.'[76] They responded by reorganising into a cellular structure that was much more difficult for the security forces to penetrate effectively. They countered the policy of criminalisation with their own policy of politicisation that was to culminate with the hunger strikes and Sinn Fein's electoral successes in the 1980s.[77] But while the IRA were not defeated, they were contained. Whereas in 1976, 297 people were killed in Northern Ireland, the following year the number fell to 112, in 1978 to 81 and in 1979 rose but only to 113.

While the importance of police primacy and criminalisation have to be insisted on, relations between the security forces and the Catholic working class remained bad throughout the years of the 1974–79 Labour government. Changes in security force methods, the army's lower profile, more covert surveillance and less aggressive intrusions into Catholic areas, into people's homes, meant that there was less confrontation, but the culture of antagonism remained in place. An important factor here was the common knowledge that confessions were being beaten out of people in RUC barracks and that these confessions were then resulting in long terms of imprisonment handed down by the Diplock courts. On the one hand, the IRA was being successfully contained and ground down by a process of attrition, but on the other hand the methods used were continuing to alienate the Catholic working class. Rees's successor as Secretary of State, Roy Mason, exacerbated this contradiction that could only have been resolved by some sort of political initiative. He was, in the words of a senior Northern Ireland civil servant, 'an instinctive unionist', although, to be fair, he had complete contempt for Ian Paisley and had defeated the abortive Protestant general strike of May 1977, an attempt to repeat their 1974 victory.[78] Mason certainly kept the pressure up on the IRA with Martin McGuinness later acknowledging that 'he beat the shit out of us'.[79] In the process, however, he successfully alienated the likes of Gerry Fitt MP for Belfast West, a determined opponent of the IRA. On one occasion, Fitt described Mason as 'an arrogant bumptious little bastard. A nasty wee c***'.[80] This alienation of even Catholic opponents of the IRA was to have serious consequences for the Labour government. Even though he was a strong supporter of the government, Fitt was appalled by the deals it had struck with the Ulster Unionists in return for their votes in the House of Commons, but, more particularly, he was outraged by its failure to put a stop to beatings that were taking place in police holding centres. By the time the Labour government faced a vote of confidence in the Commons at the end of March 1979, Fitt, under considerable pressure from his constituents, was no longer prepared to support them. He told the Commons that his mind was made up

> the Friday before last when I read the Bennett Report on police brutality in Northern Ireland. That has not received sufficient attention in this House or in the country. The report clearly states that men were brutalised and ill treated in the holding centres in Northern Ireland...That report was only the tip of the iceberg...When the true story emerges of what has been happening in the interrogation centres, the people in the United Kingdom will receive it with shock, horror and resentment. That is why I take this stand.[81]

His vote would have saved James Callaghan's government.

The hunger strikes

Margaret Thatcher took office as Prime Minister in May 1979 as a determined opponent of terrorism and steadfast supporter of the Union. Just over a month before her general election victory, one of her closest friends and advisers, the Secretary of State for Northern Ireland designate, Airey Neave, had been assassinated by the Irish National Liberation Army (INLA) in the House of Commons car-park.[82] On 27 August, soon after she took power, the IRA succeeded, on the same day, in assassinating the 79-year-old Lord Mountbatten on holiday in Donegal, and in killing 18 soldiers in the devastating Warrenpoint ambush. She immediately flew to Northern Ireland where the GOC, Sir Timothy Creasey, a bitter critic of police primacy, tried to persuade her to hand back responsibility for security to the army. One of his officers actually handed her the shoulder tabs that were all that remained of the Commanding Officer of the Queen's Own Highlanders, blown up at Warrenpoint. Creasey urged the reintroduction of internment, hot pursuit across the border and the appointment of a Director of Operations to exercise overall command over the security forces. At RUC headquarters, Newman put the case for continuing with the internal security strategy and, however reluctantly, she followed the advice of the officials and backed police primacy.[83] The only concession Creasey secured was the appointment of the former head of the Secret Intelligence Service (MI6), Maurice Oldfield, as Security Co-ordinator. His most important contribution was to be the abortive 'supergrass' initiative.[84] The likelihood is that if Creasey had had his way, the level of violence would have returned to that of the early 1970s.

When it came to the IRA hunger strikes (1 March–3 October 1981), however, Thatcher was able to demonstrate her iron resolve and steadfastly refused to make any concessions over special category status that might have defused the situation. Her stance was undoubtedly very popular among Protestants in Northern Ireland and among many people in Britain, but it created the most tremendous bitterness within the Catholic working class, indeed among all sections of the Catholic minority. Instead of criminalisation helping to isolate the IRA, the hunger strikes served to rally popular support. The ten hunger strike deaths (Bobby Sands, Francis Hughes, Raymond McCreesh, Patsy O'Hara, Joe McDonnell, Martin Hughes, Kevin Lynch, Kieran Doherty, Thomas McElwee and Michael Devine) had a cumulative impact as great as 'Bloody Sunday' and provided the IRA with a massive boost in popular support sufficient to sustain it throughout the 1980s. They were, in the words of J. Bowyer Bell, 'one of the great watersheds...Nothing could be the same again.' He emphasised 'the enormous store of bad will and alienation generated during the strike'.[85] There was a dramatic increase in support for republicanism and a real danger that Sinn Fein would actually replace the SDLP as the party representing the Catholic minority. Bobby Sands's victory on 9 April in the Fermanagh–South Tyrone by-election and election as a Westminster MP certainly gave the government early warning of the extent to which it was alienating Catholic opinion and should have led to greater flexibility. This was not to be. A good case can be made that Thatcher's stand prolonged the conflict by perhaps as much as a decade. There seems considerable justice to historian Joe Lee's judgement that her handling of the crisis was 'inept to the point of criminality'.[86]

Thatcher herself argued that she had inflicted a significant defeat on the IRA by standing fast but, at the same time, acknowledged that the hunger strikes had allowed the republicans to make 'headway in the nationalist community', to regroup and turn 'to violence on a larger scale, especially on the mainland'. The IRA were, in her own words, 'on the advance politically'.[87] This seems an almost textbook account of a pyrrhic victory, although the author seems completely oblivious to the fact. She appointed someone with no such illusions, Jim Prior, as Secretary of State for Northern Ireland on 13 September 1981, at which time there were still eight men on hunger strike. He visited the Maze and looked in on Liam McCloskie, who had been on hunger strike for 46 days:

> I was struck by how much this man looked at peace with himself. I began to realise at that moment that Northern Ireland, and perhaps the history of Ireland, has been made up of a number of people on both sides of the religious and political divide of utter determination and conviction, prepared to commit acts of violence and in a stubborn, yet courageous, way to accept the inevitable and to die. This was my first inkling as to what the problem of Northern Ireland was all about.

Prior recognised that the months of the hunger strikes had 'undoubtedly provided a boost for the IRA', leading many Catholics who were otherwise 'good citizens' to vote for Bobby Sands and Owen Carron, men who stood for 'violence, murder, intimidation, and, quite simply, anarchy'. There was 'a real danger that the Provisional Sinn Fein could yet become the leading Catholic party'.[88]

Prior quickly ended the hunger strikes, offering concessions to the prisoners that included the right to wear their own clothes, increased visits, more free association and restoration of lost remission. If these concessions had been offered before the hunger strikes then it is quite likely they would never have taken place. Too late! The damage had been done. Prior's concern was to try to lower tension in the province and to strengthen the credibility and influence of the SDLP. In his memoirs he openly admits, quite astonishingly for a British politician, that the security forces 'were firing a prodigious number of plastic bullets', killing 'a number of innocent people, including children...Their deaths adding to all the bitterness caused by the deaths of the hunger strikers.' He has nothing to say about allegations of a 'shoot-to-kill' policy, however, and goes out of his way to endorse the supergrass trials which were to collapse quite disastrously after his memoirs were written. While his political initiative (rolling devolution and a new Northern Ireland Assembly) failed, Prior began the difficult task of once again conciliating and building up the SDLP as a bulwark against Sinn Fein and, as part of this process, established that any viable domestic settlement would have 'to be acceptable to the Nationalist community...and to the Republic, which had a legitimate interest in Northern Ireland affairs because of the security position and because the Nationalists in Northern Ireland felt otherwise unrepresented'. This prepared the way for the Anglo-Irish Agreement.[89]

Some brief discussion of the 'supergrass' initiative is necessary here. This was modelled on the Italian *pentiti* system, devised by General Dalla Chiesa of the Carabinieri, which played an important part in the defeat of the Red Brigade. It was hoped that similar methods would defeat the IRA. The first supergrass was IRA member Christopher Black, whose evidence led to the arrest of 38 people in 1981. Eventually some 25 supergrasses were assembled producing nearly 600 arrests. There is no doubt that potentially the IRA could have been dealt a serious blow, but the courts refused to play their allotted role. Richard Clutterbuck subsequently complained bitterly that 'the Appeal Court judges in Northern Ireland were concerned with the process of law rather than with keeping killers off the streets' and blamed their 'squeamishness' for the continuation of the war.[90]

The Anglo-Irish Agreement

The great irony of the Thatcher decade as far as Northern Ireland is concerned is that her uncompromising stand over the hunger strikes was to create the circumstances that actually forced her government into concessions to the Catholic minority and the Irish government, concessions that completely alienated the Protestants and led to her being publicly denounced throughout the province, with Ian Paisley leading the way, for her treachery and appeasement of terrorism. Fear that the SDLP risked electoral eclipse was a decisive factor in securing her acceptance of the Anglo-Irish Agreement concluded at Hillsborough on 15 November 1985. Debate on the nature and implications of the Agreement was intense, with the Unionists condemning it as a betrayal, as a first step towards the surrender of sovereignty and a united Ireland, while the British government argued that it was largely symbolic and that the wishes of the majority in Northern Ireland would always remain paramount, at least on the question of the border. Certainly the longer-term implications of the Agreement, with its institutionalisation of a role for the Dublin government in the affairs of Northern Ireland, was the establishment of some sort of joint authority or shared sovereignty. For the time being it remained 'direct rule with a green tinge'.[91] The Protestants mounted a determined campaign to destroy the Agreement, hoping to repeat their success over the Sunningdale Agreement and the power-sharing executive. Inevitably, Paisley called upon his God to 'in wrath take vengeance upon this wicked, treacherous lying woman...take vengeance upon her O Lord and grant that we shall see a demonstration of thy power'.[92] The 'Ulster Says No' rally in Belfast on 23 November 1985 had a massive attendance of some 200 000 people, one in five of the Protestant population. Their protests were ignored. More important, the loyalist general strike of 3 March 1986 failed. On this occasion the RUC confronted the loyalist paramilitaries. By now their first loyalty was to the British State, not to Stormont, the Unionist parties or the Orange Order. The RUC was still a sectarian force, but one in the service of the British. Nevertheless, according to the Chief Constable, Sir John Hermon, 1986 and the defeat of the Protestant revolt was still their 'hardest year'.[93]

How was such a controversial initiative sold to Margaret Thatcher, of all people? On the face of it, the Agreement seemed to violate all of her instincts. It prompted the resignation from her government of one of her most trusted supporters and advisers, Ian Gow, and damning condemnation by one of her political heroes, Enoch Powell. Once again this is a matter of debate, with some arguing that the Agreement was a typically courageous initiative on her part, brushing aside any opposition, while others argue that she was misled, almost tricked into agreeing to something she did not fully understand. Her own subsequent repudiation of the policy in her memoirs suggests that those commentators who saw it as less her handiwork and more that of ministers and officials (Douglas Hurd and Sir Robert Armstrong in particular) are right. Her own account is that she was persuaded to back the Agreement on the grounds that Unionist opposition would be half-hearted and short-lived and that there would be substantial security benefits accruing from a grateful Catholic minority and increased cross-border co-operation. This latter consideration seems to have been decisive. In her own words: 'The real question now was whether the agreement would result in better security.' While the Agreement certainly played an important part in enabling the SDLP to resist the rise of Sinn Fein, as far as security was concerned, the results were less favourable. Once again in her own words, the security situation 'in the province...worsened' after 1985. It soon became clear that 'the wider gains for which I had hoped from greater support by the nationalist minority in Northern Ireland or the Irish Government and people for the fight against terrorism were not going to be forthcoming'.[94]

In fact, in retrospect we can see the Anglo-Irish Agreement as preparing the way for the Downing Street Declaration of December 1993, the Provisionals' first ceasefire of 31 August 1994 and the Good Friday Agreement of 10 April 1998. It provided the framework for gradual progress towards a political settlement and even more importantly it survived an all-out Protestant assault. The defeat of the Protestants was a necessary pre-condition for any successful compromise. From this point of view the Agreement can be seen as providing the political underpinning for the internal security strategy that had been put in place in the mid-1970s. While the security forces successfully contained the IRA, even in the aftermath of the hunger strikes, the Anglo-Irish Agreement was eventually to open the way for secret negotiations to end the war. There was still a long way to go, however.

The dirty war goes on

The Provisional IRA's expectation was that the increased popular support for their cause that had accrued during the hunger strikes would provide the basis for a renewed offensive that would make the British position in Northern Ireland untenable. The slogan of 'the armalite and the ballot box' encapsulated a strategy of advancing on two fronts simultaneously: intensifying the war and at the same time consolidating popular support on both sides of the border by building up Sinn Fein as an electoral machine. At the same time as the war was stepped up, the Provisionals proceeded to abandon abstentionism (November 1986) and embraced political participation. There was, however, an inevitable tension between these two approaches which was hidden while the movement seemed to be going forward, but was increasingly to come out into the open once it began to falter. For the time being, the armed struggle received a tremendous logistic boost in 1985–86 when the Provisionals succeeded in importing substantial quantities of weapons and explosives from Libya. Altogether over a hundred tons of material were successfully smuggled in and hidden away before the last and biggest shipment on the *Eksund* was captured in October 1987.[95] Undoubtedly this was a serious intelligence failure on the part of both the British and Irish intelligence services, leaving the Provisionals better armed than ever before. With this new weaponry the IRA hoped they would be able to increase security force casualties to a level that British public opinion would not be prepared to tolerate. This would, they hoped, put withdrawal on the agenda. With a solid electoral base giving it political legitimacy, Sinn Fein would be able to negotiate with the British government from a position of strength. This was not to be.

Throughout the 1980s, the security forces continued successfully to contain the level of conflict in Northern Ireland; indeed, the fact is that fewer British soldiers were killed in that whole decade (96) than had been killed in 1972 alone (103). Whenever the IRA tried to increase their level of activity, the security forces were able to inflict too high a level of casualties for it to be sustained. While the Provisionals had become increasingly sophisticated, so had the British. Surveillance techniques, intelligence-gathering, agent-handling and covert operations had all improved out of all recognition compared with the early 1970s. The death of eight heavily armed IRA volunteers, all wearing body armour, in an attack on Loughall RUC station on 8 May 1987 was the most dramatic testimony to this. The SAS killed them from ambush.[96]

This so-called 'dirty war' did have unfortunate drawbacks as far as the British were concerned. The officially condoned 'shoot-to-kill' practice of covert RUC and SAS squads might have been effective as a way of permanently eliminating INLA and IRA volunteers, but it was widely perceived within the Catholic working class as little better than murder. The security forces were shooting republican paramilitaries, as often as not unarmed, while signally failing to take such action against the loyalist paramilitaries who were taking such a terrible toll of Catholic lives. There is no doubt that the 'mimetic effect' Charles Townshend warned about came into effect in the 1980s. In November and December 1982, RUC undercover squads shot dead six unarmed

IRA and INLA volunteers in three separate incidents. Between December 1983 and February 1985 another ten men were shot dead by SAS undercover squads. As Mark Urban has convincingly shown, this involved a dramatic change in approach by the security forces. He argues that if one accepted the official line then one would have to conclude that the difference between those years when the SAS invariably succeeded in arresting IRA members, including those carrying weapons (1978–83), and those years when they invariably shot them, including those not carrying arms (1983–85), was that in the latter years the Provisionals developed a suicidal tendency to make threatening movements and gestures when challenged.[97]

The grim sequence of events initiated by the Gibraltar shootings of 6 March 1988 demonstrates the apparently intractable nature of this low level 'dirty war'. The killing of three unarmed IRA members by the SAS (they were riddled with bullets) was inevitably regarded by the Provisionals' working-class supporters as another instance of the security forces murdering their opponents. Sean Savage, Daniel McCann and Mairead Farrell might well have been on active service intending to carry out a bomb attack that would certainly have killed and maimed civilians, but they could have been arrested. There was no need for them to be 'executed' in the way they were. Moreover, this incident initiated a dreadful cycle of violence. Ten days later when the three were being buried at Milltown Cemetery in Belfast, a lone loyalist paramilitary, Michael Stone, made a gun and grenade attack on the mourners, killing three people and wounding another 50. When one of these three victims was being buried on 19 March, two undercover soldiers, members of the clandestine Force Research Unit, were seized and beaten by the mourners, handed over to the IRA and promptly killed.[98] What was clear was the extent to which the undercover war fed upon itself. If the three IRA volunteers in Gibraltar had been arrested instead of shot, then the subsequent events that left another five people dead, and led to a dramatic increase in tension in the province, would never have taken place. As Ian Kearns has argued, one consequence of the undercover war was 'to undermine the benefits of Ulsterization, to limit the impact of the Agreement and to provide the Provisional IRA with propaganda victories'.[99]

The killing of the two undercover soldiers on 19 March was the last straw for Margaret Thatcher. With the IRA campaign continuing without any apparent end in sight, she demanded a full security review. This, she insisted, must consider the ending of police primacy, the reintroduction of internment, the banning of Sinn Fein, the introduction of identity cards, the ending of dual citizenship for the citizens of the Irish

Republic, the relaxation of yellow card instructions and the banning of IRA spokesmen and women from the broadcast media. These proposals would have involved a decisive change in British strategy, with the ending of the internal security approach and a return to counterinsurgency. They would have meant the end of the Anglo-Irish Agreement, worsened relations with the Irish government and have made possible a rapprochement with the Unionists. It was not to be. Whatever the Prime Minister's frustration at not achieving a decisive victory over the IRA, her security advisers recognised that such measures would throw away the considerable advances already made and would instead seriously aggravate the situation, escalating the conflict and, far from weakening the IRA, would actually strengthen it. The security review's actual recommendations involved a strengthening of police primacy and only satisfied Thatcher with regard to the much-derided prohibition on Sinn Fein spokesmen and women speaking their own lines on the broadcast media! Security strategy remained one of containment rather than the pursuit of an illusory military victory.[100]

One important point when discussing 'shoot-to-kill' operations is to recognise that while they undoubtedly took place, they only took place on a limited scale. Many commentators on the right have argued that if the army, and in particular the SAS, had been allowed just to assassinate significant numbers of known republican activists and IRA members, then the conflict would have been over in months, if not weeks. Certainly there have been occasions when such methods have produced the required results, with the Argentinian 'disappearances' of the 1970s as the best example.[101] This was never a serious option in Northern Ireland. The balance of class forces in Britain, the political culture of liberal democracy, the British government's international relationships and the certainty of the conflict spreading to the South precluded such a strategy. Only a military dictatorship could have implemented an 'Argentinian' solution, and while this was talked about in some circles in the 1970s it was more to do with the class struggle in Britain than the war in Northern Ireland. In practice the loyalist paramilitaries were to substitute for state death squads, but even their level of activity never approached South American levels. What might have changed this situation is if the IRA attempt to assassinate Thatcher and other Cabinet members in Brighton in October 1984 had been successful. While the republicans seem to have believed that this might well have broken British resolve, it is much more likely that the response would have been increased repression, in particular the shooting, whether by undercover soldiers or loyalist paramilitaries, of senior Sinn Fein and IRA members.

Nevertheless, the IRA campaign was in serious difficulties. The organization had been seriously penetrated by the British to an extent that is still unclear but that clearly constituted a major success for British intelligence. The revelation in May 2003 that Freddie Scappaticci, code name 'Stakeknife', a senior IRA man, had been a British agent since 1978 came as a complete shock to the republican leadership.[102] He seems to have been the tip of the iceberg. Attacks on the security forces were proving extremely costly for the IRA, while attacks on soft targets resulted in civilian casualties which lost the movement support. The Remembrance Day bombing in Enniskillen on 8 November 1987 which left 11 people killed and over 60 injured was a particularly appalling example of this. Indeed, the situation could have been much worse on that day because, incredibly, the IRA had targeted two other bombs on the Tullyhommon War Memorial and the British Legion headquarters in Belfast but these were discovered and made safe. This sort of incident, with the attendant casualties, whether intentional or not, undermined Catholic working-class support for the IRA and cost Sinn Fein votes as well as provoking Protestant retaliation. Gerry Adams personally repudiated the Enniskillen attack which he described as 'a terrible mistake'.[103] Whereas in the 1983 Westminster general election Sinn Fein had polled 13.4 per cent of the votes compared with the SDLP's 17.9 per cent, by the 1987 general election the Sinn Fein vote had fallen to 11.4 per cent while the SDLP's had risen to 21.1 per cent. The 1992 general election showed the Sinn Fein position continuing to deteriorate with 10 per cent of the vote compared with the SDLP's 23.5 per cent. A growing proportion of the Catholic working class were voting SDLP, with Sinn Fein increasingly becoming the party of the Catholic unemployed.[104] The reality was that, by the end of the 1980s, both the IRA and Sinn Fein threats had been successfully contained and the republican movement was without any realistic prospect of victory. The Adams–Morrison leadership decided to open negotiations and seek terms but not, it must be said, from the position of strength they had intended.

Bombing Britain

One way in which the Provisionals tried to strengthen their hand was through a renewed bombing campaign in Britain, carried out by the IRA's England Department. This was not the first bombing offensive to be carried out in Britain. Indeed, earlier campaigns had produced the

Guildford pub bombings of 5 October 1974, which killed five people and injured 54, and the Birmingham pub bombings of 21 November that same year that killed 21 people and injured 180. These two incidents seriously undermined support for the IRA in Northern Ireland at the time, but were later to be turned into propaganda victories by the refusal of the British government to release those wrongly convicted of the attacks. The mishandling of the cases of the Maguire Seven and the Birmingham Six did tremendous damage to the reputation of the British judicial system both at home and abroad.[105] As we have seen, on 12 October 1982, the IRA were nearly to wipe out Margaret Thatcher and her Cabinet when they bombed the Grand Hotel in Brighton during the Conservative Party Conference. At the end of the 1980s they launched a new campaign.

On 22 September 1989 ten Royal Marine bandsmen were killed when the IRA bombed their barracks at Deal in Kent (security at the barracks had been privatised!). This opened an intensive campaign that saw the Carlton Club bombed (26 June 1990), the Stock Exchange bombed (20 July) and Conservative MP Ian Gow assassinated by a car bomb (30 July). The following year during the Gulf War the IRA made a daring mortar attack on Downing Street. The most devastating attack, however, was the bombing of the Baltic Exchange in the City of London on 10 April 1991. This left three people dead and caused widespread damage that was to cost the British government more in compensation than had been paid out in total in Northern Ireland since the start of the war. Attacks continued throughout 1992 and into 1993. The most serious was the bombing in Warrington on 20 March 1993 which killed two children (one aged 3 and another aged 12) and injured 55 people. This was followed by the bombing of the Nat West Tower in the City of London on 24 April 1993, which left one person dead and caused damage to offices over a mile away. The cost of the damage caused by this bomb was estimated at over a billion pounds.[106] As Paul Dixon has pointed out, these operations show that British penetration of the IRA, while very successful, nevertheless did have its limits.[107] These attacks were the explosive accompaniment to the peace feelers that the Provisionals were putting out, an attempt to strengthen their position in the negotiations that were to come. Martin McGuinness supposedly asked for British help in bringing the war to an end: 'The conflict is over but we need your advice on how to bring it to a close.' In fact, this message was fabricated by the mediator, Father Denis Bradley to ensure that the British took the republican overtures seriously.[108]

The road to ceasefire

The war in Northern Ireland had clearly stalled as far as the Provisionals were concerned even before the 31 August 1994 ceasefire. In 1991 the IRA had killed five British soldiers, in 1992 three and in 1993 three. Operations in Belfast had become almost impossible to mount. Moreover, an indication of British success in penetrating the organisation is provided by the fact that in 1992 it executed six of its own members as 'touts', double the number of soldiers killed.[109] At the same time, both the republican movement in particular and the Catholic minority in general were coming under renewed loyalist attack. In the 1980s British covert agencies began to make increasing use of the loyalist paramilitaries, providing them with intelligence and giving their activities direction. The Brian Nelson affair revealed a degree of collusion between the Force Research Unit (FRU) and UFF that points quite clearly to the loyalist death squads acting as proxies for the British.[110] This campaign was an important factor in bringing about the IRA ceasefire. With South African weapons and British intelligence the loyalists became increasingly effective, killing more people than the IRA. In 1992 the loyalists killed 37 people while the IRA killed 33, and in 1993 the loyalists killed 46 to the IRA's 36. These attacks were increasingly targeted on republican activists, their families and friends, although random killings continued as well. On 23 October 1993, in what seems to have been an act of desperation, the IRA attempted to eliminate the UDA leadership which was believed to be meeting over Frizzel's fish shop on the Shankill Road. Their intelligence was wrong and the bomb killed nine shoppers, including two children and one of the bomb team. The loyalist response was immediate with an attack on the crowded Greysteel bar in which eight people were shot dead, seven of them Catholics. This seems to have convinced the republican leadership that the worsening sectarian conflict could not be stopped by an armed response. Indeed, this only made the situation worse. The arguments in favour of a ceasefire were overwhelming. John Taylor, the then Deputy Leader of the Ulster Unionists was clear that the loyalist paramilitaries had 'achieved something which perhaps the security forces would never have achieved'. They had 'actually begun to overtake the IRA as being the major paramilitary and terrorist organisation in Northern Ireland'. They had made 'a significant contribution to the IRA finally accepting that they couldn't win'. The part played by the loyalist terror campaign in wearing down the Catholic community has not yet received enough attention in the academic literature.[111]

The first IRA ceasefire lasted from the end of August 1994 until February 1996. It was called off because of the lack of progress that was being made in negotiations due to the dependence of John Major's Conservative government on Unionist votes in the House of Commons. This lack of progress strengthened the hand of those elements within the republican movement opposed to ending the war. The renewal of hostilities, with the Provisionals taking considerable care to avoid provoking the loyalist paramilitaries, was a disaster for the IRA in the North. Its Belfast units were arrested and its key South Armagh sniper team were captured.[112] By this time the British had called a halt to 'shoot-to-kill' operations, recognising that this would get in the way of reopening negotiations. For their part, IRA volunteers were increasingly reluctant to die in a cause that was likely to be settled by some sort of negotiated compromise. British successes inevitably strengthened the hand of the Adams–McGuinness leadership within the movement, while, at the same time, the return to hostilities also forced the British into serious negotiations. While on the defensive in Northern Ireland, the IRA still carried out the bombing of Canary Wharf on 9 February, killing two civilians and causing damage to the tune of £100 million, and of Manchester city centre on 15 June causing £400 million in damage. These attacks showed that the organization could still mount 'spectaculars'. All this further strengthened the Adams–McGuinness position. In the run-up to the 1997 general election, the Provisional IRA mounted a 'chaos' campaign in Britain. This involved the planting of small bombs accompanied by numerous hoax bomb warnings that successfully paralysed 'large parts of England'.[113] The election of Tony Blair's New Labour government with a large majority, which effectively ended the Unionists' ability to hold up proceedings, saw a reopening of negotiations. In July 1997 the Provisional IRA renewed its ceasefire, preparing the way for the Good Friday Agreement of 10 April 1998 and the establishment of the devolved executive at the end of November 1999. Two Sinn Fein ministers took office in a Northern Ireland government headed by David Trimble, one of the men who had brought down Sunningdale.

What of the Good Friday Agreement? How can it be characterised? There is no doubt that it represented a 'strategic defeat' for Irish republicanism.[114] Adams and McGuinness had embraced a settlement that only a few years ago would have been regarded as treason. If anyone had ever suggested either of them would become ministers in a Northern Ireland government, such person would have been considered insane. Nevertheless, there is little doubt that most Catholics considered the

Agreement a victory, not least a victory over the Protestant supremacists. The republicans had successfully won political equality for the Catholic minority. There is an important element of truth in this. The Adams–McGuinness leadership's success in avoiding a serious split in the republican movement is a reflection of this. The breakaway republicans were not a serious military factor, capable only of making symbolic gestures, which can go horrifically wrong as at Omagh in August 1998. On the Unionist side, it seems clear that while the Trimble leadership regard the settlement as a defeat for republicanism, much of Protestant opinion still considers anything short of a return to Stormont as defeat and betrayal. The annual Drumcree confrontation, the Orange 'Groundhog Day', as it was described, provided an opportunity for Protestant supremacists to show their strength.[115] The Agreement survived this challenge. At this point it is worth admitting that the author in the first edition of this book still thought it lay very much within the power of the Protestants to eventually make the Agreement unworkable. In fact, even the Paisleyite DUP's election victory in the November 2003 Assembly elections did not derail the so-called peace process. Indeed on 8 May 2007, Ian Paisley became First Minister of Northern Ireland with Sinn Fein's Martin McGuinness as deputy First Minister.[116] This settlement is, of course, still fragile and could yet collapse with a return to direct rule and renewed violence if the DUP ever found itself in the position to impose its demands on a British government, either Conservative or Labour, that needed its votes at Westminster. At the time of writing, talks have taken place between the DUP and the Conservatives over just such a scenario if the 2015 general election should result in another hung Parliament. Nevertheless, for the moment the 30 years war is at an end.

As for the British, while they certainly did not achieve their preferred solution (the destruction of the IRA), they have achieved a settlement that is compatible with British interests, a settlement that involved the republican movement compromising its historic objectives, abandoning the armed struggle and embracing constitutional politics.

8
America's Wars: Afghanistan and Iraq

The 9/11 attacks were the most devastating terrorist attacks in history. The death toll of 2977 people, old, young, women, men, from all walks of life, including over 400 firefighters and other emergency workers, and the spectacle of some 200 people choosing to jump to their deaths rather than die in the flames, were a tremendous blow. Nevertheless, despite its enormity, it was still a terrorist attack – a remarkably successful attack, but of no real strategic importance. Despite the number of fatalities (more than were inflicted at Pearl Harbor, where 2403, mainly servicemen, were killed), it was more a blow to American prestige and self-regard than it was a serious threat to US interests and power. The United States was by far the world's most powerful country before the attacks and it remained by far the most powerful country after them. Indeed, 9/11 did not affect the strategic position of the United States at all. It was the ill-judged nature of the US response that did that. Al-Qaeda was a terrorist threat, at best a few hundred strong, certainly capable of symbolic, indeed spectacular, attacks, but it could not at any stretch of the imagination be seriously considered as a military threat. Instead of responding to the attacks as a terrorist threat, however, the Bush administration chose to use them as a way of reasserting US power in the Middle East, as an opportunity to move against those states – Iraq, Iran and Syria – that were seen as obstacles to US domination of the region. Indeed, the terrorist threat actually posed by al-Qaeda was quickly relegated to the back burner, apparently not taken seriously despite all the rhetoric, while the imaginary terrorist threat posed by Saddam Hussein was given absolute priority in order to provide justification for the full-scale invasion of Iraq. While President Bush proclaimed a 'War on Terror', this was primarily a propaganda exercise, an ideological construct, intended to provide justification for the aggressive unilateralist foreign policy that his administration had always intended to pursue.

What is extraordinary is that this determination to marginalise the real terrorist threat in favour of taking advantage of the situation that 9/11 had created to pursue a policy of military aggression in the Middle East was present right from the beginning. Richard Clarke, the senior counter-terrorism official, later recalled how when he arrived at the White House in the early hours of 12 September, he had expected 'a round of meetings examining what the next attacks could be, what our vulnerabilities were, what we could do about them in the short term', and instead, 'I walked into a series of discussions about Iraq'. Later in the morning, Donald Rumsfeld's deputy at the Department of Defense, Paul Wolfowitz, was insisting that no terrorist group could have carried out the attack unaided and that 'Iraq must have been helping them'. By the afternoon Defense Secretary Rumsfeld was himself advocating 'getting Iraq', prompting Clarke to remark to Colin Powell, the Secretary of State, that this would be as if the United States had attacked Mexico in retaliation for the Japanese attack on Pearl Harbor. Later in the day, Rumsfeld was to advocate bombing Iraq, to which President George W. Bush responded that it would not be enough to hit Iraq with cruise missiles, instead 'what we needed to do with Iraq was to change the government'. Looking back, Clarke remarks that any President was likely to 'have ended the Afghan sanctuary by invading' and to have 'stepped up domestic security and preparedness measures'. But he goes on: 'In the end, what was unique about George Bush's reaction to terrorism was his selection as an object lesson for potential state sponsors of terrorism not a country that had been engaging in anti-US terrorism but one that had not been, Iraq. It is hard to imagine another President making that choice.'[1] This is somewhat unfair to Bush, it has to be said. He was to a considerable extent a figurehead President, a folksy nonentity, whose role had been to win the Presidential election and thereby secure the installation in office of a group of neo-conservative ideologues with huge ambitions regarding the exercise of US power. Vice President Dick Cheney has much more claim to have been the effective head of the administration than Bush, who was from the very beginning completely out of his depth.[2] Reshaping the Middle East in America's interests was very much a priority for the neo-cons, and 9/11 was to be the perfect pretext for getting their adventure underway. The fact that 9/11 was an attack made by a Saudi-led terrorist group based in Afghanistan, financed by money from Saudi donors, and was actually carried out in the main by

Saudis (15 out of the 19 attackers were Saudis) was of little account in the bigger picture of things.

One point worth making here is that while the rhetoric has been very much about the 'War on Terror' since 9/11, in practice the United States has invaded and occupied Iraq, helped in the overthrow of Gaddafi in Libya and assisted in the attempted overthrow of Asad in Syria. All these interventions have been aimed at eliminating regimes that refused to acquiesce in US domination of the Middle East and beyond. Far from making any contribution to the defeat of the terrorist threat, they have been responsible for it developing into a real threat, to the Middle East at least, on a scale that would have been unimaginable even ten years ago. At the time of writing, the Islamic State not only controls much of Syria and Iraq, but according to one authoritative commentator may have more than 100 000 men under arms.[3] Clearly, the so-called War on Terror has been an unmitigated disaster from which the Islamist terrorists have emerged stronger than ever. But, as we have seen, it was not a war against terror at all. Instead, it was a series of interventions to remove governments that were hostile to the United States, with the downside being that the terrorists have been able to take advantage of the ensuing chaos. While the United States and its allies were strong enough to bring governments down, they have not been strong enough to determine what succeeds them.

What seems to have been responsible for this catastrophic series of misjudgements, at least as far as the Bush administration was concerned, was a belief in American invincibility now that the Cold War had been won. American power had brought down the Soviet Union and must now surely be able to deal with those petty regimes that the Russians had given protection to. Surely now the world could be remade in America's image. Moreover, there was a belief that war had been revolutionised by developments in technology and communications, the so-called Revolution in Military Affairs (RMA), and that this had immeasurably strengthened the United States. The US military was in a position to destroy rival armies almost without breaking a sweat. The United States was irresistible and all that remained was to find the will to exercise this enormous power. Vice President Cheney himself provides evidence of this new confidence in American power. He had been Secretary for Defence during the first Gulf War and had then made absolutely clear that the Americans had not proceeded to invade and occupy Iraq after they had defeated Saddam Hussein's army because of the danger of getting involved in a 'quagmire'. With remarkable prescience, he went on:

Once we got to Baghdad, what would we do? Who would we put in power? What kind of government would we have? Would it be a Sunni government, a Shia government, a Kurdish government? Would it be secular along the lines of the Baath Party? Would it be fundamentalist Islamic? I do not think the United States wants to have US military forces accept casualties and accept the responsibility of trying to govern Iraq... If you don't have a clear cut military objective, if you're not prepared to use overwhelming force to achieve it, then we don't have any business committing US military forces into that civil war.[4]

What had changed between 1991 and 2001? Certainly there was more than one factor at work, but what seems to have been decisive was the belief that US military might was irresistible, indeed so much so that 'overwhelming force' was no longer necessary. The United States was now so powerful that it could to all intents and purposes do what it liked with the world.

For the British, the problem was that the New Labour government, which had come to power in 1997, shared this view of American power. The Prime Minister, Tony Blair, in particular, was enamoured by all things American. The touchstone of his foreign policy was the so-called Special Relationship. What this amounted to was the British conviction that they benefited from being America's closest, most reliable and therefore 'special' ally, that they shared in the exercise of America's global power. To sustain this 'Special Relationship', some would say illusion of a 'Special Relationship', Blair was, as he made clear, prepared to pay a 'blood price'. Now, of course, the 'Special Relationship' had been at the centre of British foreign policy both during and since the Second World War. The Attlee Labour government had, of course, been prepared to pay the 'blood price' in Korea, although the Wilson Labour government had later refused the request for troops to be sent to Vietnam ('All we needed was one regiment. The Black Watch would have done. Just one regiment', in the words of Dean Rusk).[5] Nevertheless even Wilson had given the Americans all the support he could short of sending troops.[6] When Blair argued that not to support the Americans 'would be the biggest shift in foreign policy for 50 years', he was absolutely right, but the Bush administration was something new and dangerous, and as Wilson had shown, support did not necessarily have to involve the commitment of troops.[7] Bush's much-trumpeted phrase, 'the Axis of Evil', to describe the unlikely alliance of Iraq, Iran and North Korea, clearly owed more to American superhero comic books than it did to any serious appreciation of the international situation. Britain was eager to be Robin to America's Batman. The administration's embrace of unilateralism and pre-emptive military action should have served as a warning. Blair, however, regarded the 'Special Relationship' with particular fervour, a fervour that reflected not only his awareness of the extent to which British power had declined, the extent to which the protection of British interests was dependent on the United States, but also his belief that with the ending of the Cold War, the Americans were now all powerful. As Jonathan Powell, Blair's Chief of Staff, somewhat graphically put it to the new British ambassador to Washington DC, Christopher Meyer, his job was 'to get up the arse of the White House and stay there'.[8] This was a pretty fair summation of British foreign policy under Blair.

As was to become clear, Blair actually shared much of the neo-cons' world view and was indeed to embrace it with increasing enthusiasm as time went by. As far as he was concerned, 'our alliance with the US gave Britain a huge position' and he thought the British people 'admired the fact I counted, was a big player, was a world and not just a national leader'.[9] His modesty was only equalled by Bush's intellect. Certainly some of his colleagues were impressed, with the Foreign Secretary, Jack Straw, describing him admiringly as 'effectively the vice-president of the free world'.[10] Britain might not be a 'superpower' any more, but by positioning itself close to the United States, Britain remained, according to Blair, 'a pivotal power'.[11] Blair was prepared, indeed, determined, to pay the 'blood price' in order to maintain the 'Special Relationship'. On one occasion he was specifically asked by a reporter, Michael Cockerell, if he was willing 'to pay the blood price' for the 'Special Relationship' and replied with an unequivocal 'Yes...They need to know, are you prepared to commit, to be there when the shooting starts.'[12] As far as Blair was concerned, British troops were going to be there when the Americans went in Afghanistan, Iraq or anywhere else. They would be going in for the sake of the 'Special Relationship', but other pretexts would, of course, have to be invented for domestic consumption. This deception would not matter, though, because there was a confident expectation that given US military might, these wars would be little more than victory parades with the British and, of course, Blair himself sharing in the plaudits.

Looking back on these events in his memoirs, Blair does not have that much to say about George W. Bush, but does go out of his way to praise Vice President Cheney for his commitment to the 'War on Terror'. Cheney was wholeheartedly committed to defeating the terrorists, 'the rogue states that supported them', and their 'guiding ideology', confronting them 'head-on, with maximum American strength'. Cheney 'would have worked through the whole lot, Iraq, Syria, Iran, dealing with all their surrogates...Hizbollah, Hamas etc. In other words, he thought the world had to be made anew...he was for hard, hard power. No ifs, no buts, no maybes. We're coming for you.' While Blair conceded that Cheney underestimated the importance of diplomacy and did not appreciate the utility of 'soft power', nevertheless, 'there was much to be said for his insight'.[13] What this really reminds us is that however bad things were to become, given Blair's mindset, they could easily have been even worse.

Into Afghanistan

According to Sherard Cowper-Coles, the increasingly disillusioned British ambassador to Afghanistan from 2007 until 2009, there was a real possibility that the Taliban could have eventually been persuaded to hand over Osama Bin Laden.[14] Any prevarication was clearly going to be unacceptable to the United States, however. The Bush administration needed to demonstrate both its military might and its readiness to use it. Given this, the Taliban failure to immediately hand Bin Laden over was an act of criminal stupidity that plunged their already war-ravaged country into yet another conflict that, at the time of writing, has still not come to an end. There is a strong possibility that Bin Laden hoped to provoke a US invasion and occupation of Afghanistan, confident that such an adventure would suffer the same fate as the Russian occupation. War in Afghanistan, having brought down the Soviet Union, might yet also bring down the American Empire. The cost of driving out the Russians had been horrendous, however. Perhaps as many as one and a half million Afghans had died in the war and its bloody aftermath, another four million had been wounded, many of them permanently disabled (according to Ahmed Rashid, the Taliban leadership was 'the most disabled in the world today' because of injuries suffered fighting the Russians),[15] and another five million became refugees. This was out of a total population of some 23 million. The war was, of course, sponsored by the United States, eager to inflict a 'Vietnam' on the Soviet Union, financing and arming many of the people it would later find itself fighting against. Once the Russians had withdrawn and the Najibullah regime had been overthrown, there followed a bloody civil war that left the country in the hands of the warlords whose main source of income was opium production and trafficking.

The Taliban movement had arisen as a response to their depredations. With Pakistani support, a deeply conservative Islamist movement led by Mullah Omar had successfully taken control of most of the country. While seen in the West as misogynist enemies of women, the Taliban saw themselves as the defenders of women, putting a stop to the rape that had been endemic under the warlords. Theirs was a backwards obscurantist rural Islam,[16] however, that was certainly experienced as oppression by many Afghans, both men and women, even if the Taliban brought a degree of security and stamped out corruption. The Shura the Taliban established to govern Kabul, a city of 1.2 million people, did not include a single Kabuli and most of its members had never even visited a big city before, let alone lived in one. The prohibition on women working that they introduced was not just oppressive towards women, but also closed down much of what remained of the civil service, primary education and the health service. They did not, however, prohibit girls' education, just co-education. Indeed, according to James Ferguson, it was 'probable that more Kabuli girls were educated under the Taliban than in the preceding era'. The real problem was that the country was so poor and war-ravaged that there were few schools for anyone. Ferguson argues that given the country's poverty, 'the Kabul government's achievements were actually remarkable. The absence of official corruption meant that a little money went far.' At the same time, the Taliban prohibited just about every form of entertainment, male homosexuals were executed and a narrow puritanical Islam was imposed by force. This was clearly not an Islam adapted to the realities of modern, urban living. And, of course, by no means did all Afghan Muslims share the Taliban attitude anyway. The Shia Hazara, an over 3 million strong minority, had a much more egalitarian attitude towards gender relations, with women being both politically and economically active and even fighting alongside men in their militia. Moreover, it is important to remember that Afghanistan had once been a country known for its tolerance of religious difference. The years of war had seen the triumph of sectarian intolerance, emerging from backwards rural areas, positively encouraged by the Saudis and now embodied in the Taliban.[17]

The United States and the British would have not had any serious problem with the Taliban's reactionary domestic rule if only they had been prepared to accommodate themselves to Western interests. Public beheadings and amputations might be unsavoury and the oppression of women something to be regretted, but they had never been allowed to stand in the way of good relations with Saudi Arabia. Indeed, the

United States and Britain both positively courted the Saudis. And, of course, there were numerous occasions where both the British and the Americans had supported Islamists against secular nationalists and communists both in the Middle East and elsewhere and been remarkably unconcerned about the atrocities they committed. Instead, though the Taliban gave sanctuary to Bin Laden and al-Qaeda, he repaid them by exploiting their gullibility to once again bring the horrors of war to Afghanistan.

One measure that the Taliban did get some credit for in the West was their 2000 prohibition of the growing of the opium poppy, a prohibition that was remarkably successful. Indeed, their success was pretty much unique with only Communist China having had similar success immediately after the Revolution. The only part of the country where opium production still continued was that controlled by the Northern Alliance where some 200 tons was produced. Ironically, prohibition certainly contributed to the ease with which they were to be overthrown, having impoverished and alienated many of their erstwhile supporters. And, of course, in allying itself with the warlords of the Northern Alliance against the Taliban, the United States was allying itself with the drug traffickers.

The defeat of the Taliban is often celebrated as a remarkable feat of arms, with a handful of intrepid American CIA operatives (110) and special forces personnel (316), leading 15 000–20 000 Northern Alliance fighters to victory. The Taliban supposedly had some 60 000 troops, of whom perhaps 15 000 were foreign fighters, but were nevertheless overthrown in three months with only one American fatality from enemy action. While US air attacks were decisive militarily with up to a hundred sorties a day, nevertheless an ebbing away of support lubricated by often massive bribes was an essential feature of the success. Between 7 October 2001 and the end of January 2002, US planes flew 25 000 sorties, dropping some 12 000 bombs and firing 6700 guided munitions. AC130 gunships carried out devastating attacks on Taliban positions. They were simply obliterated by giant 15 000-lb BLU 82 'daisy cutter' bombs. Under the weight of the bombardment the Taliban broke. They suffered some 15 000 dead, 20 000 wounded and 7000 captured. Many of the prisoners were to be killed by their Northern Alliance captors. But Bin Laden himself and the Taliban leadership successfully escaped death or capture, fleeing across the border into Pakistan. America's allies themselves proved susceptible to bribery in return for letting America's enemies escape. Nevertheless, according to George Tenet, CIA Director at the time, it 'has to rank as one of the greatest successes in the Agency's history'.[18] British forces played a largely token role in this victory.

In fact, while the Taliban had been driven out of Afghanistan and al-Qaeda had certainly been dealt a serious blow, the leadership had astonishingly been allowed to escape. The man responsible for 9/11 was still at large. More important though, in order to achieve even this result, the Americans had, once again, handed Afghanistan over to the warlords and the drug traffickers. It was as if they had attacked Colombia in order to install the drug cartels in power. To some extent this was concealed by the installation of the presentable Hamid Karzai as President of Afghanistan on 10 June 2002. It is easy to forget today, but at the time, he was hailed in some quarters as another Nelson Mandela.[19] Soon after his government was installed in power its gangster character was amply demonstrated by the assassination of one of the two Vice Presidents, Abdul Qadir, shot dead on his way to a meeting with Karzai. It was widely believed that his killing had been ordered by the other Vice President, Fahim Khan, who was also Minister of Defence, the most powerful Northern Alliance warlord with an income 'estimated at nearly US$1 billion per year'. Qadir was apparently an opponent of the opium trade and was removed accordingly.[20] In fact, most of the later difficulties that were to transpire in Afghanistan were to derive from the handing over of the country to a wholly corrupt administration dominated by drug traffickers and warlords, thereby effectively ensuring the eventual return of the Taliban. What should also have given pause was the fact that there was no way that the Northern Alliance could have conceivably defeated the Taliban without US support, which surely suggested that the new government would only survive with a continuation of that support.

The United States had no real interest in what now happened to Afghanistan, and was already preparing for an attack on Iraq. Afghanistan was of no strategic importance, whereas Iraq was the key to domination of the Middle East. Britain and other NATO countries were more committed to attempting to support the Karzai government, although not to any extent that made a significant difference. The neglect of Afghanistan is startling. According to one account, Afghanistan received 'one of the lowest levels of troops, police and financial assistance in any stabilization operation since World War II'.[21] As part of this stabilization commitment, in 2002 Britain volunteered to take responsibility for the eradication of opium production. Between 2001 and 2007 opium production increased from 185 tons to 8200 tons.[22]

On to Iraq

The problem with invading Iraq was finding an adequate pretext. When neither the US nor British governments could come up with one, they invaded anyway. Nevertheless, a desperate attempt was made with Iraq's supposed links with al-Qaeda gaining some traction in the United States, while in Britain, it was Iraq's supposed possession of Weapons of Mass Destruction (WMDs) that seemed most serviceable. This was also seen by the Blair government as the best hope of securing United Nations backing for an invasion. In the event, the Bush administration argued that not only did Iraq have WMDs, but also that the country was on the verge of developing nuclear weapons that it almost certainly would hand over to Islamist terrorists. On 7 October 2002, speaking at the Cincinnati Museum Centre, Bush told his audience that: 'While there are many dangers in the world, the threat from Iraq stands alone.' He went on: 'We know that Iraq and the al-Qaeda terrorist network have had high level contacts that go back more than a decade...that after September 11, Saddam Hussein's regime gleefully celebrated the terrorist attack on America' and that 'Iraq could decide on any given day to provide a biological or chemical weapon to a terrorist group or individual terrorists.' The key passage, however, was this grim warning:

> If the Iraq regime is able to produce, buy or steal an amount of highly enriched uranium a little larger than a single softball, it could have a nuclear weapon in less than a year. And if we allow that to happen a terrible line will have been crossed. Saddam would be in a position to blackmail anyone who opposes his aggression. He would be in a position to dominate the Middle East. He would be in a position to threaten America. And Saddam Hussein would be in a position to pass nuclear technology to terrorists...Facing clear evidence of peril, we cannot wait for the final proof – the smoking gun – that could come in the form of a mushroom cloud.[23]

When Colin Powell spoke to the United Nations on 5 February 2003, he actually provided a detailed breakdown of Iraq's WMD stocks: 'up to 25 000 litres of anthrax and 400 associated bombs, 18 mobile biological weapons manufacturing facilities, 550 artillery shells with mustard gas, 30 000 empty munitions and enough precursors to stockpile as much as 500 tons of chemical agents and several dozen Scud variant ballistic missiles.'[24] None of this was true and, moreover, it can be convincingly argued that the US plans for invasion, while paying lip service to Iraqi possession of WMDs, were actually predicated on them not having them. According to one of Rumsfeld's biographers, 'although Saddam was marketed as a threat to the national security of the United States, Rumsfeld's experts privately believed that his regime was a house of cards, needing only a nudge'.[25] Despite this, in the United States, public opinion was won over. In Britain, however, the Blair government faced massive opposition from the Stop the War movement which organised the biggest protest march in British history on 15 February 2003, with well over a million people taking part. Stop the War certainly won the argument in the country but not in the House of Commons.[26] Blair became increasingly committed to the neo-con project, actually arguing on one occasion that 'if the Americans were not doing this, I would be pressing for them to be doing so'.[27] The decision to go to war on a false prospectus in the face of widespread popular opposition was to do Blair himself irreparable damage and seriously compromised the war effort once it began to go wrong.

Even if Iraq had WMDs, part of the problem with the WMD pretext was, of course, that both the United States and Britain had acquiesced and indeed assisted in Iraq's earlier use of WMDs, of chemical weapons against Iran during the Iran–Iraq War. According to Peter Galbraith, 'American help with targeting was invaluable.' Even after they were used against the Iraqi Kurds at Halabja in March 1988, and Galbraith does not rule out US assistance in targeting even this attack, the United States still continued providing Saddam Hussein with intelligence that Iraq used to target its chemical weapons 'more accurately'.[28] And, of course, the regime's overwhelming concern was always with its own survival, which made it inconceivable that it would invite the sort of massive retaliation that would inevitably follow if it did actually assist a terrorist strike against the US homeland. The most cogent, forensic, dissection of the case for war was, however, provided by Labour MP Robin Cooke in the speech he made on 17 March 2002 on his resignation from Blair's government. Here, among other things, he pointed out that on the one hand the government was arguing that Saddam Hussein was a terrible danger and on the other that he could be overthrown without any real risk. As he put it: 'we cannot base our military strategy on the assumption that Saddam is weak and at the same time justify pre-emptive action on the claim that he is a threat.'[29] But this is, of course, exactly what Blair did.

Operation Iraqi Freedom

The United States had achieved an overwhelming military superiority by the millennium. Indeed, so much had already been apparent in the first Gulf War when the Iraqis were driven out of Kuwait. The Coalition forces routed an Iraqi Army of 30 divisions, suffering only 197 battlefield fatalities while inflicting more than 40 000 fatalities, indeed some estimates of Iraqi fatalities go as high as 100 000. This was a technological massacre comparable to the colonial wars of the 19th century (Omdurman in 1898 springs to mind with its 14 000 Sudanese dead and 48 British), but on a larger scale. As Stephen Melton observed: 'Never in history had a battle been so lopsided.'[30] Even more astonishing, according to Keith Shimko, the casualty rate was so low that statistically American men were safer in the military in the Gulf war zone than they were back in the United States![31] Even so, as we have seen, in 1991 the US administration recognised that defeating Saddam Hussein's army was a very different proposition from occupying the country and risking getting involved in a protracted guerrilla/civil war. By the new millennium, not only were the Americans quite correctly confident of their ability to defeat the Iraqi Army, but they had convinced themselves that they would be welcomed as liberators. The British shared these beliefs. John Simpson, the war correspondent and a veteran of 34 wars, was himself convinced that the Iraqi people 'would come out and greet the British and American troops with gratitude as liberators'. After all, in 1991 there had been large-scale rebellions against Baathist rule in the south of the country in the expectation of American intervention, rebellions that had been put down with considerable brutality and bloodshed. Why should it be any different now? What he underestimated was the bitterness and distrust generated by the US failure to intervene in 1991 together with the horrific impact of 'twelve years of American and British sponsored sanctions...The poor starved and their children died in unprecedented numbers.'[32] In retrospect, it was, he confessed, 'pretty stupid, you might think, to believe the Americans and British could destroy a country and then expect the victims to come out and cheer them in the street'.[33] The scale of the suffering inflicted on the Iraqi people by UN sanctions has never really been adequately acknowledged in the West, but there is considerable justice to Patrick Cockburn's description of sanctions as inflicting 'one of the great man-made disasters of the last half century'.[34]

While well aware of the damage that sanctions had done to Iraqi military capability, so that the enemy they faced in 2003 was known to be considerably weaker than the one they had defeated so easily in 1991, the Americans seriously underestimated the damage they had done to the Iraqi state and society. They believed that there was a strong secular Iraqi middle class that would not only welcome liberation but would also enthusiastically embrace free market values and put in place a functioning US-style democracy. This both exaggerated the strength that the Iraqi middle class had once had and completely underestimated the damage done to it over the previous 12 years by sanctions. An overwhelming case can be made that Rumsfeld's appreciation of the force needed to defeat Saddam Hussein was correct, but the problem was, as numerous participants and commentators have pointed out, the failure to plan for the day after the Iraqi defeat.

In the event, the attack on Iraq was launched on 19 March 2003, two days before the British expected, because the Americans thought they had an opportunity to kill Saddam Hussein by means of an air strike. The 'Special Relationship' is put in perspective by the fact that they told the Israelis of the change to the timetable while the British learned of it over the phone at the same time it was being broadcast on the TV news.[35] The British contributed 46 000 troops to the invasion, operating in the south of the country and taking Basra. Once again, the conflict was spectacularly one-sided, although this time, many Iraqi soldiers well aware of the disparity between the two sides wisely deserted. Many of the tanks destroyed by the advancing Allies had already been abandoned by their crews. A country that was invaded because of the danger it posed to the world, to the United States in particular, was defeated, with US troops occupying Baghdad, for the loss of 122 American and 33 British soldiers, and many of these fatalities were the result of 'friendly fire'. The disparity between the two sides is nicely illustrated by the account of the invasion provided by Bing West and Ray Smith, two former US Marines, accompanying the Marine contingent of the invasion force. They describe how, on one occasion, the Marines they were with had three Iraqi 122mm rockets fired at them and responded with 72 radar-guided rocket-assisted projectiles, each containing 108 bomblets. 'The arithmetic', they note, 'was daunting. The Iraqis had fired three rockets – the Marines answered with 7,776 bomblets.'[36] The invasion was best summed up by Keith Shimko when he described it as 'a wildly asymmetric affair in which the most powerful military the world has ever known took on an ill-equipped, poorly motivated and incompetently led opponent..."a walkover"'.[37] Nevertheless, defeat was to be almost immediately snatched from victory.

The force that had proven able to defeat the Iraqi Army comparatively effortlessly was completely unable to secure the country. Rumsfeld was confident that 100 000 US troops was an adequate number to occupy a country of 400 000 square miles, inhabited by 38 million people. As Shimko once again points out, in New York City, with a population of only 8 million, inhabiting 500 square miles, and which had not been wrecked by war and sanctions, there were 34 000 armed police.[38] And the Pentagon hoped to reduce this force to a maximum of 70 000, but hopefully only 30 000 within six months. The chronic inadequacy of the forces available was compounded by the fact that there was no plan for what to do once the war was won. This is not strictly true of course. There were plans but they were not acceptable to Rumsfeld. In 1998, General Anthony Zinni and his staff had drawn up OPLAN 1003–98, a detailed plan for the occupation of Iraq that recommended the deployment of 500 000 troops.[39] It was ignored. There was the 2002 'Future of Iraq Project' report, prepared by Tom Warrick of the State Department, which warned that the occupation would have to last a decade.[40] One senior British official wrote of an invasion plan that 'ran to 13 volumes; but it wasn't used, it was rejected'.[41] George Tenet later claimed that the CIA had accurately predicted many of the problems that would be faced in occupied Iraq, but the trouble was 'not so much in predicting what the Iraqis would do. Where we ran into trouble was in our inability to foresee some of the actions of our *own* government.'[42] Rumsfeld quite incredibly rejected the need for any post-war planning with predictably disastrous consequences.

The first indication of what was to come was the wave, indeed tsunami seems a more accurate description, of looting and destruction that followed the Iraqi defeat. US and British troops stood by and watched while the country was stripped bare by an unprecedented outbreak of individual and organised looting. Moreover, both the British and American governments seemed remarkably unconcerned. Geoff Hoon, the British Defence Secretary, 'claimed that looting was merely a case of citizens "liberating items from the regime" and "redistributing that wealth among the Iraqi people"'.[43] Instead, a good case can be made that the complete breakdown of order was the last blow for the Iraqi middle class, to whom the US looked to run the country. According to one authoritative account, the looting

> severely damaged the state's administrative capacity: 17 of Baghdad's ministry buildings were completely gutted. Looters took portable items of value such as computers, before turning to furniture and fittings. They then systematically stripped the electric wiring from the walls to sell for scrap. This practice was so widespread that copper and aluminium prices in the neighbouring countries of Iran and Kuwait dramatically dropped as a result of the massive illicit outflow of stolen scrap metal from Iraq. Overall, the looting is estimated to have cost as much as US$12 billion, equal to one third of Iraq's annual GDP.[44]

Most famously, American troops guarded the Oil Ministry, which was surrounded by tanks and razor wire with snipers on the roof, while the rest of Baghdad was abandoned to the looters. The city's museums were looted of priceless antiquities, with thousands of irreplaceable items destroyed. Some 45 000 rare books and manuscripts were destroyed when libraries were looted and set on fire. At the Iraq National Library and Archive, US troops destroyed a statue of Saddam Hussein in front of the building and then abandoned it to the looters. The Archive was burned down, destroying some '60 per cent of the archive's state records...dating from the nineteenth century under Ottoman rule up to the Saddam regime'. Among the documents destroyed were 'records of property ownership, political history, state administration and relations with other states, including treaties, border demarcations and agreements over oil and water resources'. Hospitals and clinics, schools, colleges and universities were all looted, stripped of everything and then often burned down. The infrastructure of the Iraqi state was effectively destroyed as liberation became a disaster.[45]

Peter Galbraith was particularly incensed by the spectacle of US Marines guarding the Oil Ministry while nearby 'the Ministry of Irrigation burned, destroying the plans and blueprints for Iraq's dams, barrages, pumping stations and thousands of kilometres of canals'.[46] What happened in Baghdad was replicated throughout the rest of the country, including Basra. Most astonishing, however, was the lack of concern with securing the 946 WMD sites that the US had claimed to have identified. Initially a single derisory battalion was allocated to this task, which really does seem to give the lie to the main pretext for the war. Only after protests from Major General James Marks, who had been given the responsibility for securing the sites, was a still wholly inadequate artillery brigade assigned.[47] One of the sites where the regime had supposedly been developing biological agents such as anthrax, cholera, typhus, tetanus and the plague was the Public Health Laboratory in Baghdad. On 16 April 2003, US Marines had stood by watching while it was looted! South of Baghdad was the Tuwaitha nuclear research facility where the International Atomic Energy Authority (IAEA) as part of its inspection regime had placed a number of barrels containing 'yellow-cake', unprocessed uranium, under seal. The IAEA had warned the United States of this, but to no avail.

> When US troops arrived at Tuwaitha, the yellow cake was in a locked warehouse that had been secured by the IAEA before the inspectors left at the start of the war. While US troops were actually at Tuwaitha, looters broke into the warehouse. They took the barrels

and apparently dumped the yellowcake. Almost two tons went missing. In his 2003 State of the Union address, President Bush said Iraq's efforts to acquire yellowcake from Niger were so dangerous that they justified war, even though the intelligence about Iraq's Niger connection was transparently fraudulent. Yet his Administration did not consider Iraq's actual stockpile of yellowcake important enough to justify ordering US troops at the location to protect it.

According to Galbraith, the looters 'wanted the barrels to store rainwater'. Looking back, the occupation has all the characteristics of a *Carry On* film, although considerably more tragedy than comedy. Without any doubt it will serve as a textbook case of how *not* to occupy a conquered/liberated country. The American administration that took over the country was filled with Republican 'carpetbaggers', loyal neocons, often young, fresh out of college and without any experience or qualifications for the posts to which they had been appointed. Galbraith highlights Michael Fleischer, the man put in charge of privatising Iraqi state assets. He was the brother of President Bush's first press secretary: 'After explaining that he had got the job in Iraq through his brother Ari, Fleischer told the *Chicago Tribune*, without any apparent irony, that the Americans were going to teach the Iraqis a new way of doing business. "The only paradigm they know is cronyism."'[48]

Provoking insurgency

Resistance to the US occupation was inevitable, but what was not inevitable was the scale and ferocity that it was to achieve. To a considerable extent this was the direct result of the policies implemented by the Coalition Provisional Authority (CPA) under the direction of Paul Bremer. The ease with which the country had been conquered seems to have persuaded the Bush administration to cast all caution aside and set about a process of reshaping Iraq without any serious consideration for the likely consequences of their actions. They seem to have genuinely believed that they could do anything. After all, two dangerous regimes had been successfully overthrown with hardly any casualties, something which many of their critics had warned was impossible. The decisive moment was when Bremer, acting on instructions from Washington, banned senior Baath Party members from public sector employment on 15 May and dissolved the Iraqi Armed Forces and the Ministry of the Interior on 23 May 2003. He had only been in the country a few days. The ban not only affected committed

Baathists, but thousands of people whose party membership had been largely nominal, including teachers and doctors as well as civil servants. Nearly 80 000 people were affected. Bremer was warned that the policy would have disastrous effects by the CIA, the US military and the British,[49] but to no avail. The neo-cons knew best. The CIA station chief told him that the measure would drive '30,000 to 50,000 Baathists underground. And in six months, you'll really regret this.' According to George Tenet, 'something like forty thousand schoolteachers lost their jobs, closing down schools. Putting young people on the streets, with nothing to do, in a country 'armed to the teeth...was not a good thing', Tenet remembered.[50] Worse was to follow. A week later Bremer ordered the dissolution of the Armed Forces, which on paper were 385 000 strong, and of the Ministry of the Interior, which included the police and other security agencies, altogether over 280 000 strong. At the time of these decrees, the Americans on the ground were actually trying to reconstitute the army and the police so they could be used to help maintain order. Not only did Bremer put a stop to that, but by making more than half a million soldiers and policemen unemployed, he provided the insurgents with a mass base of men of military age, trained in the use of arms. This particular act of ill-judged stupidity was to have disastrous consequences. Colonel John Agoglia, military liaison with Bremer later described 23 May as the day 'that we snatched defeat from the jaws of victory and created an insurgency'.[51] Bremer himself was to tell journalists that part of the problem was that the Iraqis had 'a pervasive resentment that we liberated them' and felt guilty 'that they weren't able to liberate themselves'. In this respect, he opined, they were just like the French![52]

Not only was the occupation going seriously wrong, but the Americans were beginning to realise that they might well have inflicted a serious strategic defeat on themselves. The neo-cons' confident belief that Iraq without Saddam Hussein would become an ally run very much by people like themselves was falling apart. Instead, it was becoming clear that elections would bring to power the confessional parties supported by the Shia majority. These were either hostile to the United States, sympathetic to Iran, or both. Far from strengthening the US position in the Middle East, the invasion of Iraq and overthrow of Saddam Hussein had actually strengthened the position of Iran. The consequences of this for the Middle East were to be horrendous. It added another dimension to the violence in Iraq which the United States was to eventually find itself caught in the middle of: a proxy war between Iran and Saudi Arabia.

The British commitment

The British took responsibility for administering and maintaining stability in Iraq's four southern provinces of Basra, Muthanna, Maysan and Thi Qar, Multi-National Division (South East), covering some 60 000 square miles including 600 miles of border with Iran, Kuwait and Saudi Arabia, and 30 miles of coastline, and with a population of some 4.6 million. The assumption was that this was the sort of operation the British Army was best at. Instead, the result was to be humiliation and defeat with the 'Special Relationship' actually beginning to be called into question by the United States as the British failed to do the job. Why was this? A number of reasons have been put forward. First, the British fell victim to the incompetence of the US authorities that provoked a full-scale insurgency in the rest of the country that inevitably spilled over into the south. Second, that the British were either not as good at counterinsurgency as was generally believed or that they had forgotten how to do it. And third, that the British effort in the south was so under-manned and under-resourced that it was doomed from the very beginning. As we shall see there is much to be said for all three explanations.

There is no doubt the Blair government shared the illusions that gripped the Bush administration: American and British troops would be welcomed as liberators and the newly-freed Iraqis would soon be running their country along lines acceptable to the United States. There was no real consideration given to how to deal with any post-war resistance because the simple belief was that there would not be any. According to General Peter Wall, who was 'involved at high levels before the invasion': 'I can't recall having done any calculus about the sort of force densities we were going to need. I think it fair to say that there was still an expectation that we would be welcomed as liberators, that there would be sufficient of some sort of administrative capacity to at least keep things ticking on in a minimal way, and there was going to be some sort of convenient arrival of some sort of Iraqi middle class.'[53] What the British expected was to ride to glory alongside the Americans – set up a new government of grateful Iraqis and get out as quickly as possible. This was what the British Army was designed to do. The reality on the ground was completely different from what they expected and there is no doubt that the Americans made the situation considerably worse. First there were Bremer's orders banning Baathists and dissolving the Iraqi army and police. One British officer recalled how these measures were caused 'a sense of utter despondency and disbelief'. They left 'the small British force in Basra unable to work through trained and capable

Iraqi intermediaries'.[54] This was compounded by the US response once an insurgency began to develop in the Sunni areas of the country. As far as the British were concerned, the Americans made the situation worse by their excessive use of firepower, downright brutality and cultural insensitivity. The US Army, the British believed, did not have the long experience of successful counterinsurgency campaigning that the British Army had, something British officers often helpfully pointed out. British efforts to maintain stability in the south were, from this point of view, compromised by US failure in the rest of the country. One account goes so far as to argue that the British were 'effectively held hostage' by the Americans, 'whose counter-insurgency failures have not only undermined progress towards the strategic objective of a stable and democratic Iraq, but have also contributed to the spread of instability to the south'.[55] While there is no doubt that the conduct of American troops certainly fuelled the developing insurgency (according to Patrick Cockburn, their behaviour sometimes gave the impression they were actually 'determined to provoke an uprising'), this conduct was itself at least partly a product of the fact that the US Army was itself both under-manned and under-resourced, courtesy of Donald Rumsfeld. Indeed, Rumsfeld stoutly refused to acknowledge there was an insurgency long after it was apparent to just about everyone else.

One of the worst atrocities committed by US troops was at least partly attributable to too few troops being asked to do too much. On 19 November 2005, US Marines in Haditha responded to the loss of one of their number to a roadside bomb with a massacre, summarily executing five men in passing cars and then another 19 of the inhabitants of nearby houses, including six children and a 76-year-old man in a wheelchair. Oliver Poole writes of the Marines in Haditha as having 'gone feral', while Thomas Ricks regards the episode as providing some sort of key 'to understanding the failure of the first years of the American war'.[56] The violence of the US response to the insurgency was clearly making it worse, but even once one acknowledges the too-ready reliance on firepower and cultural insensitivity, this atrocity still has to be placed in the context of there being too few troops. In Haditha, there were 160 Marines ostensibly policing a town of 40 000 inhabitants. Iraqi opinion was not assuaged when the only man punished for this atrocity got a three-month suspended sentence and was demoted in rank from sergeant to private. Excesses are inevitable in this sort of situation, the more so when they go unpunished. The excesses of individual soldiers and units were, of course, to be put in the shade by the revelations regarding the mistreatment and torture of prisoners at Abu Ghraib.[57]

One other factor that has not so far figured enough in the literature is that misconduct by regular troops was in Iraq accompanied by the bad behaviour of the thousands of private security contractors who were not even subject to military discipline such as it was.[58] By the end of 2003, private security contractors made up the second largest armed force in Iraq after the US Army.[59]

The second argument that the British were not as good at counterinsurgency as they believed themselves to be is certainly valid, but as a number of commentators have pointed out, even if they had been as good as they thought in the past, the lessons of those campaigns that had been successful were either not applied or they had been misunderstood and were applied inappropriately.[60] Much more important, however, was the whole strategic underpinning of the war. The reality was that the British were not in Iraq because there were any vital British interests actually at stake in Iraq, no matter what the government said. They were in Iraq to sustain the 'Special Relationship'. This was the *'casus belli'*. No British government would ever have identified Iraq as a threat requiring a military response of its own volition, whatever Blair's protests to the contrary, if it were not for the Americans. And if the United States had chosen to attack Syria or Iran instead of Iraq, then without any doubt British forces would have participated alongside them. What this meant in practice was that the Blair government committed the resources it believed necessary to sustain the 'Special Relationship' rather than the resources necessary for military success to be more than an aspiration. While the politicians can be legitimately criticised for this, nevertheless the military high command were complicit. If the government had actually been given a realistic assessment of the manpower and resources necessary to manage the worst-case scenarios in Iraq then the commitment would either have been scaled back or would have been abandoned altogether. Blair's political career might well have been the only casualty. This was an unpopular war and arguably no government would have been able to justify the scale of the commitment over an extended period of time that the conventional counterinsurgency wisdom would have regarded as necessary. As it was, the government got the worst of both worlds, finding itself involved in a war that was far worse than it had ever contemplated and still managing to compromise the 'Special Relationship'. The Blair government hoped for the best and was completely unprepared for what was to come.

From the very beginning troop levels in the south were only appropriate if the British had been acting in support of a reliable local partner in a relatively stable situation rather than acting without a partner in a conflict zone. General Mike Jackson identified the essential problem: 'troop numbers'.

> At the height of the Troubles in Northern Ireland, for example, we had twenty thousand or more soldiers in the Province to keep the peace, and even then we were unable to suppress terrorism altogether. Northern Ireland has only around 5 per cent of Iraq's population; a similar presence would thus equate to four hundred thousand soldiers, but the Coalition struggled to reach half that figure. Furthermore, in Northern Ireland the Army was working alongside a highly competent police force, which doesn't yet exist in Iraq. On the contrary, many of the Iraqi police are corrupt and making matters worse.[61]

Of course, the situation was even worse than this because many of the Iraqi police, particularly in Basra, were actually on the side of the insurgents, and what Jackson leaves out is the fact that in Northern Ireland a majority of the population were strongly pro-British. Patrick Porter makes a similar point when he writes of 'a crippling lack of funding and troops'. He goes on: 'Even if most British soldiers did carry a mastery of minor wars in their blood, they simply lacked the minimal manpower necessary to succeed. The ratio of soldiers to civilians in Iraq was 1:370, compared to the ratio in Northern Ireland of 1:50. The Army hardly had a chance.'[62] In their discussion of the problem, David Betz and Anthony Cormack once again make the point that 'the British force was never large enough' and point to a 1:370 ratio of British troops to Iraqi civilians in Basra in 2003 compared with 1:65 in Belfast. Once again, while Porter and Betz and Cormack intend to demonstrate the scale of the problem, they actually understate it. In Belfast and Northern Ireland, the British had a reliable, well-equipped police force reinforcing them, indeed eventually taking the lead in the conflict, together with the support of the majority of the population And yet, the Northern Ireland conflict lasted 30 years before the republicans were bought to terms, terms which involved them joining the government. A British commitment of considerably more troops and resources for 30 years in a war that was being fought on behalf of the United States was never going to happen. And, of course, this was exactly the conclusion that was eventually drawn in the United States.

Basra

When the British took over Basra, much was made of their polite sensitive approach, patrolling in soft hats rather than helmets, compared with the more aggressive, shoot-first approach of the Americans. The benefits of the British approach seemed to be amply borne out by the speed with which the Americans found themselves confronted by a growing Sunni insurgency while the situation remained relatively peaceful in the south. As the Sunni insurgency intensified, a growing number of US Army officers themselves came to the conclusion that they were doing it wrong, that the British were doing it right and that the British tradition of counterinsurgency was something they could usefully learn from. The key text was John Nagl's *Learning to Eat Soup with a Knife: Counterinsurgency Lessons from Malaya and Vietnam*, written by a serving US Army officer. It had been first published in 2002 and now came into its own as offering a possible solution to the problems the US Army was having. This situation was becoming desperate. By 2006 there was a real fear that the United States was going to be defeated in Iraq unless changes were made.[63] The trouble was that appearances in the south were deceptive. From the very beginning of their occupation, the British did not have enough of a presence to actually take control and instead found themselves cooperating with / competing with a variety of rival Shia Islamist parties and militias that were also fighting each other. These became increasingly powerful, with the British, who had never really controlled Basra or the other provinces anyway, being eventually driven out by the Shia faction, the Sadrists, that had emerged victorious. Far from providing lessons, the British in the south were themselves presiding over their own disaster.

The number of British troops in the south was cut dramatically from 46 000 to only 10 500 within three months of the invasion. This was pretty much a guarantee of disaster. According to Frank Ledwidge, by the time he arrived in Basra in September 2003, 'matters were already beginning to deteriorate' and the 'era of soft hats was gone'. Troops patrolled 'fully armed and ready for trouble'.[64] That same month, soldiers of the Queen's Lancashire Regiment had arrested ten Iraqi suspects, among them a hotel receptionist, Baha Mousa. The hooded prisoners were subjected to systematic brutality including being kicked and beaten for entertainment purposes. They were beaten so that their cries made a tune, the so-called choir. Mousa died, apparently strangled to death, but not before he had suffered 93 separate injuries. Another prisoner, Ahmed al-Matairi, could speak some English, and heard bets being placed by his guards on who could hit him the hardest. He suffered 28 separate injuries.[65] Clearly the situation had changed in the south.

The turning point had been serious fighting in the town of Majar al Kebir in Maysan province on 24 June 2003 in which 'eighty to a hundred Iraqis were either killed or severely wounded'. This episode culminated in the effective lynching of six military policemen who were left unsupported in the town.[66] A good indication of the different approaches taken by the British and the Americans is provided by a comparison between the British response to the killing of the military policemen and the American response to the killing of four US military contractors, Blackwater employees, at Fallujah on 31 March 2004. There was no British attempt to storm and occupy Majar al Kebir, indeed the town was effectively abandoned, whereas Fallujah, despite fears that an attack would only make the situation worse, was to be subjected to two full-scale military assaults (5–9 April and 8–18 November 2004) that left much of the town in ruins.

The first attack was ordered against the advice of the Marine commanders on the ground who felt that 'we ought to probably let the situation settle before we appeared to be attacking out of revenge'. Instead, they were ordered to attack within 72 hours, which did not allow adequate time for preparation, by a White House that clearly wanted revenge regardless of the consequences.[67] The assault on the city provoked a widespread Sunni uprising that saw attacks on US forces escalating throughout Sunni areas. And this was at the same time as Bremer and the CPA were picking a fight with the Shia leader, Moqtada al Sadr. Bremer shut down the Sadrist newspaper, *Al Hawza*, and then issued a warrant for Moqtada's arrest on 3 April. This provoked a Sadrist uprising the very next day, an uprising that engulfed the British in the south. The Americans had managed to open a war on two fronts, provoking a Shia uprising at a time when they were barely coping with a Sunni insurgency. President Bush, showing his usual strategic insight, urged his commander in Iraq, General Ricardo Sanchez: 'Kick ass! If somebody tries to stop the march to democracy, we will seek them out and kill them' and 'Stay the course! Kill them! Be confident! Prevail! We are going to wipe them out!'[68] The attack on Fallujah was called off soon after Bush's inspirational rant.[69]

In Basra, the British had reached an accommodation of sorts with the pro-Iranian Shia faction, the Supreme Council for the Islamic Revolution in Iraq (SCIRI) that was prepared to cooperate with them. The SCIRI militia, the Badra brigade, was pretty much allowed to take over the police in Basra. In practice both Basra and the other provinces had been surrendered to the various Shia Islamist parties, each with its own armed militia. They were already in the process of imposing their rule over the population, enforcing their interpretation of Islam. On 24 December 2003, the militia had publicly executed a Christian merchant for selling alcohol in Basra's main marketplace, without any interference from either the police or the British. He was certainly not the first Christian killed for this offence. They were already beginning to drive out the Sunni minority (about 15 per cent of the population in the south). This was the price of peace in the south. The American decision to confront the Sadrists was to demonstrate the fragility of the British position.

For the British the confrontation with the Sadrists was disastrous. They were given no notice that a warrant had been issued for Moqtada's arrest, so that the Sadrist response came as a complete surprise. On 7 April, the Sadrist militia, the Jaysh al-Mahdi (JAM), took to the streets across the south seizing town centres and attacking the British. In Basra itself, 'they attacked British forces about 70 times in an hour and a half, with shootings and bombings'. In the town of Amarah in Maysan province, the situation was even worse with 'the most concerted assault on a British battalion since Korea'.[70] For a three-week period, the British HQ was mortared or rocketed every day. Over a seven-month period, the Princess of Wales Regiment was attacked 658 times. On one occasion, British troops actually ran out of ammunition and fixed bayonets.[71] Amarah was 'the epicentre of the Mahdi uprising in the British-occupied zone', with clashes continuing with some interruption until 28 August when a ceasefire was negotiated.[72] Nevertheless, the violence was contained, although as General Stewart acknowledged, he had hoped 'to neutralise the militia' but 'overall we failed'. His concern was above all else to avoid exacerbating the situation, not least because of how few troops he had available. This did not go down well with Bremer, who ordered that more severe action should be taken against the Sadrists. Stewart was 'charged with not killing enough people' and the CPA 'asked for my removal' because, instead of trying to crush the Sadrists, he was 'a chicken-livered Brit...trying to get the locals to resolve the problem themselves...trying to kill as few people as possible'. His policy with regard to Bremer's directives was 'to consent and evade'.[73] The British ambassador in Washington, David Manning, was actually summoned to the State Department to receive a reprimand 'of the kind more often delivered to "rogue states" such as Zimbabwe or the Sudan', for Stewart's refusal to follow orders. Relations between the allies on the ground were not good at this point in time. Stewart's Chief of Staff, Colonel J.K. Tanner, described the Americans as 'a group of Martians' for whom 'dialogue is alien'. As far as he was concerned, despite 'our so-called "special relationship", I reckon we were treated no differently to the Portuguese'. As far as the Americans were concerned 'there is only one way: the American way'.[74] The reality was that while the Americans were undoubtedly in serious difficulty and making the situation progressively worse, the British were themselves failing in a different way. The difficulty they faced is bought home by the results of the January 2005 elections in Iraq that saw the various Islamist parties sweep the board in Basra. A SCIRI-dominated coalition won 20 seats out of 41 in Basra but was nevertheless kept out of power by a coalition of all the other parties. Muhammad al-Waeli, no friend of the British, was installed as governor. In Maysan province, the Sadrists emerged as the strongest party.

The road to defeat

Despite the Sadrist uprising, the British still only suffered 10 fatalities in Iraq in 2004 (compared with 719 US fatalities). The situation continued to deteriorate into 2005, however, as the militia came to exercise increasing control, operating as a law to themselves, intimidating, kidnapping and on occasion killing opponents and engaging in outright gangsterism. Attacks on the British were stepped up, with any attempts to curb militia activity provoking a violent response. One particular episode highlighted the British lack of control. On 15 March, students at Basra University held a picnic for men and women in Andalus Park. Sadrist militiamen beat and publicly shamed one young woman by ripping her clothes off. They shot and wounded two male students who went to her assistance. She subsequently committed suicide. The whole episode was watched by the police. This episode demonstrated the impunity with which the militia behaved, the complicity of the police and the weakness of the British. Occasional attempts to assert British control and authority were invariably futile because of the lack of troops. Nevertheless, the criminal and sectarian depredations of one particular police unit, the Serious Crimes Unit (SCU), a 300-odd strong 'gang of rapists, torturers and murderers' operating out of Jamiat police station, eventually necessitated a response.[75] The British decided to arrest one of the SCU commanders, Captain Jafar, and he was placed under SAS surveillance. On 19 September 2005, the Iraqi police 'made' the two man surveillance team and after a gunfight, in which one policeman was killed, and a car chase, succeeded in arresting them. British troops then surrounded the police station, coming under attack from armed crowds. The two men were smuggled out and handed over to a militia group with, the British believed, Iranian connections, to be either held as hostages or killed. The British responded by storming the police compound and simultaneously raiding the house where the two men were being held and successfully rescuing them.[76] The pictures of British armoured vehicles being petrol bombed while storming a police station, that were shown around the world, stripped away any pretence that all was well in Basra. Far from working with the British, Muhammad al-Waeli, the governor, broke off all contact with them in protest against the attack on the police station and ordered the police to end all co-operation. He held a number of anti-British rallies demanding their withdrawal. At the same time, the provincial council ended all contact with the British, a boycott that continued until May the following year. In the aftermath of the Jameat episode the level of violence continued to rise. One important development creating serious difficulties for both the Americans and the British was the emergence of the increasingly sophisticated roadside bomb, the Improvised Explosive Device (IED), as a weapon in the insurgent armoury.

There is considerable irony in the fact that just as it was becoming clear that the British had lost what little control they might have had in the south and were themselves confronting a 'full-fledged insurgency'[77], the US Army journal, the *Military Review* published an article by Brigadier Nigel Aylwin-Foster, 'Changing the Army for Counterinsurgency Operations', criticising the Americans. Here he told them, very politely, where they were going wrong, absolutely denying that his was 'an arrogant exercise in national comparisons'. He pointed out that the Coalition 'has failed to capitalise on initial success' and argued that at least in part this was a result of military failings. The US military was 'weighed down by bureaucracy, a stiflingly hierarchical outlook, a predisposition to offensive operations, and a sense that duty required all issues to be confronted head-on'. He went on to argue that 'at times their cultural insensitivity, almost certainly inadvertent, arguably amounted to institutional racism'. The US Army was 'too "kinetic"...too inclined to consider offensive operations and destruction of the insurgent as the key to a given situation and, and conversely failed to understand its downside'. The Americans had a 'sense of moral righteousness combined with an emotivity...that could serve to distort collective military judgement'. He cited the attacks on Fallujah as an example of an outraged response to an obvious 'come-on'. The Americans were deliberately provoked into 'a disproportionate response, thereby further polarising the situation and driving a wedge between the domestic population and the Coalition forces. It succeeded.' The answer was a counterinsurgency approach and he recommended Nagl's *Learning to Eat Soup with a Knife* as showing the way.[78] Such a forthright critique did not come out of the blue, but was very much an intervention in the ongoing debate that was already taking place within the US military. Aylwin-Foster was invited to reinforce the arguments that were already being advanced by John Nagl and others and that were to propel General David Petraeus into prominence as the saviour of the US Army in Iraq. By the time Petraeus was appointed to command in Iraq in January 2007, the scale of the debacle in Basra meant that the British were no longer listened to.

Despite increasing levels of violence, British troop levels in Iraq were cut further during 2005 to only 7200. The thinking behind this was that their work in Iraq was nearly done and to make ready for a new commitment of troops to Afghanistan where the Taliban threat was reviving. In effect, the troops in Iraq were left to make the best of it. The ferocity of the fighting was bought home to General Dannatt when he asked his son, Bertie, about a patrol he led into a town in Muthanna province in January 2006. They had come 'under intense fire from all directions with small-arms, machine-guns and rocket-propelled grenades'. He asked his son what it had been like and in reply Bertie 'asked if I had seen the film *Black Hawk Down*'.[79]

By the time General Richard Shirreff arrived in Basra to take command of Coalition forces in the MND-SE early in 2006, the situation was dire. As far as he could see, there was 'no security at all in Basra' where all he had available was 'a single battalion looking after a city of approximately 1.3 million people'. At any one time, he only had '200 soldiers on the ground at any one time'. Amarah in Maysan province was effectively a 'no-go area' and the military base outside the town at Abu Naji was under constant attack.[80] While he was only expected to ensure a smooth evacuation from Iraq with as little trouble and embarrassment as possible, Shirreff determined instead to break the Sadrist hold on Basra before handing the city over to the Iraqi Army. He wanted 'an orderly exit from Iraq', whereas the MOD 'appeared to want an exit under any circumstances'. Any withdrawal 'without decisive action would amount to defeat and humiliation'.[81] He decided to concentrate his forces in Basra, pulling out of the other provinces, where the troops were too few to accomplish anything other than serve as targets for the militia. One night in June, no less than 67 mortar rounds were fired into the base at Abu Naji, with Colonel David Labouchere and his officers taking shelter under a table. The base was finally evacuated on 24 August, ostensibly because the Iraqi Army was now capable of taking over, even if it was not reliable to be told more than a few hours in advance. Once the British had left, hundreds of grateful locals descended on the camp to tear it down, filmed by Al-Jazeera and broadcast worldwide. The camp was 'gutted in what appeared to be a wholesale rejection of the occupation'.[82] All this time, the Blair government and the Ministry of Defence were still maintaining the pretence that everything was going according to plan, that the job in Iraq had been accomplished successfully and that the British Army was leaving with its reputation intact.

Shirreff planned a protracted operation, Operation Sinbad, to break the JAM hold over the city. He had assembled some 3000 troops for the operation and, recognising that this force was still inadequate, asked the Americans for assistance. They offered to contribute a battalion, but he was ordered to turn down the offer apparently on the grounds that it would be humiliating to accept US help. He did keep some US attack helicopters and unmanned drones. London was most unenthusiastic about the operation, which began on 28 October 2006 and continued until 18 February the following year. By the time it came to an end, some 340 militia had been killed along with 46 British soldiers with another 350 wounded, but the British were no more in control of the city than they had been on day one. Operation Sinbad was a failure, with the troops themselves deriding it as 'Operation Spinbad'. There were successes with the Serious Crimes Unit finally being dismantled and the Jameat police station demolished on 25 December, but the troops were under constant attack, had to fight their way everywhere in the city and were not strong enough to hold any of the districts they had supposedly cleared. In the words of one US officer, the whole Operation was 'an exercise in futility'.[83] Indeed, by the time Shirreff was replaced by General George Shaw in January 2007, the British base at the Basra Palace 'had become the most attacked location in Iraq'.[84] Even while this debacle was still unfolding, the British continued to lecture the Americans on how to do counterinsurgency. One senior US officer described Shaw as 'insufferable'. He still 'lectures everybody in the room about how to do counterinsurgency. The guys were just rolling their eyeballs...it would be okay if he was best in class, but now he's worst in class. Everybody else's area is getting better and his is getting worse.'[85]

Despite the appalling security situation, as soon as Operation Sinbad ended, the government withdrew another 1600 troops. In May, a militia attack nearly overran the British base at the Provincial Coordination Centre in central Basra. By July 2007, British soldiers were being killed 'at the rate of one every three days with almost 120 attacks alone in the week beginning 20 July'. By this time, British losses 'were proportionately higher than those of the US in Baghdad'.[86] With the number of troops in the city falling to only 4000 in the summer, the British set about negotiating a withdrawal with the Sadrist militia. The British, who had been operating an unacknowledged policy of internment in Basra, had held the commander of the JAM, Ahmed al-Fartosi, prisoner for three years, together with some 70-odd other militiamen. The MI6 station chief, James Proctor, opened negotiations with Fartosi, offering the release of these prisoners in return for an unmolested withdrawal from all their bases in the city to the airport. The deal was struck and the evacuations began. When the British pulled out of Basra Palace on 4 September, their withdrawal was policed by the JAM militia. As Frank Ledwidge puts it, they 'were guarded by their enemies...like the defenders of some medieval castle being given safe passage by their victorious besiegers'.[87] The prisoners were released in batches of four or five up until Sartosi's own release on 31 December. Once he was freed, attacks on the airport resumed.[88] By now, the British had to ask permission to enter the city.

The British had suffered a defeat that was made all the more humiliating by the fact that as they were effectively being driven out of Basra, the US Army under General Petraeus had launched its 'Surge'.[89] This together with a Sunni revolt against al-Qaeda, the so-called Awakening, with which the Americans successfully allied themselves, allowed the United States to claim at least some measure of success in the closing stages of the conflict. The US put over 100 000 Sunni militia on their payroll.[90] How fragile this success was has, of course, been decisively demonstrated by the recent Sunni revolt under the aegis of the Islamic State against the Maliki government, a revolt that continues at the time of writing. For the British, however, more humiliation was to come when the Maliki government in Baghdad launched its own military operation to break the Sadrist hold on Basra, Operation Charge of the Knights in March 2008. With considerable American help they succeeded, while the British watched from their base at the airport. As far as Maliki was concerned, the British were 'of no consequence'.[91] The somewhat brutal assessment of one influential US military commentator, Anthony Cordesman, was that by the end of 2007, the British were just 'hiding in the airport'.[92] The last British troops were withdrawn in May 2009. For the United States, the 'Surge' did not, in practice, amount to the embrace of a wholehearted counterinsurgency strategy. In retrospect, it can be seen rather as a short-term stratagem, a holding-action, to allow them to withdraw from the country without it collapsing into chaos around them.

Return to Afghanistan

The decision to abandon Basra, a city of considerable economic and strategic importance, and to dramatically increase the British commitment to the International Security and Assistance Force (ISAF) in Afghanistan instead has never been adequately explained. The defeat in Iraq seriously damaged British relations with the United States. Tony Blair had suffered considerable political damage going into Iraq and now the supposed benefits were thrown away. Without any doubt, the 'Special Relationship' was compromised. Britain was no longer regarded as *the* reliable ally. True, the Iraq war was unpopular at home, but if the British had reinforced their forces in Basra, instead of winding them down, had mounted their own 'surge' alongside the Americans, then something could have been saved. An Operation Charge of the Lions with British troops fighting alongside the Iraqi Army could have been presented as some sort of success with a lot more conviction than the empty claims of victory that were made in the attempt to cover up the scale of the actual defeat. By way of a contrast, Afghanistan was of little strategic importance, one of the poorest countries in the world, with, moreover, a reputation as 'the graveyard of empires'. Did the government see Afghanistan as an opportunity to redeem themselves in American eyes? Did they believe that it would be a less dangerous commitment than Iraq had turned out to be? John Reid, the Defence Secretary, famously remarked that he would be happy if after their three-year mission in Afghanistan, British troops 'had not fired a shot'. At the very same time, according to Tony Blair, Reid was warning him that 'it would be a tough and dangerous mission. The Taliban would fight very hard,'[93] Certainly a good case can be made that the government wanted to minimise the danger in order to avoid stirring up domestic opposition to the commitment. Getting involved in a new war in the aftermath of Iraq certainly involved some fancy footwork. Of course, once the troops actually found themselves under fire, the government could rely on the 'support for our boys' sentiment to undermine any opposition to this new war, although only so long as there were not too many casualties. Or did they really believe that Afghanistan would be easy? It is difficult to untangle the real motives for the dispatch of troops to Afghanistan. Given the strategic importance of Basra and the strategic unimportance of Helmand, the whole affair seems positively quixotic. More British soldiers were to be killed in this campaign than in any other of Britain's post-1945 counterinsurgencies.

As we have already seen, once US power had been demonstrated in Afghanistan and the Taliban overthrown, the United States lost interest and instead pursued its Middle Eastern adventures. The subsequent neglect of the country has been generally acknowledged as a serious mistake, but there has been less attention paid to the nature of the regime the Americans had installed in power. In Karzai's Afghanistan, power was in the hands of the warlords who dominated the drugs trade. These people were never going to be the agents of 'good governance'. This was true in 2001 and it remains true today. Meanwhile, as Tim Bird and Alex Marshall point out, on the ground, 'far from improving, basic indicators of development actually fell in Afghanistan between 2003 and 2005; life expectancy fell from an already dire 44.5 to 43.1 years, and adult literacy from 28.7 to 23.5%'.[94] In 2005, a joint Afghan-UN study found that 'using metrics of hunger, violent death, malaria, employment, longevity, infant mortality and more', Afghanistan came out worst in the world, 'even worse than Mali'. That same year, a US State Department report estimated that 'Afghanistan has the highest level of malnutrition in the world – 70 percent'. By 2005, of the $13.4 billion pledged to Afghanistan by donor countries, only $1.5 billion had been disbursed.[95] At the same time, Kabul was being transformed by the construction of luxury hotels, expensive villas known locally as 'poppy palaces', and luxury shopping malls for the benefit of the drug barons who were running the country.

Inevitably, the Taliban returned. This was due not just to the situation in Afghanistan itself but also to the active encouragement of the government of Pakistan, acting through the Inter-Services Intelligence directorate (ISI). As far as the Pakistan government was concerned, Karzai and the Northern Alliance warlords were the allies of the Indian government and this was not acceptable. Indeed, it was regarded as a serious strategic threat to the country that would have to be dealt with regardless of the involvement of the United States. The ISI was used to covertly support the Taliban and other insurgent networks, encouraging them to return to Afghanistan and providing them with weapons and finance. This was done at the same time as the Pakistan government professed its absolute commitment to the realisation of US objectives in the region. By 2003, there were at least seven Taliban training camps in Baluchistan, and in June of that year, Mullah Omar set up a new ten-member Leadership Council, the 'Quetta Shura', that was to run the Taliban insurgency from inside Pakistan. By 2003, the insurgency was already beginning to establish itself and was spreading throughout the south of the country.

War in Helmand

The British decision to take responsibility for and to commit troops to Helmand province, the centre of opium production in the country, was a serious mistake. With fighting still continuing in Basra, where a lack of troops and resources had hamstrung the military effort, it was proposed to commit to another large-scale enterprise. While the government still hoped to restore its credibility with the Americans, there seems little doubt that it was misled as to the nature of the commitment it was making. Rather than volunteering for a task that was within the capability of the troops and resources available, even though this might further diminish Britain in US eyes, the Army insisted on taking responsibility for Helmand, something well beyond the capability of the troops and resources available. Looking back on both the Basra and Helmand conflicts, General Elliott holds both politicians and soldiers culpable: 'the British High Command gave its support to wars without ensuring that the wider Whitehall elite had a clear understanding of what was involved or the risks presented, and that sufficient political will existed to see the expeditions through in the longer term. The bleat in Whitehall afterwards was that the "generals told us it would be so difficult."'[96] Another factor was the belief that once the commitment was undertaken, the government could be persuaded or even compelled to make the necessary resources available. Sherard Cowper-Coles went so far as to argue that the Army went to Helmand, 'not to defeat the Taliban, but to defeat the British Treasury, the Royal navy and the Royal Air Force'. A shooting war was a good way to safeguard, even increase, spending on the Army.[97]

The original 'Helmand Plan' was to construct a secure base, Camp Bastion, and focus on the two main towns, Lashkar Gah and Gereshk, establishing a secure environment where good governance could be implanted and a development programme got underway. They would create a 'security triangle' and once that was accomplished, making use of the good example it provided, extend outwards. The British commander, Brigadier Ed Butler, asked for 'a force of 14,000 troops, for which he was ridiculed'.[98] He got 3300. This was inadequate even for the implementation of the 'Helmand Plan', but as we shall see that was soon abandoned anyway. As a first step, in the interest of good governance, the British demanded the removal of the notoriously corrupt provincial governor, Sher Muhammad Akhundzada, one of the most powerful of Helmand's drug barons, who had once been caught in possession of 9 tons of opium. He used his office to operate a glorified protection racket. Karzai consoled him for his sacking with a seat in the Afghan Senate and appointed his brother deputy governor so he could keep an eye on the family business. The downside for the British was that Akhunzada had maintained his own armed militia, and he now paid off some 3000 of them, telling them, he told the *Daily Telegraph*, to join the Taliban. Indeed, according to one account, he began contributing to the Taliban cause financially, keeping a foot in both camps, with men he was still paying fighting the British. His sole concern was with maintaining his own power base.[99] In the interest of good governance, a corrupt governor with local influence had been replaced by an honest governor, Engineer Daoud, who was completely dependent on the British.

In 2006, the British were moving into an area where the Taliban were actively organising, but where alliances were often formed more in relation to local disputes and power struggles than some great conflict between Islamism and democracy. One former British officer has gone so far as to argue that the 'insurgency narrative' just 'does not fit with my experiences in Helmand'. The British often found that they were a intervening in local power struggles and were resisted as foreign interlopers. Where one tribe had the support of the government, its rivals would embrace the Taliban.[100] According to journalist Stephen Grey, the whole idea that the war was about democracy or any of the other causes put forward was fanciful: 'the war was more than anything about drugs.' He went on: 'One tribe might choose the government to support its claim on the opium trade; another might choose the Taliban; and another might play off one side against the other.'[101] One last point worth making about the Taliban themselves is the extent to which they were, in Patrick Porter's words, 'cultural realists'. He insists that the Taliban 'are actors with agency...who try to make their own history'. The movement is not monolithic and there are disagreements 'over issues including treatment of civilians, death in combat, and the use of technology'. They were not trapped by 'rigid cultural codes', but could when necessity required be both 'pragmatic and innovative'. As he points out, a movement that had banned music, now in the effort to rally support 'enlists singers in its propaganda output, creating cassettes with songs praising martyrdom, denouncing infidels, and even taking on a style similar to American rap music'. Military necessity has led sections of the Taliban 'to embrace pragmatism strategically trading off and redefining their codes'.[102]

Confronted with the growth of Taliban influence, Daoud demanded that the British send troops to protect the police and local administration in areas outside the 'security triangle'. Under intense pressure from Kabul, the British agreed, thereby consigning the 'Helmand Plan' to the scrapheap. This was a fateful decision from which the whole Helmand commitment never really recovered. While the 'Helmand Plan' was probably never really viable with the forces available, at least the troops would have been better placed to defend themselves. Instead, they were to find themselves dispersed and vulnerable to no good purpose whatsoever over an area of 600 square miles with only eight Chinook helicopters to keep them supplied. Fortified 'platoon houses' were established at Sangin, Now Zad, Musa Qala and elsewhere. The garrisons soon came under relentless attack. To rub salt into the wound, they had been deployed to Sangin to support a corrupt child rapist police chief and when the first British troops had approached Now Zad, they had come under fire from the local police, which was officially put down to a mistake, but unofficially was believed to be to give them time to move their opium stocks.[103]

According to one British officer, Leo Docherty, the Platoon Houses became 'honey-pot targets' for 'anyone who fancied a crack at the infidel'. Instead of establishing good governance and development programmes, the troops found themselves fighting for their lives, 'sucked into lethal high intensity war-fighting', relying on overwhelming fire power to avoid being overrun. This was not how it was meant to be. Artillery, Apache gunships and Harrier jets were called on to break up Taliban attacks, laying waste to the very areas the troops were supposed to be protecting.[104] Stephen Grey wrote that 'Whole towns and villages have been laid waste, and others are almost ghost towns.' Hundreds of 'ordinary Afghan villagers caught in the fighting have been slain'.[105] Brigadier Butler himself later acknowledged that 'we were doing more destruction than construction. We were killing a lot of ordinary Afghans, we were levelling a lot of Now Zad and Musa Qala and elsewhere.'[106] According to General David Richards, 'If we hadn't received a huge amount of air support, we'd have been hard pressed to avoid defeat, let alone achieve victory.'[107] While Sangin was the bloodiest battlefront for both the British and later the Americans in Helmand, the crisis point was first reached at Musa Qala. Here the overriding fear was the loss of one of the handful of Chinooks, shot down either resupplying or evacuating the wounded. Butler was warned that under no circumstance should he lose a Chinook, indeed he was told 'it will lose the war. If we lose a Chinook with people in the back we will certainly lose it politically.'[108] So dangerous was the situation in Musa Qala that the loss of a Chinook was really only a matter of time. Butler decided to seek a truce with the Taliban with a view to a mutual evacuation of the town. The British actually approached Akhunzada, the former governor, for his intercession, a wise move considering that many of the fighters besieging the British were believed to be on his payroll. The Taliban were exhausted from the fighting, had suffered heavy casualties and welcomed a respite. At 9.41 p.m. on 12 September 2006, a ceasefire came into effect, heralding 'the first night's peace for two months'. The town's elders, desperate for the fighting to stop, agreed to take over the town when both sides withdrew and it, in effect, became neutral in the war. The British were due to evacuate on 17 October, but remarkably did not have the necessary transport available. The troops 'were obliged to leave Musa Qala in a convoy of Jingly trucks provided by the village elders'. They were watched by hundreds of locals, including 'dozens of black-turbaned Taliban'.[109] Once again, the British had suffered a humiliating self-inflicted defeat. The Americans were not happy. The truce collapsed in February 2007 when a local Taliban leader was killed in an American air strike which they considered a violation. Privately, British officers believed the Americans had deliberately sabotaged the truce.[110]

In Garmser district, the Taliban had surrounded the British positions with a network of 'fighting positions – small trenches, fighting holes, makeshift bunkers' and every day for 20 months they fought each other 'across the Garmser no-mans-land'. In January 2007, the British launched an attack on a Taliban HQ in a fortified compound. The attack was preceded by a devastating air bombardment. On 11 January a B-1 bomber dropped four 2000-lb and six 500-lb bombs on the target, wrecking the compound. On the 15th, before the ground attack went in, what was left of the compound was subjected to an artillery barrage and had another twenty 2000-lb bombs dropped on it. Despite this, when the Royal Marines went in 'there was no easy killing to be had. Heavy resistance resulted in an eight hour firefight.' More air support was called in to pound the Taliban positions, but eventually the troops were forced to retreat under fire. Clearly, the British had suffered a defeat, but this was not how it was reported at the time.[111] Later, when Cowper-Coles visited Garmser, he was not particularly impressed: 'the Taliban were dug in along a line of poplars only about 150 yards south of the Combat Outpost from which we peered out at them.' They were being strafed by an Apache gunship. The troops had Afghan police in support: 'In filthy torn uniforms, glassy eyes staring vacantly, they lay around on flattened cardboard boxes ... They reminded me most of similarly intoxicated vagrants under Charing Cross railway bridge.'[112]

Despite the vulnerability of the British in Helmand, the Taliban failed to overrun a single outpost and suffered very heavy casualties in the attempt. Their losses forced a change of tactics and instead of attempting to take the British outposts, they placed them under siege, surrounding them with mines, with IEDs. This minimised their casualties while increasing those suffered by the British. Despite the arrival of reinforcements, the British still did not have the resources to turn the situation round, and the situation deteriorated throughout 2007 and into 2008.

Good news

While the war was not going well, the government was much more successful in keeping this from the British public. The Army claimed that the situation was always improving, that corners were being turned and that victory was in sight. The journalist Ben Anderson, who regularly visited Afghanistan over a five-year period, found the gap between what he saw and what he was told got wider every visit. He sometimes found himself doubting the evidence of his own eyes, but, in the end, he came to the conclusion that 'the situation was even more calamitous and our ambitions more fantastic than I had first thought'. Soldiers were given instructions on what to say to the media, LTTs or Lines to Take, schooled in what to say. Often once the camera was off they would come up to him and say 'and now I'll tell you the truth'. One soldier told him 'we were achieving nothing, it was not our fight, just Blair sucking up to Bush. He claimed this was a majority view.' When he visited Helmand in the summer of 2007 he had a look at one particular success story, the Afghan National Police (ANP):

> There were far more police on the payroll than actually existed. Some of those that did exist had been found setting up unofficial checkpoints where they taxed locals until they had enough money to get high. The British police officers (all six of them), who were training the ANP told me they had pulled up at one checkpoint to find a fifteen-year-old with an AK-47 in charge, while the actual policeman lay nearby in an opium-induced coma. Stories of young boys being abducted and raped were common. 'Ninety per cent of crime in Helmand is committed by the police', I was told by one of the British police mentor.[113]

Equally appalled by the discrepancy between what was being claimed and what was actually being achieved was the British ambassador, Sherard Cowper-Coles, who arrived in Kabul in 2007. One of the first things that struck him when he took the posting was 'the towering scale of British ambition in ... Helmand, and across Afghanistan more generally'. The word that came to mind was 'hubris'. He quickly realised 'that the outlook on the political and security fronts was trending downwards', but only later did he grasp quite how bad the situation was. His downbeat reports home caused some consternation in London, and towards the end of 2007 he was due to have an uncomfortable meeting at the Embassy with the Chief of the Defence Staff, Air Chief Marshal Sir Jock

Stirrup. His critical stance regarding the security situation was dramatically vindicated while he was having a shave when 'without warning, the whole house shook, and there was a huge bang. I was squeezed by a sudden blast wave.' His bodyguard rushed in, handing him body armour and a helmet. A car bomb had detonated at the US Embassy. So much for security. The government was very worried about casualties, with Sangin being a particular concern. Sometimes the losses were 'staggeringly high, as in the case of the 3rd Battalion The Rifles, who had nearly one in four of a battle group of 600 killed or seriously injured during their bloody tour in Sangin'. While Cowper-Coles had a high regard for the British troops, he did not have such a high regard for the Army High Command and soon concluded that the war could not be won. A major part of the problem was the corrupt nature of the Karzai regime, fuelled by the drugs trade. He writes of 'the vast sums of money allegedly siphoned off by certain Afghan ministers'. There were ministers and officials 'living way beyond their means in Kabul and, especially in London, the Emirates or America'. It was widely believed that 'almost everyone in influential positions in public life was somehow tainted by the trade'.[114]

'Mafia syndicate'

The nature of the Karzai regime is obviously of considerable importance in assessing the military campaign in Afghanistan. The veteran journalist Sandy Gall dismisses the Karzai government as 'an exact replica of a Mafia syndicate'.[115] This view is endorsed by Vanda Felbab-Brown, who visited the country in 2012 as a member of a NATO-sponsored research team. She described the regime as not just a 'mafia state', a 'thuggish mafia racket', but that even 'by the standards of mafia rule, the post-2002 Afghanistan system comes up short'. For many Afghans, the regime 'has been characterized by rapaciousness, nepotism, corruption, tribal discrimination, and predatory behaviour from government officials and power brokers closely aligned with the state'. The international aid budget has been ruthlessly pillaged by ministers and officials with huge amounts

> siphoned off by clever power brokers for their personal profit. The inability of donor countries and international agencies to track the funds allowed large sums to be removed from Afghanistan, often in suitcases stacked with foreign currency and carried out through Kabul airport...the amount of cash officially declared to leave Afghanistan

in such a manner in 2011 was $4.6 billion, roughly the same as the annual budget of the Afghan government.[116]

According to Rory Stewart, there was almost no economic activity in Afghanistan 'aside from international aid and the production of illegal narcotics'.[117] Ministers and officials were also heavily involved in the drugs trade. In a country where positions in the government, police and army are sold or given to relatives with the investment being recouped in bribes, extortion and embezzlement, as one would expect, the most expensive jobs are in the Ministry of Counter-Narcotics. Some Counter-Narcotics posts cost as much as $200 000 a year. The minister, General Daoud Daoud, was, somewhat predictably, 'according to multiple, separate strands of information, one of the biggest drug traffickers in the country'. The Canadian journalist Graeme Smith was told that officials took 'bribes of $50 000 to $100 000...for each major shipment' with extra for the top man. He actually secured documentary evidence in the form of safe conduct passes for a trafficker signed by Daoud, but to no avail. Indeed, he wisely left the country for his own safety.[118]

Afghanistan is acknowledged to be one of the most corrupt countries in the world. How seriously the Karzai government took the problem was perhaps best demonstrated in 2007 when Karzai appointed Izzatullah Wasifi as his anti-corruption chief. Wasifi had a conviction for trying to sell heroin worth $2 million in Caesars Palace, Las Vegas. It is, however, wrong to describe corruption as a problem, because it was, in fact, the raison d'être of the Afghan government. Sarah Chayes argues that the Karzai government could be best understood as 'a vertically integrated criminal organization – or a few such loosely structured organizations, allies but rivals, coexisting uneasily – whose core activity was not in fact exercising the functions of a state but rather extracting resources for personal gain'. Indeed, the government actually performed this 'core function with admirable efficiency'.[119] The war with the Taliban might not have been going too well, but the men in control of the Afghan government were getting extremely rich even by international standards.

The full significance of this for the war in Afghanistan has not been fully appreciated in many accounts. As Sarah Chayes has pointed out, this was not true of General Petraeus during his time in command. She had been corresponding with him for two years 'about corruption and the insurgency' and had heard him refer to the Karzai government as a 'criminal syndicate' during a White House policy debate. She and her colleagues prepared a PowerPoint presentation ('fully forty-eight slides') which Petraeus acknowledged demonstrated that his Field Manual 3–24 required revision. It had dealt with 'the art of tactical-level counterinsurgency', neglecting the political context. If the military effort is propping up a corrupt predatory government 'then all the efforts by all the brave soldiers on a tactical level will add up to nothing'.[120] This, it could be argued, is precisely what they did add up to.

Pretexts and excuses

While the grim reality was that British troops were fighting and dying to protect a corrupt regime of warlords and drug traffickers, how did the Labour government justify the war to the British people? Over the course of the war, a number of pretexts for British involvement were put forward with varying degrees of sincerity. The idea that the war was to bring democracy, good governance and prosperity to the Afghan people was, given the nature and conduct of the regime, clearly false. The August 2009 presidential elections saw massive electoral fraud. Officials were not only stuffing ballot boxes, but even created fake polling stations that recorded thousands of votes for Karzai. At some polling stations turnout was between 1 and 5 per cent, but the count revealed a 100 per cent or more turnout, all for Karzai. The scale of the fraud was 'so egregious and widespread as to stun even seasoned election monitors, several of whom declared it the most pervasive they had ever seen'.[121] The result was allowed to stand, making a complete mockery of any pretext of democracy or good governance. Another pretext sometimes put forward was that the war was being fought to advance women's rights in Afghanistan. While there were certainly people working on the ground in Afghanistan for whom this was a cause worth fighting for and risking their lives for, it was not a cause that British governments have ever gone to war for. Indeed, in Basra, the British had stood by while women's rights were relentlessly rolled back and, as we have seen, the British have for many years assiduously courted Saudi Arabia. The government considered the question of women's rights as a useful club with which to beat opponents of the war rather than it being one of the actual reasons for the commitment. More generally, as a senior British intelligence officer admitted to Jason Davidson, the whole question of human rights was 'part of the public rationale, but it was not a driver of the decision...It is always helpful for governments who want to get the *Guardian* readers of the world on board to have a humanitarian logic.'[122]

The other pretext was that the troops were there to protect Britain from attack. On Armistice Day, 11 November 2008, the Defence Secretary,

John Hutton, told an audience at the Institute for Strategic Studies that British troops were in Afghanistan to prevent al-Qaeda unleashing 'destructive forces on our streets'. He went on to describe the terrorist threat as a security priority comparable to 'the world wars or the Cold War'. The threat from terrorism was 'every bit as unambiguous as the threat presented by the invasion of Belgium in 1914 and the invasion of Poland in 1939'. He insisted that terrorism 'poses a direct threat to the security of the British people...That is why we have 8000 troops in Afghanistan.'[123] The conflating of the threat posed by Hitler with the threat posed by Mullah Omar is so dishonest that it is difficult to believe that anyone ever took it seriously. And of course, the proud boast that Britain had 8000 troops there dealing with this apparently existential threat rather gave the game away. If there had been any truth to his statement whatever, if he had believed anything he said himself, there would have been considerably more than 8000 troops in Afghanistan. As Stephen Grey wrote: 'The war's defenders clutched at so many explanations to justify the conflict that they began to appear cynical and transparently half-hearted...you did get a sense of people clutching at straws to justify a war that many in high command and across government would say in private was a ghastly mistake.'[124] The real reason for the commitment was never publicly acknowledged: British troops were in Afghanistan to maintain the 'Special Relationship'.

Saved by the Americans?

The British were worn down by a process of attrition in Helmand, with the level of casualties threatening to turn a passive hostility to the war back home into an active hostility. After all the sacrifice, the Taliban still 'effectively controlled 60 per cent of Helmand'.[125] All the British had achieved was described by one senior officer as 'mowing the grass', clearing the Taliban from an area only for them to return as soon as the troops were withdrawn.[126] In 2009, 108 British soldiers were killed, with many more suffering serious life-changing injuries. At a time when the United States had initiated a 'Surge' in Afghanistan, the British had reached exhaustion point. By the summer of 2010, the British press was reporting that the death rate for British soldiers in Afghanistan was four times that of the Americans. The government wanted the United States to step in and relieve the pressure, but it did not want the humiliation of actually asking them. Instead, the Americans were privately asked without any paper trail if they would offer help unsolicited so that the British could save face. Despite a widespread belief that the British had 'made a mess of things in Helmand', the Americans agreed. John Kael Weston, a US diplomat, told the journalist Rajiv Chandrasekaran: 'We couldn't have a situation that made Basra look like child's play. Helmand was much more important in terms of British self-respect and the US–UK partnership. We had to help our best friends in the world.' Weston

> drafted a cable for Ambassador Eikenberry titled 'US–UK at a Crossroads'. It argued that the United States needed to ease its closest ally out of the toughest parts of Helmand, not force the British to stick it out. Eikenberry agreed, but the subject was too sensitive for even a top secret cable, which would have been viewed by hundreds of people within the American bureaucracy. The Ambassador drafted a memo that he sent directly to [Hillary] Clinton.[127]

The British handed over Helmand to the Americans. At last, it had been recognised that the task was beyond anything the British Army could accomplish. By the spring of 2010 there were 20 000 US troops in Helmand. What difference did the US 'Surge' make? Clearly, it has been a holding operation, similar to the Iraqi 'Surge', but less successful because there has been no Afghan 'Awakening' to accompany it. With the announcement by President Barack Obama that the US commitment would come to an end in 2014, followed by a similar British announcement, the war has been, in effect, abandoned, with the Taliban undefeated. This was always the most likely outcome. Rory Stewart brutally summed up the situation in 2009 when he wrote that:

> It is unlikely that we will be able to defeat the Taliban. The ingredients of successful counter-insurgency campaigns in places like Malaya – control of the borders, large numbers of troops in relation to the population, strong support from the majority ethnic groups, a long-term commitment and a credible local government – are lacking in Afghanistan.[128]

But what did the British achieve? Frank Ledwidge argues that after all the expenditure of blood and treasure,

> Britain's efforts have resulted in the 'stabilization' (ie. The temporary pacification) of three of the 14 districts that make up the province of Helmand – just one of the 34 provinces in a country with a population that is half that of the UK. In terms of overall political significance, this might be the equivalent of three large market towns in

rural Lincolnshire... After three years of British presence, the province was the most savage combat zone in the world. With British forces and their commanders out of their depth, it was only the intervention of a powerful US force of marines that brought some level of control to the situation.[129]

Whatever credibility the British had as America's partner in war was gone.

Notes

New Introduction

1. David French, *The British Way in Counter-Insurgency 1945–1967*, Oxford 2011, p. 65.
2. David Anderson, *Histories of the Hanged*, London 2005; Caroline Elkins, *Britain's Gulag*, London 2005; Huw Bennett, *Fighting the Mau Mau: The British Army and Counter-Insurgency in the Kenya Emergency*, LondonCambridge 2013 ; Andrew Mumford, *The Counter-Insurgency Myth: The British Experience of Irregular Warfare*, London 2012; Benjamin Grob-Fitzgibbon, *Imperial Endgame: Britain's Dirty Wars and the End of Empire*, Basingstoke 2011. It is also worth noticing a recent attempt to challenge this consensus: Aaron Edwards, *Defending the Realm? The Politics of Britain's Small Wars since 1945*, Manchester 2012. Britain, Edwards still insists, 'has good reason to regard itself as a market-leader in fighting small wars' (p. 291).
3. See Jones and Smith, 'Myth and the small war tradition: Reassessing the Discourse of British Counter-insurgency'. They argue that 'running parallel to a record of prevailing in small wars it chose to fight, Britain has an equally well established tradition of cutting-and-running in wars where it did not' (2013) (p. 456).
4. One of the most startling achievements of the Bush Aadministrations was the way theyit inherited a $237 billion budget surplus and by late 2004 had turned it into a $413 billion deficit. By the time Bush left office, the deficit, taking into account various attempts to distort the figures, had reached $790 billion. See Deepak Tripathi, *Overcoming the Bush Legacy in Iraq and Afghanistan*, Washington DC 2010, pp. 16–17. Astonishingly, as Alasdair Roberts points out, the Bush Aadministration was committed to 'a program of tax reductions' so that 'the 9/11 crisis became the first security crisis in modern American history in which the tax burden imposed by the federal government actually declined'. See Alasdair Roberts, *The Collapse of Fortress Bush*, New York 2008, p. 60.
5. Mumford, op. cit., pp. 1, 153.
6. Edwards, op. cit., p. 238.
7. H. R. McMaster, *Dereliction of Duty: Lyndon Johnson, Robert McNamara, the Joint Chiefs of Staff and the Lies That Led to Vietnam*, New York 1997. McMaster, a serving US Army officer, was promoted to Lieutenant General in 2014. He is a veteran of both the Iraq and Afghan Wars.

1 At War with Zion

1. David R. Devereaux, *The Formulation of British Defence Policy towards the Middle East, 1948–56*, London 1990, p. 22.
2. Michael J. Cohen, *Palestine and the Great Powers, 1945–48*, Princeton 1982, pp. 15–16.

3. Howard M. Sachar, *A History of Israel*, Oxford 1976, p. 156.
4. J.C. Hurewitz, *The Struggle for Palestine*, New York 1968, p.109. For Wingate in Palestine see Moshe Dayan, *Story of My Life*, London 1976, pp. 28–30, and Leonard Mosley, *Gideon Goes to War*, London 1955, pp. 34–78. See also A.J. Sherman, *Mandate Days*, London 1997, pp. 108–16. The Emergency regulations used by the British to defeat the Arab revolt were to be later used by the Israelis: Naomi Shepherd, *Ploughing the Sand: British Rule in Palestine*, London 1999, p. 246.
5. Sachar, *op. cit.*, pp. 222–26.
6. Yigal Allon, *Shield of David*, New York 1970, p. 140.
7. Yehuda Bauer, *From Diplomacy to Resistance*, Philadelphia 1970, pp.114–18; Sachar, *op. cit.*, pp. 232–42.
8. For the Revisionist movement see Lenni Brenner, *The Iron Wall*, London 1984.
9. For the LEHI see Y.S. Brenner, 'The Stern Gang 1940–48', *Middle Eastern Studies*, 2 (1), October 1965, and more recently by Joseph Heller, *The Stern Gang: Ideology, Politics and Terror 1940–1949*, London 1995.
10. Geoffrey J. Morton, *Just the Job*, London 1957, pp. 137–49; Edward Horne, *A Job Well Done*, Tiptree 1982, pp. 274–78. For a recent account see Patrick Bishop, *The Reckoning*, London 2014.
11. Menachem Begin, *The Revolt*, London 1979, pp. 42–43.
12. J. Bowyer Bell, *Terror Out of Zion*, Dublin 1977, p. 91.
13. For an account of the assassination of Lord Moyne see Gerald Frank, *The Deed*, New York 1963. According to his nephew, Sir Henry Channon, Lord Moyne was 'the only modern Guinness to play a social or political role... He collected yachts, fish, monkeys and women', Robert Rhodes James (ed.), *Chips: The Diaries of Sir Henry Channon*, London 1967, p. 241.
14. Nicholas Bethell, *The Palestine Triangle*, London 1979, p. 181.
15. Michael J. Cohen, *Churchill and the Jews*, London 1985, p. 258.
16. Hurewitz, *op. cit.*, p. 201.
17. Tom Segev, *One Palestine Complete: Jews and Arabs under the British Mandate*, London 2000, pp. 471–72.
18. Benjamin Grob-Fitzgibbon, *Imperial Endgame: Britain's Dirty Wars and the End of Empire*, Basingstoke 2011, pp. 18–19.
19. Bowyer Bell, *op. cit.*, pp. 128–34; Eitan Haber, *Menahem Begin*, New York 1978, pp. 142–43.
20. Begin, *op. cit.*, pp. 133–53.
21. For the Labour Party and Palestine see Joseph Gorny, *The British Labour Movement and Zionism, 1917–1948*, London 1983, pp. 164–88.
22. David Horowitz, *State in the Making*, Westport 1953, pp. 3–4.
23. See David Cesarani, *Justice Delayed: How Britain Became a Refuge for Nazi War Criminals*, London 1992.
24. Sacher, *op. cit.*, pp. 245–46.
25. Alan Bullock, *Ernest Bevin: Foreign Secretary*, London 1983, pp. 173–81. For Bevin's anti-Semitism see Peter Weiler, *Ernest Bevin*, Manchester 1993, p. 170. According to one account, Bevin's hostility to the Zionists derived from his belief that Ben Gurion and Co. were dangerously left-wing; see W. Roger Louis, 'British Imperialism and the End of the Palestine Mandate', from W. Roger Louis and Robert Stookey, *The End of the Palestine Mandate*, London 1986, p. 24.

26. Gregory Blaxland, *The Regiments Depart*, London 1971, pp. 32–33.
27. Bowyer Bell, *op. cit.*, pp. 152–53.
28. Norman Rose, *A Senseless Squalid War: Voices From Palestine 1945–1948*, London 2009, p. 107.
29. For discussions of the development of British counterinsurgency and for its weaknesses in Palestine see Thomas Mockaitis, *British Counter-Insurgency, 1919–60*, London 1990; Bruce Hoffman, *The Failure of British Military Strategy within Palestine, 1939–1947*, Tel Aviv 1983; and David Charters, *The British Army and Jewish Insurgency in Palestine, 1945–47*, London 1989.
30. See David Charters, 'British Intelligence in the Palestine Campaign, 1945–47', *Intelligence and National Security*, 6 (1), January 1991; Nigel West, *The Friends*, London 1988, p. 35.
31. R.D. Wilson, *Cordon and Search*, Aldershot 1949, pp. 75–76. The author was a paratroop officer who served with 6th Airborne in Palestine.
32. *Ibid.*, p. 47.
33. Nigel Riley, *One Jump Ahead*, London 1984, p. 185.
34. Robert Lackner, *Zionist Terrorism and Imperial Response*, Saarbrucken 2010, p. 64.
35. Bethell, *op. cit.*, pp. 233–34.
36. Bullock, *op. cit.*, p. 257.
37. Sacher, *op. cit.*, pp. 263–64; Bethell, *op. cit.*, pp. 237–38.
38. Hugh Thomas, *John Strachey*, London 1973, p. 229.
39. Bernard Montgomery, *Memoirs*, London 1958, pp. 387–88.
40. For accounts of the King David Hotel incident see Thurston Clarke, *By Blood and Fire*, London 1981, and Bethell, *op. cit.*, pp. 253–67.
41. Bowyer Bell, *op. cit.*, p. 174; Blaxland, *op. cit.*, p. 44. Barker later claimed that his remarks were an ill-considered outburst that did not reflect his considered views, but his correspondence with his Arab lover, Katy Antonius, reveals a vicious anti-Semite: 'Yes I loathe the lot of them – whether they be Zionists or not. Why should we be afraid of saying we hate them – it's time this damned race knew what we think of them – loathsome people', in Segev, *op. cit.*, p. 480. Matt Golani (ed.), *The End of the British Mandate for Palestine 1948: The Diary of Sir Henry Gurney*, Basingstoke 2009, p 11.
42. See Joseph Heller, '"Neither Masada–Nor Vichy": Diplomacy and Resistance in Zionist Politics, 1945–1947', *International History Review*, 3, 1981.
43. Samuel Katz, *Days of Fire*, London 1968, p. 110.
44. Hoffman, *op. cit.*, p. 26. For a sympathetic account of Cunningham see W. Roger Louis, 'Sir Alan Cunningham and the End of British Rule in Palestine', *Journal of Imperial and Commonwealth Studies*, XVI (2), May 1988.
45. Wilson, *op. cit.*, p. 112.
46. Colin Mitchell, *Having Been a Soldier*, London 1969, pp. 58–59.
47. Montgomery, *op. cit.*, pp. 428, 429.
48. Roy Farran, *Winged Dagger*, London 1948, p. 348.
49. Bernard Fergusson, *The Trumpet in the Hall*, London 1970, pp. 210–40. For discussion of the Farran affair see Horne, *op. cit.*, pp. 564–66; David Charters, 'Special Operations in Counter-Insurgency: The Farran Case: Palestine 1947', *Journal of the Royal United Services Institution*, 124 (2), June 1979; and David Cesarani, *Major Farran's Hat: Murder, Scandal and Britain's War Against Jewish Terrorism 1945–1948*, London 2009.
50. Cohen, *Palestine and the Great Powers*, pp. 242–43.

246 Notes

51. Bowyer Bell, *op. cit.*, pp. 236–38; Smith, *op. cit.*, p. 76; and Rose, *op. cit.*, pp. 136–38
52. Ze'ev Venia Hadari, *Second Exodus*, London 1991; Ruth Gruber, *Destination Palestine*, New York 1948; and Jon and David Kimche, *The Secret Roads*, London 1955. And most recently Aviva Halamish, *The Exodus Affair: Holocaust Survivors and the Struggle for Palestine*, London 1998.
53. Ritchie Ovendale, *Britain, the United States and the End of the Palestine Mandate, 1942–1948*, Woodbridge 1989, pp. 210, 217.
54. Grob-Fitzgibbon, *op. cit.*, p. 90.
55. For the fate of the Arabs at Zionist hands see Simha Flapan, *The Birth of Israel*, New York 1987; Michael Palumbo, *The Palestinian Catastrophe*, London 1987; and Benny Morris, *The Birth of the Palestinian Refugee Problem*, Cambridge 1988. See also Benny Morris, *Righteous Victims: A History of the Zionist–Arab Conflict 1881–1999*, London 2000.

2 The Running Dog War: Malaya

1. Robert Thompson, 'Foreword' to Richard Clutterbuck, *The Long Long War*, London 1966, p. VIII. Major General Clutterbuck, himself a veteran of the Malayan Emergency, was another prominent advocate of the British 'model' for counterinsurgency operations and this book was written with the explicit intention of offering lessons for the Americans in Vietnam. For an interesting comparative discussion of Malaya and Vietnam see Robert Tilman, 'The Non-Lessons of the Malayan Emergency', *Asian Survey*, 6 (8), 1966.
2. For Thompson and Vietnam see 'Robert Thompson and the British Advisory Mission to South Vietnam 1961–1965', *Small Wars and Insurgencies*, 8 (3), Winter 1997.
3. J.J. McCuen, *The Art of Counter-Revolutionary Warfare*, London 1966, p. 320. McCuen thanks the then Colonel Clutterbuck, attached at the time to the US Army Command and General Staff College at Fort Leavenworth for his assistance with this book.
4. Martin Gilbert, *Never Despair: Winston Churchill 1945–1965*, London 1988, p. 934.
5. J.H. Brimmell, *Communism in South East Asia*, London 1959, p. 96.
6. Rene Onraet, *Singapore – A Police Background*, London 1947, pp. 116–17.
7. F. Spencer Chapman, *The Jungle is Neutral*, London 1949, p. 18. See also Brian Moynahan, *Jungle Soldier: The True Story of Freddy Spencer Chapman*, London 2009.
8. Charles Cruikshank, *SOE in the Far East*, London 1983, pp. 63–64.
9. Lee Tong Foong, 'The MPAJA and the Revolutionary Struggle 1939–1945', in Mohamed Amin and Malcolm Caldwell, *Malaya: The Making of a Neo-Colony*, Nottingham 1977, pp. 99–100. See also Brian Montgomery, *Shenton of Singapore*, London 1984, p. 161.
10. Spencer Chapman, *op. cit.*, pp. 147, 160, 162. For other accounts by British soldiers and civilians living with the Communist guerrillas see Robert Cross and Dorothy Thatcher, *Pai Naa*, London 1959; John Cross, *Red Jungle*, London 1958; and Robert Hamond, *A Fearful Freedom*, London 1984. See also Joseph Kennedy, *British Civilians and the Japanese War in Malaya and Singapore*, London 1987, pp. 104–21.

11. For the effectiveness of the MPAJA see Cheah Boon Kheng, *Red Star Over Malaya*, Singapore 1983, pp. 63–64. See also Paul H. Kratoska, *Malaya and Singapore During the Japanese Occupation*, Singapore 1995.
12. Spencer Chapman, *op. cit.*, p. 381.
13. Michael R. Stenson, *Repression and Revolt*, Athens, Ohio 1969, p. 1.
14. Cheah Boon Kheng, *op. cit.*, pp. 122–23.
15. Edgar O'Ballance, *Malaya: The Communist Insurgent War*, London 1966, pp. 62–63.
16. Cheah Boon Kheng, *op. cit.*, pp. 96–100. See also Leon Comber, '"Traitor of all Traitors" – Secret Agent Extraordinaire: Lai Tek, Secretary General, Communist Party of Malaya 1939-1947', *Journal of the Malaysian of Branch the Royal Asiatic Society*, **80** (2), 2010.
17. *Ibid.*, pp. 82–100.
18. *Ibid.*, pp. 195–241.
19. For industrial conflict see Michael R. Stenson, *Industrial Conflict in Malaya*, London 1970. See also T.N. Harper, *The End of Empire and the Making of Malaya*, Cambridge 1999, p. 80.
20. Hua Wu Yin, *Class and Communalism in Malaya*, London 1983, pp. 76–85. A recently elected Labour MP, Woodrow Wyatt, described how, on a visit to the country, 'young Chinese and young Malays, intelligent, willing to be democratic, anxious for self-government, asked me repeatedly when I was there...what there was to show the difference in Malaya between a Labour Government and any other Government'. His conclusion was that there 'has been a Labour Government in Britain but not in Malaya': Woodrow Wyatt, *Southwards from China*, London 1952, p. 157.
21. For useful discussions of this question see in particular Ruth T. McVey, *The Calcutta Conference and the Southeast Asian Uprisings*, New York 1958; Charles B. McLane, *Soviet Strategies in Southeast Asia*, New Jersey 1966; Michael R. Stenson, *The 1948 Communist Revolt in Malaya: A Note on Historical Sources and Interpretation*, Singapore 1971; Frank Furedi, *Colonial Wars and the Politics of Third World Nationalism*, London 1994.
22. Michael Morgan, 'The Rise and Fall of Malayan Trade Unionism 1945–1950', from Amin and Caldwell, *op. cit.*, p. 182.
23. Stenson, *Repression and Revolt*, *op. cit.*, p. 182.
24. Harper, *op. cit.*, p. 144.
25. Morgan, *op. cit.*, p. 157.
26. Ritchie Ovendale, 'Britain and the Cold War in Asia', from Ritchie Ovendale (ed.), *The Foreign Policy of the British Labour Governments 1945–1951*, Leicester 1984, p. 125.
27. Lee Kam Hing, 'Malaya: New State and Old Elites', from Robin Jeffrey (ed.), *Asia: The Winning of Independence*, London 1981, p. 234.
28. D.K. Fieldhouse review of D.J. Morgan, *The Official History of Colonial Development* Vols 1–5, in *English Historical Review* **97** (2), April 1982, pp. 386–94. See also A.J. Stockwell, 'British Imperial Policy and Decolonization in Malaya 1943–1952', *Journal of Imperial and Commonwealth History*, **13** (1), October 1984.
29. Nicholas J. White, *Business, Governments and the End of Empire: Malaya 1942–1952*, Kuala Lumpur 1996, p. 5. See also Tilman Remme, *Britain and Regional Cooperation in South-East Asia 1945–19*, London 1995, pp. 11–12.

30. Hua Wu Yin, *op. cit.*, p. 91.
31. Cheah Boon Kheng, *The Masked Comrades*, Singapore 1979, pp. 63–72.
32. Sir Robert Thompson, *Make for the Hills*, London 1989, p. 94.
33. Morgan, *op. cit.*, pp. 190–92.
34. Gerald de Cruz, 'Reply' from Stenson, *The 1948 Communist Revolt*, *op. cit.*, p. 24.
35. J.B. Perry Robinson, *Transformation in Malaya*, London 1956, pp. 118–22.
36. For the influence of Maoist ideas on the MCP see Khong Kim Hoong, *Merdeka! British Rule and the Struggle of Independence in Malaya 1945–1957*, Selanger 1984, p. 138. See also E.D. Smith, *Malaya and Borneo*, London 1985, pp. 7–8 and Gene Z. Hanrahan, *The Communist Struggle in Malaya*, New York 1994, p. 63.
37. Perry Robinson, *op. cit.*, pp. 46–47.
38. Norton Ginsburg and Chester Roberts, *Malaya*, Seattle 1958, pp. 54, 87.
39. See Michael Stenson, 'The Ethnic and Urban Bases of Communist Revolt in Malaya', from John Wilson Lewis (ed.), *Peasant Rebellion and Communist Revolution in Asia*, Stanford 1974. For 'divide and rule' in Malaya see Frank Furedi, 'Britain's Colonial Wars: Playing the Ethnic Card', *Journal of Commonwealth and Comparative Studies*, **28** (1), March 1990.
40. O'Ballance, *op. cit.*, p. 85.
41. Noel Barber, *The Running Dog War*, London 1971, p. 53.
42. Michael Carver, *War Since 1945*, London 1980, pp. 17–18.
43. Malcolm Caldwell, 'From "Emergency" to "Independence" 1945–1957', from Amin and Caldwell, *op. cit.*, pp. 221–22.
44. Hanrahan, *op. cit.*, p. 65; David French, *The British Way in Counterinsurgency 1945–1967*, Oxford 2011, p. 110. One account describes the scene in Port Swettenham where deportees were assembled: 'its main street echoes to their revolutionary songs and their shouted insults. They have the satisfaction of shaking their fists at the police': Vernon Bartlett, *Report from Malaya*, London 1954, p. 48.
45. Anthony Short, *The Communist Insurrection in Malaya 1948–1960*, London 1975, pp. 383–85.
46. Thompson, *Make For the Hills*, *op. cit.*, p. 93.
47. Short, *op. cit.*, pp. 211–12.
48. Lawrence James, *Imperial Rearguard*, London 1988, p. 137.
49. David A. Charters, 'From Palestine to Northern Ireland: British Adaptations to Low-Intensity Operations', from David A. Charters and Maurice Tugwell (eds), *Armies in Low-Intensity Conflict*, London 1989, pp. 190–92.
50. Huw Bennett, '"A very salutary effect": The Counter-Terror Strategy in the Early Malayan Emergency, June 1948 to December 1949', *Journal of Strategic Studies*, **32** (3), 2009, p. 417.
51. Harry Miller, *Menace in Malaya*, London 1954, p. 89.
52. Perry Robinson, *op. cit.*, p. 79.
53. Bennett, *op. cit.*, p. 433.
54. For the Batang Kali massacre see Ian Ward and Norma Miraflor, *Slaughter and Deception at Batang Kali*, Singapore 2008 and Christopher Hale, *Massacre in Malaya: Exposing Britain's My Lai*, Stroud 2013.
55. Christopher Bayly and Tim Harper, *Forgotten Wars: The End of Britain's Asian Empire*, London 2007, p. 455.

56. Bennett, *op. cit.*, p. 432.
57. Susan Carruthers, *Winning Hearts and Minds: British Governments, the Media and Colonial Counter-Insurgency*, London 1995, p. 100.
58. Richard Stubbs, *Hearts and Minds in Guerrilla Warfare*, London 1989, pp. 66, 73.
59. Clutterbuck, *op. cit.*, p. 57.
60. Charles Townshend, *Britain's Civil Wars*, London 1986, p. 159.
61. Sir Robert Thompson, *Defeating Communist Insurgency*, London 1966, pp. 51, 116. For recent discussions of the relevance of Thompson's thinking to the wars in Iraq and Afghanistan see Andrew Mumford, 'Sir Robert Thompson's Lessons for Iraq', *Defence Studies* 10 (1–2), 2010 and James Pritchard and MLR Smith, 'Thompson in Helmand', *Civil Wars* 12 (1–2), 2010.
62. Geoffrey Fairbairn, *Revolutionary Guerrilla Warfare*, London 1974, p. 139.
63. Short, *op. cit.*, pp. 239–40.
64. Caldwell, *op. cit.*, p. 235. See also Francis Loh Kok Wah, *Beyond the Tin Mines*, Oxford 1988, for the impact of resettlement in the Kinta Valley.
65. E.D. Smith, *East of Katmandu*, London 1976, p. 19.
66. Perry Robinson, *op. cit.*, p. 115.
67. Wah, *op. cit.*, p. 161.
68. See Michael Tracey, *A Variety of Lives*, London 1983. Greene had considerable experience in the field of psychological warfare, having been head of the BBC's German Service during the War and subsequently of its East European Service where he had, among other things, attempted to destabilise Communist Albania.
69. Short, *op. cit.*, pp. 318–21.
70. Chin Peng, *Alias Chin Peng: My Side of History*, Singapore 2003, p. 299. See also A.J. Stockwell, 'Chin Peng and the Struggle for Malaya', *Journal of the Royal Asiatic Society*, 16 (3), 2006.
71. John Coates, *Suppressing Insurgency: An Analysis of the Malayan Emergency 1948–1954*, Boulder, Colorado 1992, p. 118 and Karl Hack, *Defence and Decolonisation in Southeast Asia: Britain, Malaya and Singapore 1941–1968*, Richmond 2001, pp. 124–25. For a strong urging of Templer's importance see Kumar Ramakrishna, '"Transmogrifying" Malaya: The Impact of Sir Gerald Templer 1952–1954', *Journal of Southeast Asian Studies*, 32 (1), 2001.
72. Michael Carver, *Out of Step*, London 1989, pp. 280–81, 283.
73. For the development of British tactics see in particular Sir William Jackson, *Withdrawal from Empire*, London 1986, pp. 91–92, 120–21; Smith, *Malaya and Borneo*, *op. cit.*, pp. 25–31; and Raffi Gregorian, '"Jungle Bashing" in Malaya: Towards a Formal Tactical Doctrine', *Small Wars and Insurgencies*, 5 (3), Winter 1994. There is a large body of memoir literature available: Richard Miers, *Shoot to Kill*, London 1959; Oliver Crawford, *The Door Marked Malaya*, London 1958; A.E.C. Bredin, *Happy Warriors*, Gillingham 1961; J.P. Cross, *In Gurkha Company*, London 1986; J.W.G. Moran, *Spearhead in Malaya*, London 1959; Arthur Campbell, *Jungle Green*, London 1953; Roy Follows with Hugh Popham, *Jungle Beat*, London 1990, among others. For a more critical view of the British performance by another participant see Frank Kitson, *A Bunch of Five*, London 1977. For a number of accounts by British conscripts, among them Neil Ascherson, see Adrian Walker, *Six Campaigns*, London 1977.

74. For an account of the pacification of a district see Clutterbuck, *op. cit.*, pp. 112–21. Also see F.A. Godfrey, *The History of the Suffolk Regiment*, London 1988, pp. 46–54.
75. Jackson, *op. cit.*, p. 122.
76. Harry Miller, *Jungle War in Malaya*, London 1972, p. 90.
77. There are accounts of the intelligence war in Jonathan Bloch and Patrick Fitzgerald, *British Intelligence and Covert Action*, London 1983, pp. 71–74; Nigel West, *The Friends: Britain's Post-War Secret Intelligence Operations*, London 1988, pp. 41–50; Richard J. Aldrich, Gary D. Rawnsley and Ming-Yeh T. Rawnsley (eds), *The Clandestine Cold War in Asia 1954–1965*, London 2000; Karl Hack, 'Intelligence and Counter-Insurgency: The Example of Malaya', *Intelligence and National Security*, **14** (2), Summer 1999; and Leon Comber *Malaya's Secret Police 1945–1960: The Role of the Special Branch in the* Malayan Emergency, Monash 2008. For an interesting overview of intelligence and counterinsurgency see Keith Jeffrey, 'Intelligence and Counter-Insurgency Operations: Some Reflections on the British Experience', *Intelligence and National Security*, **28** (1), January 1987.
78. Calder Walton, *Empire of Secrets: British Intelligence, the Cold War and the Twilight of Empire*, London 2013, pp. 188–93.
79. Perry Robinson, *op. cit.*, pp. 154–55.
80. Philip Anthony Towle, *Pilots and Rebels*, London 1989, p. 86.
81. Andrew Mumford, 'Unnecessary or unsung? The utilization of airpower in Britain's colonial counterinsurgencies', *Small Wars and Insurgencies*, 20 (3–4), 2009, p. 640. See also Malcolm Postgate, *Operation Firedog*, London 1992.
82. Follows, *op. cit.*, p. 110.
83. John Cloake, *Templer: Tiger of Malaya*, London 1985, pp. 254–55.
84. Short, *op. cit.*, p. 387.
85. Coates, *op cit.*, p. 92.
86. James, *op. cit.*, p. 155. See also Paul Frederick Cecil, *Herbicidal Warfare*, New York 1986, p. 17: Cecil argues that 'the positive aspects of the British experience in Malaya would form the basis for future American involvement in herbicidal warfare in Southeast Asia'.
87. Cloake, *op. cit.*, pp. 256–58; Perry Robinson, *op. cit.*, pp. 171–78. For the SAS in Malaya see Alan Hoe and Eric Morris, *Re-Enter the SAS*, London 1994 and John Strawson, *A History of the SAS Regiment*, London 1986. See also my *Dangerous Men: The SAS and Popular Culture*, London 1997.
88. Stubbs, *op. cit.*, p. 107.
89. See Richard Stubbs, 'The United Malays National Organization, the Malayan Chinese Association, and the early years of the Malayan Emergency 1948–1955', *Journal of Southeast Asian Studies*, **10** (1), March 1979 and A.J. Stockwell, 'Insurgency and Decolonisation during the Malayan Emergency', *Journal of Commonwealth and Comparative Politics*, **25** (1), March 1987.
90. Cross, *op. cit.*, p. 23.
91. Barbara Watson Andaya and Leonard Y. Andaya, *A History of Malaysia*, London 1982, pp. 261–63.
92. For the Baling Talks see Short, *op. cit.*, pp. 461–71 and Lapping, *op. cit.*, pp. 182–84.
93. For this last phase of the Emergency see in particular Clutterbuck, *Conflict and Violence, op. cit.*, pp. 220–60; Gregory Blaxland, *The Regiments Depart*,

London 1971, pp. 115–30; and Tom Pocock, *Fighting General*, London 1973, pp. 101–06. See also Kumar Ramakrishna, 'Anatomy of a Collapse: Explaining the Malayan Communist Mass Surrenders of 1958', *War and Society*, **21** (2), 2003. For the MCP decision to demobilise see Aloysius Chin, *The Communist Party of Malaya: The Inside Story*, Kuala Lumpur 1995, p. 50.
94. Victor Purcell, *Malaya: Communist or Free?*, London 1954, p. 146.
95. Short, *op. cit.*, pp. 208–10.

3 The Mau Mau Revolt

1. David Anderson, *The Histories of the Hanged*, London 2005, p. 1. Martin Thomas describes it as 'the dirtiest of Britain's colonial fights'. See *Fight or Flight: Britain, France and their Roads from Empire*, Oxford 2014, p. 218.
2. M.P.K. Sorrenson, *Land Reform in the Kikuyu Country*, Nairobi 1968, p. 79.
3. Frank Furedi, 'The Social Composition of the Mau Mau Movement in the White Highlands', *Journal of Peasant Studies*, **4**, July 1974, p. 492. For contrasting accounts of the role of the squatters in the Mau Mau Rebellion see also Frank Furedi, *The Mau Mau War in Perspective*, London 1989 and Tabitha Kanogo, *Squatters and the Roots of Mau Mau*, London 1987.
4. *Report of the East Africa Royal Commission 1953–1955*, London 1955, pp. 206–09. See also David Throup, *Economic and Social Origins of Mau Mau*, London 1987.
5. For African disappointment and its consequences see John Spencer, *The Kenya African Union*, London 1985.
6. See Donald Burnett and Karari Njama, *Mau Mau From Within*, London 1966, pp. 54–55. See also Susan Carruthers, *Winning Hearts and Minds: British Governments, The Media and Colonial Counter-Insurgency 1944–1960*, Leicester 1995, p. 132.
7. The role of the trade unions in the revolt is dealt with in the official report on Mau Mau: F.D. Corfield, *Historical Survey of the Origins and Growth of Mau Mau*, London 1960, pp. 255–58. For a path-breaking academic study see Sharon Stichter, 'Workers, Trade Unions and the Mau Mau Rebellion', *Canadian Journal of African Studies*, **9** (2), 1975. More recently see Spencer *op. cit.*, pp. 266–71.
8. Makhan Singh, *History of Kenya's Trade Union Movement to 1952*, Nairobi 1969, pp. 274–79. Throup, *op. cit.*, p. 196. For a recent account see Dave Hyde, 'The Nairobi General Strike (1950): From protest to insurgency', *Azania: Archaeological Research in Africa*, **36–37** (1), 2001.
9. Ioan Davies, *African Trade Unions*, London 1966, p. 77.
10. Frank Furedi has identified the 'Forty Group', a loose association of ex-servicemen of the age-group circumcised in 1940 as the driving force behind the revolutionary movement in Nairobi. See his 'The African Crowd in Nairobi: Popular Movements and Elite Politics', *Journal of African History*, **14** (2), 1973, p. 285, where he describes it as 'the most successful populist political initiative in Kenya's history'. This has been disputed, correctly in my opinion, by other authorities, for example, Carl Rosberg and John Nottingham, who, in their *The Myth of Mau Mau*, New York 1966, p. 240, argue that the 'Forty Group' was 'absorbed into the African trade union movement which rapidly became the most militant force for protest in Nairobi'.

11. Spencer, *op. cit.*, p. 271.
12. Bildad Kaggia, *Roots of Freedom*, Nairobi 1975, p. 110.
13. Guy Arnold, *Kenyatta and the Politics of Kenya*, London 1974, pp. 104–09.
14. Kaggia, *op. cit.*, p. 114.
15. Josiah Mwangi Kariuki, *Mau Mau Detainee*, London 1963, p. 23.
16. A. Marshal McPhee, *Kenya*, London 1968, p. 116.
17. Corfield, *op. cit.*, p. 159.
18. Ladislav Venys, *A History of the Mau Mau Movement in Kenya*, Prague 1970, p. 49.
19. Barnett and Njama, *op. cit.*, pp. 69–71; Huw Bennett, *Fighting The Mau Mau: The British Army and Counter-Insurgency in the Kenya Emergency*, Cambridge 2013, p. 14. See also Frank Furedi, *Colonial Wars and the Politics of Third World Nationalism*, London 1994, pp. 159–64.
20. Anthony Clayton, *Counter-Insurgency in Kenya 1952–1960*, Nairobi 1976, p. 7.
21. For an account of loyalism and its social background see Bethwell A. Ogot, 'Revolt of the Elders: An Anatomy of the Loyalist Crowd in the Mau Mau Uprising 1952–1956', in Bethwell A. Ogot, *Politics and Nationalism in Kenya*, Nairobi 1972.
22. Rosberg and Nottingham, *op. cit.*, pp. 286–92; John Lonsdale, 'The Moral Economy of the Mau Mau', from John Lonsdale and Bruce Berman, *Unhappy Valley*, Vol. 2, London 1992, pp. 453–54.
23. Peter Evans, *Law and Disorder*, London 1956, p. 70. As David Anderson puts it, while the story of the Lari massacre 'was hashed and rehashed, the state's counter-terror in the aftermath of the attack was only vaguely hinted at' and eventually 'forgotten; British propaganda would see to that'. See Anderson, *op. cit.*, pp. 177–78.
24. Charles Douglas-Home, *Evelyn Baring, The Last Proconsul*, London 1978, p. 228. See also John Lonsdale, 'Kenyatta's Trials: breaking and making an African nationalist', from Peter Coss (ed.), *The Moral World of the Law*, Cambridge 2000.
25. *Report to the Secretary of State for the Colonies by the Parliamentary Delegation to Kenya: January 1954*, London 1954, p. 7.
26. Ione Leigh, *In the Shadow of Mau Mau*, London 1954, pp. 166–69.
27. Corfield, *op. cit.*, p. 205.
28. Sir Michael Blundell, *So Rough a Wind*, London 1960, pp. 170–71. According to one officer in the Kenya Regiment recalling this stage of the rebellion, 'one must be honest and say the Mau Mau won', in Dennis Holman, *Elephants at Sundown*, London 1978, p. 76.
29. Wunyabari O. Maloba, *Mau Mau and Kenya*, Bloomington 1993, pp. 10–11.
30. Stichter, *op. cit.*, p. 273. See also David Goldsworthy, *Tom Mboya: The Man Kenya Wanted To Forget*, London 1982.
31. David French, *The British Way in Counterinsurgency*, Oxford 2011, p. 116.
32. Tom Mboya, *Freedom and After*, London 1963, p. 37.
33. Bennett, *op. cit.*, p. 24.
34. Anthony Clayton and Donald Savage, *Government and Labour in Kenya*, London 1974, p. 389.
35. Michael Carver, *Out of Step*, London 1989, p. 261.

36. Dennis Holman, *Bwana Drum*, London 1964, p. 26. For an important discussion of the role of women in Mau Mau see Cora Ann Presley, *Kikuyu Women, the Mau Mau Rebellion and Social Change in Kenya*, Boulder 1992 and Muthoni Likimani, *Passbook Number F.47927*, London 1985.
37. Anderson, *op. cit.*, p. 294.
38. Caroline Elkins, *Britain's Gulag: The Brutal End of Empire in Kenya*, London 2005, p. 234.
39. Rosberg and Nottingham, *op. cit.*, p. 293.
40. Joran Wamweya, *Freedom Fighter*, Nairobi 1971, p. 151.
41. Peter Hewitt, *Kenya Cowboy*, London 1999, pp. 276–302. This gruesome account of the Emergency positively glories in the violence and brutality. Hewitt routinely describes the Mau Mau as 'brutes' and 'half human half animal'. He writes of how he finished off a wounded rebel: 'The .22 soft-nosed bullet entered the moribund gangster's forehead high up and the smallest of holes appeared though instantly his left eye popped out and hung as an indeterminate blob of white and red upon his shiny black cheek...another Mau Mau brute was in the bag' (p. 257). Back at the station, Mau Mau bodies were left piled up outside as an example, a regular 'macabre exhibition of dead and occasionally dying "micks"'(p. 188).
42. See Frank Kitson, *Gangs and Counter-Gangs*, London 1960 and also my 'A counter-insurgency tale: Kitson in Kenya', *Race and Class*, **31** (4), 1990. For a discussion of the work of British intelligence see Randall W. Heather, 'Intelligence and Counter-Insurgency in Kenya 1952–1956', *Intelligence and National Security*, **5** (3), July 1990.
43. Ian Henderson with Philip Goodhart, *The Hunt for Kimathi*, London 1958.
44. Stephen Chappell, 'Airpower in the Mau Mau conflict: Tthe Government's Chief Weapon', *Small Wars and Insurgencies*, 22 (2,) 2011, p. 506. For a more circumspect view see Andrew Mumford, 'Unnecessary or unsung? The utilization of air power in Britain's colonial counterinsurgencies', *Small Wars and Insurgencies*, 20 (3–4), 2009, p. 647.
45. Huw Bennett and David French (eds), *The Kenya Papers of General Sir George Erskine 1953–1955*, Stroud 2013, pp. 188–90.
46. Sorrenson, *op. cit.*, pp. 117–18.
47. Colin Leys, *Underdevelopment in Kenya*, London 1976, pp. 52–53.
48. Sharon Stichter, 'Imperialism and the Rise of a Labour Aristocracy in Kenya 1945–1970', *Berkeley Journal of Sociology*, **XXI**, 1976–77, pp. 159, 171.
49. Maloba, *op. cit.*, p. 91.
50. D.H. Rawcliffe, *The Struggle for Kenya*, London 1954, p. 68.
51. See the exchange between myself and Thomas Mockaitis: John Newsinger, 'Minimum Force, British Counter-Insurgency and the Mau Mau Rebellion', *Small Wars and Insurgencies*, 3 (1), Spring 1992, and Thomas Mockaitis, 'Minimum Force, British Counter-Insurgency and the Mau Mau Rebellion: A Reply', *Small Wars and Insurgencies*, 3 (2), Autumn 1992. For a later contribution to this debate see Thomas Mockaitis, 'The Minimum Force Debate: Contemporary Sensibilities Meet Imperial Practice', *Small Wars and Insurgencies*, 23 (4–5), 2012.
52. L.B. Greaves, *Carey Francis of Kenya*, London 1969, p. 116.
53. Clayton, *op. cit.*, pp. 44–45.

54. Robert Edgerton, *Mau Mau: An African Crucible*, London 1990, pp. 152–53, 155, 159, 185.
55. William Baldwin, *Mau Mau Man-hunt*, New York 1957, pp. 17, 174, 179–80.
56. Leonard Gill, *Military Musings*, British Columbia 2003, p. 49.
57. See Anderson *op. cit.* and Elkins *op. cit.* For an interesting review of these two books see Bethwell A. Ogot, 'Britain's Gulag', *Journal of African History*, **46** (3) 2005.
58. David Anderson, 'Mau Mau in the High Court and the "Lost" British Empire Archives: Colonial Conspiracy or Bureaucratic Bungle?', *Journal of Imperial and Commonwealth History*, **39** (5), 2011, p. 710. See also in the same number of the *Journal of Imperial and Commonwealth History*: Huw Bennett, 'Soldiers in the Court Room: The British Army in the Kenya Emergency under the Legal Spotlight' and Caroline Elkins, 'Alchemy of Evidence: Mau Mau, the British Empire, and the High Court of Justice'.
59. Ian Cobain and Richard Norton Taylor, 'Sins of Colonialists Lay Concealed for Decades in Secret Archive', *Guardian*, 18 April 2010.
60. Bennett and French, *op. cit.*, p. 36.
61. Michael Dewar, *Brush Fire Wars*, London 1984, p. 62.
62. Simon Raven, *Bird of Ill Omen*, London 1989, pp. 210–11.
63. Bennett, *Fighting The Mau Mau*, *op. cit.*, p. 194.
64. Bruce Berman, *Control and Crisis in Colonial Kenya*, London 1990, p. 358.
65. Eric Downton, *Wars Without End*, Toronto 1987, p. 236.
66. Martin Gilbert, *Never Despair: Winston Churchill 1945–1965*, London 1988, p. 834; Carruthers, *op. cit.*, p. 176.
67. Kitson, *op. cit.*, p. 46.
68. Gregory Blaxland, *The Regiments Depart*, London 1971, pp. 280–81.
69. Holman, *Elephants at Sundown*, *op. cit.*, p. 77.
70. Lord Chandos, *The Memoirs of Lord Chandos*, London 1962, pp. 394–95, 397.
71. For the danger of a Mau Mau revival see Anthony Clayton and David Killingray, *Khaki and Blue*, Athens, Ohio, 1989, p. 129.
72. For example David Goldsworthy, *Colonial Issues in British Politics 1945–1961*, Oxford 1971, p. 28.
73. Leys, *op. cit.*, pp. 39, 42.
74. David Goldsworthy, 'Conservatives and Decolonization', *African Affairs*, July 1970, **69**, (276), p. 279.
75. Philip Darby, *British Defence Policy East of Suez*, London 1973, p. 206.
76. Nigel Fisher, *Iain Macleod*, London 1973, p. 151. For an account of the independence negotiations see Keith Kyle, *The Politics of the Independence of Kenya*, London 1999.

4 Cyprus and EOKA

1. Harold Macmillan, *Tides of Fortune 1945–1955*, London 1969, p. 664.
2. Ioannis D. Stefanidis, *Isle of Discord: Nationalism, Imperialism and the Making of Cyprus*, London 1999, p. 156.
3. David Anderson, 'Policing and communal conflict: the Cyprus Emergency, 1954–60', from David Anderson and David Killingray, *Policing and Decolonisation*, Manchester 1992, p. 190.

4. Anthony Clayton, *The British Empire as a Superpower 1919–1939*, London 1986, pp. 432–35; George Horton Kelling, *Countdown To Rebellion*, Westport 1990, pp. 8–10.
5. For Cypriot Communism see T.W. Adams, *AKEL*, Stanford 1971.
6. Kelling *op. cit.*, pp. 68, 85.
7. Nancy Crawshaw, *The Cyprus Revolt*, London 1978, p. 33.
8. Costas Kyrris, *Peaceful Coexistence in Cyprus*, Nicosia 1977, p. 38.
9. Kyriacos C. Markides, *The Rise and Fall of the Cyprus Republic*, New Haven 1977, p. 13.
10. Crawshaw, *op. cit.*, pp. 46–50.
11. Stanley Mayes, *Cyprus and Makarios*, London 1960, p. 24.
12. David R. Devereux, *The Formulation of British Defence Policy Towards the Middle East 1945–56*, London 1990, pp. 174–75.
13. Robert Holland, *Britain and the Revolt in Cyprus 1954–1959*, Oxford 1998, p. 32.
14. Richard Lamb, *The Failure of the Eden Government*, London 1987, pp. 129–30; Kelling, *op. cit.*, pp. 140–41.
15. W. Byford Jones, *Grivas and the Story of EOKA*, London 1959, p. 35.
16. Crawshaw, *op. cit.*, pp. 94–95.
17. George Grivas, *The Memoirs of General Grivas*, London 1964, pp. 28, 34.
18. Doros Alastos, *Cyprus Guerrilla*, London 1964, p. 59.
19. Grivas, *op. cit.*, p. 25.
20. *Ibid.*, p. 208.
21. Anderson, *op. cit.*, p. 194.
22. Grivas, *op. cit.*, p. 42.
23. Crawshaw, *op. cit.*, p. 139.
24. Brendan O'Malley and Ian Craig, *The Cyprus Conspiracy: America, Espionage and the Turkish Invasion*, London 1999, p. 22. For a discussion of possible British involvement in the September 1955 anti-Greek riots in Turkey see Holland, *op. cit.*, pp. 76–77.
25. Michael Carver, *Harding of Petherton*, London 1978, p. 195.
26. Holland, *op. cit.*, pp. 99–100.
27. Julian Paget, *Counter-Insurgency Campaigning*, London 1967, pp. 122–23.
28. Charles Foley, *Island in Revolt*, London 1962, p. 68; Adams, *op. cit.*, pp. 48–49.
29. Paget, *op. cit.*, p. 147; David Young, *Four Five*, London 1972, p. 247.
30. Calder Walton, *Empire of Secrets: British intelligence, the Cold War and the Twilight of Empire*, London 2013, p. 312.
31. Sandy Cavenagh, *Airborne to Suez*, London 1965, p. 72.
32. Anderson, *op. cit.*, p. 195.
33. Grivas, *op. cit.*, pp. 74–75.
34. Anderson, *op. cit.*, p. 206.
35. Anderson, *op. cit.*, p. 203.
36. The official history of the Grenadier Guards gives a good account of army crowd control procedures at this time: 'Dispersing hostile crowds in built-up areas was a difficult operation which also required sound training. If possible the platoon commander tried to persuade the crowd through an interpreter, using a loudhailer, to go home non-violently. If this failed, a magistrate read the Riot Act. Soldiers would then advance in a line with fixed bayonets as

long as there was no danger of close contact with the crowd, but hand-to-hand fighting had to be avoided. Ringleaders were photographed and, if necessary, tear gas or riot control agents were fired into the crowd. If there was no alternative, for example, if the platoon was about to be overrun, the commander, and he only, could order fire to be opened. A bugle call would first draw the attention to a banner which proclaimed that the crowd must disperse or fire would be opened. If this was ineffective, the commander would indicate to a marksman the ringleader to be shot and the number of rounds to be fired. Fire had to be effective. It was a case of shoot to kill. In the gravest emergency, rapid fire from rifles or bursts from machine guns were acceptable'. See Oliver Lindsay, *Once a Grenadier: The Grenadier Guards 1945–1995*, London 1996, pp. 98–99.

37. Michael Dewar, *Brush Fire Wars*, London 1984, p. 74.
38. Rory Cormac, *Confronting the Colonies: British intelligence and Counterinsurgency*, Oxford 2014, p. 77.
39. Thomas Mockaitis, *British Counterinsurgency 1919–60*, London 1990, pp. 171–72.
40. Charles Foley and W.I. Scobie, *The Struggle for Cyprus*, Stanford 1975, pp. 152–57.
41. Grivas *op. cit.*, pp. 76–77.
42. O'Malley and Craig, *op. cit.*, pp. 43–44.
43. Foley, *op. cit.*, p. 131. According to one British soldier who handed over EOKA prisoners for interrogation, Special Branch were 'bastards. They really knocked these blokes about; I could hear them crying...but I have to admit the terrorists talked'. See Robin Neillands, *A Fighting Retreat: The British Empire 1947–1997*, London 1996, p. 288.
44. David French, *The British Way in Counterinsurgency*, Oxford 2011, pp. 145, 147.
45. For Q patrols see Mockaitis, *op. cit.*, p. 173 and Foley and Scobie, *op. cit.*, pp. 113–14.
46. Gregory Blaxland, *The Regiments Depart*, London 1971, p. 312; Cavenagh, *op. cit.*, p. 79.
47. Dudley Barker, *Grivas*, London 1959, p. 151.
48. Mayes, *op. cit.*, p. 77.
49. Hugh Foot, *A Start in Freedom*, London 1964, pp. 48–49. See also his wife's account: Sylvia Foot, *Emergency Exit*, London 1960.
50. Grivas, *op. cit.*, p. 143.
51. Foley, *op. cit.*, p. 202.
52. Byford Jones, *op. cit.*, pp. 116–22.
53. Walton, *op. cit.*, p. 309.
54. H.D. Purcell, *Cyprus*, London 1969, p. 249.
55. Richard Vinen, *National Service: Conscription in Britain 1945–1963*, London 2014, p. 339.
56. Blaxland, *op. cit.*, p. 320.
57. French, *op. cit.*, p. 57.
58. John Reddaway, *Burdened with Cyprus*, London 1986, p. 69.
59. Richard Aldrich, *GCHQ*, London 2010, pp. 7–8.

5 The Struggle for South Yemen

1. Glen Balfour-Paul, *The End of Empire in the Middle East*, Cambridge 1991, p. 67. See also Karl Pieragostini, *Britain, Aden and South Arabia*, London 1991, p. 3. For the most recent history of both North and South Yemen see Paul Dresch, *A History of Modern Yemen*, Cambridge 2000.
2. Sir Tom Hickinbotham, *Aden*, London 1958, p. 25.
3. Tom Little, *South Arabia*, London 1968, pp. 51–59; Gregory Blaxland, *The Regiments Depart*, London 1971, pp. 421–28.
4. Harold Macmillan, *At The End of The Day 1961–1963*, London 1973, p. 265. According to David Holden the establishment of the Federation was 'forced wedlock' that 'involved violence akin to rape': David Holden, *Farewell to Arabia*, London 1966, p. 63.
5. Fred Halliday, *Arabia Without Sultans*, London 1974, pp. 156–62, 180.
6. R.J. Gavin, *Aden Under British Rule 1839–1967*, London 1975, p. 327.
7. Simon Smith, 'Revolution and Reaction: South Arabia in the Aftermath of the Yemeni Revolution', *Journal of Imperial and Commonwealth History*, 28 (3), September 2000, p. 197.
8. For developments in North Yemen see Halliday, *op. cit.*, pp. 101–26 and Dresch, *op. cit.*, pp. 89–118.
9. Macmillan, *op. cit.*, pp. 267, 273.
10. There is a growing literature on this 'covert' operation but see in particular Stephen Dorril, *MI6: Fifty Years of Special Operations*, London 2000, pp. 677–99. See also David Smiley, *Arabian Assignment*, London 1975; John Cooper, *One of the Originals*, London 1991; Xan Fielding, *One Man in His Time*, London 1990; Peter de la Billiere, *Looking for Trouble*, London 1994; Clive Jones, *Britain and the Yemen Civil War*, Eastbourne 2004; and Duff Hart-Davis, *The War That Never Was*, London 2011.
11. Joseph Kostiner, *The Struggle for South Yemen*, London 1984, p. 53.
12. According to Dresch, *op. cit.*, p. 107, the three books remembered as formative by NLF militants were Arabic translations of Jack London's *The Iron Heel*, Maxim Gorky's *Mother* and Georges Politzer's *Principles of Philosophy*, the last being a Marxist textbook.
13. Blaxland, *op. cit.*, p. 435.
14. Kennedy Trevaskis, *Shades of Amber*, London 1969, pp. 207–208.
15. Julian Paget, *Last Post: Aden 1964–1967*, London 1969, pp. 40–41.
16. Sir William Jackson, *Withdrawal from Empire*, London 1986, p. 222.
17. Halliday, *op. cit.*, pp. 198–99.
18. Sir David Lees, *Flight from the Middle East*, London 1980, p. 217.
19. Halliday, *op. cit.*, p. 199.
20. Charles Allen, *The Savage Wars of Peace*, London 1990, p. 163.
21. Thomas Mockaitis, *British Counterinsurgency in the Post-Imperial Era*, London 1995, p. 55.
22. For a different view see Paget, *op. cit.*, p. 113.
23. Little, *op. cit.*, p. 117.
24. J.B. Kelley, *Arabia, the Gulf and the West*, London 1980, p. 21.
25. Aaron Edwards, *Mad Mitch's Tribal Law: Aden and the End of Empire*, Edinburgh 2014, p. 92; Bruce Reed and Geoffrey Williams, *Denis Healey and the Policies of Power*, London 1971, p. 247.

26. See also David Ledger, *Shifting Sands*, London 1983, p. 120.
27. Paget, *op. cit.*, p. 119.
28. David Charters, 'From Palestine to Northern Ireland: British Adaptations to Low Intensity Operations', from David Charters and Maurice Tugwell, *Armies in Low-Intensity Conflict*, London 1993, p. 219.
29. Michael Barthorp, *Crater to the Creggan*, London 1976, p. 39.
30. Stephen Harper, *Last Sunset*, London 1978, p. 85. Robin Neillands, *By Sea and Land*, London 1987, p. 213.
31. Barthorp, *op. cit.*, pp. 39, 44; Paget, *op. cit.*, p. 148.
32. Tony Geraghty, *Who Dares Wins*, London 1992, pp. 400–403.
33. On torture see Halliday, *op. cit.*, pp. 203–207. For a different view see Ledger, *op. cit.*, p. 91. And more recently Edwards, *op. cit.*, p. 122.
34. Robert Holland, *European Decolonisation*, London 1985, p. 330. See also David Leigh, *The Wilson Plot*, London 1988, and Stephen Dorrill and Robin Ramsay, *Smear: Wilson and the Secret State*, London 1991.
35. John Darwin, *Britain and the Decolonisation*, London 1988, p. 291.
36. See Halliday, *op. cit.*, pp. 207–14.
37. Michael Dewar, *Brush Fire Wars*, London 1984, p. 132.
38. G.G. Norton, *The Red Devils*, London 1971, p. 199.
39. Max Arthur, *Men of the Red Beret*, London 1990, pp. 353–54.
40. Humphrey Trevelyan, *The Middle East in Revolution*, London 1970, pp. 215–16.
41. *Ibid.*, pp. 216–17.
42. Ledger, *op. cit.*, pp. 141–43.
43. Colin Mitchell, *Having Been a Soldier*, London 1969, p. 13. Edwards's account, or rather celebration, of Mitchell is an interesting example of the impression he could make. Edwards's often commendably hard-nosed discussion has an unfortunate tendency towards purple prose when looking at Mitchell himself. He 'was as fit as a fiddle, devilishly handsome and charismatic. He exuded a pugnacious, raw honesty...whether on ceremonial duties or in the field, he never had a hair out of place'. He is the hero in 'a timeless story of inspiring leadership, loyalty and betrayal in the final days of empire'. See Edwards, *op. cit.*, pp. 17, 19.
44. See Kelley, *op. cit.*, pp. 38–39; Kostiner, *op. cit.*, pp. 167–69.
45. Mitchell, *op. cit.*, pp. 195–97. One admirer subsequently wrote of how the Argylls' 'rough justice had the effect of making Crater, so long the worst hotbed of trouble, a no-go area for terrorists. The Arabs showed respect for the authority of the gun when wielded ruthlessly without normal squeamish British restraint. The Scots never troubled to hide their preference for a terrorist shot dead over a cringing prisoner': Harper, *op. cit.*, p. 114. See also Edwards, *op. cit.*, pp. 212–47.
46. Martin Dillon, *The Dirty War*, London 1988, pp. 124–60.
47. Ledger, *op. cit.*, pp. 225–26. For an alternative view see Edwards, *op. cit.*, pp. 260–64.
48. Robin Neillands, *A Fighting Retreat: the British Empire 1947–1997*, London 1996, p. 356.
49. Halliday, *op. cit.*, pp. 218–21.
50. According to Jonathan Walker this seriously understates the number of British fatalities and he argues that in South Arabia as a whole between 1962 and

1967 'the number of those killed...approaches 200'. See his *Aden Insurgency: The Savage War in South Arabia 1962–1967*, Staplehurst 2005, p. 285.
51. George Brown's biographer, clearly reflecting his subject's views, describes the episode as 'a scuttle...but handled with skill and expedition': Peter Paterson, *Tired and Emotional: The Life of Lord George Brown*, London 1993, p. 209.
52. Denis Healy, *The Time of my Life*, London, 1990, p. 284.
53. Guy Arnold, *Wars in the Third World since 1945*, London 1990, p. 89.

6 The Unknown Wars: Oman and Dhofar

1. Fred Halliday, *Arabia without Sultans*, London 1974, p. 270.
2. *Ibid.*, p. 276.
3. John Townsend, *Oman: The Making of a Modern State*, London 1977, p. 11.
4. David Smiley, *Arabian Assignment*, London 1975, p. 41.
5. Ranulph Fiennes, *Where Soldiers Fear to Tread*, London 1975, pp. 53–54.
6. Peter Thwaites, *Muscat Command*, London 1995, p. 73. He writes of the Sultan's 'corrupt regime' where 'his chosen few lived in comfort and careless ignorance, while the great mass of people barely scratched an existence from their starving herds, their children growing precariously in a world of disease and squalor, with no hope of human progress towards greater knowledge, health or experience'.
7. P.S. Allfree, *Warlords of Oman*, London 1967, pp. 162, 164.
8. Corran Purdon, *List the Bugle*, Antrim 1993, pp. 243–44.
9. John Akehurst, *We Won a War*, Salisbury 1982, p. 13.
10. James Morris, *The Sultan in Oman*, London 1957, pp. 23, 130.
11. Smiley, *op. cit.*, pp. 27–28.
12. Halliday, *op. cit.*, p. 278.
13. Michael Dewar, *Brush Fire Wars*, London 1984, p. 85.
14. Allfree, *op. cit.*, p. 98.
15. Anthony Shepherd, *Arabian Adventure*, London 1961, p. 102.
16. Smiley, *op. cit.*, pp. 49, 58.
17. Sir David Lees, *Flight from the Middle East*, London 1980, pp. 131–32.
18. Frank Kitson, *Bunch of Five*, London 1977, pp. 163–71, 201. See also A. Deane Drummond, *Arrows of Fortune*, London 1992, pp. 218–19.
19. Lees, *op. cit.*, p. 133.
20. David French, *The British Way in Counterinsurgency 1945–1967*, Oxford 2011, p. 131.
21. Allfree, *op. cit.*, p. 114.
22. Peter de la Billière, *Looking For Trouble*, London 1994, pp. 150–51.
23. For accounts of taking of Jebel Akhdar see John Cooper, *One of the Originals*, London 1991, pp. 147–55; 'Lofty' Large, *One Man's SAS*, London 1987, pp. 54–81; de la Billière, *op. cit.*, pp. 131–52.
24. Smiley, *op. cit.*, p. 89.
25. De la Billière, *op. cit.*, pp. 150–51.
26. Ian Skeet, *Muscat and Oman*, London 1974, p. 111.
27. Miriam Joyce, *The Sultanate of Oman*, Westport, Connecticut 1995, p. 60.
28. Halliday, *op. cit.*, p. 311.
29. Purdon, *op. cit.*, p. 244.

30. Abdel Razzaq Takriti, *Monsoon Revolution: Republicans, Sultans and Empires in Oman 1965–1976*, Oxford 2013, p. 78.
31. See Fred Halliday, *Revolution and Foreign Policy: The Case of South Yemen 1967–1987*, Cambridge 1990, pp. 144–54.
32. Ranulph Fiennes, *Living Dangerously*, London 1989, p. 150.
33. J.B. Kelley, *Arabia, the Gulf and the West*, London 1989, pp. 137–38.
34. John Beasant, *Oman: The True Life Drama and Intrigue of an Arab State*, Edinburgh 2013, p. 145.
35. For Landon see Beasant, *op. cit.*, pp. 188–201. His Omani connections enabled him to become one of the richest men in Britain still maintaining his intelligence connections.
36. Taktiti, *op. cit.*, pp. 217–18.
37. For the 'five fronts' strategy see Tony Geraghty, *Who Dares Wins*, London 1992, pp. 183–88.
38. De la Billière, *op. cit.*, p. 263.
39. Tony Jeapes, *SAS Operation Oman*, London 1980, pp. 11. This was the first book to be written by a post-war SAS insider.
40. Townsend, *op. cit.*, p. 106; Calvin H. Allen and W. Lynn Rigsbee, *Oman Under Qaboos: From Coup to Constitution 1970–1996*, London 2000, pp. 65–66.
41. Halliday, *Arabia without Sultans*, *op. cit.*, pp. 343, 351. See Thwaites, *op. cit.*, p. 76: he writes that Mike Harvey of the Northern Frontier Regiment 'instituted a policy of blowing up or "capping" wells all over the Jebel' and 'incarcerated a number of ancient Jebelis' early on in the war.
42. Bryan Ray, *Dangerous Frontiers: Campaigning in Somaliland and Oman*, London 2012, p. 60.
43. Takriti, *op. cit.*, p. 85.
44. Jeapes, *op. cit.*, pp. 133–42.
45. For a first-hand account of the Mirbat engagement see Michael Paul Kennedy, *Soldier '1' SAS*, London 1990, pp. 80–113. This is one of the key books in the great SAS publishing boom of the 1990s that still continues. For a discussion of this and other memoirs see my *Dangerous Men: The SAS and Popular Culture*, London 1997.
46. David Arkless, *The Secret War: Dhofar 1971–1972*, London 1988, p. 221.
47. Charles Allen, *The Savage Wars of Peace*, London 1990, p. 198; de la Billière, *op. cit.*, p. 277; Jeapes, *op. cit.*, p. 157.
48. Anthony Kemp, *The SAS: Savage Wars of Peace 1947 To The Present*, London 1994, p. 107.
49. Kelley, *op. cit.*, p. 145. See also Clive Jones, 'Military Intelligence, Tribes, and Britain's War in Dhofar 1970–1976, *Middle East Journal*, 65 (4), 2011, p. 572.
50. Dewar, *op. cit.*, p. 174. For an academic account that sees Mirbat as the turning point in the war see J.E. Peterson, *Oman's Insurgencies*, London 2007, pp. 301–2.
51. Arkless, *op. cit.*, p. 210, gives a good account of the calibre of the guerrillas at the battle of Mirbat. He describes 'how one of them, a youngish man, had been cornered on the beach by two of our groups. With nowhere to go he began to wade out into the sea until he was up to his waist in the water, perhaps his idea was to try and wade past our lads and rejoin the beach further down. He was called upon to throw down his gun and surrender. Instead he turned and fired a burst from his rifle...Immediately, two GPMG opened in

52. Marc DeVore, 'The United Kingdom's last hot war of the Cold War: Oman 1963–73', *Cold War History*, **11** (3), August 2011, p. 454. For a critical assessment of the Iranian contribution to the war see Peterson, *op. cit.*, p. 331.
53. Jeapes, *op. cit.*, p. 204.
54. Geraint Hughes, 'A "Model Campaign" Reappraised: The Counter-Insurgency War in Dhofar, Oman 1965–1975', *Journal of Strategic Studies*, **32** (2), 2009, p. 291.
55. Takriti, *op. cit.*, pp. 122, 256.
56. Peter Ling, *Sultan in Arabia*, London 2004, pp. 74–75.
57. For the last stages of the war see in particular Ken Perkins, *A Fortunate Soldier*, pp. 119–39; Akehurst, *op. cit.*, pp. 138–82; John Pimlott, 'The British Army: The Dhofar Campaign 1970–1975', from Ian Beckett and John Pimlott (eds), *Armed Forces and Modern Counter-Insurgency*, London 1985, pp. 39–43; and in particular Peterson, *op. cit.*, pp. 302–408.
58. Akehurst, *op. cit.*, p. 175.
59. While the SAS played an important part in this campaign, it ended in some embarrassment and disillusion with allegations that members of the regiment had embezzled large sums intended to reward defectors from the PFLOAG. A number of men were thrown out and de la Billière admits that, for a while, the SAS had 'the smell of corruption hanging over it'. See de la Billière, *op. cit.*, p. 289. Ken Connor, in his history of the SAS, reports disillusion with Jeapes after he said that 'if there were to be casualties he would rather lose an SAS man than a member of a firqat. He later denied making the remark, but I was there when he said it.' See Ken Connor, *Ghost Force*, London 1998, p. 172. For another SAS veteran, Peter Ratcliffe: 'I have to say that no matter how many bushels of riyals, bars of gold or barrels of oil the Sultan was paying, or the goodwill that accrued to Britain in this strategically vital part of the world, it wasn't enough.' See Peter Ratcliffe, *Eye of the Storm*, London 2000, p. 93.
60. Ian Gardiner, *In the Service of the Sultan: A Firsthand Account of the Dhofar Insurgency*, London 2006, p. 1.
61. Takriti, *op. cit.*, p. 302.
62. DeVore, *op. cit.*, pp. 455–56.
63. Thomas Mockaitis, *British Counterinsurgency in the Post-Imperial Era*, Manchester 1995, p. 93.

7 The Long War: Northern Ireland

1. Brendan O'Leary and John McGarry, *The Politics of Antagonism*, London 1993, pp. 12–13; Christopher Tuck, 'Northern Ireland and the British Approach to Counter-Insurgency', *Defense and Security Analysis*, **23** (2), June 2007, p. 178.
2. Jonathan Bardon, *A History of Ulster*, Belfast 1992, pp. 484–95; Michael Farrell, *Northern Ireland: The Orange State*, London 1976, pp. 38–65.
3. For the earlier IRA campaigns see in particular Tim Pat Coogan, *The IRA*, London 1995, and J. Bowyer Bell, *The Secret Army*, London 1979.

4. For Paisley see in particular Steve Bruce, *God Save Ulster: The Religion and Politics of Paisley*, Oxford 1986 and Dennis Cooke, *Persecuting Zeal: A Portrait of Ian Paisley*, Dingle 1996.
5. Eamonn McCann, *War and an Irish Town*, London 1980, pp. 42–43.
6. For the most recent assessment of O'Neill see Marc Mulholland, *Northern Ireland at the Crossroads: Ulster Unionism in the O'Neill Years 1960–6*, London 2000.
7. McCann, *op. cit.*, p. 53. For the standard account of the civil rights movement, see also Bob Purdie, *Politics in the Streets*, Belfast 1990.
8. David Harkness, *Northern Ireland since 1920*, Dublin 1983, p. 155.
9. McCann, *op. cit.*, p. 59.
10. For the development of Irish republicanism in the 1960s and the emergence of the Provisionals see Henry Patterson, *The Politics of Illusion*, London 1989 and Patrick Bishop and Eamonn Mallie, *The Provisional IRA*, London 1987. Also of interest is Justin O'Brien, *The Arms Trial*, Dublin 2000.
11. James Callaghan, *A House Divided*, London 1973, pp. 17–18. For the development of Labour policy see Peter Rose, *How the Troubles Came to Northern Ireland*, London 2000.
12. Callaghan, *op. cit.*, pp. 47–48, 54, 142.
13. Sunday Times Insight Team, *Ulster*, London 1972, p. 215.
14. Tony Geraghty, *The Irish War*, London 1998, p. 33.
15. Paddy Devlin, *Straight Left*, Belfast 1994, pp. 129–30.
16. Kevin Kelley, *The Longest War*, London 1982, p. 147.
17. Michael Dewar, *The British Army in Northern Ireland*, London 1985, pp. 39–40.
18. Callaghan, *op. cit.*, p. 148.
19. Devlin, *op. cit.*, p. 134. According to Gerry Adams, the conduct of the British Army 'was quite stupid...they acted as an oppressive occupying force', see Gerry Adams, *Before the Dawn*, London 1997, p. 135.
20. On 'the culture of fear' with reference to Argentina see Juan E. Corradi, 'The Culture of Fear in Civil Society', from Monica Peralta-Ramos and Carlos H. Waisman, *From Military Rule to Liberal Democracy in Argentina*, Boulder, Colorado 1987.
21. Robert Ramsay, *Ringside Seats: An Insider's View of the Crisis in Northern Ireland*, Dublin 2009, p. 89.
22. Brian Faulkner, *Memoirs of a Statesman*, London 1978, pp. 24–25.
23. John Maguire, IRA *Internments and the Irish Government: Subversives and the State 1939–1962*, Dublin 2008, pp. 3, 11.
24. Michael Carver, *Out of Step*, London 1989, p. 408.
25. John Campbell, *Edward Heath*, London 1993, p. 427. See also Ciaran de Baroid, *Ballymurphy and the Irish War*, London 1990, pp. 74–94. McCann, *op. cit.*, pp. 91–100 and Farrell, *op. cit.*, pp. 281–84.
26. M.L.R. Smith and Peter R. Neuman, 'Motorman's Long Journey: Changing the Strategic Setting in Northern Ireland', *Contemporary British History*, **19** (4), December 2005, p. 423.
27. Reginald Maudling, *Memoirs*, London 1978, p. 184. His memoirs do not even mention 'Bloody Sunday'.

28. See John McGuffin, *The Guineapigs*, London 1974. See also Huw Bennett, 'Detention and Interrogation in Northern Ireland 1969–75', from Sibylle Scheipers (ed.), *Prisoners In War*, Oxford 2010.
29. John Peck, *Dublin from Downing Street*, Dublin 1978, pp. 128–29.
30. Bardon, *op. cit.*, p. 688.
31. Eamonn McCann, *Bloody Sunday in Derry*, Dingle 1992. See also Don Mullan, *Eyewitness Bloody Sunday*, Dublin 1997; Peter Pringle and Philip Jacobson, *Those Are Real Bullets Aren't They?*, London 2000, and Niall O. Dochartaigh, 'Bloody Sunday: Error or Design?', *Contemporary British History*, 24 (1) March 2010.
32. Charles Allen, *The Savage Wars of Peace*, London 1990, pp. 253–55 and Peter Harclerode, *Para!*, London 1992, pp. 288–92.
33. Dewar, *op. cit.*, p. 111.
34. Robin Evelegh, *Peacekeeping in a Democratic Society*, London 1978, pp. 54–55.
35. Frank Kitson, *Bunch of Five*, London 1977, p. 261.
36. Frank Kitson, *Low Intensity Operations*, London 1971. Kitson has since revisited his earlier views in his little-noticed *Warfare as a Whole*, London 1987. For critical discussion of his views see Charles Townshend, *Britain's Civil Wars*, London 1986, pp. 16–17; Philip Schlesinger, 'On the Shape and Scope of Counter-Insurgency Thought', from Gary Littlejohn (ed.), *Power and the State*, London 1978; and Richard Davis, 'Kitson versus Marighela: The Debate over Northern Ireland Terrorism', from Yonah Alexander and Alan O'Day, *Ireland's Terrorist Dilemma*, London 1990.
37. Carver, *op. cit.*, p. 429.
38. Keith Jeffery, 'Security Policy in Northern Ireland: Some Reflections on the Management of Violent Conflict', *Terrorism and Political Violence* 2, (1), Spring 1990, p. 27.
39. J. Bowyer Bell, *The Irish Troubles*, Dublin 1993, p. 404.
40. There are a growing number of revealing memoirs by soldiers relating to this conflict. See in particular Michael Asher, *Shoot to Kill*, London 1990; Harry McCallion, *Killing Zone*, London 1995; Frank Collins, *Baptism of Fire*, London 1997; and Bernard O'Mahoney with Mick McGovern, *Soldiers of the Queen*, Dingle 2000. For a discussion of the impact of the troops' conduct on the Catholic working class see Jeffrey Sluka, *Hearts and Minds, Water and Fish: Support for the IRA and INLA in a Northern Ireland Ghetto*, Washington DC, 1989, p. 172.
41. Adams, *op. cit.*, p. 126.
42. Evelegh, *op. cit.*, pp. 29–31.
43. Townshend, *op. cit.*, pp. 32–33.
44. Martin Dillon, *The Enemy Within*, London 1994, p. 120.
45. Sean MacStiofain, *Memoirs of a Revolutionary*, London 1975, p. 72.
46. Roger Faligot, *Britain's Military Strategy in Ireland*, London 1983.
47. Paddy Devlin,*The Fall of the Northern Ireland Executive*, Belfast 1975, p. 119.
48. Ed Maloney, *Voices From The Grave*, London 2010, p. 105.
49. Smith and Neuman, *op. cit.*, pp. 413, 422.
50. William Whitelaw, *The Whitelaw Memoirs*, London 1989, pp. 104–105.
51. Paul Dixon, 'Counter-Insurgency in Northern Ireland and the Crisis of the British State', from Paul B. Rich and Richard Stubbs, *The Counter-Insurgent*

State, London 1997. He criticises, with some justice, earlier work of mine for underestimating the importance of Operation Motorman.
52. Adams, *op. cit.*, p. 211.
53. M.L.R. Smith, *Fighting For Ireland: The Military Strategy of the Irish Republican Movement*, London 1995.
54. Merlyn Rees, *Northern Ireland*, London 1985, p. 43.
55. Devlin, *The Fall, op. cit.*, p. 89.
56. Robert Fisk, *The Point of No Return*, London 1975, pp. 92–93. See also the more recent account by Don Anderson, *14 May Days*, Dublin 1994. Acting as political and legal adviser to the UWC and co-editing their daily strike bulletin was one of the leading members of William Craig's Vanguard, David Trimble.
57. Faulkner, *op. cit.*, p. 267.
58. Desmond Hamill, *Pig in the Middle*, London 1985, p. 148.
59. Rees, *op. cit.*, pp. 69–70, 90.
60. Hamill, *op. cit.*, p. 153.
61. Paul Wilkinson, *Terrorism and the Liberal State*, London 1977, pp. 158–59.
62. Bernard Donoghue, *Prime Minister*, London 1987, pp. 130–31.
63. See Don Mullan, *The Dublin and Monaghan Bombings*, Dublin 1999.
64. The first book to highlight the activities of the Protestant murder gangs was Martin Dillon and Dennis Lehane, *Political Murder in Northern Ireland*, London 1973, but see also David Boulton, *The UVF*, Dublin 1973; Martin Dillon, *The Shankill Butchers*, London 1989; and Steve Bruce, *The Red Hand*, Oxford 1992. See also Jeffrey Sluka, '"For God and Ulster", The Culture of Terror and Loyalist Death Squads in Northern Ireland', from Jeffrey Sluka (ed.), *Death Squad: The Anthropology of State Terror*, Philadelphia 2000; David Lister and Hugh Jordan, *Mad Dog: The Rise and Fall of Johnny Adair and 'C' Company*, Edinburgh 2004; Ian S Wood, *Crimes of Loyalty: A History of the UDA*, Edinburgh 2006; and Henry McDonald and Jim Cusack, *UVF – The Endgame*, Dublin 2008.
65. For contrasting views see Bruce, *ibid.* and Ned Lebow, 'The Origins of Sectarian Assassination: The Case of Belfast', from A.D. Buckley and D.D. Olson (eds), *International Terrorism*, Wayne, New Jersey 1980.
66. For security force collusion with the Protestant paramilitaries see Fred Holroyd, *War without Honour*, Hull 1989; Martin Dillon, *Stone Cold*, London 1992; and Coogan, *op. cit.*, pp. 598–608.
67. Paul Wilkinson, 'British Policy on Terrorism: An Assessment', from Juliet Lodge (ed.), *The Threat of Terrorism*, Brighton 1988, p. 38.
68. Colm Keena, *Gerry Adams*, Cork 1990, p. 69. See also Robert White, *Provisional Irish Republicans*, Westport, Connecticut, 1993, pp. 138–39.
69. See Bob Rowthorn and Naomi Wayne, *Northern Ireland: The Political Economy of Conflict*, Cambridge 1988, p. 46 and Coogan, *op. cit.*, p. 481.
70. See in particular Tom Baldy, *Battle for Ulster*, Washington D.C. 1987. See also Paddy Hillyard, 'The Normalization of Special Powers: From Northern Ireland to Britain', from Phil Scraton (ed.), *Law, Order and the Authoritarian State*, Milton Keynes 1987 and Graham Ellison and Jim Smyth, *The Crowned Harp: Policing in Northern Ireland*, London 2000, pp. 81–85. Ellison and Smyth present an account that differs in important respects from mine.

71. See Leonard Weinberg and William Lee Eubank, *The Rise and Fall of Italian Terrorism*, Boulder, Colorado, 1987 and Richard Clutterbuck, *Terrorism, Drugs and Crime in Europe after 1992*, London 1990.
72. For the war in South Armagh see Toby Harnden, *Bandit Country: The IRA and South Armagh*, London 1999.
73. Rees, *op. cit.*, p. 336.
74. *Ibid.*, p. 276.
75. Steven Greer and Antony White, 'A Return To Trial By Jury', from Anthony Jennings (ed.), *Justice under Fire*, London 1988, pp. 47–65.
76. Kelley, *op. cit.*, pp. 284–85.
77. Liam Clarke, *Broadening the Battlefield*, Dublin 1987, pp. 41–43.
78. Ramsay, *op. cit.*, p. 142.
79. John Bew, Martyn Frampton and Inigo Gurruchaga, *Talking To Terrorists: Making Peace in Northern Ireland and the Basque Country*, London 2009, p. 69.
80. Michael A Murphy, *Gerry Fitt: Political Chameleon*, Cork 2007, p. 248.
81. House of Commons Hansard, 28 March 1979, column 519. See also Roy Mason, *Paying the Price*, London 1999, pp. 222–23. For a different view of Mason's record see Peter Neumann, 'Winning the "War on Terror"? Roy Mason's Contribution to Counter-Terrorism in Northern Ireland', *Small Wars and Insurgencies*, **14** (3), 2003.
82. For the INLA see Jack Holland and Harry McDonald, *INLA*, Dublin 1994.
83. Hamill, *op. cit.*, pp. 251–59.
84. On the supergrass initiative see Andrew Boyd, *The Informers*, Cork 1984 and Steven Greer, 'The Supergrass System in Northern Ireland', from Paul Wilkinson and A.M. Stewart (eds), *Contemporary Research on Terrorism*, Aberdeen 1987.
85. Bowyer Bell, *Irish Troubles*, *op. cit.*, p. 630.
86. Joseph Lee, *Ireland 1912–1982*, Cambridge 1989, p. 454. On the hunger strikes more generally see Tom Collins, *The Irish Hunger Strike*, Dublin 1986; David Beresford, *Ten Dead Men*, London 1987; Padraig O'Malley, *Biting at the Grave*, Belfast 1990; Brian Campbell, Laurence McKeown and Felin O'Hagan (eds), *Nor Meekly Serve My Time*, Belfast 1995; Richard O'Rawe, *Blanketmen: An Untold Story of the H – Block Hunger Strike*, Dublin 2005; and Thomas Hennessey, *Hunger Strike: Margaret Thatcher's Battle with the IRA 1980–1981*, Sallins 2014.
87. Margaret Thatcher, *The Downing Street Years*, London 1993, p. 393.
88. James Prior, *A Balance of Power*, London 1986, pp. 178, 181.
89. Richard Clutterbuck, *Terrorism in an Unstable World*, London 1994, pp. 162–63.
90. *Ibid.*, p. 240.
91. Paul Bew, Peter Gibbon and Henry Patterson, *Northern Ireland 1921–1994*, London 1995, pp. 217–24.
92. Jonathan Tonge, *Northern Ireland: Conflict and Change*, London 1998, p. 118.
93. For Protestant opposition see Arwel Ellis Owen, *The Anglo-Irish Agreement*, Cardiff 1994; Steve Bruce, *The Edge of the Union*, Oxford 1994; and Sir John Hermon, *Holding the Line*, Dublin 1997, pp. 180–93.
94. Thatcher, *op. cit.*, pp. 402, 406–07.
95. Brendon O'Brien, *The Long War*, Dublin 1993, pp. 138–50.
96. Mark Urban, *Big Boys' Rules*, London 1992, pp. 224–37.

97. *Ibid.*, p. 204.
98. See Dillon, *Stone Cold, op. cit.*
99. Ian Kearns, 'Policies Towards Northern Ireland', from Stuart Croft (ed.), *British Security Policy: The Thatcher Years*, London 1992, p. 122.
100. Thatcher, *op. cit.*, pp. 408–12.
101. See Donald C. Hodges, *Argentina's Dirty War*, Austin 1991 and Martin Edwin Andersen, *Dossier Secrets: Argentina's Desaparecidos and the Myth of the Dirty War*, Boulder, Colorado 1993. More generally see Bruce B. Campbell and Arthur D. Brenner (eds), *Death Squads in Global Perspective*, Basingstoke 2000.
102. See Martin Ingram and Greg Harkin, Stakeknife: *Britain's Secret Agents in Ireland*, Dublin 2004.
103. Keena, *op. cit.*, p. 143.
104. David McKittrick, *Endgame*, Belfast 1994, pp. 24–25.
105. See in particular Chris Mullin, *Error of Judgement*, London 1986 and Robert Kee, *Trial and Error*, London 1986.
106. For the bombing campaign and the secret negotiations see Dillon, *Enemy Within, op. cit.*, pp. 224–63; Coogan, *op. cit.*, pp. 639–69; James Adams, *The New Spies*, London 1994, pp. 208–20; Gary McGladdery, *The Provisional IRA in England: The Bombing Campaign 1973–1997*, Dublin 2006; and A.R. Oppenheimer, *IRA: The Bombs and Bullets*, Dublin 2009.
107. Paul Dixon, 'Was the IRA Defeated? Neo-Conservative Propaganda as History', *Journal of Imperial and Commonwealth History*, **40** (2), 2012, pp. 314–15.
108. Bew, Frampton and Gurruchaga, *op. cit.*, pp. 118–19.
109. Jack Holland, *Hope against History: The Ulster Conflict*, London 1999, p. 328.
110. See Nicholas Davies, *Ten-Thirty-Three*, Edinburgh 1999. See also Paul Larkin, *A Very British Jihad: Collusion, Conspiracy and Cover-Up in Northern Ireland*, Belfast 2004; Justin O'Brien, *Killing Finucane*, Dublin 2005; Chris Anderson, *The Billy Boy*, Edinburgh 2007; Neil Root and Ian Hitchings, *Who Killed Rosemary Nelson?*, London 2011; Anne Cadwallader, *Lethal Allies: British Collusion in Ireland*, Dublin 2013.
111. Peter Taylor, *Loyalist*, London 1999, p. 234. For an important academic account see Maurice Punch, *State Violence, Collusion and the Troubles: Counter Insurgency, Government Deviance and Northern Ireland*, London 2012.
112. Holland, *op. cit.*, pp. 278–79.
113. McGladdery, *op. cit.*, pp. 206–07.
114. Martyn Frampton, 'Agents and Ambushes: Britain's "Dirty War" in Northern Ireland' from Samy Cohen (ed), *Democracies At War Against Terrorism: A Comparative Perspective*, New York 2008, p. 94.
115. For Drumcree as the Orange 'Groundhog Day' see Mark Devenport, *Flash Frames: Twelve Years Reporting Belfast*, Belfast 2000, p. 1777. On the Drumcree crisis see McDonald, *op. cit.*, pp. 167–64, 255–57 and Susan McKay, *Northern Protestant: An Unsettled People*, Belfast 2000, pp. 142–86.
116. For an interesting discussion see Thomas Hennessey, *The Northern Ireland Peace Process*, Dublin 2000. His proclamation of British victory is the truth but not the whole truth.

8 America's Wars: Afghanistan and Iraq

1. Richard A. Clarke, *Against All Enemies: Inside America's War on Terror*, London 2004, pp. 30–31, 244.
2. Clarke, who does not accept that Bush was just a 'dumb, lazy rich kid', although it is not clear why he doesn't, nevertheless remembers being warned that the President wasn't one for reading and was always in bed by 10pm. Bush 'looked for the simple solution, the bumper sticker description of the problem ... The problem was that many of the important issues like terrorism, like Iraq were laced with important subtlety and nuance.'. This seems to be a pretty devastating indictment of any Commander-in-Chief! He contrasts this unfavourably with President Bill Clinton's tremendous work ethic and thirst for information and argument before a decision. See Clarke, *op. cit.*, p. 243. For Cheney see Barton Gellman, *Angler: The Shadow Presidency of Dick Cheney*, London 2008.
3. Patrick Cockburn, 'Paranoid but determined, ISIS is ready for a fight to the death in Mosul', *The Independent*, 18 February 2015. For the Islamic State see Patrick Cockburn, *The Jihadis Return: ISIS and the New Sunni Uprising*, New York 2014.
4. From a TV interview he gave on 7 April 1991. See Adam Cobb, 'A Strategic Assessment of Iraq', *Civil Wars*, 9, (1), (2007), p. 55. Another senior member of the first Bush administration, James Baker, the Secretary of State, made clear that what they were concerned to avoid was 'the Lebanonization of Iraq, which we believed would create a geopolitical nightmare'. From Jeffrey Record, *Dark Victory: America's Second War Against Iraq*, Annapolis 2004, p. 3.
5. John Dumbrell, *A Special Relationship*, Basingstoke 2001, p. 154.
6. Wilson, it seems clear, wanted to send a token force, but the Labour Lleft was too strong for him to dare to do so. On one occasion, he confided to Barbara Castle that he had told President Johnson that if he committed troops 'I would be finished'. See Chris Wrigley, 'Now yYou sSee It, Now You Don't: Harold Wilson and Labour's Foreign Policy 1964–1970' from R. Coopey, S. Fielding and N. Tiratsoo, (eds), *The Wilson Governments 1964–1970*, London 1993, p. 130. And on another occasion, he asked Jack Jones, the general secretary of the Transport and General wWorkers Union, if he could be persuaded to support the despatch of 'a token force ... maybe 30 men or so, and they could be virtually non-combatants'. Jones said no. See Jack Jones, *Union Man*, London 1986, p. 176.
7. Alistair Campbell, *The Blair Years*, London 2007, p. 630.
8. Christopher Meyer, *DC Confidential*, London 2003, p. 1.
9. Tony Blair, *A Journey*, London 2010, p. 410.
10. Campbell, op cit*op. cit.*, p. 630.
11. Patrick Porter, 'Last cCharge of the kKnights: Iraq, Afghanistan and the sSpecial rRelationship', *International Affairs*, 86, (2), (2010), p. 359.
12. Alex Danchev, 'Tony Blair's Vietnam: The Iraq War and the Special Relationship in Historical Perspective', *Reviews of International Studies*, 23, (2), (2007), p. 199.
13. Blair, op cit*op. cit.*, p. 409.
14. Sherard Cowper-Coles, *Cables from Kabul*, London 2011, p. 290.

15. Ahmed Rashid, *Taliban: Islam, Oil and the New Great Game in Central Asia*, London 2001, p. 17.
16. As Rashid points out: 'The Taliban leaders were all from the poorest, most conservative, and least literate southern Pashtun provinces of Afghanistan. In Mullah Omar's village women had always gone around fully veiled and no girl had ever gone to school because there were none. Omar and his colleagues transposed their own milieu, their own experience or lack of it, with women, to the entire country and justified their policies through the Koran.' Rashid, *op. cit.*, p. 110.(p 110)
17. James Ferguson, *Taliban*, London 2010, pp. 68–69, 76–78. According to Rashid, 'Traditionally, Islam in Afghanistan has been immensely tolerant-to other Muslim sects, other religions and modern lifestyles... Until 1992 Hindus, Sikhs and Jews played a significant role in the country's economy... After 1992 the brutal civil war destroyed this age-old Afghan tolerance and consensus.' Rashid, *op. cit.*, (pp. 82–83).
18. George Tenet, *At the Centre of the Storm: My Years in the CIA*, New York 2007, p. 225.
19. Sarah Chayes, *The Punishment of Virtue*, New York 2006, p. 135.
20. Nicky Hager, *Other People's Wars: New Zealand in Afghanistan, Iraq and the War on Terror*, Nelson, NZ 2011, pp. 90–91. An International Assistance Security Force (ISAF) team was appointed to investigate but did not get far: 'Most of the evidence had disappeared, key officials refused to be interviewed, bullet cartridges had not been fingerprinted, witnesses seemed scared to talk to them and when the ISAF investigation committee visited the scene they found that a day or two before, even the bullet holes in the ministry wall had been plastered over and painted' (p. 92).
21. Seth G. Jones, *In the Graveyard of Empires: America's War in Afghanistan*, New York 2009, p. 118.
22. Julien Mercille, *Cruel Harvest: US Intervention in the Afghan Drug Trade*, London 2013, Pp. 81.
23. Jeffrey Record, *Wanting War: Why the Bush Administration Invaded Iraq*, Washington, DC 2010, pp. 55–57.
24. Record, *Dark Victory*, op citop. *cit.*, p. 108.
25. Andrew Cockburn, *Rumsfeld: An American Disaster*, London 2007, p. 153.
26. For Blair's road to war see John Kampfner, *Blair's Wars*, London 2004; David Coates and Joel Krieger, *Blair's War*, Cambridge 2002; and Steven Kettell, *Dirty Politics: New Labour, British Democracy and the Invasion of Iraq*, London 2006. For the Stop the War movement see Andrew Murray and Lindsay German, *Stop The War: The Story of Britain's Biggest Mass Movement*, London 2003 and Chris Nineham, *Politics, the Media and the Anti-War Movement*, Winchester 2014. An interesting anecdotal testimony to the strength of opposition to the invasion is provided by Major General Christopher Elliott, in his account of the Iraq and Afghan Wars. He retired just before the invasion of Iraq, but recalls how while he supported the invasion, the 'rest of my family disagreed with that and went on the million-person protest march against the invasion through London'. See Christopher Elliott, *High Command: British Military Leadership in the Iraq and Afghanistan Wars*, London 2013, p. 20. And, the Blair government was not even successful in convincing the military of the need for war with Iraq. In his memoirs, General Richard Dannatt makes

clear that what struck him about the intelligence he saw was 'just how thin it was...I found the intelligence about weapons of mass destruction most uncompelling'. The outcome was 'one of the most devastating decisions in modern times', although he is thankful that 'the neo-cons great...strategic moment' was 'only short-lived'. From Richard Dannatt, *Leading From The Front*, London 2010, pp. 216, 218.
27. Kampfner, op cit*op. cit.*, p. 279.
28. Peter Galbraith, *The End of Iraq: How American Incompetence Created a War Without End*, London 2006, p. 19. Galbraith was a senior US diplomat.
29. Coates and Krieger, op cit*op. cit.*, pp. 60–61.
30. Stephen Melton, *The Clausewitz Delusion: How the American Army Screwed Up the Wars in Iraq and Afghanistan*, Minneapolis 2009, p. 112.
31. Keith Shimko, *The Iraq Wars and America's Military Revolution*, Cambridge 2010, p. 77.
32. Famously, the US Secretary of State, MadelaineMadeleine Albright, when asked on the '60 Minutes' TV show in the United States on 12 May 1996 about the death of perhaps half a million children, 'more children than died at Hiroshima', as a result of the sanctions on the '60 Minutes' TV show in the United States on 12 May 1996, she replied that it was 'a very hard choice, but the price — we think the price is worth it'.
33. John Simpson, *The Wars Against Saddam*, London 2003, p. 305.
34. Patrick Cockburn, *The Occupation: War and Resistance in Iraq*, London 2006, p. 25. According to Warren Chin, 'the indiscriminate nature of the sanctions regime...was highlighted in the West by John and Karl Mueller who estimated that "economic sanctions had probably already taken the lives of more people in Iraq than have been killed by all the weapons of mass destruction in history"'. From Warren Chin, *Britain and the War on Terror*, Farnham 2013, p. 81.
35. *Ibid.*, p. 292.
36. Bing West and Ray Smith, *The March Up: Taking Baghdad with the 1st Marine Division*, London 2003, p. 169. Another US account describes how a company came under small arms fire from the village of Az Zubadayah. They responded by calling in four Cobra helicopters to strafe the village with rocket and cannon fire, a 155mm artillery barrage and an air attack by a F/a-18 which dropped a 1,000-lb bomb. And all the while, they kept up non-stop fire on the village with their own weaponry. See Seth Folsom, *The Highway War*, Washington, DC 2006, p, 235–236. For a discussion of US Marine memoirs of the Iraq invasion see my 'Taking Baghdad: sSome US Marine mMemoirs of the iInvasion of Iraq', *Race and Class*, 52, (4), (2011).
37. Shimko, op cit*op. cit.*, p. 158.
38. *Ibid.*, p. 174.
39. Alistair Finlan, *Contemporary Military Strategy and the Global War on Terror*, New York 2014, p. 111. See also Cobb, op cit*op. cit.*, pp. 45–46.
40. Charles-Philippe David, 'How Not to dDo Post-iInvasion: Lessons Learned from US Decision-mMaking in Iraq 2002–2008', *Defense and Security Analysis*, 26, (1), (2010), p. 32.
41. Hilary Synott, *Bad Days in Basra*, London 2008, p. 153. He goes on that 'one of its architects was thrown out of Baghdad once the US Defence Secretary learned that he was part of the post-conflict management team'.

42. Tenet, op cit*op. cit.*, p. 426.
43. Steven Kettell, *New Labour and the New World Order*, Manchester 2011, p. 57.
44. Toby Dodge, *Iraq: From War to a New Authoritarianism*, London 2012, p. 38.
45. Greg Muttitt, *Fuel on the Fire: Oil and Politics in Occupied Iraq*, London 2011, pp. 63–67.
46. Galbraith, op cit*op. cit.*, p. 113.
47. Cobb, op cit*op. cit.*, pp. 45–47.
48. Galbraith, op cit*op. cit.*, pp. 102–104, 126.
49. According to one senior British intelligence officer, 'Our advice to Downing Street was very strongly against widespread de-Baathification. We argued that it was necessary to keep the Iraqi army and security forces in place to maintain order. There was unanimity on this throughout the intelligence community and the Foreign Office. The message was loud and clear. But Washington simply took no notice.'. A senior diplomat at the Foreign Office explained the difference between British and US neocon thinking: 'The Americans were drawing comparisons with the Nazis in 1945. We preferred to draw comparisons with the Russians in 1991, when the communists were overthrown but many communist party members continued in their jobs.'. He went on: 'The only place that was deciding policy on Iraq was the Pentagon, and the one place where we had no influence was the Pentagon.'. From Con Coughlin, *American Ally: Tony Blair and the War on Terror*, London 2006, pp. 324–325.
50. Tenet, op cit*op. cit.*, p. 427.
51. Thomas Ricks, *Fiasco: The American Military Adventure in Iraq*, London 2006, pp. 161–163. When the British Chief of the General Staff, General Mike Jackson visited Baghdad around this time, the briefing he was given by Tim Cross, the British officer supposedly second in command in the occupation authority ,was entitled 'Snatching Defeat from the Jaws of Victory'. See Tim Cross, 'Rebuilding Iraq 2003: Humanitarian Assistance and Reconstruction' from Jonathan Bailey, Richard Iron and Hew Strachan, (eds), *British Generals in Blair's Wars*, Farnham 2013, p. 78.
52. Jonathan Steele, *Defeat: Why They Lost in Iraq*, London 2008, p. 23.
53. Jon Moran, *From Northern Ireland to Afghanistan: British Military Intelligence Operations, Ethics and Human Rights*, Farnham 2013, p. 74.
54. Justin Maciejewski, 'Best Effort: Operation Sinbad and the Iraq Campaign' from Bailey, op cit*op. cit.*, pp. 159–160.
55. Thomas Waldman, 'British "Post-Conflict" Operations in Iraq: Into the Heart of Strategic Darkness', *Civil Wars*, 9, (1), (2007), p. 73.
56. Oliver Poole, *Red Zone: Five Bloody Years in Baghdad*, London 2008, p. 123; Thomas Ricks, *The Gamble: General Petraeus and the Untold Story of the American Surge in Iraq*, London 2010, p. 4.
57. For Abu Ghraib see Philip Gourevitch and Errol Morris, *Standard Operating Procedure*, New York 2008.
58. According to Thomas Mockaitis, 'Private security firms often showed even less restraint than the military.'. See Thomas Mockaitis, *Iraq and the Challenge of Counterinsurgency*, Westport 2008, p.111.
59. James Tyner, *The Business of War: Workers, Warriors and Hostages in Occupied Iraq*, Aldershot 2006, p. 69–70. The casualties suffered by contractors do not show up in the Coalition figures for soldiers killed and wounded, but, according to Patrick Cockburn, between March 2002 and October 2005, no

less than 412 contractors were killed, one for every five US soldiers killed. See Cockburn, *op. cit.*, p. 175.
60. The British Army, it was argued, had failed to institutionalise the lessons that Robert Thompson had laid down for the waging of counterinsurgency warfare. There have been two interesting attempts to apply Thompson's approach to Iraq and Afghanistan: Andrew Mumford, 'Sir Robert Thompson's Lessons for Iraq: Bringing the "Basic Principles of Counter-Insurgency" into the 21st Century', *Defence Studies*, 10, (1–2), (2010) and James Pritchard and M. L. R. Smith, 'Thompson in Helmand: Comparing Theory to practice in British Counter-Insurgency Operations in Afghanistan', *Civil Wars*, 12, (1–2), (2010). It is Thomas Mockaitis, however, who highlights the crucial element in his thinking that was relevant in Iraq and Afghanistan. In 1987, Thompson had told him: 'Don't go anywhere unless you plan to stay for 20 years.'. See Thomas Mockaitis, *Iraq and the Challenge of Counterinsurgency*, Westport 2008, p. ix.
61. Jackson, op cit*op. cit.*, pp. 419–420.
62. Patrick Porter, op cit*op. cit.*, p. 369.
63. John Nagl, *Learning to Eat Soup with a Knife: Counterinsurgency Lessons from Malaya and Vietnam*, Chicago 2002. According to Nagl, the book was taken up by Newt Gingrich, who set about getting it published in paperback and recommended it to the US Army Chief of Staff, General Peter Schoonmaker. Schoonmaker 'then sent expensive hardcover copies of the book to all his subordinate four-star generals to read'. See John Nagl, *Knife Fights: A Memoir of Modern War in Theory and Practice*, New York 2014, pp. 92, 119.
64. Frank Ledwidge, *Losing Small Wars: British Military Failure in Iraq and Afghanistan*, New Haven 2011, p. 24.
65. See A. T. Williams, *A Very British Killing: The Death of Baha Mousa*, London 2002 and Huw Bennett, 'Baha Mousa and the British Army in Iraq', from Paul Dixon, (ed.), *The British Approach to Counterinsurgency: From Malaya and Northern Ireland to Iraq and Afghanistan*, Basingstoke 2012.
66. Mark Nicol, *Last Round: The Redcaps, the Paras and the Battle of Majar*, London 2006, p. 264.
67. Ricks, Fiasco, op cit*op. cit.*, p. 333.
68. Terry H. Anderson, *Bush's Wars*, Oxford 2011, p. 175.
69. The attack on Fallujah was to be renewed in November 2004 when 10, 000 US troops and Marines, supported by 2,000 Iraqi troops, assaulted the city. In the course of the battle the Marines 'fired four thousand artillery rounds and ten thousand mortar bombs into the city, while warplanes dropped ten tons of bombs. At least two thousand buildings were destroyed and another ten thousand were badly damaged.'. From Ricks, *Fiasco*, op cit*op. cit.*, p. 402.
70. Andrew Stewart, 'Southern Iraq, 2003–2004', from Bailey, op cit*op. cit.*, p. 85.
71. Poole, op cit*op. cit.*, p. 141. He describes a helicopter pilot telling him on a flight from Amarah to Bara that: 'The government doesn't care even though they sent us here. All it wants to do is suck up to the Americans and we're collateral damage for that' (p. 199).
72. North, op cit*op. cit.*, p. 49.
73. Stewart, op cit*op. cit.*, p. 85.

74. Andrew Gilligan, 'Hostility between British and American military leaders revealed', *Daily Telegraph*, 22 November 2009.
75. Ledwidge, op cit*op. cit.*, p. 33.
76. See Mark Urban, *Task Force Black*, London 2010, pp. 94–110.
77. Moran, op cit*op. cit.*, p. 104.
78. Nigel Aylwin-Foster, 'Changing the Army for Counterinsurgency Operations', *Military Review*, November–December 2005, pp. 2–8. It is very hard to imagine any British in-house military forum subjecting itself to such a devastating critique from an American, which demonstrates two things: the relative openness of debate in the US Army and the extent of the loss of confidence by 2005. When the *British Army Review* proposed to publish an issue with five articles on Basra, despite the fact that 'access was already restricted to the army, just two articles ended up being published, and both were subjected to close scrutiny — even censorship – – by the MOD; three other articles deemed too critical were dismissed'. From David Ucko and Robert Egnell, *Counterinsurgency in Crisis: Britain and the Challenges of Modern Warfare*, New York 2013, pp.129–130.
79. Dannatt, op cit*op. cit.*, p. 232.
80. Chin, op cit*op. cit.*, p. 133.
81. Maciejewski, op cit*op. cit.*, pp. 161, 163.
82. Jack Fairweather, *A War of Choice: The British in Iraq 2003–2009*, London 2011, p. 274.
83. Peter Mansoor, *Surge: My Journey with General David Petraeus and the Remaking of the Iraq War*, New Haven 2013, p. 236.
84. Fairweather, op cit*op. cit.*, p. 302.
85. Ledwidge, op cit*op. cit.*, p. 47.
86. James Wither, "Basra's not Belfast: the British Army, "Small Wars" and Iraq', *Small Wars and Insurgencies*, 20, (3–4), 2009, pp. 622–623.
87. Ledwidge, op cit*op. cit.*, p. 48.
88. Fairweather, op cit*op. cit.*, pp. 310, 331.
89. For a while it seemed as if the rise of General Petraeus signalled the triumph of the advocates of counterinsurgency within the US military. His best-selling Field Manual 3–24 seemed to implant counterinsurgency as doctrine, but in practice the costs of protracted commitment quickly bought the ascendency of its advocates to an end.
90. One senior British officer, General Graeme Lamb, working at the US HQ, was heavily involved in pushing the policy of supporting the 'Awakening'. General McChrystal, who had the highest opinion of him, described how the British retreat in Basra, led some US officers to mistakenly regard 'the reconciliation Graeme was pushing' as 'a British-concocted scheme to save face, rather than what it was — a vital component of an aggressive surge'. See McChrystal, op cit*op. cit.*, p. 262.
91. Bing West, *The Strongest Tribe: War, Politics and the Endgame in Iraq*, New York 2008, p. 351.
92. Ricks, *The Gamble*, op cit*op. cit.*, p. 277. Cordesman argued in a Center for Strategic and International Studies paper that the British had effectively lost the south by 2005, which was a defeat of some significance as it 'produces over 90% of government revenues and has over 70% of Iraq's proven oil reserves'. See Anthony Cordesman, *The British Defeat in the South and the Uncertain*

Bush 'Strategy' in Iraq: 'Oil Spots', 'Ink Blots', White Space', or 'Pointlessness', Washington 2007, p. 3.
93. Blair, op cit*op. cit.*, p. 610.
94. Tim Bird and Alex Marshall, *Afghanistan: How the West Lost its Way*, New Haven 2011, p. 119.
95. James Nathan, 'Poppy Blues: The Collapse of Poppy Eradication and the Road Ahead in Afghanistan', *Defense and Security Analysis*, 25, (4), (2009), p. 339.
96. Elliott, op cit*op. cit.*, p. 217.
97. *Ibid.*, p. 21. Ledwidge makes a similar point: 'the army had its own reasons for wanting a large-scale deployment: it was threatened with cuts.'. From Frank Ledwidge, *Investment in Blood: The True Cost of Britain's Afghan War*, New Haven 2013, p. 20.
98. Elliott, op cit*op. cit.*, p. 155.
99. Emile Simpson, *War from the Ground Up: Twenty-First century Combat as Politics*, London 2012, p. 45; Mike Martin, *An Intimate War: An Oral History of the Helmand Conflict*, London 2014, pp. 153–155.
100. Martin, *ibid.*, p. 4.
101. Stephen Grey, *Operation Snakebite*, London 2009, p. 23.
102. Patrick Porter, *Military Orientalism: Eastern War through Western Eyes*, London 2009, pp. 144, 149,168,170. For a useful discussion of the Taliban movement in Helmand see Theo Farrell and Antonio Giustozzi, 'The Taliban at wWar: iInside the Helmand iInsurgency 2004–2012', *International Affairs*, 89, (4), (2013).
103. *Ibid.*, p. 160.
104. Leo Docherty, *Desert of Death*, London 2007, p. 188.
105. Grey, op cit*op. cit.*, p. 31.
106. Sandy Gall, *War against the Taliban: Why it all Went Wrong In Afghanistan*, London 2012, p. 120.
107. Eric Sangar, *Historical Experience-Burden or Bonus in Today's Wars: The British Army and the Bundeswehr in Afghanistan*, Berlin 2014, p. 85.
108. Gall, op cit*op. cit.*, p. 111.
109. James Ferguson, *A Million Bullets*, London 2009, pp. 358–359.
110. Antonio Giustozzi, *Koran, Kalashnikov and Laptop: The Neo-Taliban Insurgency in Afghanistan*, London 2007, pp. 211–212.
111. Carter Malkasian, *War Comes to Garmser*, London 2013, pp. 109–110. Malkasian does not go so far as to claim a British victory, but he quotes a Taliban fighter as saying that the Taliban had suffered a defeat.
112. Cowper-Coles, op cit*op. cit.*, p. 192.
113. Ben Anderson, *No Worse Enemy*, Oxford 2011, pp. 14–15, 18, 49.
114. Cowper-Coles, op cit*op. cit.*, pp. 6, 80–81, 112, 173.
115. Gall, op cit*op. cit.*, p. 270.
116. Vanda Felbab-Brown, *Aspiration and Ambivalence: Strategies and Realities of Counterinsurgency and State Building in Afghanistan*, Washington, DC 2013, pp. 82, 85,105.
117. Rory Stewart, 'The Irresistable Illusion', *London Review of Books*, 9 July 2009.
118. Sarah Chayes, *Thieves of State: Why Corruption Threatens Global Security*, New York 2015, p. 64; Graeme Smith, *The Dogs Are Eating Them Now: Our War in*

Afghanistan, Toronto 2013, pp. 256–257. He argues that the drug traffickers also conduct a very profitable trade carrying weapons, many of which end up in the hands of the Taliban, back across the border with the assistance of the same officials and policemen.

119. Chayes, *Thieves*, op cit*op. cit.*, pp. 62–63.
120. *Ibid.*, pp. 134, 138–139.
121. Ahmed Rashid, *Pakistan on the Brink*, London 2012, pp. 82–83; Chayes, *Thieves*, op cit*op. cit.*, p. 42.
122. Jason Davidson, *America's Allies and War*, Basingstoke 2011, p. 112, 136.
123. See my *America Right or Wrong: New Labour and Uncle Sam's Wars*, London 2009, pp. 3–4.
124. Grey, op cit*op. cit.*, p. 321.
125. Moran, op cit*op. cit.*, p. 138.
126. Anthony King, 'Understanding the Helmand Campaign: British military operations in Afghanistan', *International Affairs*, **86**, (2), (2010), p. 317.
127. Rajiv Chandrasekaran, *Little America: The War Within the War for Afghanistan*, London 2012, pp. 206, 214.
128. Stewart, op cit*op. cit.*
129. Ledwidge, *Investment in Blood*, op cit*op. cit.*, p. 217.

Select Bibliography

Akehurst, John, *We Won a War*, Salisbury 1982.
Anderson, David, *The Histories of the Hanged*, London 2005.
Arkless, David, *The Secret War: Dhofar 1971–1972*, London 1988.
Bennett, Huw, *Fighting the Mau Mau*, Cambridge 2013.
Bethell, Nicholas, *The Palestine Triangle*, London 1979.
Blaxland, Gregory, *The Regiments Depart*, London 1971.
Carruthers, Susan, *Winning Hearts and Minds: British Governments, the Media and Colonial Counter-Insurgency*, London 1995.
Carver, Michael, *Harding of Petherton*, London 1978.
Carver, Michael, *Out of Step*, London 1989.
Cesarani, David, *Major Farran's Hat: Murder, Scandal and Britain's War against Jewish Terrorism*, London 2009.
Charters, David, *The British Army and Jewish Insurgency in Palestine*, London 1989.
Clayton, Anthony, *Counter-Insurgency in Kenya 1952–1960*, Nairobi 1976.
Cloake, John, *Templer: Tiger of Malaya*, London 1985.
Clutterbuck, Richard, *The Long Long War*, London 1966.
Crawshaw, Nancy, *The Cyprus Revolt*, London 1978.
de la Billière, Peter, *Looking for Trouble*, London 1994.
Dewar, Michael, *Brush Fire Wars*, London 1984.
Dillon, Martin, *The Dirty War*, London 1988.
Edgerton, Robert, *Mau Mau: An African Crucible*, London 1990.
Edwards, Aaron, *Defending the Realm? the Politics of Britain's Small Wars Since 1945*, Manchester 2012.
Elkins, Caroline, *Britain's Gulag: The Brutal End of Empire in Kenya*, London 2005.
Furedi, Frank, *Colonial Wars and the Politics of Third World Nationalism*, London 1994.
Grivas, George, *The Memoirs of General Grivas*, London 1964.
Grob-Fitzgibbon, Benjamin, *Imperial Endgame: Britain's dirty Wars and the End of Empire*, Basingstoke 2011.
Hack, Karl, *Defence and Decolonisation in Southeast Asia: Britain, Malaya and Singapore 1941–1968*, London 2000.
Halliday, Fred, *Arabia Without Sultans*, London 1974.
Heller, Joseph, *The Stern Gang: Ideology, Politics and Terror*, London 1995.
Jeapes, Tony, *SAS Operation Oman*, London 1980.
Kelley, J.B., Arabia, the Gulf and the West, London 1980.
Kelley, Kevin, *The Longest War*, London 1982.
Kitson, Frank, *Gangs and Counter-Gangs*, London 1960.
Kitson, Frank, *Low Intensity Warfare*, London 1971.
Kitson, Frank, *A Bunch of Five*, London 1977.
Kostiner, Joseph, *The Struggle for South Yemen*, London 1984.
Ledger, David, *Shifting Sands*, London 1983.
Ledwidge, Frank, *Losing Small Wars: Britain's Military Failure in Iraq and Afghanistan*, New Haven 2011.

McCann, Eamonn, War and an Irish Town, London 1980.
Mitchell, Colin, *Having Been A Soldier*, London 1969.
Mockaitis, Thomas, *British Counter-Insurgency 1919–1960*, London 1990.
Mockaitis, Thomas, *British Counter-Insurgency in the Post-Imperial Era*, London 1995.
Mumford, Andrew, *The Counter-Insurgency Myth: The British Experience of Irregular Warfare*, London 2012.
Paget, Julian, *Counter-Insurgency Campaigning*, London 1967.
Paget, Julian, *Last Post: Aden 1964–1967*, London 1969.
Peterson, J.E., *Oman's Insurgencies*, London 2007.
Short, Anthony, *The Communist Insurrection in Malaya 1948–1960*, London 1975.
Stubbs, Richard, *Hearts and Minds in Guerrilla Warfare*, London 1989.
Takriti, Abdel Razziq, *Monsoon Revolution: Republicans, Sultans and Empires in Oman 1965–1976*, Oxford 2013.
Thompson, Sir Robert, *Defeating Communist Insurgency*, London 1966.
Thompson, Sir Robert, *Make for the Hills*, London 1989.
Urban, Mark, *Big Boys' Rules*, London 1992.

Index

9/11 (2001), 201–203

aboriginal tribes, 57–58
Abu Ghraib, 219
Abu Naji, evacuation of, 227
Acre rescue, 28
Adams, Gerry, 174–175, 176, 177–178, 184, 196, 199
Aden
  British withdrawal, 127–128, 133–135
  incorporation into Federation of South Arabia, 113–114
  strategic importance, 112
Aden police, 130–131
Aden Trades Union Congress (ATUC), 114–116
Afghan National Police, 235–236
Afghanistan
  corruption, 237–239
  pretexts for British involvement, 239–240
  Russian occupation, 239–240
Afxentiou, Grigoris, 97, 106
Agoglia, John, 217
Ahmed, Imam, 113
Akehurst, John, 139, 154, 155
Akhunzada, Sher Muhammad, 232–234, 235
Al Qaeda, 201
Alastos, Doros, 94
bin Ali, Imam Ghalib, 140
bin Ali, Talib, 140
al-Asnag, Abdullah, 115, 128
Allfree, P. S., 138, 142–143
Alwyn-Foster, Nigel, 226–227
Anderson, Ben, 236
Anderson, David, 2, 62, 82
Anglo-American Commission, 15, 20
Anglo-Irish Agreement, 190–192
anti-semitic rioting, 30
Arab Revolt of 1936–39, 6
'Argentinian solution', 195–196

Argyll and Sutherland Highlanders, 132–133
Armitage, Sir Robert, 96
Armstrong, Sir Robert, 192
Arnold, Guy, 134
Art of Counter-Revolutionary Warfare, The, 33
Attlee, Clement, 20, 26, 31, 44
Avgorou, 108

Baader-Meinhof, 185
Baath Party, proscribing of, 216–217
Baldwin, William, 81
Balfour Declaration, 6
Baling Talks, 59
Baring, Sir Evelyn, 68, 77–78, 86
Barker, Evelyn, 23, 26
Barnett, Donald, 69, 70
Batang Kali massacre, 50
Batu Arang, 46, 50
Begin, Menachem, 9
Ben Gurion, David, 7, 10
Bennett, Huw, 2, 49, 70
Bet-Zouri, Eliahu, 10
Betz, David and Anthony Cormack, 221
Bevin, Ernest, 14–15, 22, 31
'Bevingrads', 27
Bird, Tim and Alex Marshall, 231
Birmingham pub bombing, 197
Black, Christopher, 190
Blair, Tony, 199, 204–206, 230
Blaxland, Gregory, 113
'Bloody Friday' bombings, 177
'Bloody Sunday' massacre, 172
Blundell, Sir Michael, 73
Bogside, battle of, 162
bombing
  Afghanistan, 208
  Kenya, 77–78
  Malaya, 57
  Oman, 141–142
  South Yemen, 120–121

Bourn, John, 185
Bourne Geoffrey, 60
Bower, Sir Roger, 60
Bowyer Bell J., 16, 189
Bremer, Paul, 216–217, 223
Briance, John, 18
Briggs, Sir Harold, 50–51, 53
Brighton bombing, 195, 197
Britain's Military Strategy in Ireland: The Kitson Experiment, 176
British Military Administration (BMA), 37
Brockway, Fenner, 65
Brown, George, 130, 132
Burntollet Bridge ambush, 160
Bush, George W., 3, 201, 202, 210, 223
Butler, Ed, 232, 234

Calcutta Conference, 40
Caldwell, Malcolm, 52
Callaghan, James, 162, 164–165, 168
Carver, Michael, 75, 174
Cassels, James, 20
casualties
  Aden, 134
  Cyprus, 111
  Iraq, 213
  Kenya, 84
  Northern Ireland, 157
  Palestine, 32
Catling, Richard, 18
Central Intelligence Agency (CIA), 208–209, 217
Cesarani, David, 30
Chandrasekaran, Rajiv, 241
Chapman, Spencer, 35–36
Chayes, Sarah, 238–239
Cheney, Dick, 202, 203–204, 205–206
Chichester-Clark, James, 161, 170
Chiesa, Dalla, 190
Chin Peng, 36, 41, 54, 60
Churchill, Winston, 6, 10, 34, 83
Civil Aid teams, 159–160
Civil Rights Association, 159–160
Clarke, Richard, 202
Claudy bombing, 177
Clayton, Anthony, 80

Clutterbuck, Richard, 51, 190
Coalition Provisional Authority (CPA), 216
Cockburn, Patrick, 212, 219
Communist Party of Cyprus (KKK), 89
Conduct of Anti-Terrorist Operations in Malaya, The, 55
Cooke, Robin, 211
Cooper, John, 117
Cordesman, Anthony, 229
Corfield Report, 72–73
Corry, Patrick, 162
Cowper-Coles, Sherard, 206, 232, 235, 236–237
Craig, William, 159
Crater, 130–133
Crawshaw, Nancy, 97
Creasey, Sir Timothy, 188
Creech-Jones, Arthur, 50, 86
Cross, John, 59
Crossman, Richard, 21
Cunningham, Sir Alan, 16, 20, 22, 25–26
Cutliffe, Catherine, shooting of, 110
Cyprus
  strategic importance, 88
Cyprus Farmers' Union (PEK), 94

Daily Worker, 50
Dalton, Hugh, 12, 32
Dannatt, Richard, 227
Daoud, Daoud, 238
Daoud, Engineer, 233
D'Arcy, John, 20, 21
Davidson, Jason, 239
Davis, John, 36
De Cruz, Gerald, 45
de la Billiere, Peter, 117, 143–144, 146
Defeating Communist Insurgency, 51
Democratic Unionist Party, 178, 200
Dennison, Malcolm, 151
Dereliction of Duty, 4
detention without trial
  Cyprus, 98
  Kenya, 75–76
  Malaya, 47
Devlin, Paddy, 167, 168, 176, 179

Dewar, Michael, 141, 152, 168
Dhofar Liberation Front, 144–145
Diplock courts, 186, 187
'dirty war', 193–195
Dixon, Paul, 197
Docherty, Leo, 234
Doran, Desmond, 18
Downing Street Declaration, 192
Drakos, Markos, 97, 106
Drumcree, 200
Drummond, Tony Deane, 143
Dublin and Monaghan bombings, 183

East African Trades Union Congress (EATUC), 65, 66
Eden, Anthony, 92
Edgerton, Robert, 80–81
Edwards, Aaron, 3, 123, 127
Eksund, 193
Eliav, Yaacov, 31
Elkins, Caroline, 2, 82
Elliott, Christopher, 232
Enosis, 90
Erskine, Sir George, 70, 71, 82–83
Evelegh, Robin, 173, 175
Exodus, 31

Faligot, Roger, 176
Fallujah, 223
Falls Road curfew, 167
Farran, Roy, 29–30, 127
al-Fartosi, Ahmed, 228–229
Faulkner, Brian, 170, 178, 181
Felbab-Brown, Vanda, 237
Ferguson, James, 207
Fergusson, Bernard, 29, 31
Fiennes, Ranulph, 137–138, 145
Firqats, 148
Fisk, Robert, 180
Fitt, Gerry, 159–160, 187
Fleischer, Michael, 216
Foley, Charles, 99, 104
Foot, Hugh, 107
Fort Morbut interrogation centre, 127
Forward Research Unit (FRU), 194, 198
Francis, Carey, 80
French, David, 2, 75, 105, 142

Front for the Liberation of South Yemen (FLOSY), 128, 130
Furedi, Frank, 63–64

Galbraith, Peter, 211, 215–216
Gall, Sandy, 237
Ganapathy, S. A., 44
Gardiner, Ian, 155
Garmser, 235
general strike
  Aden, 115
  Cyprus, 102, 107
  Kenya, 66
  Malaya, 39, 40
  Northern Ireland, 179–182
  Palestine, 15
Gent, Sir Edward, 42
Georgadjis, Polycarpos, 101
al-Ghassani, Muhammad Ahmad, 145
Gibraltar shootings, 194
Gill, Leonard, 81–82
Glasgow *Sunday Mail*, 133
Golani, Matt, 23
Good Friday Agreement, 199
Goulding, Cathal, 163
Gow, Ian, 197
Gray, Nicol, 29
Greek Orthodox Church, 90–91, 94–95
Greene, Hugh Carleton, 53
Greenwood, Anthony, 123–124
Grey, Stephen, 233, 234, 240
Griffiths, James, 64
Griffiths-Jones, Eric, 82
Grivas, George, 90, 92–94, 96–97, 102–103, 109, 110
Grob-Fitzgibbon, Benjamin, 2
Guildford pub bombing, 197
Gulf War, 211–212
Gurney, Sir Henry, 50, 53

Haditha massacre, 219
Haganah, 7, 22–23, 30
Hakim, Eliahu, 10
Halliday, Fred, 114, 136–137, 144, 148–149
hanging, 30, 47, 83, 102, 104
Hanslope Park archive, 82

Harding, Sir John, 98, 99
Harper, Stephen, 126
Haughey, Charles, 170
Healey, Denis, 123, 134
'hearts and minds', 51, 148
Heath, Edward, 166, 178
'Helmand Plan', 232
Hermon, Sir John, 191
Hewitt, Peter, 76–77
Hickinbotham, Sir Tom, 112
Hola camp massacre, 86
Home Guard
  Kenya, 71
  Malaya, 55–56
Hoon, Geoff, 214
Hopkinson, Henry, 92
Hor Lung, 60
Horowitz, David, 12
house searches in Northern Ireland, 174
Hughes, Brendon, 177
hunger strikes, 188–190
Hurd, Douglas, 192
Hutton, John, 240

'Imperial Policing', 17
Improvised Explosive Device (IED), 226, 235
infecting London's water supply, 31
intelligence, 17–18, 56, 99, 104, 122
Inter-Services Intelligence directorate (ISI), 231
International Security and Assistance Force (ISAF), 230
internment in Northern Ireland, 170–172
Iranian battle group, 152–153
Iraq
  looting of, 214–215
Iraqi Army, dissolution of, 216–217
Irgun Zvei Leumi (IZL), 7–9, 10–12, 16, 18–20, 22–23, 28
Irish National Liberation Army (INLA), 188
Irish Republican Army (IRA), 158, 163
Islam, role of, 154
Islamic State, 203

Jabotinsky, Vladimir, 7
Jackson, Mike, 221
Jaysh al-Mahdi (JAM), 224, 228, 229
Jeapes, Tony, 146–147, 151
Jebel Akhdar, 140–141
Jewish Agency, 6–7, 10, 13, 23–24
Johnston, C. M., 78
Johnston, Roy, 163
Jones, J Byford, 109
Jungle is Neutral, The, 35
Jungle Warfare School, 55, 59

Kaggia, Bildad, 65, 66, 71
Kamba involvement in Mau Mau, 72
Kariuki, Josiah, 68
Karzai, Hamid, 209, 232, 238
Katz, Samuel, 24
Kealy, Mike, 149
Kearns, Ian, 194
Kelley, J. B., 123
Kelley, Kevin, 168, 186
Kemp, Anthony, 151
Kendrew, Douglas, 109
Kenya African Union, 64, 67
Kenya Federation of Registered Trade Unions (KFRTU), 73–74, 75, 79
Kenyatta, Jomo, 67–68, 71, 87
Kesatuan Melayu Muda (KMM), 37
Khalifa, Abdullah Hasan, 117, 122
'Khi', 90, 93
Kikuyu, 63
Kikuyu Central Association (KCA), 65
Kimathi, Dedan, 76
King David Hotel bombing, 22
King, Frank, 181
Kitson, Frank, 76, 84, 142, 174–175
Korean War, 58
Kubai, Fred, 65, 66–67, 71
Kyrris, Costas, 90

Labour government
  1945–51, 5, 12–13, 15, 43, 47, 64–65
  1964–70, 123, 129, 204
  1974–79, 179, 187
bin Laden, Osama, 206, 208
Lagoudontis, George, 101
Lai Tek, 36, 38, 41
Land and Freedom Armies, 69–70, 76

Landon, Tim, 146
Lari massacre, 71
Lau Yiu, 44, 46
Learning to Eat Soup with a Knife: Counterinsurgency Lessons from Malaya and Vietnam, 222, 226
Ledger, David, 133
Ledwidge, Frank, 222, 241–242
Lee, Joe, 189
Lees, Sir David, 141, 142
Lennox-Boyd Constitution, 85–86
Leys, Colin, 86
Lohamei Herut Israel (LEHI), 8, 10–12, 16, 18–20, 22–23, 28, 30–31
Loughall ambush, 193
Low Intensity Operations, 174
Loyalist murder gangs, 183–184, 198
Lynch, Jack, 172
Lyttleton, Oliver, 57, 85

McCann, Eamonn, 159–160, 162, 172
McCloskie, Francis, 162
McCloskie, Liam, 189
McCuen, J. J., 33
Macgregor, Alistair, 29
McGuinness, Martin, 176, 187, 197, 199, 200
McGurk's Bar bombing, 183
McLean, Neil, 117
Macleod, Iain, 86–87
McMaster, H. R., 4
MacMichael, Sir Harold, 9
MacMillan, Gordon, 28
Macmillan, Harold, 86, 88, 114
Macstiofain, Sean, 163, 176
Mahra nomads, 155
Majar el Kebir, 222–223
Major, John, 199
Makarios, Archbishop, 91, 93, 102, 106, 111
al-Makkawi, Abdul, 124–125
Malaya
  economic importance, 42–43
Malayan Chinese Association (MCA), 58–59
Malayan Communist Party (MCP)
  defeat, 59–61
  ethnic composition, 38, 41–42
  guerrilla strategy, 44–45
  preparation for armed struggle, 41
  retreat, 54
Malayan People's Anti-British Army (MPABA), 46
Malayan People's Anti-Japanese Army (MPAJA), 35
Malayan People's Anti-Japanese Union (MPAJU), 35–36
Malayan Races Liberation Army (MRLA), 47, 60
Malobi, Wunyabari, 79
Martin, T. G., 23
Mason, Roy, 187
Mathenge, Stanley, 69
Mau Mau, 65
Mau Mau from Within, 69
Mau Mau Man-Hunt, 81
Maudling, Reginald, 166–167
Mboya, Tom, 74, 79
Melton, Stephen, 212
Menaul, Air Vice Marshal, 123
Meyer, Christopher, 205
MI5, 18
MI6, 18
Miller, Harry, 49
Min Yuen, 46–47, 48, 56
Mirbat, battle of, 149–152
Mitchell, Colin, 26, 132
Mitchell, Sir Philip, 67
Montgomery, Bernard, 21, 26–27
Morris, James, 139, 140
Mountbatten, Lord, 188
Moussa, Baha, 222
Moyne, Lord, 10
Mumford, Andrew, 2, 3
Musa Qala, 234–235
mutiny, 130–131

Nagl, John, 222, 227
Nairobi
  revolutionary movement in, 65–66, 73
National Liberation for Occupied South Yemen (NLF), 117–118, 122, 128, 133
National Organisation of Cypriot Fighters (EOKA), 93–94, 96, 100, 106–107

Neave, Airey, 188
Nelson, Brian, 198
Newman, Kenneth, 186, 188
'Night of the Bridges', 21
'Night of the Trains', 13
Nixon, Richard, 33
Njama, Karari, 69
Northern Alliance, 208

O Bradaigh, Ruari, 163
O Connaill, Daithi, 163, 174
Obama, Barack, 241
Oldfield, Maurice, 188
O'Neill, Terence, 159, 161
Operation
  Agatha, 22, 24
  Anvil, 74–75
  Charge of the Knights, 229
  Demetrius, 170–171
  Elephant, 28
  Jaguar, 149
  Jock Scott, 69
  Lucky Alphonse, 102
  Motorman, 177–178
  Nutcracker, 118
  Pepperpot, 102
  Polly, 27
  Shark, 23, 24
  Simba, 149–150
  Sinbad, 228
  Tiger, 30
opium production, 208, 209
Orange parades, 163–164, 166
Orange State, 158
Ovendale, Ritchie, 31

Paget, Julian, 119–120
Paisley, Ian, 159, 178, 191, 200
Palestine
  strategic importance, 5
Palestinians, 25
Palmach, 7, 13
Pancyprian Federation of Labour (PEO), 90, 107
Pancyprian Trade Union Committee (PTUC), 90
Pan-Malaysian Federation of Trade Unions (PMFTU), 40, 42
Parachute Regiment, 129, 133, 172

Passive Wing, 71
People's Democracy, 160
People's Front for the Liberation of the Occupied Arabian Gulf (PFLOAG), 145, 148
People's Republic of South Yemen, 154–155
People's Socialist Party, 116, 121–122, 124
Petraeus, David, 227, 238–239
'pitchfork murders', 132
police primacy, 185–186
Poole, Oliver, 219
Poole, Peter, 86
Porter, Patrick, 221, 233
Potter, Henry, 67, 68
Powell, Colin, 210
Powell, Enoch, 191
Prior, Jim, 189–190
private security contractors, 220
Progressive Party of the Working Class (AKEL), 89–91, 96, 99
Provisional IRA, 163–164, 168–169, 176, 184, 192–193
pseudo gangs, 76
Purdon, Corran, 138

Q patrols, 105
Qaboos, Sultan, 145–146, 147
Qadir, Abdul, 209

Radfan campaign, 118–122
Rahman, Tunku Abdul, 59
Rasid, Ahmed, 206
Rawcliffe, D. W., 79–80
Raziel, David, 8
Red Brigade, 185
Reddaway, John, 111
Rees, Merlyn, 179, 182, 186
Reid, John, 230
Remembrance Day bombing, 196
Resettlement
  Kenya, 75–76
  Malay, 52–53
Revolution in Military Affairs (RMA), 203
Richards, David, 234
Ricks, Thomas, 219
Rooney, Patrick, 163

Rose, Norman, 31
Royal Anglian Regiment, 126–127
Royal United Services Institute (RUSI), 123
Rubowitz, Alexander, 30
Rumsfeld, Donald, 202, 213, 214

Saddam Hussein, 201, 210, 211, 213
al Sadr, Moqtada, 222
Sadrists, 225
Saison, 10–12
as-Sallal, Abdullah, 116
Sampson, Nicos, 106
sanctions, 212
Sands, Bobby, 188, 189
Scappaticci, Fred, 196
schoolchildren's protest, 101
Servas, Plautas, 89
al-Shaabi, Qatan, 128
Shamir, Yitzhak, 8, 23
Shaw, George, 228
Shepherd, Anthony, 141
Shimko, Keith, 212, 213–214
Shirreff, Richard, 227–228
Short, Anthony, 48, 54
shot while trying to escape, 49–50, 70
Simpson, John, 212
Singh, Makhan, 65–66
Sinn Fein, 192–193, 196
SIS, *see* MI6
Six Day War, 130
Slavery in Oman, 137
Smiley, David, 117, 137, 139, 141, 143–144
Smith, Graeme, 238
Social Democratic and Labour Party (SDLP), 178, 190, 196
Sook Ching, 35
Soong Kwong, 39
South Arabian Army, 130–131
South Armagh, 185
Special Air Service (SAS), 29, 58, 119, 126–127, 136, 142–143, 148, 193–194
Special Branch
  Aden, 125
  Malaya, 53, 56
  Northern Ireland, 174
Special Constabulary, 158, 160

Special Night Squads, 6
Special Operations Executive (SOE), 7, 29, 36
'Special Relationship', 204–205, 220
Spencer, John, 67
Spraying, 58
squatters
  Kenya, 63–64
  Malaya, 57–58
State of Emergency
  Cyprus, 98
  Kenya, 69
  Malaya, 42, 47
Stern, Abraham, 8
Stern Group, 8
Stewart, Andrew, 224
Stewart, Rory, 238, 241
Stichter, Sharon, 79
Stone, Michael, 194
Stop the War Movement, 211
Stormont, fall of, 176
Storrs, Sir Ronald, 89
Strachey, John, 21
Struggle for Kenya, The, 79
Stubbs, Richard, 50, 58
Suez invasion, 104
Sunningdale Agreement, 178–179
supergrass initiative, 190
Supreme Council for the Islamic Revolution in Iraq (SCIRI), 223
Swynnerton Plan, 78

bin Taimur, Sultan Said, 137–139, 144, 145
Takriti, Abdel Razzaq, 149
Taliban, 207–208, 231, 233
Tanner, J. K., 224
Taylor, John, 198
Templer, Gerald, 53–55, 57, 59, 170
Tenet, George, 208–209, 214, 217
Thatcher, Margaret, 157, 188, 190–192, 194–195
Thompson, J. B. Perry, 45
Thompson, Robert, 33, 44, 47, 51
Thorneycroft, Peter, 121
Thwaites, Peter, 138
The Times, 139
Torture, use of, 56, 77–82, 104–105, 127

Townshend, Charles, 137, 175, 193
Transport and Allied Workers' Union (TAWU), 65, 73
Trevaskis, Sir Kennedy, 117, 122, 124
Trevelyan, Sir Humphrey, 130
Trimble, David, 199
Truman, President, 20
Turkish Cypriots, 101, 108, 109, 111
Turkish government, 111
Turnball, Sir Richard, 124, 129
Tuwaitha nuclear research facility, 215–216
Tuzo, Sir Harry, 171
Twomey, Seamus, 176

Ulster Defence Association (UDA), 183
Ulster Freedom Fighters (UFF), 183
Ulster Volunteer Force (UVF), 183
Ulster Workers Council, 179
'Ulsterisation', 184–185
United Resistance Movement, 13, 23
Urban, Mark, 194

Volkan, 107, 108

Wakahangara, Chief, 71
Wall, Peter, 218
Walton, Calder, 56
'War on Terror', 201–202
Warrenpoint ambush, 188
Warrington bombing, 197
Waruhiu, Chief, 68
Wasifi, Izzatullah, 238
Watts, John, 122, 146, 151
'Way Ahead', 185
'Weapons of Mass Destruction', 210–211
Weizmann, Chaim, 7, 14, 22
West, Bing, 213
Whitelaw, William, 176–177
Wickham, Sir Charles, 29
Widgery Tribunal, 172
Wilkins, Tom, 10
Wilson, Harold, 123, 127, 158, 164, 179, 204
'Wilson Plot', 127
Wilson, R. D., 18
Windley, E. H., 63
Wingate, Orde, 6
Wolfowitz, Paul, 202
Woodley, Bill, 84

Yellin-Mor, Nathan, 8, 10
Yemen Arab Republic YAR), 116
Yishuv, 6–7, 9, 14–15

Printed and bound by CPI Group (UK) Ltd, Croydon, CR0 4YY